AF006392

Mobile and Ubiquitous Media

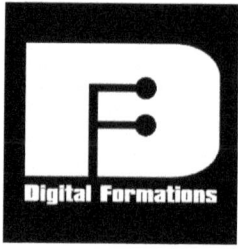

Steve Jones
General Editor

Vol. 116

The Digital Formations series is part of the Peter Lang Media and Communication list.
Every volume is peer reviewed and meets
the highest quality standards for content and production.

PETER LANG
New York • Bern • Berlin
Brussels • Vienna • Oxford • Warsaw

Mobile and Ubiquitous Media

Critical and International Perspectives

EDITED BY Michael S. Daubs
AND Vincent R. Manzerolle

PETER LANG
New York • Bern • Berlin
Brussels • Vienna • Oxford • Warsaw

Library of Congress Cataloging-in-Publication Data

Names: Daubs, Michael S., author | Manzerolle, Vincent, R. author.
Title: Mobile and ubiquitous media: critical and international perspectives /
edited by Michael S. Daubs and Vincent R. Manzerolle.
Description: New York: Peter Lang, 2018.
Series: Digital formations; Vol. 116 | ISSN 1526-3169
Includes bibliographical references and index.
Identifiers: LCCN 2017038366 | ISBN 978-1-4331-4841-5 (hardback: alk. paper)
ISBN 978-1-4331-4636-7 (pbk.: alk. paper)
ISBN 978-1-4331-4842-2 (ebook pdf)
ISBN 978-1-4331-4843-9 (epub) | ISBN 978-1-4331-4844-6 (mobi)
Subjects: LCSH: LCSH: Ubiquitous computing—Social aspects. | Social media.
Classification: LCC HM851 .M626 2018 | DDC 303.48/34—dc23
LC record available at https://lccn.loc.gov/2017038366
DOI 10.3726/b11817

Bibliographic information published by **Die Deutsche Nationalbibliothek.**
Die Deutsche Nationalbibliothek lists this publication in the "Deutsche
Nationalbibliografie"; detailed bibliographic data are available
on the Internet at http://dnb.d-nb.de/.

© 2018 Peter Lang Publishing, Inc., New York
29 Broadway, 18th floor, New York, NY 10006
www.peterlang.com

All rights reserved.
Reprint or reproduction, even partially, in all forms such as microfilm,
xerography, microfiche, microcard, and offset strictly prohibited.

Table of Contents

Figures and Tables vii
Acknowledgements ix

Introduction: From Here to Ubiquity 1
    Michael S. Daubs and Vincent R. Manzerolle

Part One: Archaeologies: Histories and Futures of Ubiquitous Media

Chapter One: How We Got Here: The Technologies and Policies Behind
    Ubiquitous Computing and Ubiquitous Media 19
    Laura Steckman
Chapter Two: The Ubiquitous Media War 41
    Tanner Mirrlees
Chapter Three: From Contagion and Revealing to Recovery and Healing:
    Examining the Lifecycle of Ubiquitous Control Through the
    Sony/BMG Rootkit 59
    Eric Lehman

Part Two: Mobilities: Mobile Devices, Wearables, and Locative Media

Chapter Four: Google Street View and Representational Ubiquity 77
    Aaron Shapiro
Chapter Five: Wearable Technology in the Production, Diffusion, and Active
    Use of Ubiquitous Knowledge 93
    Marco Centorrino and Sebastiano Nucera

Part Three: Visualities: Ubiquitous Media and Visual Culture

Chapter Six: Towards a New Visuality of "Mobile Infogrpahy": Examining
    Contemporary Visual Applications as New Ways of Seeing 109
    Ana Rita Morais

Chapter Seven: Entrepreneurial Journalism and Ubiquitous Media: Considerations for Digital Labor 127
   Maggie Reid
Chapter Eight: Youth Practices Online and Offline: Ubiquitous Tools and Meaningful Contexts 143
   Pilar Lacasa, Julián de la Fuente, and Katiuska Manzur
Chapter Nine: Everywhere and Nowhere, Simultaneously: Theorizing the Ubiquitous, Immaterial, Post-Digital Photograph 163
   Kris Belden-Adams

Part Four: Economies: Critical Political Economy Perspectives

Chapter Ten: Ubiquitous Media and Monopolies of Knowledge: The Approach of Harold Innis 183
   Edward Comor
Chapter Eleven: The Mediated Experiences of Our Everyday/Everynight Lives: Notes From a Case Study on Digital Labor 201
   Susan Bryant

Part Five: Localities and Communities: Spaces, Places, and Time

Chapter Twelve: Push Narratives: Ubiquitous Mobile News and Participatory Local Media in Himalayan India 219
   Jacqueline H. Fewkes and Abdul Nasir Khan
Chapter Thirteen: Towards Journalism Everywhere: The New Opportunities and Challenges of Real-Time News Streams in Finland 237
   Turo Uskali

Part Six: Surveillances: Privacy, Surveillance, and Ubiquitous Media

Chapter Fourteen: "Framelessness," or the Cultural Logic of Big Data 251
   Mark Andrejevic
Chapter Fifteen: The Relationship Between Ubiquitous Media and Surveillance of Dissent From the Civil Rights Movement to Black Lives Matter 267
   Sarah Harney
Chapter Sixteen: Ubiquitous Emotion Analytics and How We Feel Today 287
   Susan Currie Sivek

Contributors 303
Index 307

Figures AND Tables

FIGURES

Figure 8.1.	Theoretical model: Main concepts	144
Figure 8.2.	Multiple spaces and times. Scenarios at the workshop	151
Figure 8.3.	Nadia's first posts on Instagram, 2014 10 04	151
Figure 8.4.	Nadia on Instagram: Changes over time	153
Figure 8.5.	Photography from the mobile phone screen	155
Figure 8.6.	Artistic effects	155
Figure 8.7.	It's the Hard Knock Life. Nadia on *Musical.ly*	156
Figure 9.1.	Akihiko ("Aki") Hoshide, *Space Selfie, International Space Station Imagery: ISS032-E-025258*, Sept. 5, 2012	166
Figure 12.1.	Anti-corruption campaign discussion, with photo, text, and video commentary (S TV Ladakh 2015. WhatsApp message to author, October 2). The phonetically spelled Urdu comment reads, "It looks like now our community is awakening."	229
Figure 12.2.	A comment on news that other group members found was not reliable, a WhatsApp screenshot from Al Noor News Ladakh 2015 (Al Noor News Ladakh. 2015. WhatsApp message to author, February 22).	231

TABLES

Table 11.1.	The Survey	207
Table 16.1.	Gathering Emotion Data: User Characteristics Included in Apple Patent	291

Acknowledgements

The editors would like to sincerely and wholeheartedly thank the following individuals for their important role in helping to complete this project. Most importantly we would like to thank Mary Savigar, Steve Jones, and Kathryn Harrison for providing the foundational encouragement and support necessary to include this in Digital Formation series as well as Michael Doub and the whole editorial team at Peter Lang who made the process seamless and manageable.

We would also like to thank Marcelo Guarini and the Faculty of Arts, Humanities and Social Sciences at the University of Windsor for their support. Similarly, we want to acknowledge the additional support provided by the Faculty of Humanities and Social Sciences at Victoria University of Wellington and particularly thank Sarah Leggott for making that support possible and Philippa Race for her administrative support.

We also owe a great deal of gratitude to our copyeditor Rudy Leon, who provided a thorough, professional, and much need set of fresh eyes to the manuscript, strengthening its overall clarity and coherence. Her comments and suggestions quite simply made this a better book.

Michael S. Daubs would like to specifically thank his colleagues in the Media Studies department at Victoria University of Wellington for their encouragement and support, particularly Jo Smith, Joost de Bruin, Peter Thompson, Kathleen Kuehn, Minette Hillyer, and Geoff Stahl for their guidance and willingness to discuss topics, issues and themes that became central issues in this text (often over pints; also, thanks for the pints). I would also like to thank the many friends and colleagues who helped shape my understanding of and foment my interest in the topics in this volume, not just Vincent Manzerolle, but also Brian Brown, Chrstopher Cwynar, Alison Hearn, David Jackson, Atle Mikkola Kjøsen, Lee McGuigan, Henry Svec, Sy Taffel, Elise Thorburn, Sasha Torres, and Liam C. Young—and probably others I'm forgetting. Many of these names will appear in Vincent's own acknowledgements below which is both a testament to their intellects and our enduring friendships. Their discussions, suggestions and own work have been invaluable and they have made me a better scholar as well as provided unending enjoyment and good humour. I would also like to thank the students I've taught at both the University of Western Ontario and Victoria University of Wellington, especially the students in my "New Media: Theory and Practice" and "Mobile and Ubiquitous Media" courses at Victoria for both putting up with my nerdy excitement for this topic and for contributions to class discussions which helped inform my thinking about this topic. Finally, extra special thanks to Vincent for his patience during this process (and for putting up with several 3-hour Skype calls at odd hours), Benson and Figgis (for sleeping on my feet during those calls and only rarely asking to play fetch), and—most of all—my partner Wendy Daubs for never complaining when I'd get up at 4am, for taking care of everything I neglected while working, and for her continued love and support, without which nothing I've achieved would be possible.

Vincent Manzerolle would like to first thank his colleagues in the Department of Communication, Media, and Film for the supportive environment they've provided. Conversations around this topic have been essential to the intellectual development of this project. Several individuals have helped shaped my thinking around this volume's various topics. Over the last several years I've had the great fortune to have many enriching conversations with the following friends and colleagues: Michael Daubs, Lee McGuigan, Liam C. Young, Atle Mikkola Kjøsen, Leslie Meier, Edward Comor, Ben Birkinbine, Alison Hearn, Andrew Herman, Brett Caraway, Valerie Scatamburlo-D'Annibale, Kamilla Petrick, Brian Brown, Henry Svec, David Jackson, Kyle Asquith, and Elise Thorburn. Thanks to these and other inspiring colleagues for providing me with an embarrassment of intellectual riches to draw from. I'm also indebted to the undergraduate students I've taught at University of Western Ontario and the University of Windsor in the Department of Communication, Media & Film who have offered both a chance to both refine my thinking, but have also allowed me to learn from their experiences with ubiquitous media. Special thanks to my family and friends as their relationships continually remind me of the most important things in life. Final and extra special thanks due to Stacy Lynn for her unwavering support and encouragement throughout the course of this project and beyond.

Introduction

From Here to Ubiquity

MICHAEL S. DAUBS AND VINCENT R. MANZEROLLE

INTRODUCTION

The impetus for this edited collection was the increasingly frequent appearance of the word "ubiquitous" in reference to a wide variety of media and technologies in both the popular and academic press. A Google Ngram search on the phrase "ubiquitous media" reveals the term has been appearing sparingly in texts since 1964, but shows a sharp increase in use since 1984.[1] Even a cursory online search will reveal multiple articles claiming that we live in a "world of ubiquitous media," a "ubiquitous media landscape," or some variation thereof. The wireless technology developer Qualcomm (2011) has released statements referring to "ubiquitous connectivity and seamless experiences that are developing across mobile phones, computing and consumer electronics" and articles that reference ubiquitous media examine its problems and promise in fields ranging from advertising (Åkesson and Ihlström Eriksson 2010), to journalism (Gillmor 2010), to politics (Garon 2012; Mihailidis and Thevenin 2013), to education (Cope and Kalantzis 2010). Other texts, such as a 2009 volume of the journal *Theory, Culture & Society* edited by Mike Featherstone (2009), and the book *Culture, Aesthetics, and Affect in Ubiquitous Media: The Prosaic Image* by Helen Grace (2013) examine ubiquitous media within specific geographic regions or cultures, such as Asian communities in Japan or Hong Kong.

Despite these thoughtful examinations, there is a general tendency to treat this "world of ubiquitous media" as a given, or at least as something of which everyone has an intrinsic understanding. As a result, there is a tendency to define ubiquitous media specifically in relation to a particular field in lieu of developing broader understandings of the term. Such an approach would seek to understand the concept of media ubiquity as a phenomenon with wide economic, social, and cultural ramifications. One of the goals of this book is to directly contribute to the development of a more comprehensive literature on ubiquitous media. Our examination begins with a simple question: what does it mean to live in a world of ubiquitous media? As Featherstone (2009, 3) argues: "Theorizing ubiquitous media becomes an integral part of theorizing culture and society today." Answering this question requires a consideration of the conditions—including material, technological, and social—that enabled the development of ubiquitous media as well as an investigation of how such a media environment affects social formations and institutions, our interactions with others, and our conceptualizations of space/place.

HISTORICAL PRECEDENTS

We begin here with an attempt to situate ubiquitous media within the larger history of the development of media and communication technology. Featherstone (2009, 2), whose introduction to the *Theory, Culture & Society* issue dedicated to ubiquitous media has become a seminal text on the topic, argues that the emergence of a ubiquitous media environment has been rapid:

> We have moved within a generation from the terminology of 'mass media,' or 'the media,' with debates about the monopolistic concentration of media power and dangers of pervasive manipulation ('the culture industry,' 'the consciousness industry,' 'the hidden persuaders'), to the sense that media are now differentiated, dispersed, and multi-modal.

While it is important to acknowledge that changes in the current mediascape, both social and cultural, have their roots in the pre-digital era,[2] it is undeniably true that understandings of media and their sociocultural role has seen a dramatic transformation in the last two decades, particularly because of the emergence of digital media devices, networks, and services.

A comprehensive summary of the innovations that led to the development and wide-spread adoption of digital media technologies could fill a book in itself. In fact, there are several excellent books dedicated to the topic, such as Martin Campbell-Kelly's and William Aspray's *Computer: A History of the Information Machine* (2004) or Manuel Castells' renowned book *The Rise of the Network Society* (2000). However, there are some important antecedents that we feel it is important to highlight in order to provide a historical foundation for the discussions of ubiquitous media in the following chapters.

Digitalization

One of most important movements that enabled the development of a ubiquitous media environment is a shift away from analog technologies due to the emergence of digital operating systems. Simone Murray (2003) refers to the digitalization of media technologies as the "second wave" of media convergence, following an initial wave of industrial convergence in the form of horizontal and vertical integration enabled by the deregulation of the media industry. Digitalization is often considered in terms of technologies rather than social impacts. Robert Burnett and David Marshall (2003, 1), for example, describe digitalization as enabling a "blending of the media, telecommunications and computer industries, and the coming together of all forms of mediated communication in digital form." Murray (2003, 9) considers digitalization from an industrial perspective, arguing that the establishment of common digital operating systems "radically challenges the media industry compartmentalization traditionally favored by political economy."

Discourse on convergence reached new level of frenzy in the 1980s–90s because of the "exponential growth effect that occurs with the integration of media and products" (Cartwright 2002, 417). The shift to digital operating systems, for example, allowed content previously restricted to one medium or platform (e.g., televisual content) to be conveyed via other channels (e.g., the Internet). For the first time, people could access multiple forms of content flowing across multiple technologies in ways never before experienced, reshape that content, or even create and distribute content of their own. As a result, content "has come to be redefined as a highly transferable commodity inscribed in—but not exclusively embodied by—any one specific media platform" (Murray 2003, 10). The ability for media content to flow freely between media platforms is key to Jay David Bolter's and Richard Grusin's (2000, 45) concept of "remediation," or the "representation of one medium in another." As Featherstone (2009, 2) argues, digitalization "restructures the ways in which material is stored and accessed in the archive….In effect, the *digital media become both a topic and resource, something researchers need to study and theorize to make sense of the world, but also the resource, the interface which cuts into and opens up that world*" (emphasis added).

The flow of media texts across platforms, combined with increased opportunities for participation and interactivity are similarly central to Henry Jenkins' (2006, 2) concept of "convergence culture," which he famously describes as "where old and new media collide, where grassroots and corporate media intersect, where the power of the media producer and the power of the media consumer interact in unpredictable ways." Jenkins sees digitalization and convergence culture as a significant shift; one that, in his words, would result in a "new cultural order" (2006, 93). Jenkins is arguably a bit celebratory in his claims, but the emergence and rapid adaptation of digital technology, platforms and media has indeed created opportunities for shifts in the "cultural order" as well as opportunities to reinforce the status quo, as some of the chapters in this volume demonstrate. Digitalization has made content available anywhere, anytime, and on virtually any platform, defying the conventional economics of scarcity and triggering a profound, and ongoing, restructuring of the content producing industries.

Ubiquitous Computing

As a practical matter, the pervasive flow of data, information, and content is enabled by the proliferation of digital devices. Paul Dourish and Genevieve Bell (2011) link the emergence of the current spate of digital devices to the historical development of computing technologies. To illustrate this trajectory, they refer to the work of Mark Weiser, a computer scientist who led the Computer Science Laboratory at the Xerox Palo Alto Research Center (PARC) in the late 1980s and early 1990s. Weiser (1996) argued that developed societies in the early 1990s were witnessing the beginning of a "third wave" of computing, following the first wave of shared computer mainframes ("one computer, many people") and a second wave characterized by personal computers ("one person, one computer"). The third wave, according to Weiser (1996), is one of "ubiquitous computing, or the age of *calm technology*, when technology recedes into the background of our lives" (emphasis in the original). This third wave of ubiquitous computing (UC or UbiComp) will be characterized by "many computers sharing each of us" (Weiser and Brown 1996).

Weiser, who is sometimes referred to as the "father of ubiquitous computing," believes that the goal of ubiquitous computing research is "to make a computer so imbedded, so fitting, so natural, that we use it without even thinking about it." Weiser and Brown (1996) further elaborate:

> Some of these computers will be the hundreds we may access in the course of a few minutes of Internet browsing. Others will be imbedded in walls, chairs, clothing, light switches, cars—in everything. UC is fundamentally characterized by the connection of things in the world with computation.

They refer to these technologies as "calm" or "encalming" because they are designed "so that the people being shared by the computers remain serene and in control" and contrast them with "information technologies" such as the Web, mobile phones and email that "bombard us frenetically" (Weiser and Brown 1996). Instead of attention-demanding devices, Weiser (1991, 94) advocates for "a new way of thinking about computers, one that takes into account the human world and allows the computers themselves to vanish into the background."

Despite Weiser's and Brown's attempt to contrast it from "information technologies," information and data are integral to UbiComp, as their emphasis on the "connection of things in the world with computation" suggests. This information is then used to enhance our way of life. Canadian computer scientist Bill Buxton (1997) expanded upon Weiser's conceptualization of ubiquitous computing, arguing that there is a "seeming paradox that arises between the principle of ubiquity and that of transparency" he hoped to resolve. He introduces the related concept of "ubiquitous video" (UbiVid) in which "there are a range of video cameras and monitors in the workspace, and that all are available. By having video input and output available in different sizes and locations, we enable the most important concept underlying UbiVid: exploiting the relationship between (social) function and architectural space" (Buxton 1997).

Buxton (1997) made a key observation about his UbiVid concept, namely, that it serves as a "complement to UbiComp in that it shares the twin properties of ubiquity and transparency." He ultimately argues that there is only a "seeming" paradox; in reality, by smartly adding *more* equipment (ubiquity) "there actually appears to be less technology and far less intrusion of the technology in the social interactions that it mediates" (transparency). Moreover, he argues that UbiVid and UbiComp "work hand-in-hand" and should collectively be called "ubiquitous media" (Buxton 1997). In contrast to "multimedia computers, in which functionality is inherently bundled into a single device, located at a single location, and operated by a single individual," ubiquitous media represent "an architectural concept in that it is concerned with preserving, or building upon, conventional location-function-distance relationships" that augment reality rather than present an artificial world (e.g., virtual reality).

Buxton's article contains some of the earliest references to terms that are more familiar today, namely "augmented reality" and—important to this volume—"ubiquitous media." However, while his working definition for augmented reality, which is based on the concept of computer-augmented environments in which computers are used to "augment objects in the real world" (Wellner, Mackay, and Gold 1993), is still relatively cogent, his conceptualization of ubiquitous media is somewhat limited, focusing on video conferencing (and a multitude of cameras and screens that attempt to make interaction over great distances more natural). Even so, his arguments for a design approach that "shift to builds upon users' existing skills, rather than demanding the learning of new ones" is central to ubiquitous media design approaches today that try to naturalize or make effortless our interactions with technology.

Some of the most recognizable attempts to naturalize media experiences can be seen in the haptic interfaces and voice-based artificial intelligence (AI) systems common to smartphones, such as Siri on Apple devices. Mark Deuze and the Janissary Collective (2012, 297) argue that these interfaces represent the "seamless integration among human beings, nature, and technology." Mobile technologies in general are a key precursor—if not central element—of the modern ubiquitous media environment. Past and current mobile technologies from pagers to PDAs, and cell phones to modern smartphones and wearables, are some of the most visible manifestations of the progression toward ubiquitous media in nearly every corner of the world. Mobile giants such as Google Android and Apple dominate markets in the US and Europe, and mobile technologies are particularly important in emerging and developing nations where mobile data subscriptions outpace fixed broadband connections by a significant margin (International Telecommunication Union 2016). Hence, mobile devices are one of the key harbingers of ubiquitous media as both a technical/material and discursive reality for individuals around the world.

Other mobile devices extend this trend and incorporate the data collection and processing characteristic of UbiComb. Bechmann and Lomborg (2015, 1), for example, argue that wearable technologies including fitness trackers that "log, accumulate, and organize sensory, biometric, geo-locational, and other types of personal data are introduced to users in pursuit of, among other things, self-monitoring and augmentation of lived experience." This idea is echoed by Featherstone (2009, 3), who seemingly connects the ideas of UbiComp and ubiquitous media, stating:

> Increasingly, as media become ubiquitous they become embedded in material objects and environments, bodies and clothing, zones of transmission and reception. Media pervade our bodies, cultures and societies—a shift made possible by miniaturized electronic circuitry, the cheap ubiquitous computer chips embedded in environments and mobile devices that sustain a new communicative infrastructure.

Of course, for content and data to flow between devices and channels, a communication system is required to connect them. The Internet fulfils that role today, existing both as one of the infrastructures supported by and supportive of UbiComp.

Networking and the Internet

Bechmann and Lomborg (2015, 1) argue that the Internet itself has become ubiquitous and "extends itself across a wide variety of digital technologies." But much like ubiquitous computing, the development of the Internet into a ubiquitous network has a long and complex history. Campbell-Kelly and Aspray (2004, 255–256) note that one of the theoretical predecessors of the Internet is the encyclopedia, since a primary goal of both is to bring order to the world's knowledge and make readily available to all. This basic idea inspired science fiction author H. G. Wells to write a series of essays on what he called the World Encyclopedia or World Brain between First and Second World War. He envisioned this as having an open, international, scholarly cooperative with a distributed infrastructure and networked management. Wells' World Brain similarly influenced scientist, inventor, and M.I.T. Professor Vannevar Bush to conceive, pre-WWII, of the Memex, a theoretical information storage-and-retrieval and proto-hypertext machine remarkably similar to Wells' World Brain (Campbell-Kelly and Aspray 2004, 256–259).

Neither the World Brain nor the Memex were ever realized, but the basic ideas of a distributed architecture with networked management for information sharing and collaborative work were incorporated into ARPANET, a "fault tolerant computer network" developed under the supervision of Joseph Carl Robnett Licklider (1963–1966) and Larry Roberts (taking over in 1966) at the United States Department of Defense's Advanced Research Projects Agency (ARPA) beginning in 1963 (Campbell-Kelly and Aspray 2004, 260). The establishment of ARPANET was dependent upon the previous developments in computing and information communication technology (ICT) including, but not limited to, general purpose computers, starting with ENIAC at the University of Pennsylvania in 1946; the "computer on a chip" or the microprocessor, invented by Intel engineer Ted Hoff in 1971; and packet-switching communication technologies, a communications paradigm in which packets (i.e., discrete blocks of data) are routed between nodes over data links shared with other traffic (see Castells 2000, 40–46).

Packet-switching was originally handled by a communication standard simply called the Network Control Protocol (NCP) but, eventually, a more advanced protocol was developed called Transmission Control Protocol/Internetworks Protocol (TCP/IP). Highly flexible, TCP/IP allowed different kinds of private networks to communicate with each other, meaning computers on differently structured local networks were able to encode and decode data packages for each other (Sterling 1993). Because of its flexibility, TCP/IP became an ARPANET standard in 1980 and is still the network protocol we use to communicate on the Internet today.

Packet switching not only made the network fault tolerant as desired—if part of the network is down, messages would simply be rerouted automatically—but it also allowed for the most efficient use of these data lines; a single user could not monopolize a line since data would be shuttled around the network in discrete packets. In addition, by networking ARPA's computer systems together, the users of each computer would be able to use the facilities and processing power of any other computer on the network. In essence, packet-switching enabled a (relatively) stable and ever-present network that was (theoretically, provided the right equipment and permissions) available to everyone.

ARPANET first went online on September 1, 1969, and consisted at the time of four nodes located at universities in the western United States: The University of California, Los Angeles, Stanford University, the University of California, Santa Barbara, and the University of Utah. Access was restricted to the military and university researchers. New nodes were added over time. By 1971, there were 23 total nodes; by 1977, that number had increased to 111. While the linking of computers via ARPANET was motivated by economic considerations (Campbell-Kelly and Aspray 2004, 260)—namely, the ability for various institutions to share computing resources an processing power—ARPANET was also quickly adopted for interpersonal communication and group socialization, in large part thanks to the invention of e-mail by Ray Tomlinson in 1971. As Bruce Sterling (1993) summarizes: "The main traffic on ARPANET was not long-distance computing. Instead, it was news and personal messages. Researchers were using ARPANET to collaborate on projects, to trade notes on work, and eventually, to downright gossip and schmooze." Mailing lists dedicated to topics such as science fiction became increasingly popular and, although this "was frowned upon by many ARPANET computer administrators...this didn't stop it from happening" (Sterling 1993).

Demand for access to the Internet (and tools such as e-mail), coupled with an ever-increasing amount of (primarily social) traffic led to the creation of new networks built upon the same principles. These networks included MILNET for the military, CSNET for computer scientists, the National Science Foundation's NSFNET, among others. Although the traffic was split, all of these sub-networks still used the original ARPANET as a backbone thanks to TCP/IP. Because of that, people started calling this "network of networks" the ARPA-INTERNET and then, eventually, just INTERNET[3].

At the same time, others who were excluded from participation in ARPANET or put off by "acceptable use" rules established by the US military and member universities, started establishing alternatives to the early Internet. These ad-hoc networks usually relied on the use of a modem, devices that (at the time) could modulate a signal, similar to that used by telephones, to carry digital information. Examples of thee alternative systems include Usenet, a topic-based discussion/messaging board through which people could communicate and exchange files (USENET was developed by students at Duke University and the University of North Carolina, two universities excluded from ARPANET) (Campbell-Kelly and Aspray 2004, 265); the "Whole Earth 'Lectronic Link" or WELL, a text-based "virtual world" people could connect to via modem; Bulletin Board Systems or BBSs, which could feature both synchronous (chat) and asynchronous (bulletin board) elements; and Multi-User Dungeons or MUDs, text-based predecessors to today's graphical Massive Multiuser Online Role Playing Games (MMORPGs). All of these systems worked to increase the popularity of computer networking outside of the "official" Internet.

Eventually, commercial pressures combined with the growth of private and non-profit networks led to opening up access to the Internet in 1992–1993, followed by the closing of government operated Internet backbone in April 1995, and to a full privatization of the Internet. At this point, many of the extra-Internet systems mentioned above shifted to Internet protocols and were eventually integrated into the Internet itself, which helped greatly expand the Internet with little effort. Even with this integration, the Internet was still very difficult for most people to use. It was heavily text based, often required special knowledge, had limited graphic capabilities, and lacked organization, which made it difficult to find and retrieve specific information.

The invention of a new Internet-based application would solve many of these problems and shift the Internet into the mainstream: the World Wide Web. The

Web was developed in the late 1980s and early 1990s by Tim Berners-Lee, a software engineer from the United Kingdom. The idea of the Web stemmed from his experiments with hypertext systems in 1980 during a six-month consulting position at CERN, a nuclear physics research facility in Geneva, Switzerland (*ibid.*, 268). That idea was in part based on the work of Ted Nelson who, in 1974, imagined a new system of organizing information that he called "hypertext" which used a series of horizontal links between information sources, allowing users to construct their own information maps. Berners-Lee revisited the system he developed, which he called Enquire, when he returned to CERN in 1984 and began to push for a "more expansive hypertext program" (Lambert 2005, 16).

The inspiration for this new global hypertext program was to allow physicists all over the world to collaborate and share information without having to worry about interoperability between different networks and computer systems. One of the outcomes of the proposed program, in other words, would be to make all information instantly accessible regardless of a researcher's physical, geographic location. Although the concept of ubiquity was never referenced, Berners-Lee's project represents one of the first, nascent steps towards making media, information, and even connectivity itself ubiquitous. In 1987, he began cooperatively working with his CERN colleague Robert Cailliau, who was experimenting with Apple's hypertext-based Hypercard database software, to further develop this system (Lambert 2005, 16), but it was Berners-Lee who envisioned the system as a "marriage of hypertext and the Internet" (Campbell-Kelly and Aspray 2004, 269). Finally, in 1989, the pair made a formal proposal to CERN for what they called "the World Wide Web" (Campbell-Kelly and Aspray 2004; Lambert 2005). The subsequent development of graphical web browsers meant to run on personal computers, starting with Marc Andreessen's Mosaic browser (which would eventually become Netscape Navigator), both simplified and mainstreamed the use of the Web (Campbell-Kelly and Aspray 2004, 271–273).

Later developments, including mobile technologies such as Internet-enabled smartphones and mobile apps, have further cemented the Web and the Internet into the daily lives of those with access (see International Telecommunication Union 2016). As Anja Bechmann and Stine Lomborg (2015, 1) state, "personal computers wired to the internet have become a natural part, for some even the backbone, of how people across the globe plan and execute work and leisure activities in everyday life." They speak of a "ubiquitous Internet" that "manifests itself in diffusion patterns of ubiquitous internet devices, a diverse set of cultural practices of digital media use, and a whole range of sociopolitical issues across domains" (Bechmann and Lomborg 2015, 1). Their concept of the ubiquitous Internet resonates with Castells' (2001, 1) contention that the Internet has become "the fabric of our lives." Here, Castells is building upon his concept of the "network society," i.e., a new societal configuration in which nearly all structures, activities, and institutions are influenced by, if not dependent upon, information processing via networked communications, with the Internet representing the network *par excellence* (Castells 2000, 2001). This "network society" is related to concepts that have emerged in recent years such as digital culture (e.g., Miller 2011), a culture of connectivity (van Dijck 2013), or "mediatized worlds" (Hepp and Krotz 2014). Within these "media lives" (Deuze 2012), people have become intertwined with networks, content, and devices in their everyday lives to the point that these digital media are taken for granted.

Considered alongside Featherstone's reference in the section above to computers embedded in a multitude of object and environments, once can see the way all three of these historical precedents—digitalization, UbiComp and Networking—have contributed to the conceptualization of the "Internet of Everything," an environment strongly related to ubiquitous media comprised of "a whole host of connected endpoints that in some way interact with the physical world, whether sensing, acting, or reacting" (Greene 2015). These always-on, always-connected devices "not only provide the potential for ubiquitous connectivity and greater interactivity, enabling everyone to communicate with everyone else; they also open up a further stage, that of a physical environment of things talking to each other" (Featherstone 2009, 4). As one "professional services company" put it, a ubiquitous media environment is one in which "anything—a shoe, a city, your own body—can become a touchpoint for engaging people with media" (Becker 2009).

THEMES

To reiterate, this overview of ubiquitous media's historical precedents is cursory and incomplete. However, the interrelation of the three concepts outlined above provides us with a general framework for this book, in which we consider ubiquitous media from a variety of perspectives and in a variety of contexts. Despite the multitude of approaches represented here, four major themes emerge in the chapters that follow that are worth noting, many of which emerge from the antecedents discussed in the previous section. These themes include:

- **a tension between visible and invisible media** somewhat reminiscent of the tension between transparency and ubiquity in UbiComp;
- **increasing datafication** made possible by more devices in more places capable of collecting, storing and transmitting more information;
- **a merging of digital/virtual/online and analog/real/offline environments** such as in augmented reality and, finally;
- **a merging of bodies and media** in which our bodies, in a sense, become media through the incorporation and use of wearable technologies.[4]

SECTION AND CHAPTER OVERVIEW

We asked each of the authors in this collection to consider and discuss the question of what it means to live in a world of ubiquitous media in their respective chapters. The texts they produced not only address the themes outlined above, but also discuss how the emergence of these themes impact our culture and society at the macro, meso, and micro level. These chapters have been divided into six "contexts" or major motifs that each represent a different approach to understanding the concept of ubiquitous media. These contexts, and the chapters in each, are outlined briefly below.

Archaeologies: Histories and Futures of Ubiquitous Media

This opening section fills in some of the gaps in our discussion of the historical precedents of ubiquitous media above by examining the past development and deployment of ubiquitous media. Laura Steckman's chapter begins by diving deeper into the role of Xerox's Palo Alto Research Center (PARC), outlines some of the major technological advances involved in ubiquitous computing and media, discusses the evolution of the mobile phone into a miniature, fully-functional, computing device that also is a central component in the ubiquitous media environment, and covers multiple concerns that impact US policy in light of emergent technology. Tanner Mirrlees explores the relationship between media and war in a chapter that aims to clarify the meaning of "ubiquitous media war" in the twenty-first century, in which he conceptualizes "ubiquitous media war" as a war waged by a plurality of actors who produce, distribute, exhibit, consume, and interactively prosume a war of images and messages across every available media form and platform. He positions the US war in Iraq (2003–2011) as the twenty-first century's first ubiquitous media war to demonstrate this concept. Finally, Eric Lehman similarly uses a case study, in this instance of the Sony/BMG rootkit scandal, to examine that company's attempt and failure to execute ubiquitous yet covert control over music media in the form of Digital Rights Management (DRM) as a both a literal and symbolic contagion narrative. From this example, he argues that while media and its controls are thought to be everywhere, specific incidents are not always seen even though they are present and active; only in their ability to "go viral" by entering the public imagination do these controls reveal their omnipresent nature.

Mobilities: Mobile Devices, Wearables, and Locative Media

The second section recognizes the central role mobile technologies play in the understanding and definition of ubiquitous media. Aaron Shapiro contributes to our understanding of ubiquitous media by contrasting locative ubiquity with an alternative, one that focuses not only on the ubiquity of mediating devices but also on the ubiquity of representations, specifically representations of space and place within the Google Street View platform. Rather than a user moving through and connecting with a networked environment via his or her phone, ubiquitous representations of space in this case are enabled by the proxy mobility of the Google car, which travels across the Earth's surface collecting street-level images to enable "armchair exploration" of a virtual world. Sebastiano Nucera and Marco Centorrino focus on the use contexts of wearable technologies and how they affect the ways that despatialized knowledge is propagated. They argue that wearable technologies are building a system of uses and relationships similar to technologies of the past, where the body is "co-opted" as an active part of content creation.

Visualities: Ubiquitous Media and Visual Culture

The third section examine ubiquitous media through the lens of visual culture. Ana Rita Morais introduces us to the term "mobile infography," which she defines as "the visual representation of information as projected through the mobile hardware of the camera, and subsequently translated via the software of the mobile apps." From this definition, she outlines the ways in which mobile devices work collectively with bodies and objects in a process of inscribing meaning and value into both social and spatial relations. Pilar Lacasa, Julián de la Fuente, and Katiuska Manzur examine the Bakhtinian concept of the chronotope in tandem with a two-year ethnographic study in order to examine the practices of children when interacting with ubiquitous mobile devices in their daily lives, and how these ubiquitous tools enable the construction of digital "micro-stories" that play a role in meaning-making. Finally, Kris Belden-Adams examines digital photography, particularly forms of "vernacular" photographs such as selfies, in relation to Walter Benjamin's concept of aura. Her examination demonstrates how the concept of aura can help us understand the sociocultural role of digital photography and reveal potential new approaches to vernacular photography for digital humanities scholars.

Economies: Critical Political Economic Perspectives on Ubiquitous Media

This section examines ubiquitous media in relation to issues such as capitalism, economic class, labor, and the economics of production. Edward Comor's contribution relates media ubiquity to Harold Innis's concerns regarding media, civilization, imperialism/centralization of power, and monopolies of knowledge. Innis intimately captures the power relations that ubiquitous media reflect and affect, while never losing sight of the importance of locating these in broader historical and political economic dynamics. Comor applies his remarkable understanding of Innis' concepts in order to demonstrate that the ubiquity of digital media widens and deepens status quo relations and thinking but, in so doing, it tends to bias (or forge rigidities) in knowledge/cultural capacities (thus undermining or isolating certain kinds of creativity and adaptability). Margaret Reid approaches ubiquitous media through a critical political economy approach to analyze major shifts in the business, labor, and practice of news media creation in a digital context. She analyses how the immaterial labor undertaken by journalists operates both to create value for social media sites while also creating potential value for journalists themselves through brand development. She also provides theoretical insight into the politics of ubiquitous media in the context of journalistic work, and the difficulties that emerge when media use and brand building are contextualized as labor, in an already precarious labor economy. Finally, Susan Bryant uses an analysis of a survey of undergraduate teaching assistants working in an online academic writing course to illustrate the theoretical issues related to ubiquitous media involving both digital labor and the challenges of the so-called "work-life balance," with a particular emphasis on some of the gendered aspects of social relations. She uses Dorothy Smith's feminist approach to political economy, which focuses on peoples' everyday/everynight activities, in order to highlight the artificiality of the perceived dichotomy between "work" and "life," especially for women, and to elaborate on why and how this analytical dichotomy is even more problematic in the era of ubiquitous connections.

Localities and Communities: Spaces, Places and Time

The chapters in this section examine the role of ubiquitous media in specific communities, as well has how they influence or alter our understanding of specific places and spaces. Jacqueline Fewkes and Abdul Nasir Kahn discuss how citizens and media providers in Kargil, a region in the north Indian Himalayas, use social media and mobile apps to make possible the establishment of traditional local television stations. They argue that the use of multiple media platforms allows local stations to combine global television styles with community interests in ways that are common for community-based television. With a particular focus on the use of the mobile messaging app WhatsApp, they demonstrate how digital media can enable the combination of the multiple perspectives of a talk show and the narrative approach of a documentary with the urgency of breaking news into a text based media presence integrated into users' daily lives. Tiro Uskali interrogates concepts of "ubiquitous journalism" or "journalism everywhere" by examining the emergence of long-form livestreams on Finnish and other Scandinavian television networks. Pulling from a variety of examples, he outlines the similarities and differences between livestreams and (ubiquitous) journalism while pointing out the potential and pitfalls of both concepts.

Surveillances: Privacy, Surveillance and Ubiquitous Media

This last section deals with one of the most prominent and highly-discussed issues in recent years: digital privacy and surveillance. Mark Andrejevic emphasizes how ubiquitous media enable the redoubling of the world in the form of data. The result of this datafication of everyday life is the rise of a condition of "framelessness", which is an expression of the cultural logic of big data. He explores the political, economic, and cultural implications of big data as an expression of ubiquitous media. Sarah Harney compares surveillance techniques used during the Civil Rights movement in the 1960s in the United States to those used against the Black Lives Matter movement to ask how ubiquitous media has changed how surveillance of social movements is enacted. Relying on the concepts of biopower, and the surveillant assemblage, she details how technology, covert tactics, and legislation work together to attempt to monitor dissent and enact social control. Finally, Susan Currie Sivek outlines the ways consumers' media experiences are shaped by the input from an array of sensors that gather a range of data about users. Her chapter investigates the consequences of this gathering, analysis, and application through the growing use of "emotion analytics." She incorporates case studies of Apple and the lesser-known start-up Affectiva to demonstrate how these companies are already deeply engaged in the innovative use of emotion analytics to surveil users' emotions and then to tailor media and advertising messages to their emotional status, which she argues is indicative of a type of emotional labor in which our emotional responses generate value for corporate data-gatherers.

Each of these chapters offers a unique but ultimately illustrative and critical approach to the concept of ubiquitous media. In so doing, the authors assembled here not only contribute to our understanding of the definition of ubiquitous media, but also offer detailed insights into the effects a world of ubiquitous media will have on our experiences, cultures, communities, and understanding of ourselves.

NOTES

1. An n-gram is a graph that shows how often a word or phrase has occurred in a body of texts over a selected range of years. For more information, see https://books.google.com/ngrams/info. The Google Ngram search tool is available at https://books.google.com/ngrams/.
2. Examples of pre-digital roots of ubiquitous media include the postal system (Siegert 1999); the establishment of the telephone as central via common carrier laws; the invention of transistors that allowed for the miniaturization of devices; the embrace of neoliberalism and its emphasis on

personal responsibility and choice; leading to the valorization of "vernacular" culture and creativity (Burgess and Green 2009) in the digital era.
3. The ARPANET backbone, having become obsolete, closed down on February 28, 1990, at which point the backbone of the Internet was NSFNET. This too was decommissioned, in 1995. Now the Internet consists entirely of the various commercial ISPs and private networks.
4. As Featherstone (2009, 10) argues, current technologies are increasingly "adapted and integrated into the human body and the body itself changes with technologies."

REFERENCES

Åkesson, Maria, and Carina Ihlström Eriksson. 2010. "Advertising Challenges in Ubiquitous Media Environments." In *Handbook of Research on Mobile Marketing Management*, edited by Key Pousttchi and Dietmar G. Wiedemann, 77–93. New York: Business Science Reference.
Bechmann, Anja, and Stine Lomborg. 2015. "The Ubiquitous Internet: Introduction and Conceptualization." In *The Ubiquitous Internet: User and Industry Perspectives*, edited by Anja Bechmann and Stine Lomborg, 1–5. New York: Routledge.
Becker, Gene. 2009. "What is Ubiquitous Media." *Lightning Laboratories*. Last modified June 26, accessed December 28. http://www.lightninglaboratories.com/tcw/2009/06/what-is-ubiquitous-media/.
Bolter, Jay David, and Richard Grusin. 2000. *Remediation: Understanding New Media*. Cambridge, MA: MIT Press.
Burgess, Jean, and Joshua Green. 2009. *YouTube, Digital Media and Society Series*. Malden, MA: Polity Press.
Burnett, Robert, and David Marshall. 2003. "Introduction." In *Web Theory*, edited by Robert Burnett and David Marshall, 1–6. New York: Routledge.
Buxton, William A. S. 1997. "Living in Augmented Reality: Ubiquitous Media and Reactive Environments." *billbuxton.com*. Last modified February 21, 2012, accessed January 19. http://www.billbuxton.com/augmentedReality.html.
Campbell-Kelly, Martin, and William Aspray. 2004. *Computer: A History of the Information Machine*. 2nd ed. Boulder, CO: Westview Press.
Cartwright, Lisa. 2002. "Film and the Digital in Visual Studies: Film Studies in the Era of Convergence." In *The Visual Culture Reader*, 2nd ed., edited by Nicholas Mirzeoff, 417–432. New York: Routledge.
Castells, Manuel. 2000. *The Rise of the Network Society*. Cambridge, MA: Blackwell.
———. 2001. *The Internet Galaxy: Reflections on the Internet, Business, and Society*. New York: Oxford University Press.
Cope, Bill, and Mary Kalantzis. 2010. *Ubiquitous Learning*. Urbana, Illinois: University of Illinois Press.
Deuze, Mark. 2012. *Media Life*. Malden, MA: Polity Press.
Deuze, Mark, and The Janissary Collective. 2012. "Mobile Media Life." In *Moving Data: The iPhone and the Future of Media*, edited by Pelle Snickars and Patrick Vonderau, 296–308. New York: Columbia University Press.
Dourish, Paul, and Genevieve Bell. 2011. *Divining a Digital Future: Mess and Mythology in Ubiquitous Computing*. Cambridge, MA: MIT Press.
Featherstone, Mike. 2009. "Ubiquitous Media: An Introduction." *Theory, Culture & Society* 26 (2–3):1–22.

Garon, Jon. 2012. "Revolutions and Expatriates: Social Networking, Ubiquitous Media and the Disintermediation of the State." *Ubiquitous Media and the Disintermediation of the State* 11 (2):293–310.

Gillmor, Dan. 2010. "Mediactive." *mediactive.com*. http://mediactive.com/wp-content/uploads/2010/12/mediactive_gillmor.pdf.

Grace, Helen. 2013. *Culture, Aesthetics and Affect in Ubiquitous Media: The Prosaic Image*. New York: Routledge.

Greene, Jeff. 2015. "TIM Lecture Series—The Internet of Everything: Fridgebots, Smart Sneakers, and Connected Cars." *Technology Innovation Management Review* 5 (5): 47–49.

Hepp, Andreas, and Friedrich Krotz. 2014. *Mediatized Worlds: Culture and Society in a Media Age*. Basingstoke, Hampshire: Palgrave Macmillan.

International Telecommunication Union. 2016. The World in 2016: ICT Facts and Figures. Accessed 29 January 2017.

Jenkins, Henry. 2006. *Convergence Culture: Where Old and New Media Collide*. New York: New York University Press.

Lambert, Laura. 2005. *The Internet: A Historical Encyclopedia*. Santa Barbara, CA: MTM Publishing.

Mihailidis, Paul, and Benjamin Thevenin. 2013. "Media literacy as a core competency for engaged citizenship in participatory democracy." *American Behavioral Scientist* 57 (11): 1611–1622.

Miller, Vincent. 2011. *Understanding Digital Culture*. Thousand Oaks, CA: Sage.

Murray, Simone. 2003. "Media Convergence's Third Wave Content Streaming." *Convergence: The International Journal of Research into New Media Technologies* 9 (1): 8–18.

Qualcomm. 2011. "Qualcomm to Acquire Atheros, Leader in Connectivity & Networking Solutions." *qualcomm.com*. Last modified January 6. https://www.qualcomm.com/news/releases/2011/01/05/qualcomm-acquire-atheros-leader-connectivity-networking-solutions.

Siegert, Bernard. 1999. *Relays: Literature as an Epoch of the Postal System*. Stanford, CA: Stanford University Press.

Sterling, Bruce. 1993. "Short History of the Internet." *Internet Society*. Accessed January 17. http://www.internetsociety.org/internet/what-internet/history-internet/short-history-internet.

van Dijck, José. 2013. *The Culture of Connectivity: A Critical History of Social Media*. New York: Oxford University Press.

Weiser, Mark. 1991. "The Computer for the 21st Century." *Scientific American*, September, 94–104.

———. 1996. "Ubiquitous Computing." *ubiq.com*. Last modified March 17, accessed January 16. http://www.ubiq.com/hypertext/weiser/UbiHome.html.

Weiser, Mark, and John Seely Brown. 1996. "The Coming Age of Calm Technology." *ubiq.com*. Accessed January 18. http://www.ubiq.com/hypertext/weiser/acmfuture2endnote.htm.

Wellner, Pierre, Wendy Mackay, and Rich Gold. 1993. "Back to the Real World." *Communications of the ACM* 36 (7):24–26. doi: 10.1145/159544.159555.

PART ONE

Archaeologies

Histories and Futures of Ubiquitous Media

CHAPTER ONE

How We Got Here

The Technologies and Policies Behind Ubiquitous Computing and Ubiquitous Media

LAURA STECKMAN

INTRODUCTION

The movement toward realizing the technologies and policies behind "ubiquity" in global connectivity has been decades in the making. Ubiquity, as referred to herein, is the prevalence and pervasiveness of computing, and since the turn of the twenty-first century, media, within society. In other words, ubiquity encompasses and explains why a person located almost anywhere in the world can select among a variety of communications devices, such as a mobile phone or other portable device, at any given time and connect to the Internet or another network to send and receive data. The ability to use rapid, wireless communication did not appear overnight; rather, it required significant efforts across a wide range of individuals, corporations, and governments that applied extensive research and resources to invent and improve new and pre-existing technology. To understand this phenomenon of how global communications developed into the ubiquity paradigm, it is necessary to examine the individuals who acted as key technological innovators on the path to ubiquity alongside the technologies (including Wi-Fi, Bluetooth, Radio Frequency Identification or RFID, and Global Positioning System or GPS), and the socio-political implications, such as the policy and legal debates over the issues of spectrum management and encryption, which have arisen from the mass adoption of and increasing demand for wireless communications.

Computers, as devices used to produce, process, store, and transmit data, are the precursor without which ubiquity could not exist. Charles Babbage conceived the idea of the computer in the 1830s, describing a machine that could perform calculations and analytics based on the technologies of that era. In Babbage's depiction, computers would be hand-cranked machines rather than mobile devices connected to a larger network (Purbrick 1993). Though he could not predict the route that technological development would eventually take, not knowing that the machines would be battery-powered or electrical, he nonetheless devised an idea that would change the future. The next major steps in computing occurred a century later in the 1940s, with the Atanasoff Berry Computer, which was quickly superseded by ENIAC (Electronic Numerical Integrator and Computer) (Sankaran 1995). These machines were large, heavy, and costly. Few people apart from university or corporate staffs had the opportunity to see or use them, as opposed to the present, when large numbers of people carry mobile devices capable of computing in their pockets to perform day-to-day lifestyle functions.

While computers continued to advance, and shrink in size and cost, the effort that catalyzed the movement toward today's ubiquity began in the late 1970s. Xerox's Palo Alto Research Center (PARC), located in Palo Alto, California, embarked on a project to create the "office of the future." For this effort, PARC assembled a team of social scientists, computer engineers, and physical scientists to rethink how people interacted with technology in order to develop and integrate multiple small devices seamlessly into people's daily lives. In the late 1980s, under the leadership of Mark Weiser (the man who coined the term "ubiquitous computing"), PARC established the Ubiquitous Computing program within its Computer Science Laboratory. The program intended to provide a "radical answer to what was wrong with the personal computer: too complex and hard to use; too demanding of attention; too isolating from other people and activities; and too dominating as it colonized our desktops and lives" (Weiser, Gold, and Brown 1999, 693). More precisely, PARC's researchers believed that technology should be easily accessible, such as reaching for a pad and pencil, rather than being complicated and bulky (Markoff 1991). Some of PARC's major inventions included LiveBoard, a large wall display; Active Badge, a name badge that transmitted its location to infrared sensors and tracked the wearer's location throughout a sensor-enabled building; and ParcTab, a palm-sized tablet, the prototype for Personal Digital Assistants. These inventions constituted early milestones in the trajectory to achieve ubiquitous computing.

Ubiquitous computing, as an idea, took off in the 1990s. Information specialists predicted that it would transition to actualization, meaning that people would begin using the small, portable devices to communicate whenever and wherever they chose (Mills and Scholtz 1999). PARC's program made great advances in computer development, and also uncovered many issues, such as questions about privacy and transparency in who sees and controls the data produced by the devices' electronic transmissions. In the mid-1990s, the program also shifted its focus to what it termed "calm computing," the idea that computers should be tools that fade into the background of a user's consciousness while remaining accessible. Calm computing used the analogy that just as a carpenter's hammer becomes an extension of the carpenter, allowing him or her to seamlessly integrate it into the work and focusing on the bigger project than directly on the hammer, computers must also become tools to help people solve problems rather than being something separate (Weiser, Gold, and Brown 1999, 695). Ultimately, calm computing has not functioned as PARC envisioned due to the product branding; instead of portable technology fading into the background, devices stand out and are often sought out because of their manufacturer. For example, Apple product users perceive the brand very highly and are devoted to it, showing their willingness to stand in long lines for hours to purchase new products (Matyszczyk 2016). Consumer's interest in owning devices from specific brands—and having loyalty to those brands—was not configured into the calm computing paradigm where devices fade into the background of daily life. Instead, for many people, owning a particular brand can have intrinsic value and can positively affect their social image or prestige (Cătălin and Andreea 2014; Liu and Liang 2014). However, in spite of the role of customer preference toward branding, some major facets of calm computing have become realized: computers are integrated seamlessly into society today, and those devices have played a role in the prevalence and usage of ubiquitous computing, and later, ubiquitous media.

Following PARC's lead, other organizations made their own marks on the ubiquitous computing paradigm. IBM, Hewlett-Packard, and MIT, among other research giants in industry and academia, initiated their own programs to explore the potentialities and opportunities within the realm of ubiquitous computing (IBM Annual Report 2003; Infosys 2001; Microsoft Annual Report 2016). Early efforts focused on wireless networking, processing capability, storage capacity, and well-formulated displays. In the early 2000s, the focus prioritized location-aware and location-based applications and their applicability to users. During this period, the interest in ubiquitous computing inspired the European Union to inaugurate its Disappearing Computer project (Russell, Streitz, and Winograd 2005). From the late 2000s to the mid-2010s, the research field placed priority on sensing and data analytics. Combined, industry and academic efforts laid the groundwork for present-day ubiquitous computing's mobility, through technologies required for wireless communications, such as Wi-Fi, Bluetooth, and RFID; portability, with the ever-growing number of devices and wearables that connect to the Internet and transmit information; and locality, where GPS geo-locates a user's exact coordinates. These advances have led to heightened interest in the "Internet of Things," a phrase coined in 1999, as an alternative to ubiquitous or pervasive computing.

The Internet of Things (IoT) is a "network of connected objects that link the physical world with the world of information through the web" (NMC 2015, 46). Kevin Ashton, a British employee at Proctor & Gamble, coined the neologism in

1999. The term was derived from his experience trying to determine why a certain shade of lipstick was always sold out, and why stores didn't know they needed to restock the item. After successfully solving the problem by integrating RFID technology into a tracking system, he saw the potential to revolutionize commercial industry (Maney 2015). IoT has required the collaboration of many people, organizations, corporations, and governments to implement. It is an extension of the ubiquitous computing concept, though it has not followed all of the precepts inherent in the original concept, particularly the idea that ubiquitous computing should be calm, meaning that devices are present and so readily available that they fade into subconsciousness and are used without a second thought. Instead, it has led to manufacturers branding the devices so that they do stand out, and in some cases, have developed community followings that swear loyalty to that brand and will stand in line for hours to acquire the newest upgrades. IoT is also sometimes used interchangeably with the Internet of Everything (IoE), a confusion that proves how important branding has become within the paradigm. Cisco, a multinational IT firm headquartered in San Jose, California, created the term IoE in 2013 to put its own spin on the concept[1] (LinkLabs 2015). The IoE concept builds on the original, implied intention of IoT and adds people, process, and data to the definition, officially (Banafa 2014). Within the IT world, IoT has now been relegated to objects connected over the web. It is not a small number; in 2016, 6.4 billion devices comprised the IoT, with the number projected to reach 20.7 billion by 2020 (Gartner 2015). These devices fall into the literal interpretation of IoT, though the initial dream for IoT implicitly involved people, processes, and data.

The technological revelations stemming from advances in ubiquitous computing have also applied to the mobile phone and other media. In fact, in the early 2000s, research teams started delving into what they termed "ubimedia," which combined ubiquitous computing and physically-linked hypermedia, to focus research and design on how emerging technological systems could forge links between physical and digital media (Barton, Goddi, and Spasojevic 2003). Ubimedia combines "technologies in location and context adaptation, inter-device interaction and reaction, as well as media and data communication for the well-being of humans" (Lau *et al.* 2011, 218). Ubiquitous media encompasses more than just the technological aspects related to the proliferation of pervasive media. As a concept, it applies to aspects of human culture, such as how a particular group chooses some forms of media over others as well as how people interact with media to share information. Therefore, ubiquitous media is an advanced application of ubiquitous computing to the media, specifically to top-down and bottom-up journalism, in addition to the devices and technologies used to disseminate news.

Ubiquitous media, as a term and as a practice, has already led to some key revelations about society. The first known reference of the term, for example, occurred when mainstream media was able to report on a major US disaster before the government released the information. In 2001, Michael K. Powell, chairman of the Federal Communications Commission (FCC), stated that the country's "ubiquitous media environment" made it unnecessary to use the national Emergency Alert System after September 11, 2001, because media outlets were already reporting on the tragic events that day (Collins 2001). Though the term was initially used to exemplify the presence of major media outlets such as CNN, MSNBC, and FOX, the concept expanded to include bottom-up reporting from individuals on the scene or in the know, who now use mobile devices to make videos and upload them for immediate consumption. An example of how bottom-up reporting demonstrated the power of ubimedia happened when Sohaib Athar, a Pakistani IT consultant, noted a helicopter flying over Abbottabad at one o'clock in the morning on May 1 2011. He went to Twitter, where he mentioned the rarity of a helicopter at that hour, and subsequently commented on a local bombing. Athar quickly received international media attention for reporting first on the raid against Osama bin Laden, making him one of the early examples of the power and legitimacy of ubiquitous media from non-traditional outlets (Gross 2011). Following in the wake of the rising popularity of social media, particularly during the so-called Arab Spring, ubiquitous media had gained purchase in societies around the globe.

Bottom-up reporting, the idea that any person on the ground can report from anywhere, would not be possible without wireless-enabled cellular phones. Motorola produced the first mobile phone in 1973, later introducing the first commercial mobile phone in 1983 (Seward 2013). Improvements in design, portability, and technological advances from 1990 to 1995 allowed Nokia to make the mobile phone market more competitive. Initially, phones were cost prohibitive and designed only for speaking. Functionally, phone designers did not add many features until the late 1990s, when mobile phones started to gain in popularity; in fact, PDAs features were integrated into phones to prevent users from carrying multiple devices. BlackBerry, for example, released its first model in 1999, and became known as a quality brand for communications and scheduling. Over time, the mobile phone has evolved into more of a mobile device; its functions now allow an owner to access, use, and customize a wide variety of multimedia, including but not limited to accessing to the Internet, taking and sharing photos, connecting via social media, and streaming television and radio. By 2016, there were 4.30 billion mobile phone users worldwide, accounting for about 58.7% percent of the population (eMarketer 2016). In the United States alone, 198.5 million people owned smartphones, accounting for 79.1% of the mobile market (ComScore 2016). The mobile phone, with the ability to access wireless communications networks through browsers and specialized applications, or apps, has now become a mobile computing device. It is a part of the ubiquitous computing paradigm, and at the same time, also functions as an enabler of ubiquitous media.

Today's mobile devices exemplify both types of the ubiquities, computing and media. The upgrades over the years that have enabled their transition from voice communications to every type of communications, including the incorporation of sophisticated applications, and the ability to transmit data wirelessly. These advances have allowed people to use the appropriate enabled device when they wanted, where they wanted, and how they wanted. Some of the most important technologies in mobile phone development are Wi-Fi, Bluetooth, RFID, and GPS capabilities.

Wi-Fi

Wi-Fi is a short-range wireless broadband technology that permits enabled devices to connect to the Internet without cords. Wi-Fi is usually projected through a router that in turn is usually wired to an Internet connection and permits enabled devices to connect wirelessly as long as they remain in range[2]. The US government acquiesced to the development of Wi-Fi when the FCC decided to open specific bands of the wireless spectrum to unlicensed use in 1985. Specifically, the FCC decided to open the 802.11 technology, opening bands previously used for microwave transmission to communications, provided that connected devices would not interfere with other non-communications signals (Economist 2004). However, the initial announcement did little to further the Wi-Fi concept.

In 1990, the Institute of Electronic Engineers (IEEE) placed Vic Hayes, a gentleman who would become known as the "Father of Wi-Fi," at its head. Along with Wireless Ethernet Compatibility Alliance (WECA), and the Wi-Fi Alliance, the IEEE worked to promote and regulate wireless technologies. Their initial standards put forward new data transfer standards that could reach up to 300 Mbps, which were fast for the early 2000s, but not as fast as the technology could eventually go. In fact, the technology developed more slowly than Wireless Local Area Networks (WLANs), as the first 802.11 WLAN protocol was released in 1997, after which there were subsequent updates as 802.11 technology improved (Tektronix 2013). More recently, the latest version of 802.11 as of August 2013, is 802.11ac, often called 5G Wi-Fi. This newest protocol, on its second wave as of 2016, has a theoretical speed of 866.7 Mbps over eight 160MHz channels, though most users will access only one or two bands, giving them a maximum speed of 1.7 Gbps to 2.5 Gbps (Brodkin 2016). This increase is significant when compared to the precursor, 802.11n, with a maximum speed of 600 Mbps (Lendino 2016). The technology is only expected to increase in transmission speed as it continues to develop.

The biggest early proponent of Wi-Fi was Apple. It told Lucent, one of the companies concerned with perpetuating Wi-Fi, that if it could supply an adaptor for less than $100 USD, Apple would add a slot to all of its computers. In 1999, Lucent delivered and Apple complied (Economist 2004). Apple's decision to incorporate Wi-Fi adaptors into its computers revolutionized technology and communications, leading to the predominance of Wi-Fi today on portable electronic devices today. It did, however, take several years for Wi-Fi to integrate the 802.11 technology with their networks and be interoperable on WLAN systems. The Wi-Fi Alliance (WFA) certified the first mobile phones to carry Wi-Fi capabilities and interface with WLANs in 2004 (Smith 2004).

Bluetooth

Bluetooth (named after eighth century Norse King Harald Blåtand) links electronic devices together wirelessly, particularly cellular phones and tablet computers, with other electronics via radio waves over short distances. Often, the linkage is performed to connect phones or tablets with a wireless headset or other listening device and is primarily used to transmit data and voice communications. The technology developed from Swedish graduate student Sven Mattisson's 1986 PhD dissertation at the California Institute of Technology, though it did not materialize until 1997 when Mattisson, then an employee of Ericsson Mobile Communications, convinced a conglomerate of electronics corporations to collaborate; in 1998, they launched Bluetooth (Karlsson and Lugn). This conglomeration immediately became known as the Bluetooth Special Interest Group (SIG).

The Bluetooth SIG, one year after its formation, started promoting its capabilities, ultimately demonstrating how its Bluetooth could contribute to making ubiquitous computing a reality. In 1999 it issued its 1.0 specification, and in 2000 it released its technology in multiple products, including cell phones, a laptop, and a headset. From that point its releases snowballed in number, continuing with enabling printers, a mouse and keyboard, a camera, MP3 player, headphones, and many others. By 2004, Bluetooth existed in more than 250 million devices (Bluetooth 2016). Consumers and companies alike saw the promise of the technology and the value in how enabled products could meet their personal and professional needs.

After 2004, the Bluetooth SIG continued to grow, both in the number and diversity of enabled products and in the number of companies that had joined the consortium. Bluetooth can connect almost any device to another, so long as they are Bluetooth-enabled; when one of the devices has Internet connectivity, Bluetooth can function as a bridge to give the non-enabled device wireless Internet connectivity. The number and types of devices that can use Bluetooth are almost infinite. Some examples of the more unusual devices are sports equipment that reports on users' habits, keyless entry for locks and doors, a pressure cooker, and even buttons for ordering food. Because of its limitless applications, by 2016, over 30,000 companies had become SIG members (Bluetooth 2016).

The introduction of Bluetooth revolutionized global communications because it permitted secure and rapid access to wireless networks and hotspots. With the ease of access came growing consumer demand for new applications, or apps, and other services that functioned through the capability.

Radio Frequency Identification (RFID)

Radio frequency identification (RFID) is a wireless system that uses radio frequency signals to communicate and capture data. The use of RFID allows a computer or another programmed device to read inexpensive tags or chips over short distances by placing readers at key points to track them. The tags are kept low-cost because they do not require an embedded battery. It is an old technology that, with recent advancements in other communications technology, can now be used in modern commercial applications, including enabling RFID readers in wireless-enabled devices such as smartphones or tablets.

RFID, originally developed in the 1940s, was first implemented during World War II to identify enemy airplanes (Jones and Chung 2011, 43–44). With additional development in the 1950s and 1960s, it became integrated into non-military uses, such as in counter-theft devices in high-end department stores (Magill 1996, 993–994). Those RFID tags were often 1-bit tags that could either be on or off; just like anti-theft chips today, they needed to be turned off at the time of purchase before a shopper could leave the store with the item.

By the 1970s, RFID technology and usage expanded to additional markets. The Los Alamos Scientific Laboratory, which started using RFID technologies to track nuclear materials in the early 1970s, branched off and along with other companies, automated toll road payments on a 915 MHz frequency with minimal transmitted data (Partanen 2015). This system is similar to the one that exists today for high-volume roads in busy areas as well as to ensure that certain state or municipal governments receive payments for traffic on certain highways or interstates. In 1973, the US awarded its first patents for improved RFID technology and application. It awarded Mario Cardullo with the first patent for RFID tags with rewritable memory and to Charles Walton, who invented a passive transponder that could unlock a door without a key (Roberti 2005). As RFID technologies showed promise to improve multiple industries, they received more money for research and development.

Building on the initial successes of RFID in the 1970s, many commercial industries started adopting RFID tags and technologies in the 1980s and 1990s, most notably for shipping, toll roads, animal tags, and personnel access badges. These uses increased and spread to new industries in the 2000s, particularly after the Massachusetts Institute of Technology (MIT) established its Auto-ID Center in 1999, with the goal of establishing a worldwide Electronic Product Code (EPC) standard for RFID readers. The center was spearheaded by Sanjay Sarma, David Brock, and Kevin Ashton, known today as the "Father of the Internet of Things." The Auto-ID Center initiative transformed into the Auto-ID Labs project in 2003

(Roberti 2005), having grown into a federation of seven international research universities working to improve RFID and emerging sensor technologies, with the ultimate goal of revolutionizing sensors, the Internet of Things, and the newly-coined "Cloud of Things" for global commerce.

RFID technology has become integrated into some mobile devices. With the technology, the devices can have a RFID tag identifier that contains information about them, and/or have a RFID reader that can interpret data transmitted from a RFID tag. For example, some security personnel may have RFID-tagged mobile communications devices that ping their locations on rounds. Their employers can then monitor if they patrolled their assigned locations on schedule and can investigate if there are unexpected gaps of time before the employee passes the next location on the patrol route. In this instance, the readers are the sensors that determine the employee's location. Smartphones themselves can also have RFID readers. Retail businesses are starting to use phones and special applications to track loyalty cards and merchandise. RFID-enabled devices with readers can improve the speed and quality of some services, such as appliance repair because a technician can download a service order instantly, or assure that airline baggage is deposited on the correct plane.

Global Positioning System (GPS)

Global Positioning System (GPS) has become an integral part of all wireless-enabled devices in order to track their precise locations, velocities, and elevation in real time. GPS is a decades-old technology with some similarities to RFID in that it relies on radio frequencies. It is somewhat newer than RFID in that it was born out of the Cold War's Space Race. When the Russians launched Sputnik in 1957, Johns Hopkins University scientists noticed that when the satellite changed directions, the radio frequencies it emitted also changed. The scientists devised a way of using receivers on the ground to track the satellite's position, and noticed that the reverse also worked, becoming more precise as more satellites were used to track positions on the ground (Sullivan 2012). The US military was the first to use the scientists' observations. As GPS proved successful for military and government use, it was eventually expanded to commercial applications.

The first major development in GPS was when the US Navy completed and launched the TRANSIT satellite in 1964, after years of research and development. The system specifically tracked submarines and fishing vessels. Later its coverage extended to civilian vessels and even drifting buoys. With TRANSIT's success, the Navy allowed commercial entities access to the system in 1967 (Stansell 1983). The military found additional uses for GPS capabilities and employed them in the defense of US national security.

In 1983, the Soviets shot down Korean Airlines Flight 007 after it veered off-course. President Ronald Reagan responded by allowing civilians some access to GPS technology, particularly wanting airlines to employ the capability to avoid future avoidable damage. In 1989, after launching the first privately-owned satellite, the Magellan NAV 1000 became the first portable, handheld GPS receiver to appear on the market (Ha 2010).

The first commercially available phone with GPS, the Benefon Esc!, was sold in Europe in 1999. It was not until 2001 after costs lowered substantially and size was significantly reduced that corporations started including GPS technology on their devices. Congress cleared the way for widespread GPS adoption when it permitted civilian uses of GPS in 2000. Drivers were among the first mass GPS users with devices created by Garvin and TomTom. In 2004, Qualcomm Corporation announced a successful trial of placing GPS on cellular devices and tracking users to their approximate locations. From 2004, GPS became a standard feature on most mobile phones.

Cellular phone companies were not enthralled with the idea of including GPS initially on their phones. In fact, it was only after the FCC required them to locate 911 calls in case of emergencies did they start to incorporate the technology. Even with the government mandate, cellular companies tried to keep the information on the phones but locked away from users due to privacy concerns (Charles 2006). Over time, GPS has become a standard feature on mobile phones and privacy concerns, while they do still exist, are folded into issues of "big data" rather than being the purview of the phone company. In 2016, most phones and devices offer the option to turn GPS tracking on and off, though some app makers now require the feature to track who uses their products and where. GPS tracking is one of the key features used in geolocation today, which pinpoints mobile phone and social media user accounts to a precise location during communications.

The next technological advancement for wireless-enabled mobile devices is to make them "cognitive" devices. Researchers, scientists, and computer engineers are currently using big data to understand people's activities and daily routines, translate them into meaningful algorithms, and then teach electronic devices to read the data outputs of their users and choose programs and apps that better facilitate the user's lifestyle. Ultimately, a phone might be able to use a calendar app to learn when the user makes appointments, whether or not the user typically arrives early or late, and adjust the schedule with enough flexibility or rigidity to ensure the user can attend every event on the calendar. The technology could even go a step forward by employing data about transportation habits, such as mode, and then remind the user to depart the current location to arrive at the correct time.

Without Wi-Fi, Bluetooth, RFID, and GPS, mobile devices would not be the same. These technologies form the basis of the computing innovations that have made phones and other electronic devices "smart." Wi-Fi permits connections to the World Wide Web over the Internet without physical cords. Bluetooth enables devices to communicate via a link, which leads to faster information and data sharing while at the same time, often assist in creating invisible circuits that connect devices to the Internet. GPS locates a device with a degree of accuracy anywhere in the world that a satellite, or other tracking device, can obtain data. RFID is another type of location beacon that conveys positioning and can track products as they transit locations. Most mobile phones contain these technologies. In 2014, 90% of mobile phones were equipped with Wi-Fi and Bluetooth capabilities, while almost 100% of mobile phone handsets contained GPS[3] (Afshar 2014; Berg Insight 2014; Telecompaper 2014). As more and more devices are created or updated to be "smart," they also require the integration of these or similar capabilities. As time progresses, there will be upgraded and new technologies incorporated into these devices, which will further embed ubiquitous media into human society.

POLICY IMPLICATIONS

There are social implications to the technologies of ubiquitous computing and media. The idea that every person, everywhere, can create news on multiple devices, share on multiple platforms, and access information and communicate from almost everywhere, impacts policymaking at all levels. Information has now been localized and globalized at the same time, and almost limitless information is available at the touch of a button or a verbal request. Some of the issues that US policymakers must tackle include spectrum management, privacy, and encryption-related concerns. The communications spectrum, a finite number of frequencies, is currently allocated between public and private usage. With the increasing number of gadgets attached to the Internet, using more and more of that limited bandwidth, spectrum management become a challenge for the FCC and regulators worldwide (Deagon 2016; European Commission 2016; Pociask 2015; UK Spectrum Policy Forum 2015). Privacy is also a concern, as laws lag behind technological development and cannot keep up with the pace of ubiquity. Governments and corporations worldwide collect personal information on individual citizens for surveillance and marketing purposes. Encryption, also affected by laws that cannot keep up with emerging technologies, has led to intense encounters between the government, especially law enforcement, and the tech companies. While law enforcement seeks greater access to electronic data, the tech companies argue it has no legal right or precedent and that proposals to ease government access, such as the standard creation of back-doors in the software, would create vulnerabilities for data encryption. Discussions on encryption have led to wide-spread debates on data privacy rights versus crime fighting, especially in the media and within the US government (Alter 2015; Comey 2016; Judiciary Committee 2016; Nakashima and Gellman 2015).

Electromagnetic Spectrum Management

The electromagnetic spectrum is the range of electromagnetic radiation—which includes light, X-rays, radio waves, microwaves, and gamma rays, and which is usually organized from the shortest to longest waves. Most of the spectrum has historically been under US government control, as it was assigned for military and nonmilitary uses. Those portions that had been licensed for non-government uses have slowly grown over the years, with interested corporations or other licensees having to wade through long bureaucratic processes to gain the rights to operate over very specific frequencies. In the past, these processes were generally adequate, if sometimes challenging. However, the unprecedented technological developments that have emerged over the last two and a half decades—with some pieces having even earlier origins—have made wireless and broadband technologies an indispensable part of the present and an absolute requirement for the future. While more and more devices demand the use of wireless connectivity, there is only a finite amount of spectrum. Because the government is the primary owner and spectrum manager, it falls to government to address the immediate, and imminent, need to reform policies connected to the spectrum.

Spectrum management officially began in the early 1900s when wave-based communications fell under the US Department of the Navy's control. While the history is unique in its own right and follows the trajectory of technological developments related to radio, television, telephones, and the Internet, the most relevant points for modern-day spectrum management include the founding of the FCC in 1934, the Communications Act of 1934, and the Telecommunications Act of 1996. Outside of the policy realm, when Tim Berners-Lee, a British scientist working at CERN, invented the World Wide Web (WWW) in 1990, the future importance of the invention was not immediately understood. It was originally intended to allow universities or research institutions to share information through Hypertext Markup Language (HTML) that would allow for the inclusion of links that would take a reader to another section or page with additional information. Once he posted the first HTML webpage in 1991, the WWW spread, becoming popular worldwide, albeit it at different rates in various locations. The WWW and its structural backbone, the Internet, opened up a world of virtually unlimited information sharing and had the (now realized) potential, of revolutionizing communication. It also started the US, as well as the other countries of the world, to focus on revamping spectrum allocation and management, as all of these devices called for additional spectrum access, and even more so with the invention of wireless technologies.

The US government is not oblivious to the importance of wireless connectivity. The Commercial Spectrum Enhancement Act of 2004 focused on reallocating spectrum for non-federal uses and de-conflicting spectrum frequency conflicts. Under President Barack Obama's administration, the United States government embarked on a multi-year policy reform to keep the country economically competitive in a world that has begun to rely heavily on wireless technologies and communications. Policies on wireless connectivity automatically involve electromagnetic spectrum management when they seek to modify how the spectrum is used and allocated. In 2010, the White House released the memorandum "Unleashing the Wireless Broadband Revolution," which acknowledged the growing levels of investment in wireless since the 1990s and the vital economic role it played for business, research, and other daily activities. The first section of the memorandum focused on spectrum management reform, and specified that the Secretary of Commerce, the National Telecommunications and Information Administration (NTIA), and the FCC work together to "make available a total of 500 MHz of Federal and nonfederal spectrum over the next 10 years, suitable for both mobile and fixed wireless broadband use" (White House 2010). This policy shift to open the spectrum promised to alter the system established by the Communications of Act of 1934 (one that is still predominantly followed), whereby the FCC allocated specific bands for narrowly-defined under defined rules for what could operate on those bands. This memorandum marked one of the first official initiatives to promote broadband access by re-assessing past spectrum management policy and update it to compete in an increasingly connected world; it also set limits on how long the FCC and NTIA have to release 500 MHz of bandwidth, a gigantic task that must be completed by 2020.

It was soon understood that the government's efforts had some positive effects but that federal involvement would be continually required to meet the ever-growing need to use the spectrum. Declaring the efforts conducted after the 2010 memorandum a success, in 2013 the Obama administration pushed spectrum management reform even further. Through the Office of the Press Secretary, the administration issued a second memorandum. "Expanding America's Leadership in Wireless Innovation" focused on making more of the spectrum available and encouraging development of wireless technologies and applications. It established a Spectrum Policy Team decided to advancing the full utilization of the spectrum and spearheading spectrum sharing arrangements designed to allocate the spectrum to more diverse users without interfering with critical government spectrum needs, such as 911 emergency response and national security requirements (White House 2013). Among other functions, the Spectrum Policy Team would explore recommendations for sharing the spectrum on bands previously unavailable for non-government licensing. Essentially, the advances in spectrum reallocation since 2010 revealed that there were additional opportunities to open and allocate more spectrum bands; the necessity to promote rapid reform that still permitted the government's key spectrum usage requirements was also paramount.

Over time, it became clear that the White House and selected agencies were not sufficient to perform the research and make the recommendations explicitly required for spectrum management reform; it was time to involve additional government agencies and bring the Department of Defense permanently into the conversation. In 2015, the Obama administration issued a follow up memorandum to continue expanding the availability of broadband and opening up more portions of the electromagnetic spectrum. The memorandum, entitled "Expanding Broadband Deployment and Adoption by Addressing Regulatory Barriers and Encouraging Investment and Training," intended to lower barriers to accessing broadband, to include lowering costs to make it more financially accessible, and encouraging more competition in local markets to prevent one company from having an unofficial monopoly over a certain geographic area (White House 2015). The initiative also established the Broadband Opportunity, which includes representatives from all major US government departments, and directed each agency to develop recommendations to support the broadband expansion policy. With society leaning more solidly into the Internet of Things, a concept which leads to a steadily increasing number of gadgets requiring wireless access, the need to expand broadband access in addition to dealing with more of the minutia involved in spectrum management were key points that needed imminent attention.

The three White House memoranda were not, of course, the only policy documents proposed for dealing with the spectrum. Rather, they were some of the landmark documents that sought quick solutions to a complicated problem. Just as all of these documents indicated to some extent, there are challenges regarding the future of spectrum management policy. The first is that the system to reallocate bands, distribute licenses, and open up enough spectrum to meet growing demand is cumbersome. Currently, there are many government agencies involved in deliberations and policy regarding spectrum management; logically, each organization represents its own interests while trying to determine policy, creating a dichotomy that increases obstacles to obtaining transparency on ownership and actual federal spectrum requirements. To streamline the system, policy analysts recommend a single, independent enforcement agency to make, assess, and implement recommendations (Skorup 2013). Whether this body would be temporary or permanent is more controversial, and there would be additional challenges on the authorities and enforcement piece.

Debate over current policy, and the understanding that demands on the spectrum will grow exponentially with time, portends that the issue requires the active involvement of the US federal government, as spectrum owners, as well as communications regulatory bodies such as NTIA and the FCC , in order to come up with short and long-term solutions. The major challenges that will need to be navigated, or monitored, are the sharing relationship between the government and non-government entities, the enforcement mechanisms for policy, the exploration of monetizing use of the spectrum for government revenue instead of the static auction model used previously, and the repurposing of some bandwidths for additional uses

(Techonomy 2015). Spectrum management will continue, in the near and short term, to require a balance between efficiency and demand for a limited resource.

Privacy and Encryption

Two issues affecting government policy are the interrelated concerns around privacy laws and encryption. Both of the issues, both separately and individually, have been the center of policy debates. The continuously expanding use of wireless enabled devices leads to the transmission of tremendous amounts of data over connections that are often unsecure or hackable. When people use their devices, they either consent to, or unknowingly, share personal information to corporations, unsavory entities such as scammers or criminals, or even governments who will use that data as they choose. Personal data can include demographic information, personal identifiers such as Social Security Numbers, financial information, passwords, and other data that can jeopardize a person's identity, lives, or the lives of people they interact with in some fashion. Identity theft is a serious issue in the United States; in 2014, 17.6 million Americans experienced identity theft (Harrell 2015). For the victims, trying to restore accounts can take months and weigh heavily on a person's emotional well-being.

Identity theft is, however, a small part of the online privacy debate; the larger questions relate to the powers that corporations have to gather and use personal data. In the United States, there are few regulations regarding what information can be collected, transmitted, repackaged, and sold for corporate gain. Personal data has high market value, so without regulations and restrictions, corporations have no need to govern their own data collection apart from following the regulations that do exist. For example, Google collects data on all of its users' searches to improve targeted advertising. Over time, that data collection reveals a lot of information about a person's interests, medical questions, preferences, and possibly future plans. Because the searches are localized to an IP address and a location, the company can also track user location and movement. Through the use of cookies, it can also track where a person goes on the web, how long they stay, the links that they click, and other such usage behaviors. In the United States, where privacy policies are less regulated than in Europe, Google can do almost anything it wants with the data it collects under its broad terms of service and privacy policy, which includes information given to the company; information derived from using any of its services, including data about the device, location, search histories, and even some information recorded to a device's storage, emails, browsing preferences, interactions with advertisements and websites, etc.; royalty-free universal rights to any uploaded content, such as pictures; and some of its services use facial recognition technologies (Google 2016). Most other large firms that can make money through their user data, such as Facebook and Microsoft, have similar policies on collecting and utilizing the personal information that they collect.

US policy has not kept up with the rapid advances in technology, to include how personal data is collected and used online. In contrast to Europe, where users enjoy stricter privacy laws, a company's ability to collect, store, and transmit data has been legally curtailed. Using the Google example, since 2014 the European Union requires Google to "forget" information about users that meets a certain threshold per their request (Douglas 2016). Though the process has neither been easy nor transparent, it is a privilege that Europeans have while Americans do not. On the policy side, there is a fear that the "right to forget" in the US would curb freedom of speech. Similarly, another way that companies deal with data is by shifting it to places with fewer privacy restrictions. Max Schrems, an Austrian law student, won an uphill legal battle against Facebook in 2015. He sued the company in European courts for violating European privacy rights and won, a victory that translated to new privacy protection regulations for all tech companies with offices in Europe, but only applies to data on European nationals (Satariano and Bodoni 2016). Similar policies have not been adopted in the US, as there is a divide between those who want federal regulation and those who believe government should not be involved in activities that appear to restrict free speech.

US law on online privacy primarily revolves around the circumstances by which the government can access personal data stored on electronic devices or cloud-based information storage services. The Electronic Privacy Act of 1986 set some limitations on the storage and transmission of electronic communications, namely in application to law enforcement and surveillance. It also protected electronic data from improper public disclosure and wrongful use by third parties. While the law was sufficient for the 1980s, technology has advanced well beyond the confines of the law. The US House of Representatives has recognized that it needs updating, and in 2016 passed the Email Privacy Act. It will travel to the Senate and, if approved, to the president to become law (Brill 2016). Neither, however, address how corporations collect, store, and use data.

Ubiquitous media is also changing the shape of policy in fundamental ways. The ability of citizens to record events has led to questions about whether police officers apply force unnecessarily or have overstepped their legal constraints. Many US jurisdictions are considering the legality of recording the police; many have also started requiring certain officers to wear body cameras to record incidents from their perspectives. The Baltimore Police Department, for example, inaugurated a program to equip its police force with body cameras at the end of 2015. The program roll out ensures that by the end of 2017, 75% of its police officers will wear the cameras on duty (Baltimore County 2016). Many other states have passed legislation on law enforcement's usage of body cameras, or have legislation pending (Urban Institute 2016). Camera use can have implications for privacy, and some states do not permit audio recordings, but the videos can also protect police officers. Policies regarding recordings and body cameras have been implemented across the country, though there is not yet a standard, nor has federal policy been issued.

Privacy concerns and regulations, or the lack thereof, are often tied into debates about encryption. In 2015, the Federal Bureau of Investigation (FBI) asked Apple to unlock Syed Farook's iPhone after he and a partner executed a terrorist attack in California that killed fourteen people in December of that year. Apple, a company which has prided itself on advanced encryption since its first iPhone release, explained that they could not and refused to write a program to de-encrypt the phone (Barrett 2016). The incident launched a national-level debate about encryption, stirring up feelings about NSA surveillance and the right to electronic privacy. The debate comes not too long after the Snowden debacle, where a federal government contractor stole and released classified documents in 2013 pertaining to illegal National Security Agency surveillance. While the incident stirred up an important national debate about encryption and led to the curtailing of many NSA, and other agency, practices, it did not otherwise greatly impact federal policy.

The FBI eventually had the iPhone unlocked. In an unorthodox play, it hired professional hackers to crack the phone using a previously unknown security flaw. The program, which allegedly works on only the iPhone 5C running the iOS 9 operating system, removed Apple entirely from the process (Nakashima 2016). It also opened a debate regarding whether the government had the obligation to share the flaw with Apple, further straining the already tense relationships between the government and tech companies. What it has done is keep encryption discussions focused squarely on the government's right to access and use data, rather than on how corporations collect and disseminate citizen's personal information. Both events, the FBI-Apple dispute and allegations surrounding the NSA, fit into the wider debate about government and encryption policies. Both led to the drafting of bills on policy updates, national-level encryption policies and laws have yet to be enacted, and will create future challenges for policymakers, tech companies, and citizens alike.

CONCLUSION

Achieving ubiquity, for both computing and media, is the culmination of decades of invention, innovation, and progress. The concept, stemming from the 1980s and the early 2000s for computing and media, respectively, has only come to fruition to the extent it has due to the advancement and development of technology. While some of the technology involved in realizing ubiquity has a decades-long history, other pieces are relatively new; together, they culminate into complex systems that involve portable devices, electromagnetic waves, and humans. The systems have fundamentally altered the pace and speed at which people communicate, and has impacted human society on multiple levels, with no end in sight as new upgrades and development occurs, pushing the boundaries of how people and technology intersect.

Ubiquity, arguably, is a concept that is constantly under revision, constantly looking to make improvements. On one hand, ubiquity has been achieved to an extent, not only in the actualization of the number of portable devices that can transmit and receive data without physical connections, but even more so in how it has revolutionized the media, a world that used to be dominated by large agencies and now allows the average person to record and report on the events around them. On the other hand, there are still ways in which progress is still needed to realize the vision completely. In the same vein, there are current and future challenges inherent not only in the technology, but also in terms of policy creation and revision. Ubiquity has changed the world; it will continue to shape how and where people communicate as the mission to attain true ubiquity continues.

NOTES

1. Cisco has moved away from IoE as a concept, choosing to replace it in early 2016 with the term "digitization." The change occurred because of industry confusion with IoT and because the new term, according to Cisco, better reflects the human dimension the company intended IoE to project. For a brief explanation, see McCaskill 2016.
2. Wi-Fi range depends on a number of factors, such as the router model and the router's physical location. A typical range is 150 feet indoors and 300 feet outdoors, but may vary based on interference and the power supply.
3. Similar statistics are not available for RFID-tagged mobile phones or phones that have downloaded apps that function as RFID readers.

REFERENCES

Afshar, Vala. 2014. "50 Incredible WiFi Tech Statistics that Businesses Must Know [Slide Deck]." *Huffington Post*, February 12. http://www.huffingtonpost.com/vala-afshar/50-incredible-wifi-tech-s_b_4775837.html.

Alter, Jonathan. 2015. "Manhattan DA: Smartphone Encryption Foiled 120 Criminal Cases." *Daily Beast*, December 28. http://www.thedailybeast.com/articles/2015/12/28/manhattan-da-smartphone-encryption-foiled-120-criminal-cases.html.

Baltimore County Government. 2016. "Body-Worn Camera Program." http://baltimorecountymd.gov/Agencies/police/bodycameras.

Banafa, Ahmed. 2014. "The Internet of Everything." *LinkedIn*, March 19. https://www.linkedin.com/pulse/20140319132744-246665791-the-Internet-of-everything-ioe.

Barrett, Brian. 2016. "The Apple-FBI Battle Is Over, But the New Crypto Wars Have Just Begun." *Wired*, March 30. https://www.wired.com/2016/03/apple-fbi-battle-crypto-wars-just-begun/.

Barton, John, Patrick Goddi, and Mirjana Spasojevic. 2003. "Creating and Experiencing Ubimedia." *Hewlett-Packard Company*. http://www.hpl.hp.com/techreports/2003/HPL-2003-38.pdf.
Berg Insight. 2014. GPS and Mobile Handsets. http://www.berginsight.com/reportpdf/productsheet/bi-gps4-ps.pdf.
Bluetooth. 2016. "Our History." https://www.bluetooth.com/media/our-history.
Brill, Julie. 2016. "It's time to update the Electronic Communications Privacy Act (ECPA)." *The Hill*, May 25. http://thehill.com/blogs/congress-blog/technology/281106-its-time-to-update-the-electronic-communications-privacy-act.
Brodkin, Jon. 2016. "Wi-Fi Gets Multi-Gigabit, Multi-User Boast with Upgrades to 802.11ac." *ArsTechnica*, June 29. http://arstechnica.com/information-technology/2016/06/wi-fi-gets-multi-gigabit-multi-user-boost-with-upgrades-to-802-11ac/.
Cătălin, Munteanu Claudiu, and Pagalea Andreea. 2014. "Brands as a Mean of Consumer Self-expression and Desired Personal Lifestyle." *Procedia—Social and Behavioral Sciences* 109 (8): 103–107. doi:10.1016/j.sbspro.2013.12.427.
Charles, Dan. 2006. "GPS is Smartening up Your Cell Phone," *NPR*, September 25. http://www.npr.org/templates/story/story.php?storyId=6097216.
Collins, Glenn. 2001. "The Silence of the Alert System; Experts Urge Overhaul of Plan Unused Even on Sept. 11." *New York Times*, December 21. http://www.nytimes.com/2001/12/21/nyregion/silence-alert-system-experts-urge-overhaul-plan-unused-even-sept-11.html.
Comey, James B. 2016. "Encryption Tightrope: Balancing Americans' Security and Privacy." *FBI*, March 1. https://www.fbi.gov/news/testimony/encryption-tightrope-balancing-americans-security-and-privacy.
ComScore. 2016. "comScore Reports January 2016 US Smartphone Subscriber Market Share." March 3. https://www.comscore.com/Insights/Rankings/comScore-Reports-January-2016-US-Smartphone-Subscriber-Market-Share.
Deagon, Brian. 2016. "Auctioning the Sky: Wireless Providers Bid on FCC Spectrum." *Investor's Business Daily*, June 3. http://www.investors.com/research/industry-snapshot/wireless-carriers-ready-for-network-expansion-with-spectrum-auction/.
Douglas, Michael. 2016. "Google Expands the 'Right to be Forgotten', but Australia Doesn't Need It." *The Conversation*, March 7. http://theconversation.com/google-expands-the-right-to-be-forgotten-but-australia-doesnt-need-it-54887.
Economist. 2004. "A Brief History of Wi-Fi," June 10. http://www.economist.com/node/2724397.
eMarketer. 2016. "Mobile Phone, Smartphone Usage Varies Globally." November 23. https://www.emarketer.com/Article/Mobile-Phone-Smartphone-Usage-Varies-Globally/1014738.
European Commission. 2016. "Wireless Europe." https://ec.europa.eu/digital-single-market/en/wireless-europe.
Gartner. 2015. "Gartner Says 6.4 Billion Connected 'Things' Will Be in Use in 2016, Up 30 Percent from 2015." November 10. http://www.gartner.com/newsroom/id/3165717.
Google. 2016. "Welcome to the Google Privacy Policy." https://www.google.com/intl/en-GB/policies/privacy/.
Google Play. 2016. "Search: Apps." December 5. https://play.google.com/store/search?q=rfid%20readerandhl=en.
Gross, Doug. 2011. "Twitter User Unknowingly Reported Bin Laden Attack." *CNN*, May 2. http://www.cnn.com/2011/TECH/social.media/05/02/osama.twitter.reports/.
Ha, Peter. 2010. "Magellan NAV 1000." *Time*, October 25. http://content.time.com/time/specials/packages/article/0,28804,2023689_2023753_2023787,00.html.

Harrell, Erika. 2015. *Victims of Identity Theft, 2014*. Bureau of Justice Statistics, United States Department of Justice.
IBM. 2003. Annual Report. ftp://public.dhe.ibm.com/annualreport/2003/2003_ibm_ar.pdf.
Infosys. 2001. Press Release: Infosys and Massachusetts Institute of Technology (MIT) Host Joint Symposium in Bangalore. January 5. https://www.infosys.com/newsroom/press-releases/Documents/2001/MIT--05Jan01.pdf.
Jones, Erick C., and Christopher A. Chung. 2011. RFID and Auto-ID in Planning and Logistics: A Practical Guide for Military UID Applications. Boca Raton, FL: CRC Press.
Judiciary Committee, House of Representatives. 2016. "Encryption: Balancing Americans' Security and Privacy." https://judiciary.house.gov/issue/encryption/.
Karlsson, Svenlof, and Anders Lugn. "The History of Bluetooth." *Centre for Business History, Stockholm and Telefonaktiebolaget LM Ericsson*. https://archive.fo/Wnln/.
Lau, Rynson W. H., Ralf Klamma, Shu-Ching Chen, and Benjamin Wah. 2011. "Advances in Ubiquitous Media Technologies and Applications." *World Wide Web* 14 (3): 217–222. doi:10.1007/s11280-011-0123-7.
Lendino, Jamie. 2016. "What is 802.11ac Wi-Fi, and How Much Faster than 802.11n is It?" *ExtremeTech*, August 22. http://www.extremetech.com/computing/16037-what-is-802-11ac-and-how-much-faster-than-802-11n-is-it.
LinkLabs. 2015. "The Story Behind the Evolution from M2M to IoT to IoE." December 29. https://www.link-labs.com/m2m-to-iot-to-ioe/.
Liu, Chia-Ju, and Hao-Yun Liang. 2014. "The Deep Impression of Smartphone Brand of the Customer's Decision Making." *Procedia—Social and Behavioral Sciences* 109 (8): 338–343. doi:10.1016/j.sbspro.2013.12.468.
Magill, Frank N. 1996. Chronology of Twentieth-Century History: Business and Commerce, Vol. II. New York: Routledge.
Maney, Kevin. 2015. "Meet Kevin Ashton, Father of the Internet of Things." *Newsweek*, February 23. http://www.newsweek.com/2015/03/06/meet-kevin-ashton-father-Internet-things-308763.html.
Markoff, John. 1991. "And Not a Personal Computer in Sight: Xerox Bobbled a Brilliant Computer Vision in the 70's. It's Trying Again with 'Ubiquitous Computing." *New York Times*, October 6. F1.
Matyszczyk, Chris. 2016. "Apple (Still) Inspires Most Love from Consumers, Says Study." *CNET*, February 24. https://www.cnet.com/news/apple-inspires-most-love-from-consumers-says-study/.
McCaskill, Steve. 2016. "Cisco Live: What Happened to the Internet of Everything?" *Silicon*, February 18. http://www.silicon.co.uk/networks/voip/cisco-live-what-happened-to-the-Internet-of-everything-186240.
Microsoft. 2016. Annual Report. https://www.microsoft.com/investor/reports/ar16/index.html
Mills, Kevin L., and Jean Scholtz. 1999. Situated Computing: The Next Frontier for HCI Research." *National Institute of Standards and Technology*. http://ws680.nist.gov/publication/get_pdf.cfm?pub_id=151045.
Nakashima, Ellen. 2016. "FBI Paid Professional Hackers One-Time Fee to Crack San Bernardino iPhone." *Washington Post*, April 12. https://www.washingtonpost.com/world/national-security/fbi-paid-professional-hackers-one-time-fee-to-crack-san-bernardino-iphone/2016/04/12/5397814a-00de-11e6-9d36-33d198ea26c5_story.html.
Nakashima, Ellen, and Barton Gellman. 2015. "As Encryption Spreads, US Grapples with Clash Between Privacy, Security." *Washington Post*, April 10. https://www.washingtonpost.com/world/

national-security/as-encryption-spreads-us-worries-about-access-to-data-for-investigations/2015/04/10/7c1c7518-d401-11e4-a62f-ee745911a4ff_story.html?utm_term=.9c54eed6550d.
NMC. 2015. *NMC Horizon Report—2015 Higher Education*. Austin, TX: New Media Horizon.
Partanen, Juho. 2015. History of RFID. *Rain RFID Alliance Publication*. http://rainrfid.org/wp-content/uploads/2015/12/History-of-RFID.pdf.
Pociask, Steve. 2015. "We're Three Years Away from Spectrum Shortages. *Forbes*, June 30. http://www.forbes.com/sites/realspin/2015/06/30/the-spectrum-shortage-is-coming/.
Purbrick, Louise. 1993. "The Dream Machine: Charles Babbage and His Imaginary Computers." *Journal of Design History* 6 (1): 9–23. doi:10.1093/jdh/6.1.9.
Roberti, Mark. 2005. The History of RFID Technology. *RFID Journal*. http://www.rfidjournal.com/articles/view?1338.
Russell, Daniel M., Norbert A. Streitz, and Terry Winograd. 2005. "Building Disappearing Computers." *Communication of the ACM* 48 (3):42–48.
Sankaran, Neeraja. 1995. "Looking Back at ENIAC: Commemorating A Half-Century of Computers in The Reviewing System." *The Scientist*. http://www.the-scientist.com/?articles.view/articleNo/17531/title/Looking-Back-At-ENIAC--Commemorating-A-Half-Century-Of-Computers-In-The-Reviewing-System/.
Satariano, Adam, and Stephanie Bodoni. 2016. "The 28-Year-Old Activist Who Took on Facebook. And Won." *Bloomberg*, August 3. http://www.bloomberg.com/news/articles/2016-08-03/the-28-year-old-activist-who-took-on-facebook-and-won.
Seward, Zachary M. 2013. "The First Mobile Phone Call was Made 40 Years Ago Today. *The Atlantic*, April 3. http://www.theatlantic.com/technology/archive/2013/04/the-first-mobile-phone-call-was-made-40-years-ago-today/274611/.
Skorup, Brent. 2013. "Reclaiming Federal Spectrum: Proposals and Recommendations." Working Paper. Fairfax, Va.: Mercatus Center, George Mason University.
Smith, Tony. 2004. "Wi-Fi Trade Body Approves First WLAN Mobile Phones." *The Register*, October 22. http://www.theregister.co.uk/2004/10/22/wifi_phones_certified/.
Stansell, Thomas A. 1983. The TRANSIT Navigation Satellite System. *Magnavox*. https://www.ion.org/museum/files/TransitBooklet.pdf.
Sullivan, Mark. 2012. "A Brief History of GPS," *PC World*, August 9. http://www.pcworld.com/article/2000276/a-brief-history-of-gps.html.
Techonomy. 2015. "FCC (R&D) on Spectrum and the Policy Future for Tech." June 11. http://techonomy.com/conf/policy/policy-evolution/fcc-rd-on-spectrum-and-the-policy-future-for-tech/.
Tektronix. 2013. "Wi-Fi: Overview of the 802.11 Physical Layer and Transmitter Measurements Primer." http://www.nortelcoelectronics.se/document-file5116?lcid=1053andpid=Native-ContentFile-File.
Telecompaper. 2014. "Bluetooth Penetration Reaches 90% across All Mobile Phones." April 9. https://www.telecompaper.com/news/bluetooth-penetration-reaches-90-across-all-mobile-phones--1007063.
UK Spectrum Policy Forum. 2015. "UK Spectrum Usage and Demand: Second Edition." https://www.techuk.org/insights/reports/item/6825-uk-spectrum-usage-demand-second-edition.
Urban Institute. 2016. "Police Body-Worn Cameras: Where Your State Stands." http://apps.urban.org/features/body-camera/.
Weiser, Mark, Rich Gold, and John. Seely Brown. 1999. "The Origins of Ubiquitous Computing Research at PARC in the Late 1980s." *IBM Systems Journal* 38 (4): 693–696.

White House, Office of the Press Secretary. 2010. "Presidential Memorandum: Unleashing the Wireless Broadband Revolution." *Whitehouse.gov*. June 28. https://obamawhitehouse.archives.gov/the-press-office/presidential-memorandum-unleashing-wireless-broadband-revolution.

White House, Office of the Press Secretary. 2013 "Presidential Memorandum—Expanding America's Leadership in Wireless Innovation." *Whitehouse.gov*. June 14. https://obamawhitehouse.archives.gov/the-press-office/2013/06/14/presidential-memorandum-expanding-americas-leadership-wireless-innovatio.

White House, Office of the Press Secretary. 2015. "Presidential Memorandum—Expanding Broadband Deployment and Adoption by Addressing Regulatory Barriers and Encouraging Investment and Training." *Whitehouse.gov*. March 23. https://obamawhitehouse.archives.gov/the-press-office/2015/03/23/presidential-memorandum-expanding-broadband-deployment-and-adoption-addr.

CHAPTER TWO

The Ubiquitous Media War

TANNER MIRRLEES

INTRODUCTION: MEDIA WAR IN A UBIQUITOUS MEDIA AGE

From the First World War to the Global War on Terror of the present, the US Department of Defense (DOD) has tried to influence the way the media industries frame the policy, personnel, practices and events surrounding the wars it fights, so as to effectively command and control how war is perceived and responded to by citizens. With great efficacy, the DOD has combined persuasion and censorship to shape the war-time conduct of media firms and the content of their products and exerted tremendous influence upon public opinion (Andersen 2006; Carruthers 2011; Freedman and Thussu 2012; Knightley 1975; Taylor 1997, 2008). All too often, newspapers, advertisers, radio and TV news broadcasters, film studios, and even video game companies have aligned with DOD campaigns aimed at "manufacturing consent" to war (Boggs and Pollard 2007; Freedman and Thussu 2012; Martin and Steuter 2010; Stahl 2010). The DOD does not own or control the market-embedded media industries, but media firms have nonetheless served the DOD well by cooperating, collaborating and synergizing with the DOD's public affairs agencies.

The goal of this chapter is to explore media war dynamics in an age of ubiquitous, interactive, and many-to-many digital networks and platforms. By attending to the dialectics of change and continuity in the recent history of media war and exploring how the dynamics of media war today are quite different from those which characterized the bygone age of scarcity, mass transmissive, and few-to-many TV broadcasting, this chapter theorizes and interrogates the early twenty-first century's "ubiquitous media war." Featherstone (2009) says that "theorizing ubiquitous media" is an "integral part of theorizing culture and society today" (3) and that the intensity of change "invite[s] a range of responses" (13). My response conceptualizes the ubiquitous media war as one in which many actors use many devices and platforms to interactively produce, distribute, exhibit, and consume a glut of content (e.g., texts, images, videos, films, TV shows, video games, likes, shares, retweets and more) about the circumstances, happening and events of a real war, anytime and anywhere.

This chapter contextualizes, conceptualizes, and concretizes the ubiquitous media war in three interrelated sections. The first section offers a brief review of relevant political economy of communications and critical media studies literature on the topic of war, militarism, and the media. The second section centers on a shift from "mass media war" to ubiquitous media war as occurring in the space between the "Shock and Awe" that launched "Operation Iraqi Freedom" (2003–2011) and the present US war against ISIS in Iraq, or "Operation Inherent Resolve" (2014–present). The third section highlights seven significant characteristics of the ubiquitous media war. It shows the ubiquitous media war to be ubiquitous with regard to: (1) sources of content; (2) workers; (3) types of stories; (4) access points; (5) time; (6) space; and (7) data. Overall, the chapter aims to periodize and clarify the new conditions and characteristics of ubiquitous media war to problematize old paradigms that put the military-media complex in command and control of media wars.

FROM THE MICC TO UBIQUITOUS MEDIA: CONTINUITY AND CHANGE

In the political economy of communications tradition, the interlinking of the DOD and the media industries is well known. In the late 1960s, Herbert Schiller conceptualized the mediated wars marching lockstep with the DOD's real wars as arising from the "military-industrial-communications-complex" (MICC) (Schiller 1969, 1973, 2000). Schiller's MICC concept pointed to an "institutional edifice" comprised of the military and the media industries, a nexus of DOD and corporate communications power (Maxwell 2003, 32). The MICC concept explained the existence of mediatized wars with regard to the interests, resources, and actions of the militaries and media companies that control the means of producing, distributing, and exhibiting the products that constitute it. Schiller (1992) gave empirical weight to the concept by documenting how military "mind managers" sourced the private news media with packaged propaganda designed to influence public perceptions of war, and contracted out war propaganda jobs to PR and advertising firms.

At the turn of the millennium, Der Derian (2001) forwarded the MICC-related concept of the "military-industrial-media-entertainment network" (MIME-NET) to highlight the DOD's incorporation of popular culture into its arsenal of persuasion. In the first decade of the twenty-first century, critical media studies scholars interrogated this complex's annual roll out of "militainment" products, or media and cultural forms that mix military propaganda and entertainment formats (e.g., Andersen 2006; Andersen and Mirrlees 2014; Mirrlees 2016; Stahl 2010). Throughout the second half of the twentieth century and into the early twenty-first, this complex routinely transformed each war the DOD fought into a gigantic televised spectacle, and delivered this to a mass audience who consumed war's violence, perhaps with a TV dinner. For example, the DOD built public relations into every stage of the 1990 Persian Gulf War, from planning, to preparation, to execution, to aftermath, and CNN helped the DOD sell this war to the public as a consumable spectacle (Kellner 1992). The DOD also attempted to manage the TV image of war when it returned to waging a full-fledged war in Iraq during 2003's "Operation Iraqi Freedom."

The military-media complex persists, and studies of its old and new structures and effects continue to be very important to the political economy of communication and critical media studies. Yet, the early twenty-first century's new digital communications and media environment invites researchers to interrogate paradigms of the military-media complex that came of age when mass media—epitomized TV broadcasting—was the dominant means through which the DOD tried to build public consent to war.

Since the turn of the millennium, TV broadcasting's old mass media paradigm has been eclipsed by a new one constituted by social media business models and websites. These models collect and commoditize data about users by enabling them to connect and interact with others by producing, distributing and consuming digital content via ubiquitous personal computers, smartphones, and tablets (Treem *et al.* 2016, 770). The age of mass mediated communication–one in which massive government and corporate organizations produced and transmitted a limited supply of audio-visual content to a mass and largely passive audience vulnerable to manipulation—was said to have come to an "end" in the same year that the US launched the Global War on Terror (Chaffee and Metzger 2001). As of late, scholars have examined changes to the communications environment with periodizing concepts like "post-broadcast era" (Turner and Tay 2009), "post-network era" (Lotz 2007), "era of convergence culture" (Jenkins 2006), "spreadable media" (Jenkins, Ford, and Green 2013), and the even more recent "platform paradigm" (Burgess 2015, 282).

Political economists of communication have shown these new changes are driven significantly by capitalist logics. The profit-motive spawned technological innovations that disrupted old and established media sectors, unleashed new start-ups like Google and Facebook, and instigated fierce competitions between them for market dominance, and it now propels these same firms to concentrate their holdings of networks and platforms, commodify data about users in pursuit of maximal advertising revenue, and exploit the digital labor of prosumers around the world (Andrejevic 2007; Fuchs 2011, 2012, 2014; Schiller 1999, 2007, 2008; McChesney 2013; McGuigan and Manzerolle 2014). Political economists of communication have also shown how the digital media's early constitutive hardware and software did not emerge from the "invisible hand" of the free-market, but was underwritten by the DOD, which allocated public monies to the R&D arm of its partner universities and corporations to bring military, security, and war-useful technological innovations into the world, and into markets as commodities (Schiller 2007, 2008). The pace and extent of digital capitalism's transformative effects are uneven, with the already affluent, digitally literate, and networked populations of most powerful countries of the world system being early experiencers while the poor, digitally downtrodden and disconnected remain excluded. Nonetheless, digital capitalism's pursuit of maximal profit and the DOD's pursuit of strategic supremacy intertwine in significant ways, reconfiguring the business of war and media war-making.

In a period in which ISIS releases "modded" versions of the 2004 Rockstar Games hit *Grand Theft Auto: San Andreas* through Web 2.0 platforms to recruit followers and spread its ideology, armchair peace activists rage against "chicken hawks" in the comments section of *The New York Times*, and US soldiers and civilians use YouTube to "prosume" videos for and against war, the power of the military-media complex to command and control a mass media war may be subverted.

When did this transformation occur? The following section centers on a shift from mass media war to ubiquitous media war as occurring in the space between the Shock and Awe that launched Operation Iraqi Freedom (2003–2011) and the present US war against ISIS in Iraq, or "Operation Inherent Resolve" (2014–present). The Iraq war began with a military-media-complex made-for-TV war spectacle ("Shock and Awe"), but changes to the communication and media environment over the thirteen years that followed transformed this TV war into a ubiquitous media war, a war read about, seen, listened to, watched, played, debated, and interactively prosumed, participated in by millions around the world through a range of mediums (e.g., TV sets, personal computers, game consoles, smartphones, and tablets), and fought, almost anytime, anywhere.

SHOCK AND AWE: IRAQ, REAL WAR, MEDIA WAR, TOWARD UBIQUITY

Penned in 1996 by strategic thinkers Harlan K. Ullman and James P. Wade (1996) for the National Defense University, *Shock & Awe: Achieving Rapid Dominance* was the US military doctrine applied in the early stages of Operation Iraqi Freedom, or, the 2003 US-led pre-emptive invasion and occupation of Iraq. Aligned with the US Department of Defense's post-Cold War and post-Fordist efforts to bring about a "revolution in military affairs" (Murray 1997) that shifts to an age of "network centric warfare" (Cebrowski and Garstka 2003), Ullman and Wade's *Shock & Awe* (1996, xi) aims "to destroy or so confound the will to resist that an adversary will have no alternative except to accept our strategic aims and military objectives" (xi). They say Shock and Awe is exerted when a military destroys a country's infrastructure and controls its communications media by "shut[ting] down key electronic communications to, from, and within a country" (49), "controlling radio and television" (49), "denying an adversary's ability to communicate" and "reaching the population with appropriate messages" (50) that may inform and manipulate. This combination of brute force and ideological persuasion—military command and media control—are identified as "key components" of a total "assault on the will and understanding of the opponent" (xxvii) that aims to "cause the perception and anticipation of certain defeat and the threat and fear of action that may shut down all or part of the adversary's society or render his ability to fight useless short of complete physical destruction" (92).

On March 19, 2003, the DOD unleashed Shock and Awe upon Iraq. F-15s launched about 1700 missiles at Iraq for nearly two full days while Commando Solo, a mobile information operations aircraft, jammed the communication networks of Ba'athist leaders, dropped hundreds of thousands of leaflets demanding surrender, and broadcast a radio program carrying Iraqi folk music, 1980s American rock, and new wave Euro-pop mixed with a propaganda messages in Arabic (Armistead 2004, 155). Three weeks following Shock and Awe, the DOD's Coalition Provisional Authority (CPA) had taken control of Iraq's government, privatized much of the country, seized Iraq's oil fields, and built the Iraqi Media Network (IMN) (Klein 2007). In the Iraq War's early stages, Washington and the DOD's lead-up to and execution of Shock and Awe drummed up public support for the war with the help of US-based media corporations.

To lead the American public into war, the Bush Administration manufactured a pretext of lies that framed Saddam Hussein as in cahoots with al-Qaeda's 9/11 terrorist attacks, claimed Iraq possessed weapons of mass destruction and intended to use them against the US and its allies, and depicted Iraqis as wanting Americans to liberate them (Krugman 2015; Stein and Dickinson 2006). The TV news media parroted this pretext of lies, legitimizing as opposed to challenging the official source's story. The lead up to and execution of the Shock and Awe campaign were made-for-TV global military events, military-media-manufactured war spectacles transmitted to millions.

Consider the following manipulations. Colin Powell and Donald Rumsfeld appeared on TV news networks citing Judith Miller's *New York Times* trumped up story about Iraq's possession of WMDs (Boyd-Barrett 2004). In the time and space not privileged for ads for soft drinks, automobiles and other commodities, Fox News Channel hosts beat the war drum against Saddam Hussein and presented support for war as patriotic, increasing ratings and ad revenue while lowering the bar for quality journalism. The DOD dispatched retired US military generals and lobbyists for munitions corporations to TV news networks to fatten the case for pre-emptive war in the guise of neutral analysts and experts. When the bombing of Iraq began, TV gave spectators a "clean war" of bombs falling and exploding on Baghdad with no trace of civilian terror, injury and death (Stahl 2010, 25); invited them to relish in "techno-fetishism" by glorifying the power and efficacy of weaponry (28); and as usual, rallied them to "support the troops," "equating support for official policy with support for the soldiers" (29) and diverting public attention away from the point of war policy's creation and toward its point of execution (30).

When the ground assault and siege of Baghdad began, hundreds of journalists (carefully vetted according to pro-military political correctness criteria by the Rendon Group, a PR firm) were embedded with the troops, living and working with them, and covering the war from their point of view. More DOD-serving analysts appeared on TV news networks, talking up the good of the war, the weapons and the troops, and downplaying its awful consequences. The DOD hired Hollywood to create a soundstage from which military public affairs officers drip fed briefings and vids to reporters. It also censored images taken of dead US soldiers and corpses of Iraqi civilians to prevent them from flowing back to the US, while flacking and sometimes attacking the news workers with non-aligned media firms like Al-Jazeera. The Shock and Awe media spectacle climaxed when a US soldier wrapped the face of a Saddam Hussein statue in the American flag as a few Iraqis gathered in Firdos Square, and then attacked and pulled down the statue, with help from US psychological operations personnel. The grand finale? On May 1, 2003, US president George W. Bush, flying in a Lockheed S-3 Viking aircraft with a fighter pilot, landed on the USS Abraham Lincoln. Surrounded by hundreds of sailors, standing and grinning under a star-spangled banner proclaiming "Mission Accomplished." Bush declared: "Major combat operations in Iraq have ended." Hubris followed applause. More hoopla. That was the end of Shock and Awe.

The DOD's orchestration of Shock and Awe in Iraq and through the mass media highlights how when the DOD prepares for war and wages it, two kinds of war thus occur: a "real war" and a "media war" (Taylor 1997, 119). Although the former war requires the latter, they are not identical, as these wars happen in different places, are experienced differently by those partaking in them, and have incommensurable consequences. The real war takes place upon the geographies where the fighting, killing and dying occurs (the territorial battlefield); the media war is what civilians see and hear at a safe distance from embodied risk, threat and harm (a de-territorialized media battle-space) (*ibid.*). Throughout the twentieth century and into the twenty-first, developments in communication technologies—the telegraph, motion picture, radio and TV broadcasting, the Internet and video games—have shrunk the space between real war and media war (Stahl 2010, 8). These border crossing communication technologies instantaneously bring faraway wars closer to home, textually and audio-visually at least, and they make what's happening "over there" on deadly battlefields, seem closer to "here," in safer mediated battle-spaces.

Real wars, happening in a different time and place become audio-visually present to publics as a media war. So, when the DOD was subjecting Iraqis to the terrors and horrors of Shock and Awe in Iraq, bits and pieces of this "real war" were being transformed by the DOD and media corporations into stories, sounds, images, and videos about Shock and Awe, circulated back to and consumed by US civilians. The Shock and Awe experienced by the Iraqi civilians whose cities, towns, families, and lives were destroyed by it was not the same as the Shock and Awe Americans read about in *The New York Times*, heard about it on conservative talk radio shows, watched in near real-time compliments of the Fox News Channel and CNN cable TV networks. The real Shock and Awe was inescapable and full of death; its media war products were avoidable and docile. The circumstances, embodied experiences and consequences of real Shock and Awe were different from, diluted, dumbed down, and distracted by its made-for-TV mass media spectacle.

The DOD and corporate media's transformation of Shock and Awe into a massive spectacle that aimed to dazzle viewers into compliance is common practice in the US history of war propaganda. Yet, the Shock and Awe mass media event was perhaps the last time the DOD would be able to exert such control over the media war. After all, Bush's *Top Gun*-esque "Mission Accomplished" performance belied the reality of an Iraqi insurgency that was just beginning, and the fact that combat operations in Iraq have continued, save a brief withdrawal (2011–2014), for the past 13 years. In retrospect, the finale of Shock and Awe reads as a twisted parody of itself. The mission was not accomplished. The Iraq war continues and is now called "Operation Inherent Resolve."

Nonetheless, the US communications and media environment has undergone significant changes since the Iraq war began. In 2003, only 11.1% of the world population had an Internet connection; about 60% of the American population was using the Internet. Now, about 40% of the world population has an Internet connection and almost 90% of the American population does (Internet Live Stats 2016). In 2003, the Apple iPhone was barely an R&D concept and Blackberry was just starting to roll out its first "convergent" smartphone, one equipped with mobile telephony, email, text messaging, Internet, faxing, and Web browsing services. As of late, about 50% of the global adult population owns a smartphone; by 2020, it is projected that 80% will. When the DOD launched Shock and Awe, the TV set was the go-to medium for one-way content transmission and viewing; Web 2.0 business models and social media sites enabling of two-way content communication, interactivity and collaboration were not in wide operation. Since 2003, the dominance of TV networks has been displaced by the rise of Web 2.0 companies such as Facebook (social networking) YouTube (video-sharing), Twitter (microblogging service), Pinterest (content sharing) and Instagram (mobile-photo sharing). Currently, these and other Web 2.0 businesses and platforms are widespread, and their use has become routine, even compulsory (Fuchs 2014).

The DOD's opening of Operation Iraqi Freedom in 2003 with Shock and Awe occurred in an age when TV-age mass-media business models, technologies, practices and paradigms were on the cusp of being disrupted. The DOD's Shock and Awe media war was largely manufactured, transmitted to a mass audience, and effectively managed, with help from TV news firms, as a conventional spectacle. The Internet and World Wide Web (Inter-Web) played a role in this media war, but a small one. The peace movement used the Internet to pre-emptively oppose the Iraq war before it began and continued protesting—virtually and actually—while it was happening (Berenger 2006; Wall 2005). Peace activists used the Inter-Web as a "means of communicating grievances, sharing and expanding communication across various transnational constituencies, and ultimately, increasing the interconnectedness and consciousness of groups and individuals on a global scale" (Carty and Onyett 2006, 230). Peace activists certainly took advantage of the Inter-Web to contest US military aims and legitimacy in waging the Iraq war (Berenger 2006; Gillan, Pickerill and Webster 2008), but their reach and influence was marginal as compared to the military-media complex. The Pew Internet and American Life Project reported that only 8% of US Internet users sought out information about the Iraq war on alternative news sites, while 61% relied on TV news network and elite press run websites (Jordan 2007; Fox, Rainie, and Fallows 2003).

Although the Internet was being used by trans-national peace activists in the early stages of the Iraq war, TV news networks and their websites were the major and most authoritative source of the media war. But as years passed and conditions changed, the dynamics of the media war changed as well. How specifically, then, did the new communications and digital media environment transform the media war? What are the emerging conditions and characteristics of the ubiquitous media war?

The Conditions and Characteristics of the Ubiquitous Media War

This section presents an overview of the new conditions and characteristics of "ubiquitous media war." I conceptualize the ubiquitous media war as ubiquitous with regard to the following: (1) sources of content; (2) workers; (3) types of stories; (4) access points; (5) time; (6) space; and, (7) data.

Sources. We once lived in a world where the DOD and a handful of giant media firms controlled the means of producing, distributing, and exhibiting most audio-visual war content, and these firms had the power to tell large numbers of people what war topics and issues were appropriate to think about and how to think about them, as well as the power to exclude the voices and viewpoints of pacifists who did not subscribe to the mainstream media war agendas and frames of reality they constructed. The DOD and media firms exerted substantial control over the 2003 Iraq media war, and the military-media complex is still a big, significant and powerful organizational source of media war content, but it is not the only one in the digital age. The producers of the media war are no longer few, but many. An abundance of media war sources—domestic and foreign, corporate and government-run, professional and amateur, allied and enemy-operated—compete for attention and influence, producing and circulating content that infrequently aligns with the agendas and frames of reality made by the military-media complex.

International broadcasters (e.g., Doha-based Al-Jazeera, Russia's Russia Today and Iran's Press TV), non-profit news organizations (e.g., Democracy Now, Wikileaks, The Intercept), and non-governmental organizations (NGOs) like Veterans for Peace produce and circulate content about war that conflicts with Washington. Al-Jazeera shows the world the human consequences of war, Democracy Now gives voice to the anti-war movement and Wikileaks is a trove of content that sheds light on military misdeeds that in a previous age would likely remain in the dark. For example, "Collateral Murder,"[1] a Wikileaks-produced mini documentary available on YouTube and shared via social media sites, shows a US helicopter gunship killing Namir Noor Eldeen, a Reuters photographer, and 11 Iraqi civilians in a Baghdad suburb on June 12, 2007. Furthermore, social media bursts with anti-war content sources. On Twitter, Anti-Imperial (@Anti_Empire)[2] claims to be "dedicated to the dismantling of imperialism in the twenty-first century" and a Facebook group called "The Grassroots Anti-Imperialist Network"[3] encourage users to "end the unjust wars waged by the U.S. government in the Middle East, Asia, Africa, and Latin America." Enemy sources, like ISIS's Al Hayat Media Center, produce gruesome videos of its acolytes sniping American soldiers and beheading security contractors, and then circulates these worldwide to score propaganda points. As more and more organizations are learning to use digital media-making software and hardware to produce content about war, as it happens, from all over the world, the source primacy of the US military-media complex begins to wane.

Workers. In the age of mass made-for-TV war, the division of labor underlying the production of the media war and public opinion management was relatively small and highlight professionalized. The professionals behind the curtain of the US Empire's media wars were conceptualized as "America's media managers" (Schiller 1973, 1). Today, they continue to do the work of making media wars: the Shock and Awe media spectacle, for example, was produced by DOD public affairs experts in conjunction with some of the media industries' workers. Yet, the era of a few professional mind managers is giving way to one in which many amateur influencers participate in the do-it-yourself manufacture of consent (and dissent too). In the past, the mind managers who made media wars could be distinguished from the people on the receiving of their spectacles. They usually boasted a "professional" status (they possessed a communications degree or credential of some kind), craft (they, perhaps following the pioneering work of Edward Bernays in both public relations and propaganda, had applied themselves to mastering the art and vocation of persuasion), and an employee status role vis-à-vis an employer (they were paid a wage by the DOD or PR firms in exchange for their labor power). The military-media complex still relies on and enlists the labor power of many professionals to make media wars, but more and more people with no formal training in media war-making, and who are not employed by the DOD or the media industries, are developing and using low-cost media production capacities to create media war content, without pay or the expectation of it. Social media sites like YouTube, Facebook, and Twitter encourage and expect "prosumers" to engage in productive labor, "from producing commercials to engaging in online word-of-mouth endorsements, to integrating brand messages into their own communication platforms" (Napoli 2010, 512). These prosumers—soldiers and civilians—are also productively using their devices, software and social media sites to engage in the labor of creating, uploading, tweeting, commenting upon, and sharing original, derivative, and remixed content about the Iraq war.

Take the following: US soldiers in Iraq create and upload videos of themselves fighting to YouTube (Christensen 2008). "Apache Kills in Iraq,"[4] for example, shows U.S. soldiers firing high powered munitions at Iraqis which, on contact, explode their bodies, splattering arms and legs and heads and blood everywhere. They also use their smartphones to take, edit and share digital photos on the photo-sharing website NowThat'sFuckedUp.com (NTFU) (Anden-Papadopoulos 2009). Some of these digital photos depict deserted landscapes and troops in barracks, but others are gruesome close-up shots of dead, dismembered and mutilated Iraqis accompanied by sadistic comments such as "What every Iraqi should look like" and "These fuckers get what they deserve" (*ibid.*). In the Comments section for Paul Krugman's (2015) "Errors and Lies," a piece in The Opinion Pages of *The New York Times'* Web 2.0 site, over 1461 readers from Frankfurt, Germany to Seoul, Korea, to San Francisco, USA, produced and "shared their thoughts on this article." And these user-generated comments also aim to influence thoughts about why the Iraq War happened. For example, SKG claims: "a major motivation for the Iraq War was simply to help George W. Bush to get re-elected [....] The Mission Accomplished charade was more than a self-congratulatory spectacle; it was the opening act of the 2004 campaign" (*ibid.*). SDW says: "The fact that the *casus belli* for the military adventure which cost so many lives and drained our treasury was an intentional fabrication used to mislead Americans is the most important of all" (*ibid.*) As the US war machine and Web 2.0 firms expand on a planetary scale, they mobilize and exploit the digital labor of the entire networked planet of prosumers. As result, the media war's division of labor is now ubiquitous: an age of few media war workers has passed to one of many workers. And the media war work of the few is often contested by the many.

Stories. In the age of TV broadcasting, a few big TV networks (ABC, NBC, CBS, CNN and FOX News Channel) scheduled a limited supply of war stories on a select number of TV stations, and these were watched by a mass audience of millions (a mass audience sold to advertisers for millions too) (Smythe 1981). Although war stories that convey sorrowful rejoinders and radical criticism of the glorious and virtuous war narratives assembled by the military-media complex have always existed, these were barely audible or visible on mainstream TV. They circulated at a subterranean level, through subcultural print culture and public orality. Moreover, the Hollywood major studios did not produce anti-war film narratives while wars were happening, and distributors and exhibitors were not screening pleas for pacifism to the world. In the early twenty-first century, the military-media complex may still try to author one-dimensional audio-visual stories of war. The 2003 Shock and Awe of Iraq, for example, was a made-for-TV "branded war, a co-production of the Pentagon and Newsrooms, processed and cleansed so that it could appeal to the well-established tastes of people who were veteran consumers of popular culture" (Rutherford 2004, 4). Yet, the military-media complex cannot limit the supply of war stories or prescribe their contents. As the cultural industries trans-nationalize and pursue smaller and smaller groupings of audiences with corresponding commercial stories, and the ubiquitous media lets almost anyone cut their teeth as a digital storyteller, we see a rapid increase and diversification of the types of war scripts financed, sold, told, and watched.

In the early twenty-first century, a glut of war stories circulate, competing for hearts and minds and revenue. Since the 2003 Iraq War began, the TV industries have produced at least nine different TV series about the Iraq War (e.g., *Djihad, Generation Kill, House of Saddam, Over There*), two made-for-TV movies (*Saving Private Lynch, The Mark of Cain*), and countless episodes (e.g., *Family Guy*'s "Saving Private Brian" and *South Park*'s "I'm a Little Bit Country"). Globalizing Hollywood, trying to capture box office receipts from a trans-national as opposed to distinctly American audience, has produced over forty Iraq War films (e.g., *American Sniper, Grace is Gone, Green Zone, The Hurt Locker, The Lucky Ones, Redacted*) while prolific documentary film studios have made approximately eighty docs on this topic (e.g., *Bush Family Fortunes: The Best Democracy Money Can Buy, Fahrenheit 9/11, Iraq for Sale: The War Profiteers, Heavy Metal Baghdad, Iraq in Fragments, My Country, My Country, The War Tapes, Why We Fight*). Trans-national news organizations and the army of prosumers add to this surfeit of content. A September 1, 2016 "Google News" search for "Iraq war" retrieved 2,770,000 results in 21 seconds; a YouTube video search on the same date returned 1,370,000 Iraq War videos such as "John Perkins: The Secret History of the American Empire," "John Galtung: The Fall of the U.S. Empire and then What?" Digital copies of books like *War Porn* by Rory Scranton, *Fobbit* by David Abrams and *Nobody Told Us We Are Defeated: Stories from the New Iraq* by Rory McCarthy tell harrowing and horrifying stories about the Iraq war. Digital games like *Army of Two*, *Battlefield 3* and *Six Days in Fallujah* invite civilians play stories of the Iraq war, level by level. In the age of "information overload" and digital "glut" (Andrejevic 2013), many stories about the Iraq war circulate, and these are written by and from the point of view of everyone from DOD public affairs officers to weathered war correspondents to homesick soldiers to liberal scriptwriters to trans-national peace activists to novelists to Iraqi civilians themselves. Some stories may align with those manufactured by the military-media complex and others may communicate dissent.

The ubiquitous media war in Iraq may be comprised of more stories about and derived from a real war than any other war in human history. In this context, one must ask: can military-media complex produced propaganda be successful?

Access Points. In the age of TV broadcasting, people accessed the media war—audio-visual content—by turning on their TV sets, and tuning into the mediated violence (or lack thereof). Televised war content was received through free-to-air broadcast transmission or through cable or satellite subscription. For Americans, the Vietnam War was the first war watched on TV. But the 1991 Persian Gulf War was the first—compliments of satellites, the DOD and CNN—to let viewers watch a war begin and unfold, live, in real time, on cable TV. The 2003 Shock and Awe of Iraq was also a made-for-TV event, and to watch it unfold one would have go to the TV set, wherever it was placed and plugged in, turn it on, and tune in. While the TV set has long been the go-to technology for watching war as it happens, due to media convergence (Jenkins 2006), all kinds of devices—personal computers, smartphones and tablets—have become new and pervasive gateways to the media war. These give access to all kinds of different sites and platforms that traffic all kinds of different stories about war events and happenings. The TV set is still an important access point to the media war, but it is not the only access point. Today ubiquitous devices drive "anytime, anywhere" connectivity to the media war. The ubiquitous media of access also frees the media war from the cage of broadcast TV's temporality and spatiality.

Time. In the era of broadcast TV, the time of watching the media war was largely determined by TV networks, which ruled the viewer's leisure time by meticulously scheduling TV shows for consumption on behalf of advertising clients. Media war stories were delivered (through transmission) to viewers in ways that adhered to network scheduled time (particular time slots in the TV schedule). Ubiquitous media devices, however, enable prosumers to read and watch and hear and interact with the media war whenever they like. Time-shifting digital video recorders like TiVo, on-demand and subscription based digital streaming services like Netflix, video sharing platforms like YouTube, and Facebook social networking services, allow prosumers to search for, browse, and take in media war stories when they want, at whatever time they like, and without abiding by TV schedules. Prosumers may download war stories in digital form at one time, upload their own story some other time, and then attack someone else's any time they like. The temporality of the made-for-TV media war—the scheduling of media war at certain times on certain channels—is unsettled by the ubiquitous media, which lets prosumers self-schedule, do-it-yourself program, playlist-generate and curate, and interact with media war stories, any time they like.

Space. In the era of broadcast TV, the space of accessing and watching the media war was the household. The TV set, often placed in a living room and plugged into an electricity supply, gathered people—sometimes a family—around it for the media war. So, the Vietnam War was called a "living room war" because it was the first to be watched on TV by millions of Americans in their living rooms. The ubiquitous media, however, takes the media war outside of the home, and lets it be watched, heard and engaged with almost anywhere, at work and at play. As "media become ubiquitous they become embedded in material objects and environments, bodies and clothing, zones of transmission and reception" (Featherstone 2009, 3). The ubiquitous media war overflows from the household, through the pipes and circuitry of personal computers, smartphones and tablets, following every move one's body makes into a multitude of private and public spaces. In a time when millions cannot seem to live without being connected to others via mobile devices, when the sociality of walking, sitting, seeing, speaking, hearing and talking are integrated with devices and applications, "the intensifying rhythms of capitalist cultural production and its ubiquitous flows of information are now increasingly inseparable from the human body" (Manzerolle 2010, 461). With devices "always on" and "always-on-you" (Turkle 2008), the media war is always on and always on you too, an embodied everywhere phenomenon.

As the space of accessing media war becomes ubiquitous, the media war spreads across borders, bodies, and devices into automobiles, restaurants, shopping malls, offices, and classrooms. In the past, nation-states could regulate what content flowed in and out of their territorial jurisdictions, but the cross-border media networks of the ubiquitous media war disrespect boundaries, and the state's power to limit the overflow of digital media war content from foreign contexts to domestic is constrained (Armistead 2004; Stahl 2010). As a consequence, DOD-administered information operation campaigns intended to transform the minds of enemy combatants on the battlefront now make their way back to the home front, where they may shape American minds, too. In an age where mobile devices connect to the bodies of people everywhere they go, the media war flows out of the household, exceeds the TV set, gets watched, and fought, anywhere. The battlefields of traditional territorial warfare converge and diverge from ubiquitous media-constituted battle-spaces: "it is not that the battlefield as the place where war is waged has gone in smoke or has born out of importance, it is rather the case that the battlefield has been dis-placed, re-designed, re-shaped and rethought through new spatializing practices of warfare" (Grondin 2011, 255).

Data. In the age of TV broadcasting, the audience watching the media war was constructed by TV networks, advertisers, and ratings agencies as a "mass" commodity (Smythe 1981). TV networks scheduled war on TV to lure viewers into a steady flow of advertisements, and then sold the attention of this audience to advertising companies—the main source of their revenue. When the theory of the "audience commodity" emerged (McGuigan and Manzerolle 2014; Smythe 1981), TV networks scheduled war stories at specific times, used these stories as bait to mobilize the audience's affect and attention, and delivered it to ads. Cable TV, however, broke up the mass audience commodity, sorting segments of audiences into demographically narrower audience commodity groupings. In the era of ubiquitous media war, the TV age's mass and niche audience commodities explode into millions and millions of prosumer data profiles.

Through the sites and platforms of the digital media, millions of prosumers present themselves as themselves to the world when railing against or rallying for war; others drop rhetorical bombs on intellectual opponents from behind carefully crafted digital personas; and even more lurk in the trenches of ongoing battles, gathering intelligence. The prosumer's search for and selection of existing media war content, and participation in media war battles, however, generates huge amounts of public, private and meta-data about one's actions and interactions. Assemblages of prosumer data, not an aggregated audience, is what now gets produced, sold and bought in today's digital media marketplace-battlespace. The companies that own the sites that enable ubiquitous media war monitor, collect, mine, and then assemble the data prosumers generate into profiles. They sell these—and access to these—to advertising firms, which pay them to algorithmically target prosumers with ads (Andrejevic 2007; Fuchs 2011, 2012, 2014; McGuigan and Manzerolle 2014). The ubiquitous media war kills off the mass audience commodity, with its connotations of being "duped" and "distracted" and "dumbed down," while enlivening the prosumer to engage, participate and interact in daily battles. Won or lost, all secure the growth of a global digital ad market worth over one hundred billion dollars. When prosumers publicize their private opinions about war, post culture jams of munitions corporations on Facebook, Tweet pleas for peace in the Middle East, blog oppositional readings of the latest war movie and Link in with likeminded comrades, these forms of "agency" are meaningful, and profitable too.

CONCLUSION: THE MILITARY MEDIA COMPLEX, 2.0

For the second half of the twentieth century—a period in world history which saw the rise of the US Empire, the military-media complex and cultural imperialism—the US dominated the battle for hearts and minds because it possessed the extraordinary power to influence the global TV broadcasting.

In the early twenty-first century, circumstances have changed. The power of the US military-media complex to command and control how people perceive and think about war may be diminishing. Between the US Shock and Awe of Iraq in 2003 and the present day war against ISIS, the global communication and digital media environment has become a "battle-space" in which mobile device-using, Internet-connected, and Web 2.0 prosumers, from DOD hawks to anti-war activists, struggle for hearts and minds. In the near future, the sorrows and traumas of Empire's real wars will continue to be accompanied by military-media complex-produced "media wars" (Mirrlees 2016), yet, these will likely be challenged. In a time in which anyone with smartphone can lob a radical anti-military critique at military-media complex-produced media war agenda, frame, or talking point and share this critique with likeminded others via Web 2.0 sites and platforms, in real time and from almost any location, it is doubtful that any State or firm possesses the power to command and control the total opinion of war.

The shift from mass media war to ubiquitous media war points to important changes, but not revolutionary ones. A fundamental transformation of the existing geopolitical-economic power structure of the US military-media complex has not happened, and does not seem forthcoming. Moreover, the ubiquitous media war poses an opportunity for the renewal of the military-media complex. The DOD is well aware of these momentous changes, and is trying to keep up with them. In a recent *Time Magazine* article entitled "The US Is Losing the Social Media War," Rand Waltzman (2015), the former program manager for a $50 million dollar Defense Advanced Research Projects Agency (DARPA) study of "Social Media in Strategic Communication," writes: "the use of social media and the Internet is rapidly becoming a powerful weapon for information warfare and changing the nature of conflict worldwide. Because of misaligned U.S. policies and laws, we continue to largely rely on conventional warfare techniques, which puts us at a severe disadvantage." Consequently, the DOD is responding to the disruptive and destabilizing effects of the digital communications and media environment, regrouping and asserting its power to win the ubiquitous media war. It is well positioned to do so.

US-based giants—Google, Facebook, Twitter—are global digital capitalism's dominant players, and the DOD is now leveraging their networks, sites, and platforms for cyber-war, surveillance, and public relations. The DOD hosts websites, moderates blogs, socially networks via Facebook pages, operates YouTube channels, and uploads videos to them, manages Twitter accounts, and posts photos to

Pinterest. By spreading its content through the websites that intersect with the daily lives of billions of people, the DOD bypasses the gatekeeping powers of news media. The ubiquitous media has enabled the DOD's publicity machine to turn the manufacture of consent into a direct military-to-public affair by diminishing the intermediary role of news media companies. Also, by using social media platforms that they do not own or pay to use but which are some of the most visited and trafficked in the world, the DOD can reduce costs associated with media war content distribution/exhibition while potentially increasing its reach.

The US wars are ubiquitous, as are the media wars being fought for and against them. The military-media complex is not dead, but mutating, and to discern how and with what effect this is so, further research is needed. In this regard, the geopolitical economy of communication is vital.

NOTES

1. https://collateralmurder.wikileaks.org/
2. https://twitter.com/Anti_Empire/
3. https://www.facebook.com/peoplenotprofit/
4. https://www.youtube.com/watch?v=LoFq9jYB2wo/

REFERENCES

Anden-Papadopoulos, Kari. 2009. "US Soldiers Imaging the Iraq War on YouTube." *Popular Communication* 7 (1): 17–27.

Andersen, Robin. 2006. *A Century of Media, A Century of War*. New York: Peter Lang.

Andersen, Robin, and Tanner Mirrlees, eds. 2014. "Introduction: Media. Technology, and the Culture of Militarism: Watching, Playing and Resisting the War Society." *Democratic Communiqué* 26 (2): 1–21. http://journals.fcla.edu/demcom/article/view/83940/80844

Andrejevic, Mark. 2007. *iSpy: Surveillance and Power in the Interactive Era*. Lawrence, KS: University Press Kansas.

Andrejevic, Mark. 2013. *Infoglut: How to Much Information is Changing the Way We Think and Know*. New York: Routledge.

Armistead, Leigh, ed. 2004. Information Operations: Warfare and the Hard Reality of Soft Power. Washington DC: Brassey's Inc.

Berenger, Ralph D. 2006. "Introduction: War in Cyberspace." *Journal of Computer- Mediated Communication* 12 (1): 176–188.

Boggs, Carl, and Tom Pollard. 2007. *The Hollywood War Machine: U.S. Militarism and Popular Culture*. London: Paradigm Publishers.

Boyd-Barrett, Oliver. 2004. "Judith Miller, *The New York Times*, and the Propaganda Model." *Journalism Studies* 5 (4): 435–449.

Burgess, Jean. 2015. "From 'Broadcast Yourself' to 'Follow Your Interests': Making Over Social Media." *International Journal of Cultural Studies* 18(3): 281–285.

Carruthers, Susan. 2011. *The Media at War*. New York, N.Y.: Palgrave MacMillan.
Carty, Victoria, and Jake Onyett. 2006. "Protest, Cyberactivism and New Social Movements: The Reemergence of the Peace Movement Post 9/11." *Social Movement Studies* 5 (3): 229–249.
Cebrowski, Arthur K. and John. J. Garstka. 1998. "Network Centric Warfare: Its Origins and its Future." http://www.kinection.com/ncoic/ncw_origin_future.pdf
Chaffee, Steven, and Miriam Metzger. 2001. "The End of Mass Communication?" *Mass Communication and Society* 4 (4): 365–379.
Christensen, Christian. 2008. "Uploading dissonance: YouTube and the U.S. occupation of Iraq." *Media, War and Conflict* 1 (2): 155–175.
Der Derian, James. 2001. *Virtuous War: Mapping the Military Industrial-Media-Entertainment Network*. Boulder, CO: Westview Press.
Featherstone, Mike. 2009. "Ubiquitous Media: An Introduction." *Theory, Culture & Society* 26 (2–3): 1–22.
Fox, Sussanah, Lee Rainie, and Deborah Fallows. 2003. "The Internet and the Iraq War: How Online Americans Have Used the Internet to Learn War News." *Pew Internet and American Life Project*, April 1. http://www.pew Internet.org/reports/pdfs/PIP_Iraq_War_Report.pdf.
Freedman, Des, and Daya K. Thussu, eds. 2012. *Media and Terrorism: Global Perspectives*. London: Sage.
Fuchs, Christian. 2011. "Web 2.0, Prosumption, and Surveillance." *Surveillance and Society* 8 (3): 288–309.
———. 2012. "Dallas Smythe Today—The Audience Commodity, The Digital Labour Debate, Marxist Political Economy and Critical Theory. Prolegomena to a Digital Labour Theory of Value." *tripleC* 10 (2): 692–740.
———. 2014. *Social Media: A Critical Introduction*. London: Sage.
Gillan, Kevin, Jenny Pickerill, and Frank Webster. 2008. "The Information Environment of War." *Sociology Compass* 2 (6): 1833–1847.
Grondin, David. 2011. "The Other Spaces of War: War beyond the Battlefield in the War on Terror." *Geopolitics* 16 (2): 253–279.
Internet Live Stats. 2016. http://www. Internetlivestats.com/ Internet-users/.
Jenkins, Henry. 2006. *Convergence Culture: Where Old and New Media Collide*. New York: New York University Press.
Jenkins, Henry, Sam Ford, and Joshua Green. 2013. *Spreadable Media: Creating Value and Meaning in a Networked Culture*. New York: New York University Press.
Jordan, John. 2007. "Disciplining the Virtual Home Front: Mainstream News and the Web during the War in Iraq." *Communication and Critical/Cultural Studies* 4 (3): 276–302.
Kellner, Douglas. 1992. *The Persian Gulf TV War*. Boulder, CO: Westview Press.
Klein, Naomi. 2007. The Shock Doctrine: The Rise of Disaster Capitalism. Toronto: Knopf Canada.
Knightley, Phillip. 1975. *The First Casualty*. New York: Harcourt Brace.
Krugman, Paul. 2015. "Errors and Lies." *New York Times*, May 18. http://www.nytimes.com/2015/05/18/opinion/paul-krugman-errors-and-lies.html?_r=0.
Lotz, Amanda. 2007. *The Television Will Be Revolutionized*. New York: New York University Press.
Manzerolle, Vincent. 2010. "Mobilizing the Audience Commodity: Digital Labor in a Wireless World." *Ephemera* 10 (3–4): 455–469.
Martin, Geoff, and Erin Steuter. 2010. *Pop Culture Goes to War*. New York: Rowman and Littlefield.
Maxwell, Richard. 2003. *Herbert Schiller*. New York: Rowman and Littlefield
McChesney, Robert W. 2013. *Digital Disconnect: How Capitalism is Turning the Internet Against Democracy*. New York: The New Press.

McGuigan, Lee, and Vincent Manzerolle, eds. 2014. *The Audience Commodity in a Digital Age: Revisiting a Critical Theory of Commercial Media*. New York: Peter Lang.

Mirrlees, Tanner. 2016. Hearts and Mines: The US Empire's Culture Industry. Vancouver: UBC Press.

Murray, Williamson. 1997. "Thinking About Revolutions in Military Affairs." *Joint Force Quarterly* 16 (1): 69–76.

Napoli, Philip. 2010. "Revisiting 'Mass Communication' and the 'Work' of the Audience in the New Media Environment." *Media, Culture and Society* 32 (3): 505–516.

Rutherford, Paul. 2004. *Weapons of Mass Persuasion: Marketing the War against Iraq*. Toronto: University of Toronto Press.

Schiller, Dan. 1999. *Digital Capitalism: Networking the Global Market System*. Cambridge, MA: MIT Press.

———. 2007. *How to Think about Information*. Urbana, IL: University of Illinois Press.

———. 2008. "The Militarization of US Communications." *Communication, Culture and Critique* 1 (1): 126–138.

Schiller, Herbert I. 1969. *Mass Communication and American Empire*. Boston: Beacon Press.

———. 1973. *The Mind Managers*. Boston: Beacon Press.

———. 1992. *Mass Communications and American Empire*. New Boulder, CO: Westview Press.

———. 2000. *Living in the Number One Country: Reflections from a Critic of American Empire*. New York: Seven Stories Press.

Smythe, Dallas W. 1981. *Dependency Road: Communications, Capitalism, Consciousness, and Canada*. Norwood, NJ: Ablex Publishing.

Stahl, Roger. 2010. *Militainment, Inc.: War, Media, and Popular Culture*. New York: Routledge.

Stein, Jonathan, and Tim Dickinson. 2006. "Lie by Lie: A Timeline of How We Got into Iraq." *Mother Jones*, September/October. http://www.motherjones.com/politics/2011/12/leadup-iraq-war-timeline.

Taylor, Philip M. 1997. *Global Communications, International Affairs, and the Media Since 1945*. London: Routledge.

———. 2008. "Can the Information War on Terror Be Won?" *Media, War and Conflict* 1 (1): 118–124.

Treem, Jeffrey, Stephanie Dailey, Casey Pierce, and Diana Biffl. 2016. "What We Are Talking About When We Talk About Social Media: A Framework for Study." *Sociology Compass* 10 (9): 768–784.

Turkle, Sherry. 2008 "Always-On/Always-On-You: The Tethered Self." In *Handbook of Mobile Communication Studies*, edited by J. Katz, 121–138. Cambridge, MA: MIT Press.

Turner, Graeme, and Jinna Tay. 2009. *Television Studies after TV: Understanding Television in the Post-Broadcast Era*. New York: Routledge.

Ullman, Harlan K., and James Wade. 1996. *Shock and Awe: Achieving Rapid Dominance*. Washington DC: National Defense University/Institute for National Strategic Studies. http://www.dodccrp.org/files/Ullman_Shock.pdf.

Wall, Melissa. 2005. "Blogs of War: Weblogs as News." *Journalism* 6 (2): 153–172.

Waltzman, Rand. 2015. "The US Is Losing the Social Media War." *Time Magazine*, October 12. http://time.com/4064698/social-media-propaganda/.

CHAPTER THREE

From Contagion AND Revealing TO Recovery AND Healing

Examining the Lifecycle of Ubiquitous Control Through the Sony/BMG Rootkit

ERIC LEHMAN

> The concept of contagion evolved throughout the twentieth century through the commingling of theories about microbes and attitudes about social change. Communicable disease compels attention—for scientists and the lay public alike—not only because of the devastation it can cause but also because the circulation of microbes materializes the transmission of ideas. The interactions that make us sick also constitute us as a community. Disease emergence dramatizes the dilemma that inspires the most basic of human narratives: the necessity and danger of human contact. (Wald 2008, 2)

This chapter dissects the history of the Sony/BMG rootkit and examines it as an "outbreak narrative." The outbreak narrative, according to Wald, follows a "formulaic plot" (2), where social and global connections are discussed in light of an "emerging infection" (30). While most unwanted media can be examined as a form of contagion or infestation, the Sony/BMG rootkit remains a unique case in the spread of undesired ubiquitous media as it was perceived as being doubly infectious. First, 4.7 million music compact discs (CDs) from dominant recording artists such as Neil Diamond, Ricky Martin, and Celine Dion were distributed by Sony/BMG and harbored unwelcome Digital Rights Management (DRM) software (Edgecliffe-Johnson 2005; Stanwick and Stanwick 2013). Once the DRM was installed from the CD to consumers' laptops and desktops, it was difficult to uninstall and if it was removed simply by deleting the file, it could potentially damage the computer. Furthermore, these DRM applications were installed without the consent or awareness of the computer user leaving the consumer uninformed about changes to operation procedures and privacy leaks on their computers (Mulligan and Perzanowski 2007, 1163–64). Secondly, the DRM was saddled with a potentially harmful rootkit that exposed vulnerabilities in networked systems to malicious viruses and hacker attacks. Sony/BMG rootkit whistle-blower Mark Russinovich (2005a) explains in a blog post, "Rootkits are cloaking technologies that hide files, Registry keys, and other system objects from diagnostic and security software, and they are usually employed by malware attempting to keep their implementation hidden." The covert and reproducing qualities of the rootkit on laptops and desktop computers and the rhetoric of contagion which circulated through public discourse enabled the rootkit to spread from the hard drive to biological, corporate and national bodies infecting these entities in unexpected ways. By studying this particular incident using a theoretical framework based primarily on Priscilla Wald's scholarship on the discourse of contagion and Jussi Parikka's theories on digital contagion, I propose that ubiquitous controls also have a formulaic lifecycle, much like the "outbreak narrative," and move from an incubation period, to contagion, to remission.

Mobile technologies, such as the phone or the tablet, have allowed for easy and instant access to media. Furthermore, these devices and the content they carry noticeably appear in the public, private, intimate, and digital spheres. However, specific media, such as the rootkit within Sony/BMG's DRM applications, are not always seen despite being present and active. Only in its ability to "go viral" and "reveal" itself does a rootkit enter the public imagination. Once exposed, the rootkit can then be examined in terms of its invasiveness and be quarantined or eradicated. In this way, Sony/BMG's development of copy protection software acts not as an isolated infection, but reveals connections between the virus, the host and other bodies.

Ubiquitous media also reveals connections in how it circulates. Sociologist Michael Featherstone (2009) notes a distinct shift from the monolithic authority of "mass media" to a more dispersed and democratized power of "new media" and "multi-media" (2–3). He states, "as media become ubiquitous they become embedded in material objects and environments, bodies and clothing, zones of transmission and reception" (3). Perhaps the types of "embedded" media that seem most omnipresent and noticeable are the unwanted ones which act much like a rash, and is at once both unsightly and irritating. Junk mail, television advertising, and pop ups infect valued content and consume precious time. Furthermore, whether by filing it in either the physical or digital recycling bin or by patiently waiting for the commercial to be over, unwelcome content needs to be pushed out of the way before the desired content can be accessed. At least from the perspective of the music or entertainment consumer, DRM is no exception on this list of unwanted media.

Media theorist Tarleton Gillespie (2007) describes DRM as a "speed bump" (70) and regards technological regulation as a combination of the use of technological devices aligned with laws, effort and partnership to "arrange people and activities in a coherent system" (99). Technologies are "mediational" (87) and act as a means to intervene with human activity at a distance and set forth particular consequences. Additionally, technologies have political implications in both the decision making process to adopt them and in the designated policies that govern their use (74). Finally, Gillespie argues that while legal regulation is visible both in its written form and in its enforcement, software code is hidden noting that a "trusted system" (93–94) only functions by keeping its inner workings hidden from others.

Alongside being described as impedance or a speed bump, DRM is also seen as a method of observation and, like much scholarship on online surveillance, critiqued as a Foucauldian panopticon. For instance, law scholar Alex Cameron (2005) observes that DRM and panopticism are similar in that they both maintain their power through surveillance and information collection and that those under observation are without privacy. However, he also suggests that the DRM may be superior to the panopticon because unlike the guards in the tower of Bentham's prison who may be looking away at any given time, DRM is always monitoring. Information technology law expert Ian Kerr (2010) concurs by stating that if early technical protective measures (TPMs) were "a virtual fence, then a DRM is a virtual surveillance system" (273) and sees digital locks as "primitive prototypes of what is likely to come" (275). In the case of Sony/BMG's DRM, while the End User Licensing Agreements (EULAs) claimed that the software enclosed on the CDs was for intellectual property protection only and that no private information was gathered, this statement was false.

Once installed, the copy protection software had "phone home" capabilities and reported back to Sony/BMG information including the user's IP address, what CD was played and the time the CD was played (La Belle 2006, 89–94). The 'phone home' feature served as a one-way transmission advertising Sony/BMG's cultural goods and could be "use[d] to lock users into a particular family of products" (Samuelson and Schultz 2007, 65). Kerr (2010) expands on the metaphor of the lock—from the mechanical to the digital to the legal—in stating that digital locks are something more than "instruments of exclusion" (301) that "leave no room for forgiveness" (302). For Kerr, while digital locks are a measure put in place to limit access to content, they also leave room for "virtuous conduct" (302) or the ability to choose the right, and moral, path. Furthermore, Kerr observes that ultimately, control resides not in the locks but in the keys which "give us the power to open or close, to turn on or turn off, to grant or deny, to allow, or forbid" (261). In other words, digital locks are only capable of keeping "honest" people out, and whether locks are used to exclude or as tools for marketing, power resides with whoever holds the key.

While Digital Rights Management (DRM) is often critiqued culturally using metaphors of impedance such as a speed bump or a lock, or as a means of surveillance, the presence of the rootkit bends the bars in Bentham's panopticon. By containing a rootkit, these Sony/BMG CDs demonstrated instability in what was described by Foucault (1979) as a "cruel, and ingenious cage" (205) shifting the perceived power of observation from the tower in the center of the prison to outside its peripheries and beyond. While rootkits can arguably have some legitimate purposes, such as collection of information by law-enforcement or for military tactical purposes (Hoglund and Butler 2006, 6), they are often associated with computer viruses and worms and therefore associated with criminal behavior. For that reason, individuals who exploit the rootkit, such as hackers and virus-programmers, are often maligned and put into the same category as "terrorists, communists, and pedophiles" (Parikka 2007b, 176) as they disrupt the efficiency of the panopticonic control. No longer is the power of surveillance centralized, but dispersed and made ubiquitous. The presence of a rootkit enables surveillance to not only be controlled from within, but also from the outside turning the one-way transmission of the "phone home" feature in Sony/BMG's DRM, meant for relaying information about the listener back to the parent company, into a virtual switchboard where information could be relayed to anyone, anywhere at any time. In other words, the rootkit unlocks information enabling it to go viral without the knowledge or consent of the user, and shifting the power of the key holder (Sony/BMG) to that of a picklock (the hacker).

Although the inner workings of the rootkit-infected DRM may have been hidden on the computer's hard drive, public awareness and outbreak narratives made these contagions imaginable. Wald (2008) asserts that "outbreak stories convey [scientific] expertise as the ability to make the unseen world appear" (37). Martin Heidegger (1993) notes that narratives, as well as technology (or rather the essence of technology) open doors to unseen worlds. Technology is "a way of revealing. If we give heed to this, then another whole realm for the essence of technology will open itself up to us. It is the realm of revealing" (318). For Parikka (2007a) the computer virus is also capable of revealing networked relations. "Viruses, then, are seen also as a kind of a memory of their environment and the ethology of their hosts. What they reveal are movements and connections" (289), or as he explains in two short words, "Diseases expose." (Parrika 2007b, 2) In implementing third party copy protection software on their CDs, Sony/BMG, perhaps unintentionally, also participated in revealing an unseen world. These revelations not only made the private and personal information of those who purchased the infected CDs available to Sony/BMG through phone home capabilities, but through the DRMs inclusion of a rootkit, also to anyone who had the expertise and desire to exploit it.

That said, it is worth considering that although releasing active DRM was an aggressive and invasive move on Sony/BMG's part, it is doubtful that Sony/

BMG was intending to infect the public with potential security issues that would sicken the computers of their customers. It is more likely that quite the opposite was true; they were searching for a way to inoculate their copyrighted works from spreading across cyberspace. When Sony/BMG released the first CD containing rootkit technology in January 2005, the sale of physical music formats was already in decline. From 1999 to 2003, the music industry saw a 31% decrease in CD sales which translated into a deficit of revenue from $14.6 billion to $11.2 billion worldwide (La Belle 2006, 82). Although there are a number of possible reasons contributing to the decrease in CD sales, it is speculated that piracy was largely responsible for this economic hit (82–83). The National Association of Recording Mechanizing (NARM) released a study in 2004 revealing that less than 50% of music consumers bought their recordings, either by purchasing physical product or by downloading it from a legitimate online retailer (86–87). Also, given that CD technology was developed without an encryption code, it was difficult for record labels to immunize their intellectual property against online piracy. However short-sighted, the CD was designed for consumption as a playback-only format; since the medium's only defense was a copyright bit that informed only a limited public who knew of its existence whether a work was protected or not, CD media was, for all intents and purposes, unlocked (Sterne 2012, 196–197). For better or worse, with the development of MP3 audio coding, faster Internet speeds, and ever decreasing cost for CD ripping and burning technology, the spread of music across web-based platforms had flourished. Digital technologies were "freeing" music and making them instantly accessible to the masses. Whether in the form of CD burning or downloading via peer-to-peer (P2P) networks, digital copies sounded identical to their original and making reproductions was quickly accomplished.

It is also important to note that these rootkit technologies were not the first attempts by the recording industry to control copyrighted music. However, unlike DRM, earlier methods were ineffective and nonthreatening. In 2001, record labels introduced a passive method of protection where they intentionally added an error to the Table of Contents (TOC) located on the outer region of the compact disc, which in turn was supposed to prevent the computer from reading the music on CD-ROMs/CD burner drives. This passive means of protection caused more problems for the industry than it solved. It turned out that the copy protection could easily be foiled by using tape or a felt pen on the disc itself and eventually, with the release of new drivers for CD burners, posed no impedance at all. To add insult to injury, some conventional CD players refused to play the passively protected CDs and consumers would return them to the retailers for a refund (La Belle 2006, 88; Mulligan and Perzanowski 2007, 1192–94).

The recording industry also tried circumventing P2P through 'spoofing,' where corrupt, empty or modified files were intentionally added to file sharing services to clog up the system and discourage file sharers from exchanging files (La Belle

2006, 84–85). One particularly infamous case of spoofing occurred in 2003 when a masked recording of Madonna saying "What the fuck do you think you are doing?" (CMJ 2003) was circulated on P2P networks in place of her newly released album *American Life*. Hackers responded with "this is what the fuck I think I'm doing" when they breached Madonna's website and posted free downloads of previously unreleased material (Gordon 2011, 13). Furthermore, electronic artists released remixes of the "what the fuck" soundbite in defiance of the recording industry's attempts to thwart file sharing (Mason 2009, 68–70).

Decidedly, spoofing and passive means of protection were severely limited in their effectiveness, so Sony/BMG took the next step in protecting its copyrights by switching from passive protections to active DRM on their CDs. One insider source noted that Sony/BMG turned to active DRM because protection that could easily be circumvented with the use of marker was making record companies "look stupid" (Knopper 2009, 225) and that the label needed to find "something deep" (*ibid.*) if it was going to prevent the circulation of their copyrighted music. In other words, DRM, at the time, seemed as if it was going to be the perfect remedy. As Cameron (2005) notes, "To the great dismay of copyright owners, a perceived 'plague' of infringement has been thriving on the world's digital networks. Digital rights management (DRM) technology is hailed as a cure for this modern plague." When Sony/BMG released rootkits to the masses, they had high hopes for the great potential to immunize their intellectual properties against online piracy. However, in this case, the cure was worse than the disease, and what was intended as a vaccine became a pandemic, infecting computers globally as millions of CDs were distributed with active DRM.

These active forms of DRM enforced their copy protection not on the CD media itself, but by transferring its copy protection software through an executable file on the music listener's computer. This installation would attach itself to Windows Media Player[1], infecting it in order to block the digital duplication from CD to computer file, and thus preventing copy protected works from being shared online (Schneier 2005). However, as part of its coding, these new discs also installed a rootkit which posed security risks and enabled hackers to access user's computers remotely. Perhaps more surprisingly, the rootkit remained in an incubation period for a considerable time before it was discovered and made public in a blogpost. On October 31, 2005, approximately ten months after the first CD containing this technology was released, Mark Russinovich leaked the presence of a rootkit in Sony/BMG's copy protection software which he uncovered while testing security software called RootkitRevealer (RKR). Russinovich, who went on to publish an additional four blog posts on the Sony/BMG rootkit and XCP, was concerned not only with security breaches, but with how the DRM would integrate itself with the computer. Revocability, for Russinovich (2005a), was a key issue as was stated in his initial report:

> Not only had Sony put software on my system that uses techniques commonly used by malware to mask its presence, the software is poorly written and provides no means for uninstall. Worse, most users that stumble across the cloaked files with a RKR scan will cripple their computer if they attempt the obvious step of deleting the cloaked files.

In a later blog post, Russinovich (2005b) lists in detail the pitfalls he experienced in obtaining the patch to uninstall the software:

> First you have to go to Sony's support site, guess that the uninstall information is in the FAQ, click on the uninstall link and then fill out a form with your email address and purchasing information, possibly adding yourself to Sony's marketing lists in the process. Then, after you submit the information the site takes you to a page that notifies you that you'll be receiving an email with a "Case ID." A few minutes later you receive that email, which directs you to install the patch and then visit another page if you still really want to uninstall. That page requires you to install an ActiveX control, CodeSupport.Ocx, that's signed by First 4 Internet, enter your case ID and fill in the reason for your request. Then you receive an email within a few minutes that informs you that a customer service representative will email you uninstall instructions within one business day.

Uninstalling the rootkit-laden software was beyond the capabilities of most of the general public, and Russinovich likened the experience of uninstalling the DRM to that of conventional malware. One required the research skills to track down the uninstall link, additional software to perform the uninstallation, the technical know-how to perform the uninstallation, patience while Sony/BMG took a business day to provide instructions on how to remove the software and, most fundamentally, trust in the companies who infected the computer with a rootkit in the first case. While Russinovich was finally able to remove the DRM which plagued his hard drive, it was not an easy feat and it was evident that the copy-protection software that was intended to minimize the online transmission of unauthorized MP3s was designed in a way that it could not be circumvented. It would seem that the rootkits were programmed by their developers to infect and, until Russinovich acted as whistleblower, had been allowed to spread across numerous computer systems.

Yet, the spread of the rootkit may have been contained earlier. A month before Russinovich leaked the information on his blog, a team made up computer scientists Ed Felten and Alex Halderman had stumbled across the rootkit, but as they had already been threatened previously with DMCA lawsuits, were afraid to come forth with their findings (Mulligan and Perzanowski 2007, 1198–99). It is possible that if their hands were not legally tied, Felten and Halderman may have revealed the deficiency in Sony/BMG's software to the public sooner, and the incubation period and hidden spread of the rootkit could have been shortened. While it may be tempting to fault these two researchers for not breaking the news sooner, as the "delay caused by legal uncertainty left millions at risk for weeks longer than necessary" (1199), they would be only amongst the long list of people, companies and organizations who would be challenged in not preventing this viral contagion. Even though Sony/BMG took the brunt of the fiscal and legal culpability for the fiasco, as will later be discussed, who was ultimately responsible for the spread of the outbreak was still up for debate. Nonetheless, once the presence of the rootkit had leaked, stories about who spread the infection and who failed to protect the public began to surface.

While much of the criticism, especially in Russinovich's foundational blog posts, was aimed at the music industry, *Wired* magazine reporter Bruce Schneier (2005) condemned big business computer security companies like Symantec and McAfee:

> I truly believed that even in the biggest and most-corporate security company there are people with hackerish instincts, people who will do the right thing and blow the whistle. That all the big security companies, with over a year's lead time, would fail to notice or do anything about this Sony rootkit demonstrates incompetence at best, and lousy ethics at worst.

Still, as Parikka (2007b) notes, with the privatization of the media sphere in the 1980s, computer security was meant to protect a triad of interests: individual privacy, national safety, and commercial security (54–55). Anti-viruses were put in place to monitor the health of the networked computer system and their failings at finding the breach and putting immunities in place not only put individual computers at risk, but (as will be addressed later) also threatened national and economic security. The CD, for all intents and purposes, was able to pass through society unnoticed as what Wald (2008) describes, as a "healthy carrier" (68). A healthy carrier is an individual who transmits the disease, yet shows no signs or symptoms of being sick and therefore can spread illness to those around him/her without ever being suspected. In defense of anti-virus developers, it was easy to overlook the compact disc as a viral technology. The CD was generally seen as fun and friendly media and, much like the audio cassettes and LPs before it, had been welcomed into the private home for safe entertainment. Certainly, in its 20 years on the market up to this point, the CD had never posed a threat to an individual's wellbeing.[2]

Sony/BMG didn't agree with Russinovich's diagnosis. This was exemplified by Sony/BMG executive Thomas Hesse when he made the following offhanded response in an interview: "Most people, I think, don't even know what a rootkit is, so why should they care about it?" (quoted in Mulligan and Perzanowski 2007, 1161) However, the public did care about the rootkit because once the rootkit was installed and the computer was infected, not only did it lay bare the system for computer hackers to exploit and install malware and viruses but through the rhetoric of contagion and public discourse, the rootkit also had the capability to jump from a technological body, to a corporate body, a national body, or a biological body. If the DRM had merely acted as a tool to control copyrights, while it would have been a nuisance to those who were sharing music online or shifting formats, the effect of the DRM would have been localized. However, 52 different albums representing an estimated 2.1 million CDs sold contained the rootkit (Stanwick and Stanwick 2014). As the DRM was downloaded onto computers connected to the Internet, the threat no longer remained isolated but was networked with other public and private systems and the spread of the Sony/BMG rootkit became a full blown pandemic.

While Russinovich and the public at large became concerned with privacy leaks and damages to their computers, they were not the only ones pushing to put an end to the software infection. The United States government also intervened to keep America safe from Sony/BMG's infected DRM. On November 11, 2005, Stewart Baker, the assistant secretary of policy for the Department of Homeland Security, released a statement reminding Sony/BMG, "It's very important to remember that it's your intellectual property, it's not your computer. And in the pursuit of protection of intellectual property, it's important not to defeat or undermine the security measures that people need to adopt in these days" (Bridis 2005). Homeland Security was concerned about keeping the US safe from infected hard drives which could be transformed into "zombie computers" capable of hiding communication and activities of criminal and terrorist organizations (Mulligan and Perzanowski 2007, 1173). One private decision on behalf of the corporate body to attempt to stop the piracy of music grew into a national security problem. Zygmunt Bauman (2007, 25) further elaborates:

> Society is no longer protected by the state, or at least it is unlikely to trust the protection it has to offer....'Open' and increasingly defenceless...the nation-state loses its might, now evaporating into global space, and its political acumen and dexterity, now increasingly relegated to the sphere of individual 'life-politics.'

As the rootkit opened the possibility of attacks launched not from physical, geographical space, but from cyberspace, the American governing body could not quarantine an impending epidemic from crossing over its border. Furthermore, as the nation was unable to contain the threat both at home and in the private home, the nation's blame for compromising state security shifted from the individual body to the corporate body.

Homeland Security was also concerned about the rootkit contributing to the spread of biological viruses. Baker further stated in that same November 11th release:

> If we have an Avian flu outbreak here and it's even half as bad as the 1918 flu, we will be enormously dependent on being able to get remote access for a large number of people. Keeping the infrastructure functioning is going be a matter of life and death and we take it very seriously as well (quoted in Rhodes 2005).

A malfunctioning infrastructure reveals the nation's inability to protect its citizens against global threats, whether they are criminal, biological or military in nature. The 2002–2003 SARS outbreak was an example of this, where the contagion of "the epidemic revealed that Canada's public health infrastructure was fragile" (Price-Smith 2009, 146). Priscilla Wald (2008, 51) notes, "the designation of political responsibility and funding structure is that the responsibility for collective health is understood to be primarily national." Nations who portray themselves as the protectors of their citizens mask that they are incapable of sometimes managing their responsibilities and incidents, such as the Sony/BMG rootkit, expose the nation of being incapable of withstanding the global challenges of the World Wide Web and its viral denizens.

Beyond the national body, Baker's statement shows that a computer virus can also mutate across bodies and infect the human body. Computer viruses in this sense are not merely, as Parikka (2007b) suggests, "explained *as if they* were biological viruses…where their characteristics are viewed as metaphorically transported from the discourse of biology" (120). They actually go beyond the metaphor by being able to infect a public at a biological level in breaking down public health infrastructure. In this instance, the computer virus is directly linked to the possibility of increasing the spread of the Avian flu pandemic. Parikka further acknowledges that "an inspection of a technological or computer body means analyzing a whole congregation of bodies (human, technical, social, natural) that are attached together under [a] specific force" (120). The intermingling of bloods from these varied bodies allowed for the Sony/BMG rootkit, initially unleashed as a private decision to protect intellectual property, to be contagious and mutate along several different bodily discourses spreading to a mass public and infecting a nation. Margaret Pelling's (2001) research, which notes that contagion is often analogized to a rotten fruit and that "decay spread[s] from one part of a fruit to another, and from one fruit to the next if they were in contact" (20) is particularly useful here. While a rootkit is not technically a virus, as will later be discussed, it could and did spread from one type of media (the compact disc) to another (the home computer) by means of conventional record distribution. Furthermore, this physical means of dispersion not only allowed for the system to decay by breaking down its immunities, but enabled computer viruses to enter and infect the technological body and attach itself to the human body, not simply through discourse, but by attacking the regulated bodies put in place to keep the biological body healthy.

The Trojan horse was one type of viral attack that was plotted through the rootkit vulnerability and that the American nation was especially concerned about (Mulligan and Perzanowski 2008, 1167). Parikka (2007b, 47) describes Trojan horses as follows:

> Trojan horses can be defined as programs that are not what they seem to be on the surface. Named after the Homeric legend of the Trojan horse, which allowed the Greeks to gain entry into Troy by smuggling soldiers within a wooden horse, the digital versions usually refer to shareware or freeware programs that contain malicious code or, for example, create a backdoor to the computer system.

The metaphor of the Homeric Trojan horse aptly describes how Trojan horse computer virus attacks can remain disguised within useful and seemingly benign software. That said, the Trojan horse virus works in quite the opposite way than Trojan™ brand condoms work. Where the condom is designed to stop the transmission of virus, Trojan horses expose the computer to numerous viral attacks. Here, the comparison between the prophylactic and the virus introduces discussions surrounding technological and sexual contagion. Both the computer virus and HIV came to the public attention at around the same time. Some computer viruses were even named after the disease as in the case of the "AIDS Trojan" and "PC AIDS" (Parikka 2007b 62, 142; Sontag 1989, 70). While Parikka and AIDS scholar Susan Sontag note that there is a rhetorical similarity between sexual contagion and technological contagion, AIDS and rootkits are also suitable metaphorically as neither will, in and of themselves, make their host sick. Sontag (1989) notes, "AIDS-acquired immune deficiency syndrome is not the name of an illness at all. It is the name of a medical condition, whose consequences are a spectrum of illnesses" (16). Likewise, rootkits are also not a virus but a condition which in breaking down the immunities of the computer can lead to a "spectrum" of viruses.

Rhetoric surrounding the contagion of the AIDS virus and the rootkit also placed some responsibility on the infected party. Susan Sontag (1989, 26–27) notes that since AIDS is often seen to transferred through "deviant" (homo)sexual intercourse and addiction, that fault goes to the individuals transmitting the disease. Rebecca Ruby's (1999) call to have the intentional transmission of HIV criminalized further confirms this position. "People acted as though they were invincible, engaging in what we now know to be extremely risky behavior. This attitude allowed the virus to spread to individuals who were unaware of the chances they were taking." File-sharers who were willingly downloading copyrighted MP3s from dubious parties were also responsible for transmitting viruses. The individual's responsibility in preventing the spread of computer viruses, what has become known as practicing "safe hex," includes maintaining good "digital hygiene" or abstaining from risky behavior online (Parikka 2007b, 8). This is consistent with neoliberal citizenship where in a market driven sphere, social responsibility over health is downloaded onto the individual. David Harvey (2005) notes that in in the neoliberalist state, "Personal failure is generally attributed to personal failings and the victim is all too often blamed" (76). Sontag (1989, 54–57) notes that the plague historically has been metaphorically linked to social and moral judgement where the infected parties are punished for the ill-conceived decisions that they make. The 10 biblical plagues of Egypt from Exodus is an excellent example of this type of judgement. Furthermore, Sontag states that "AIDS seems to foster ominous fantasies about a disease that is a marker of both individual and social vulnerabilities. The virus invades the body; the disease (or, in the newer version, the fear of the disease) is described as invading the whole society" (65–66).

The cloaked yet circulating Sony/BMG rootkit was made ubiquitous first through digital contagion and then through social contagion. First, it was allowed to spread and incubate on computers, opening doors for malicious attacks by hackers and Trojan Horse viruses. Second, it continued to spread through public discourse when the rootkit threat was exposed by Mark Russinovich. Blame was placed on Sony/BMG for initiating the virus, anti-virus companies for failing to keep computer systems safe, and the private individual for participating in the dubious acts of pirating CDs and sharing music on-line. Through the rhetoric of contagion, the rootkit moved from a technological body attacking national bodies who seemingly could not control threats to their networked security systems and biological bodies who were threatened by the spread of Avian flu due to potentially failing public health systems. Sony/BMG DRM revealed itself in unintended ways and to unintended onlookers when it contaminated users with a rootkit. Although the DRM was used by Sony/BMG to collect information on its customers for marketing purposes and to control the copying and dissemination of free music, it made, as Wald (2008, 37) so aptly noted, "the unseen world appear." Certainly, to hackers who could now gain access and exploit an individual's private information, but also to the public and the state who, through Russanovich's blogpost on the rootkit and the publications that followed, became aware of the potential dangers of the rootkit and began questioning the rights of private enterprise over public and national safety.

Media that is free can have inadvertent costs. Richard Stallman made an important distinction regarding the concept of free when he said "think free as in free speech, not free beer" (quoted in Lessig 2001, xxvi). However, there is another distinction that can be made. Information can also be thought of also as free-flowing, moving like water moving from a stream, into a river, and into the ocean. The Sony/BMG rootkit incident proves, not only as Stewart Brand's now clichéd statement "Information wants to be free" (quoted in Anderson 2009, 96) suggesting that media wants to be either at zero-cost or that the public has freedom to access it, but also that information wants to be *freed*, not as in the case of rights and freedoms like the freedom of speech, but unleashed like an engineered pathogen circumventing the control of any systems, even those that protect and keep the public safe. The Sony/BMG rootkit is as William S. Burroughs suggests, a "word virus," or "an organism with no internal function other than to replicate itself" (quoted in Parrika, 2007b, 138). While the rootkit also served no function other than to copy itself to the hard drive, much like AIDS, it broke down the computer system's immunity opening it up to invasive viral attacks and public discourse enabled it to spread from technology, to the private individual, to commercial entities, to the state.

However, while public discourse and metaphors of contagion served to circulate the rootkit, publication and discussion surrounding the Sony/BMG rootkit also led to its eventual quarantine. What was experienced a "coming plague" (Wald 2008, 1) would soon give way to the "triumph of science over the virus" (216) as anti-viruses were quick to catch up and eventually provide fixes for the rootkit. It was also the triumph of law over the virus. Blogs and conventional journalism, litigation and public outcry, led to CDs containing the infectious software being recalled. Sony/BMG was sued by a consolidated class action group (an imagined community it its own right) with the courts directing them to remove the DRM infected media from the shelves, and replace consumers purchases with DRM-free versions of the CDs (La Belle 2006, 98–100). Furthermore, because of the high-profile nature of the case, this was the last time any major record label experimented with active DRMs to protect their physical media (Mulligan and Perzanowski 2007, 1174). Despite the revealing of Sony/BMG's duo of contagions—first by making public the inner workings of the DRM and second by exposing the rootkit as a potential open door for malicious hackers to infiltrate security—the case of the Sony/BMG rootkit also experiences an erasure of sorts. Since CDs after this lawsuit were released DRM-free, this narrative often goes down in history as a footnote instead of as a cautionary tale of what happens when the security, privacy, and well-being of the many is jeopardized in the face of private, economic interest.

Additionally, it perhaps remains the last time DRM and computer viruses were considered to be on par in regards to social, political, and personal wrongdoing. While shifting platforms from home computers to mobile technology, rootkits continue to surface in and plague the news media. In 2016, a rootkit designed by Chinese hacker group Yingmob called Hummingbad infected over 10 million mobile devices across the globe. *The Guardian's* Dan Tynan (2016) reported, "Most people probably got infected because they installed a less-than-hygienic app from a third-party Android store or website" and that the "odds are you won't ever know" that you are infected. The alarming discourse of rootkits as hidden pathogens spread by refusing to practice "safe hex" still prevail. DRM, despite having found a new home in music media with the rise of music streaming services such as Spotify, Groove, Google Play, and Tidal, is no longer considered to be a pandemic and has been reduced comparatively to the common cold. Communication scholars Jeremy Wade Morris and Devon Powers (2015, 108) state in their study of streaming music services, "While DRM was loathed for preventing users from transferring files to other devices, making repeated copies of files and editing files for other purposes, streaming is largely celebrated despite these very same restrictions." DRM has returned to its metaphors of impedance, and these locks and speed bumps are something to be lived through as they balanced with convenience to access. Also, by no longer being discussed as part of the outbreak narrative, DRM returns, at least in terms of the public consciousness, to a state of "standing-reserve[3]," hidden and awaiting to be revealed once more as the world anticipates, as they do any compelling outbreak story, its sequel.

NOTES

1. Only Microsoft software was affected by the Sony/BMG rootkits. Apple's iTunes remained immune. For more, see Schiener 2005.
2. Although we have come to think of computer viruses as emerging from the online world, this was not the first time a computer virus was distributed through physical means. In 1989, software company PC Cyborg shipped (quite ironically) educational software about AIDS which infected computers with a malicious computer virus. See Parikka, 2007b, 62.
3. For an in-depth philosophical discussion of "standing-reserve," see Heidegger 1993, 322–324.

REFERENCES

Anderson, Chris. 2009. *Free: The Future of a Radical Price*. New York: Hyperion.

Bauman, Zygmunt. 2007. *Liquid Times: Living in an Age of Uncertainty*. Cambridge, MA: Polity Press.

Bridis, Ted. 2005. "Sony to Suspend Making Antipiracy CDs." *Washington Post*. November 11. http://www.washingtonpost.com/wp-dyn/content/article/2005/11/11/AR2005111100632.html.

Cameron, Alex. 2005. "Beyond the Panopticon: Architectures of Power in DRM." *On the Identity Trail*. March 8. http://www.idtrail.org/content/view/220/42/index.html.

CMJ Network Inc. 2003. "Caught Ya! What the Fuck Do You Think You're Doing?" In *CMJ New Music Monthly*, 13. CMJ Network, Inc. https://books.google.com/books.

Edgecliffe-Johnson, Andrew. 2005. "Sony BMG to Compensate Buyers of Flawed CDs." *Financial Times*, December 31. http://www.ft.com/cms/s/0/6e199252-79a2-11da-8d99-0000779e2340.html?ft_site=falcon&desktop=true#axzz4cZSj9WPN.

Featherstone, Mike. 2009. "Ubiquitous Media: An Introduction." *Theory, Culture and Society* 26 (2–3): 1–22.

Foucault, Michel. 1979. *Discipline and Punish: The Birth of the Prison*. Translated by Alan Sheridan. New York, NY: Vintage Books.

Gillespie, Tarleton. 2007. *Wired Shut: Copyright and the Shape of Digital Culture*. Cambridge, MA: MIT Press.

Gordon, Steve. 2011. *The Future of the Music Business: How to Succeed with the New Digital Technologies*. New York: Hal Leonard Corporation.

Harvey, David. 2005. *A Brief History of Neoliberalism*. New York: Oxford University Press.

Heidegger, Martin. 1993. "The Question Concerning Technology." In *Basic Writings: From Being in Time to the Task of Thinking*, edited by David Farrell Krell, 311–341. San Francisco, CA: Harper.

Hoglund, Greg, and James Butler. 2006. *Rootkits: Subverting the Windows Kernel*. Upper Saddle River, NJ: Addison Wesley.

Kerr, Ian. 2010. "Digital Locks and the Automation Of Virtue." In *From Radical Extremism to Balanced Copyright: Canadian Copyright and the Digital Agenda*, edited by Michael Geist, 247–303. Toronto, ON: Irwin Law.

Knopper, Steve. 2009. Appetite for Self-Destruction: The Spectacular Crash of the Record Industry in the Digital Age. New York: Free Press.

La Belle, Megan M. 2006. "The 'Rootkit Debacle': The Latest Chapter in the Story of the Recording Industry and the War on Music Piracy." *Denver University Law Review* 84 (1): 79–134.

Lessig, Lawrence. 2001. *The Future of Ideas: The Fate of the Commons in a Connected World*. NewYork: Random House.

Mason, Matt. 2009. *The Pirate's Dilemma: How Youth Culture is Reinventing Capitalism*. New York, NY: Simon and Schuster.

Morris, Jeremy Wade, and Devon Powers. 2015. "Control, curation and musical experience in streaming music services." *Creative Industries Journal*, 8 (2): 106–122.

Mulligan, Deirdre K., and Aaron K. Perzanowski. 2007. "The Magnificence of the Disaster: Reconstructing the Sony BMG Rootkit Incident." *Berkeley Technology Law Journal* 22: 1157–1231.

Parikka, Jussi. 2007a. "Contagion and Repetition: On the Viral Logic of Network Culture." *Ephemera*. 7 (2): 287–308.

———. 2007b. *Digital Contagions: A Media Archaeology of Computer Viruses*. New York: Peter Lang.

Pelling, Margaret. 2001. "The Meaning of Contagion: Reproduction, Medicine and Metaphor." In *Contagion: Historical and Cultural Studies*, edited by Allison Bashford and Claire Hooker, 15–38. New York: Routledge.

Price-Smith, Andrew T. 2009. *Contagion and Chaos: Disease, Ecology and National Security in the Era of Globalization*. Cambridge, MA: MIT Press.

Rhodes, Chet. 2005. "Homeland Security Warns Against Anti-Piracy." *Washington Post*. November 11. http://www.washingtonpost.com/wp-dyn/content/video/2005/11/11/VI2005111101160.html.

Ruby, Rebecca. 1999. "Apprehending the Weapon Within: The Case for Criminalizing the Intentional Transmission of HIV." *American Criminal Law Review* 36 (2): 313–335. http://go.galegroup.com.cat1.lib.trentu.ca:8080/ps/i.do?p=AONE&sw=w&u=ocul_thomas&v=2.1&it=r&id=GALE%7CA54823255&asid=3422416176d7643282808b240156186f

Russinovich, Mark. 2005a. "Sony, Rootkits and Digital Rights Management Gone Too Far." *Mark Russinovich's Blog*. October 31. https://blogs.technet.microsoft.com/markrussinovich/2005/10/31/sony-rootkits-and-digital-rights-management-gone-too-far/.

———. 2005b. "Sony: You Don't Reeeeaaaally Want to Uninstall, Do You?" *Mark Russinovich's Blog*. November 9. https://blogs.technet.microsoft.com/markrussinovich/2005/11/09/sony-you-dont-reeeeaaaally-want-to-uninstall-do-you/.

Samuelson, Pamela and Jason Schultz. 2007. "Should Copyright Owners Have to Give Notice of Their Use of Technical Protection Measures." *Journal on Telecommunications & High Technology Law* 6 : 41–76.

Schneier, Bruce. 2005. "Real Story of the Rogue Rootkit." *Wired*. November 17. http://archive.wired.com/politics/security/commentary/securitymatters/2005/11/69601?currentPage=all.

Sontag, Susan. 1989. *AIDS and Its Metaphors*. New York: Farrar, Straus and Giroux.

Stanwick, Peter, and Sarah Stanwick. 2014. *Understanding Business Ethics*. Thousand Oaks, CA: Sage Publications.

Sterne, Jonathan. 2012. *MP3: The Meaning of a Format*. Durham, NC: Duke University Press.

Tynan, Dan. 2016. "HummingBad Android Malware: Who Did It, Why, and Is Your Device Infected?" *The Guardian*. July 7. https://www.theguardian.com/technology/2016/jul/06/what-is-hummingbad-malware-android-devices-checkpoint.

Wald, Priscilla. 2008. *Contagious: Cultures, Carriers and the Outbreak Narrative*. Durham, NC: Duke University Press.

PART TWO

Mobilities

Mobile Devices, Wearables, and Locative Media

CHAPTER FOUR

Google Street View AND Representational Ubiquity

AARON SHAPIRO

"UBIQUITY" AS INFORMATIC ENVIRONMENTS

In his influential 1991 *Scientific American* article, Mark Weiser (1991) outlined a detailed vision of what the computer would look like in the twenty-first century. Along with his colleagues at Xerox Palo Alto Research Center (PARC), Weiser foresaw a world in which computing machines were invisible through their ubiquity and pervasive throughout built environments, analogous to the bombardment of text, images, and symbols that we experience in nearly every moment of our waking lives. This vision was "diametrically opposed" to the future of computing popularly imagined at the time: virtual reality, the "world inside the computer" (94). Virtual reality requires users to "don special goggles that project an artificial scene on their eyes" and "wear gloves or even body suits that sense their motions and gestures so that they can move about and manipulate virtual objects" (*ibid.*). Weiser and his team, however, were interested in the world outside the computer. Against the virtual-ization of reality, they proposed a real-ization of the "'virtuality' of computer-readable data—all the different ways in which it can be altered, processed and analyzed" (98). He called this vision "embodied virtuality": pulling the computer out from its "electronic shell" and bringing it into the physical world—into the home, into the office, throughout the city (*ibid.*; see also Galloway 2004; Greenfield 2006; Greenfield and Shepard 2007; Shepard 2011). "[V]irtual reality is only a map, not a territory" (Weiser 1991, 94) and Weiser's team was most interested in computing's territorial implications.

As many have argued, it was this vision of embodied virtuality—of built environments saturated with computing power—that seeded the research agenda that we know today as "ubiquitous computing" or "ubicomp" (Dourish and Bell 2007; Galloway 2004; Kinsley 2011). Although this agenda might now go by several different titles—from "pervasive computing" to "urban informatics" to "smart cities" (Burrows and Beer 2013; Dodge and Kitchin 2007; Thrift 2011), the scenarios that Weiser and the PARC researchers envisioned back in 1991 remain a dominant image for conceptualizing "ubiquity" not only in computation, but in media and technology broadly. For instance, in Mike Featherstone's (2009, 3) account of "ubiquitous media," the affordances of "miniaturized electronic circuitry, the cheap ubiquitous computer chips embedded in environments and mobile devices...sustain a new communicative architecture," reflecting a shift away from our understanding of media as a monopolistic concentration of power toward "the sense that media are now differentiated, dispersed and multi-modal." Ubiquitous informatic devices mediate the relationship between body and environs: "As media become ubiquitous, they become embedded in material objects and environments, bodies and clothing, zones of transmission and reception...creat[ing] an environment where things around us are constantly offering, passing and collecting information" (*ibid.*).

My concern with this paradigmatic vision of ubiquity is its somewhat narrow obsession with Moore's Law (Dourish and Bell 2007, 414)—with the recession of computation into the background around us, into micro-processors that become "part of the woodwork" (Kinsley 2011, 231). Surely the "sensor-ization" of environments is an important piece of the puzzle of ubiquitous digital mediation, but an inventory of today's media and technology landscape suggests that this is not the whole picture. If one were to consider Weiser's more tacit definition of ubiquitous computing, as constituted by a dynamic relationship between objects, the environment, and the "'virtuality' of computer-readable data," then a broader, more complex notion of ubiquity begins to emerge. In this broader conceptualization, "ubiquitous media" concern *the processes by which physical environments are rendered informatic through computational technologies*. This broader definition allows us to take stock of variations in the configurations of ubiquity. In this chapter, I differentiate between two such variations: *computational ubiquity* and *representational ubiquity*, which, when considered in tandem, reflect a diversity in the affordances and power geometries (Massey 1993) that ubiquitous mediation heralds.

THE DOUBLE ARTICULATION OF UBIQUITY

What does it mean to say that ubiquitous computing is about the rendering of physical environments as informatic? Suhail Malik's (2005) expounding on information and informatics is helpful in this regard. Building on thinkers such as

Gregory Bateson and Niklas Luhmann, Malik defines information as an "event that is situated within a system of organized memory" (32). In Luhmann's words, "Information is always information for a system" (quoted in Malik 2005, 33). It "presupposes organization, requires systemization" (Malik 2005, 33). Rendering physical environments informatic through the "'virtuality' of computer-readable data" and "all the different ways in which it can be altered, processed and analyzed" similarly requires systemization. It requires both the capturing of events within physical environments *and* an organization and structuring of the relationships between and within those environments. This can be grasped, for instance, by considering a data infrastructure such as the Global Position System (GPS) and its import for environmental data. GPS operates through a constellation of dozens of medium-range artificial satellites, called NAVSTAR, that are synchronized to coordinate extensive ground connectivity across the earth's surface (USNO, 2016). It presupposes a global, totalizing system of coordinates that organize and structure spatial relationships (Dalton 2013). Surely, then, GPS is a ubiquitous medium, and considering it as such emphasizes the broader conceptualization of ubiquity that I am getting at here—not only the saturation of environments with computing devices, but also access to systems of organized memory about those environments and their relationships to one another.

Since 1991, when Weiser sketched out his vision for ubiquitous computing, technological "systems of organized memory" about the environment have undergone dramatic changes. It was not until the year 2000 that the United States decided to end its "intentional degradation" of GPS signals for commercial usage (White House 2000). In the years since, we have witnessed the bulk of geographic information production shift from the relatively arcane worlds of academic geography, military strategy, and government planning, into the popular realm of consumer-oriented information technologies—not to mention advertising and marketing (Bauman and Lyon 2013; Burrows and Ellison 2004; Thrift 2011). From advances in geographic information systems (GIS) to the incorporation of "locative media," "geocoding," and the "geoweb" into mobile social media and gaming (Barreneche 2012), the ubiquity of location-aware systems has rendered the primacy of location—like that of computing, in Weiser's prognostication—nearly invisible. Web search results are algorithmically ordered by place. Online ad targeting uses physical proximity to commercial centers to tailor messaging. In its governing of access to information, location becomes "a default protocol setting of communication, and soon a taken-for-granted dimension of our media experience…to the point of rendering the prefix 'geo' in geomedia superfluous" (*ibid.*, 332). To borrow Weiser's phrasing, one could say that geo-mediatization has been woven "into the fabric of everyday life"; that the "virtuality" of geo-data (the map) and the physical embodiment of space (the territory) have become "indistinguishable" (Weiser 1991, 94; see also Thrift 2011).

Like the paradigmatic vision of ubicomp, geomedia applications, devices, and services render environments informatic through computational technologies. The processes by which they do so, however, are more multifaceted than the paradigmatic vision of ubicomp might suggest—not only the sensor-ization of environments, but also their imaging, cataloguing, databasing, sorting, mapping.

One way to conceptualize ubiquity in this sense builds on Mark Andrejevic's (2004) work on surveillance as a double articulation of both *watching* and *being watched*. Greg Elmer (2010) extends this logic to describe the operations of locative media as *finding* and *being found*—locating and being located—within spatializing systems of spatial information. Weiser's paradigmatic vision of ubiquitous media captures the *being found* half of this double articulation quite well—as environments saturated with computational technologies enact beneficent, automated forms of surveillance that locate users, register their actions and behaviors, and effect changes of state in the environment based on those inputs. The broader conceptualization of ubiquitous media that I am proposing here, however, is about the automation of the *finding* function, the locating—the ways in which new media privilege a *surveillant sorting of environments through a ubiquity of representations*. This framing of ubiquitous computing is not so farfetched considering the widespread adoption of locative smartphone apps and online platforms that provide information about places, such as FourSquare, Yelp, or GooglePlaces. These and other locative platforms invite users to sort through environments and environmental conditions as discerning consumers of urban landscapes—as potential homebuyers or renters, as romantic partners, as gamers or urban explorers (Sutko and de Souza e Silva 2011). They also invite corporate and state actors to seek out actionable relationships between space, place, and socio-economic character—a geographically-informed social sorting in pursuit of profit or discipline (Burrows and Ellison 2004; Dalton and Thatcher 2015; Graham 2005; Thatcher 2013). As with Weiser's vision, such processes recede into the background of our cultural psyche through their ubiquity (Graham 2005; Thrift and French 2002).

UBIQUITOUS REPRESENTATIONS OF SPACE AND PLACE

It is hard to imagine a single place on the planet that has yet to be photographed—or that a photograph of a particular place could not be located by internet search. Like the "avalanche of printed numbers" that Ian Hacking (1990) correlates with core features of modernity, it would seem that we are in the midst of an avalanche of digital images. Around 350 million digital photographs are uploaded to Facebook every day and over 80 million to Instagram; some reports suggest that upwards of 1.8 billion images are uploaded daily across the whole ecology of social media platforms (Eveleth 2015). Francesco Lapenta (2011) argues that the unprecedented scale at which digital images are presently produced and circulated is fomenting "a momentous technological and cultural shift that is profoundly reshaping how we represent and perceive the world." And this is especially true of digital images that capture and represent space and place (Eveleth 2015). Not only do sites like Flickr and Mapillary invite users to upload geotagged images onto their searchable public databases; web and mobile platforms such as Google Earth give users unprecedented access to satellite imagery (Parks and Schwoch 2012), wayfinding maps with live traffic information, bike routing, crowdsourced information about the location of police officers, etc. The theorization of maps as spatially productive is likely now more empirically evident than ever before (Cosgrove 2006).

Google has been at the forefront of this momentum (Dalton 2013). Through its acquisitions of digital mapping company Keyhole Corporation, Google made geographic information available to users at an unprecedented scale, with its easy-to-use "virtual globe" programs Google Earth and Google Maps (*ibid.*). But it was Google Street View—with its omnidirectional, street-level imagery of places on all seven continents, captured by roving fleets of "Google cars" mounted with specialized cameras from over five million miles of roads, across 39 countries and over 3,000 cities (Farber, 2012)—that truly solidified the cultural expectation that we should be able to pull up digital imagery about any place, anytime[1]. Photographs within Google's Street View platform (called Photo Spheres) are digitally stitched together to create an immersive experience (Anguelov *et al.* 2010), designed to give its users the sense that they can navigate city streets and "seamlessly move from one image into another in a virtual continuum of increasingly global spatial representations of the world" (Lapenta 2011, 14). In the words of former Google Maps VP Brian McClendon (2010), Street View is the "last zoom layer on the map," "a way to show you what a place looks like as if you were there in person"; it "enables armchair exploration," allowing users to move through "a virtual reflection of the real world."

Despite claims from Google engineers that the imagery displayed in Street View itself "contains a huge amount of information," in practice, the visual information contained within a single place-image is far less valuable informatically than in its amenability to aggregation within massive datasets of equally geo-informational place-images. Street View's amenability to aggregation is what makes its ubiquitous representations powerful. Aggregation is a key dimension of machine learning. It allows Street View imagery to become big data, to be incorporated into training datasets for computer vision algorithms that "learn" to identify objects (Prince 2012). As Manovich (1997) argues, "teaching" computers to "see" in the 1990s involved the supplementing of visual images with para-visual technologies for directly measuring space, such as ultrasounds or laser scanners.[2] However, recent advances in computer processing and machine learning techniques have prompted a shift away from direct-range measurement toward an emphasis on the aggregation and analysis of large datasets of images that are tagged with locational metadata (Prince 2012;

Szeliski 2010). Thanks to advanced computing power, image datasets that were previously too massive for computers to do much with are now used to train algorithms to identify target-objects with varying degrees of uncertainty. "Innovation" in this field involves new processing and storage methods that increase the speed of computation and thus enlarge the potential scale of the datasets (*cf.* Arietta, Agrawala, and Ramamoorthi 2013; Arietta *et al.* 2014; Doersch *et al.* 2012; Khosla *et al.* 2014; Quercia, O'Hare, and Cramer 2014). For example, a team at Google recently trained an algorithm to discern the location that a photograph was taken without using any locational metadata, "using only the pixels it contains" (Brokaw 2016). The training data for the algorithm contained approximately 91 million geotagged images scraped from Flickr, while an additional batch of two million geotagged photos were then used for testing the accuracy of the algorithmic predictions. The size of these datasets is what make the algorithm's predictive capabilities so powerful, even if "success" at present means correct identifications of an image's country of origin only 28.4% of the time.

The reason why this type of representational ubiquity, as well as its amenability to aggregation, are so important is that they allow for visual environmental qualities to be transformed into quantifiable data points. Here I sketch out two case studies illustrating what this has enabled computer scientists to do with informaticized environmental qualities.

Consider PlacePulse, a tool developed by the Macro Connections Group at MIT's Media Lab. PlacePulse "quantitatively measure[s] urban perception by crowdsourcing visual surveys to users around the globe" (Macro Connections 2014). PlacePulse is presented as a game to the visitors of the project website, who, by playing, become de facto participants in a "research study"; more realistically, players are generating training data for algorithms. On the website's home page, visitors are presented with two randomly-generated Street View images. Above the images is a pull-down menu of questions, prompting an evaluative judgment of the places represented: "Which place looks safer? Livelier? More boring? Which place looks wealthier? More depressing? More beautiful?" To answer, participants select one of the two images. To date, PlacePulse has recorded 1.3 million clicks.[3] This data is available for users to peruse as a series of visualizations that show how 50 or so cities rank against one another for each of the six evaluative prompts.

Aside from ranking cities, the PlacePulse researchers also employ the place-evaluation datasets as training data for algorithms designed to predict what a human's response would be to a randomly-generated place-image. The idea is that places labeled as "safe" or "lively" or "depressing" will share common visual characteristics that influence the evaluative outcome—but only in their aggregate will these clues emerge (Naik *et al.* 2014; Nasar 1998). The StreetScore algorithm, trained on the PlacePulse data, applies machine learning techniques to predict how viewers of a given street scene would perceive its level of safety, and then, again, compare these predictions with the "ground truth" of the PlacePulse data (Naik *et al.* 2014). This involves dissecting the Street View images' scene composition into discrete visual elements and identifying correlations between those elements and various evaluative outcomes. High-scoring images in the StreetScore study, for instance, tended to include "suburban houses with manicured lawns and streets lined with trees; while the typical low scoring image contains empty streets, fences, and industrial buildings" (*ibid.*, 2). From the point of view of algorithm design, these visual elements are not meaningful. Rather, they become informatically valuable—predictable—through their aggregation (Nasar 1998, 60). This allows the algorithm to create a statistical object from the seemingly "subjective" endeavor of evaluation: favorable feature selection is thus driven, the researchers argue, "not by biases in age, gender or location of the participants, but by differences in the visual attributes of images" (Naik *et al.* 2014, 2).

A group at University of California Berkeley has built a similar algorithm for studying correlations between visual and non-visual attributes of the urban environment (Arietta, Agrawala, and Ramamoorthi 2013; Arietta *et al.* 2014). But unlike PlacePulse, the Berkeley group is less concerned with user evaluations than with the identification of predictive correlations between visible features in the cityscape and the non-visual, "location-specific attributes" of social deviance or criminality. Using publicly available geocoded data on crime, housing price information (as an indicator of the relative affluence of neighborhoods), and locational data for graffiti (as a proxy for neighborhood "visual disorder"), this group's "City Forensics" algorithm is designed to predict the presence or absence of different crime types by identifying visual features discriminative for reports of those crimes. The locational metadata for each Street View image within the City Forensics database allows the researchers to build positive and negative subsets specific to the non-visual attribute of interest; this is the algorithm's training data. For example, imagery from areas where graffiti was reported would, according to this algorithmic logic, contain common visual elements that correlate with a high likelihood of graffiti being reported to the police. These visual elements stand to be "non-obvious" to the human eye (Andrejevic and Gates 2014, 186)—for example, a certain type of window frame or street lamp (Arietta *et al.* 2014).

Once a set of visual elements are identified as predictive of a specific crime type for a given city, the efficiency of the City Forensics algorithm is then tested across cities (do significant visual elements in San Francisco also predict the location of crimes in Boston?) and against human evaluations of the same images that were used to train the predictors. The City Forensics team hired a contingent of Mechanical Turk workers to examine a series of Street View images from a number cities and to "decide based on the image along whether [they] would feel safe in the area or not at any time of day" (Arietta *et al.* 2014, 5)—effectively reproducing the PlacePulse methodology of producing "ground truth" from human evaluation.

The predictors identified by the City Forensics algorithm—unique to each city and crime type—reportedly outperformed the human evaluations in correlating dangerous-looking places with crime by 33%.

Both the PlacePulse and City Forensics algorithms are examples of how Google Street View's representational ubiquity enables the informaticization of environments in ways not captured within the paradigmatic vision of ubiquitous computing. In both cases, ubiquitous representations of space and place allow for the automation of scene selection for different criteria—with PlacePulse, for the features that correspond with human preferences, and with City Forensics, for features that correspond with particular types of reported crimes. The implications of these algorithms for enacting new geographies is striking. In both examples, the automated sorting of place-images prompted the researchers to suggest their algorithms be applied as wayfinding applications to inform and customize mobility—routes that would lower the probability of encountering neighborhoods with higher crime rates or heighten the probability of encountering preferential environmental features. The "virtuality" of images as "computer-readable data" has the potential to effect new geographies of preference.

THE BIASES OF UBIQUITOUS MEDIA

The reason why it is important to take stock of the differences between computational ubiquity and representational ubiquity is that, taken together, they reflect a diversity in the affordances and power geometries (Massey 1993) that ubiquitous mediation heralds. In Weiser's vision, computational ubiquity facilitates dynamic environments that respond to the needs of their users or inhabitants through sensing, coding, and automating. In the case studies of PlacePulse and City Forensics, representational ubiquity enables computer scientists to automatically sort through place-images in order to identify particular visible, environmental qualities. At present, these two "ubiquities" operate separately, but it is not hard to see in recent visions—for example, corporate fantasies of the "smart city" (Söderström, Paasche, and Klauser 2014)—a desire to wed the two as totalizing instruments of "environmentality": a "distribution of governance within and through environments and environmental technologies" (Gabrys 2014, 43; see also Barreneche 2012). Environmentality promises the double articulation of ubiquity discussed above: the ability to locate and be located, as if every physical object, environment, condition, and human were a coordinate or address within a coordinated system of addresses. In Kittler's (1996) words: "Addresses are data which allow other data to appear... From the national postal service to the public telephone to the license plate on every registered vehicle, media are at work replacing people with their addresses." In physical environments rendered informatic through computational technologies and representational ubiquity, all are addressed.

Of course, totalizing instruments of environmentality remain a dream or fantasy of control; what we have at present are piecemeal attempts and programs to look to, which gave shape to those dreams or fantasies. Taking stock of the different affordances that the computational and representational ubiquities offer, then, can help to capture what those fantasies are about.

What does representational ubiquity offer that computational ubiquity cannot? Harold Innis' (1951) notion of media bias and James J. Gibson's (1977/2014) concept of object affordances help shed light on the differences between representational and computational ubiquity. Applying Innis, the affordances of different media-objects create biases at the level of communication regime. Contrasting, for example, stone tablets and papyrus for writing, Innis argues that communication regimes can be biased toward time over space, as in the durability of a media-object such as a stone tablet, which survives through the ages; or toward space over time, as in the mobility of a media-object like papyrus, which can travel great distances due to its light weight.

We can imagine the comparison between computational and representational ubiquity taking place along similar axes. On the temporal axis, there are two core differences between computational and representational ubiquities. The first is the lag or temporal distance between capture and analysis of objects within environments. In computational ubiquity, environments laden with networked sensors respond dynamically to the behaviors of users and environmental conditions. This is "real-time," the perception of no lag (Chun 2011). "Dumb" sensors such as thermostats or motion detectors are networked together into "smart" systems that respond to the presence or preferences of a person in the environment when he or she is in that environment: for example, by automatically adjusting temperature, or switching on a lamp or coffee machine (e.g., Weiser 1991). Recent years have seen a move to sensor-ize urban space in a similar manner, for instance, with dynamic LCD kiosks that tailor their advertising prices to the presence of large crowds in public space (*Screen Media Daily* 2014). On the other hand, with representational ubiquity, the lag between the capture of environmental qualities as information and analysis is as short or as long as necessary. The point is not necessarily real-time analysis, but the "readiness-to-hand" of environmental information (Heidegger 2008)—a latent potentiality, realized in the act of analysis, whenever the need arises: for example, when a couple checks out a neighborhood on Street View before considering renting an apartment there, or conducting research about the correlations between health outcomes and the presence of litter in a neighborhood (e.g., Wilson, Kelly, Schootman 2012). The real-time responsiveness of computational ubiquity is sacrificed for the archival, readiness-to-hand quality of representational ubiquity.

This archival quality is also related to the second temporal dimension: the durability of events. If we stick with the definition of information as an event "situated within a system of organized memory," then the question of what constitutes "an event" inevitably arises. In regimes of computational ubiquity, the answer is straightforward: an event is a change of states, as captured or registered by sensing devices. In regimes of representational ubiquity, the event is relational: it arises out of the statistical relationships between quantified features across environments. The disjointed temporality of Street View imagery—the visible time lags between Photo Spheres in Street View, for instance (Lapenta 2011)—gives preference to objects of certain durabilities, such as buildings or other topographical features.[4] In this sense, Street View's representational ubiquity betrays its bias towards durable environmental features; the event is not the feature itself, but rather its relationship to other features in the same environment or to features in other environments. This privileges a sense of immutability that can in many instances be misleading.[5]

The spatial axis displays two notable differences. The first is the issue of coverage. Computational ubiquity operates within the confines of defined environment, circumscribed by the extent to which sensing devices can capture changes of state. These environments can be linked or networked together through diffuse technologies or even mobile sensing devices (such as wifi-enabled cars or a sensor-laden smartphone). Nonetheless, the singular environment remains the unit of computational ubiquity: it is about saturation, and saturation implies limits. IBM has outfitted Rio de Janeiro with a centralized command and control center that gives city staffers access to multiple sensor-ized networks throughout the entire urban region (Singer 2012). But even this extensive meta-network is limited to the urban region. Representational ubiquity, by contrast, presupposes connectivity without limit. The stitching together of images in Google Street View creates virtual pathways mimicking the connective tissue of physical geographies. This is the fruit of the images' temporal disjointedness: "The initially mechanically divided images of the world are digitally reunited in the virtual map, geolocationally pinned down by geomedia technologies, juxtaposed and merged as the jigsaw pieces of an intricate puzzle" (Lapenta 2011, 17). The ambition of representational ubiquity is global in scope (Dalton 2013); it resides at the suture between map and territory.

The second difference along the spatial axis is mobility. Computational ubiquity is about capturing, informaticizing, analyzing, and responding to the mobility of users. Whether it is a person entering their apartment, a highway driver passing through an RFID scanning electronic toll collection device, or a worker at a firm who moves about with her "virtual office" trailing her from tablet to desktop and back again (Weiser 1991), computational ubiquity is about the transduction of mobility into machine readable data (Dodge and Kitchin 2005). Conversely, representational ubiquity mobilizes the sensor itself—in the case of Google Street View, atop the Google car. The mobility of the sensor is key to Street View and other virtual mapping platforms' *simulation of mobility*. The hiddenness of the Google car within Street View image (aside from the stray shadow) invites the user to inhabit the scene; its absence buttresses the sense of fidelity around street-level imagery whilst simultaneously shrouding the labor and business practices around the processes of image capture. Of course, the vastness of mobile sensing that makes Street View possible relies not on the mobility of an individual driver, but on entire fleets of drivers, often outsourced to various independent contractors (*cf.* White 2007). These invisibilities give users a sense of ease and automation when the process of producing the virtual globe is in reality manual and intensive. Street View is not the only instance of this: the compiling of Flickr images for computer vision algorithm training, the aggregation of traffic data from Google Maps users' smartphone apps, various applications of "citizen science" (Dodge and Kitchin 2013; Gabrys 2014)—each of these examples hinges on the mobility of human-sensor hybrids, moving through and capturing data about environments, and incorporating those data into databases that allow for the identification of statistical relationships between decontextualized features.

MUNDANE UBIQUITIES

These different affordances and biases are indicative of the diversity inherent in ubiquitous mediation. It could probably be said that the comparison between computational and representational ubiquities raises more questions than it answers; for instance, to what extent are techniques and technologies of ubiquitous mediation used to effect forms of control over populations? The vision laid out by Weiser and his colleagues is one in which humans are the masters of the machine networks that they spin around themselves. The history of ubiquitous mediation over the past 25 years, however, has illustrated not only the unevenness with which the benefits of this mastery are distributed, but also their tendency to turn into more malevolent forms of surveillant tracking, for the purposes of profit or discipline. Introducing representational ubiquity into the discussion provides no relief, as the case studies of PlacePulse and City Forensics are indicative of the ways in which the rendering of environmental qualities into information can facilitate an automation of sorting that uses space and place as a proxy for social desirability and deviancy.

What the computational and representational ubiquities share in common is their invisibility by design, their retreat into the cultural psyche, the "technological unconscious" (Thrift and French 2002). Their mundanity makes their potential for control all the more insidious. Fomenting awareness of the mediations implicit in such technological practices—for instance, their propensity to exclude as much as include data—may have the potential to diminish their techno-affective sway over us as we move through captured and networked environments. But this would be working against the grain, against the invisibility designed into such infrastructures. Ubiquitous mediation shrouds itself behind interfaces that simply nudge or notify, making them resistant to close analysis. Consider the speculations of urban technologists Adam Greenfield and Mark Shepard as they reflect on the potential of ubiquitous computing in the city, wearable technologies, and statistical relationships between urban environments:

> The importance of Oakland Crimespotting is that it makes transparent something that absolutely shapes both the affective experience of being in the city and the choices we make there—the actuality of street crime—plotting reported incidents on a map and returning that knowledge to you. But it must be said that its impact is somewhat limited by the fact of its output being limited to a PC, or at best a smartphone, screen. Why? Because geographically-organized data like this cries out for a direct mapping back to the locations in question. How much more powerful and actionable will things like Crimespotting be when they're ambient—when the information about a place comes to you when you're in that place? When, instead of shaded circles on a screen, you experience the output as a rising tone in your head-phones, as a tickle in your shoe or a sudden wash of yellow over the view through your glasses, as you're actually walking through the streets of Oakland? (Greenfield and Shepard 2007, 11)

What we talk about when we talk about ubiquity—where the computational and representational ubiquities merge—is this kind of nudging, in which decisions are made for you by automated systems of sorting and evaluation. It is the ironic task of the scholar of ubiquitous media to work against such nudging, to untangle those technologies and data infrastructures that, in Weiser's (1991, 94) words, "weave themselves into the fabric of everyday life until they are indistinguishable from it."

NOTES

1. Microsoft Streetside and Mapillary are alternative platforms similar to Google Street View.
2. Google's cars also capture this kind of para-visual information alongside its street-level imagery.
3. "Clicks" are not defined, so it is unlikely that the 1.3 million clicks represent unique visitors.
4. In certain countries, Google Street View is required to blur human faces, if not remove human bodies entirely; see Flores and Belongie 2010; Rakower 2012.
5. Nothing makes this bias clearer than disjunctures between Street View representations and dramatic changes in landscapes resulting from disasters. A grassroots effort in New Orleans, for instance, lobbied Google to update its local Street View imagery, which in 2012 still displayed images of FEMA trailers and piles of debris captured in 2007. See Annalisa Kelly and Hunter King, "Update Google Street View in New Orleans!" http://nolastreetview.blogspot.com/

REFERENCES

Andrejevic, Mark. 2004. *Reality TV: The Work of Being Watched*. New York: Rowman & Littlefield.
Andrejevic, Mark, and Kelly Gates. 2014. "Big Data Surveillance: Introduction." *Surveillance & Society* 12 (2): 185–196.
Anguelov, Dragomir, Carole Dulong, Daniel Filip, Christian Frueh, Stéphane Lafon, Richard Lyon, Abhijit Ogale, Luc Vincent, and Josh Weaver. 2010. "Google Street View: Capturing the World at Street Level." *Computer* 43 (6): 32–38.

Arietta, Sean M., Maneesh Agrawala, and Ravi Ramamoorthi. 2013. "On Relating Visual Elements to City Statistics." UCB/EECS-2013–157. EECS Department, University of California, Berkeley. https://www.eecs.berkeley.edu/Pubs/TechRpts/2013/EECS-2013-157.html.

Arietta, Sean M., Alexei A. Efros, Ravi Ramamoorthi, and Maneesh Agrawala. 2014. "City Forensics: Using Visual Elements to Predict Non-Visual City Attributes." *IEEE Transactions on Visualization and Computer Graphics* 20 (12): 2624–2633.

Barreneche, Carlos. 2012. "Governing the Geocoded World: Environmentality and the Politics of Location Platforms." *Convergence* 18 (3): 331–351.

Bauman, Zygmunt, and David Lyon. 2013. *Liquid Surveillance a Conversation*. Cambridge, UK; Malden, MA: Polity Press.

Brokaw, Alex. 2016. "Google's Latest AI Doesn't Need Geotags to Figure out a Photo's Location." *The Verge*. February 25. http://www.theverge.com/2016/2/25/11112594/google-new-deep-learning-image-location-planet.

Burrows, Roger, and David Beer. 2013. "Rethinking Space: Urban Informatics and the Sociological Imagination." In *Digital Sociology: Critical Perspectives*, edited by Kate Orton-Johnson and Nick Prior, 61–78. New York: Palgrave-MacMillan.

Burrows, Roger, and Nick Ellison. 2004. "Sorting Places Out? Towards a Social Politics of Neighbourhood Informatization." *Information, Communication & Society* 7 (3): 321–336.

Chun, Wendy Hui Kyong. 2011. *Programmed Visions: Software and Memory*. Cambridge, MA: MIT Press.

Cosgrove, Denis E. 2006. "Carto-City." In *Else/where: Mapping New Cartographies of Networks and Territories*, edited by Janet Abrams and Peter Hall. Minneapolis: University of Minnesota Design Institute.

Dalton, Craig M. 2013. "Sovereigns, Spooks, and Hackers: An Early History of Google Geo Services and Map Mashups." *Cartographica* 48 (4): 261–274.

Dalton, Craig M., and Jim Thatcher. 2015. "Inflated Granularity: Spatial 'Big Data' and Geodemographics." *Big Data & Society* 2 (2): 1–15.

Dodge, Martin, and Rob Kitchin. 2005. "Code and the Transduction of Space." *Annals of the Association of American Geographers* 95 (1): 162–80.

———. 2007. "'Outlines of a World Coming into Existence': Pervasive Computing and the Ethics of Forgetting." *Environment and Planning B: Planning and Design* 34 (3): 431–45.

———. 2013. "Crowdsourced Cartography: Mapping Experience and Knowledge." *Environment and Planning A* 45 (1): 19–36.

Doersch, Carl, Saurabh Singh, Abhinav Gupta, Josef Sivic, and Alexei A. Efros. 2012. "What Makes Paris Look like Paris?" *ACM Transactions on Graphics* 31 (4).

Dourish, Paul, and Genevieve Bell. 2007. "The Infrastructure of Experience and the Experience of Infrastructure: Meaning and Structure in Everyday Encounters with Space." *Environment & Planning B: Planning & Design* 34 (3): 414–430.

Elmer, Greg. 2010. "Locative Networking: Finding and Being Found." *Aether: The Journal of Media Geography* (March): 18–26.

Eveleth, Rose. 2015. "How Many Photographs of You Are Out There in the World?" *The Atlantic*, November 2. http://www.theatlantic.com/technology/archive/2015/11/how-many-photographs-of-you-are-out-there-in-the-world/413389/

Farber, Dan. 2012. "Google Takes Street View Off-Road with Backpack Rig." *CNET*. June 6. http://www.cnet.com/news/google-takes-street-view-off-road-with-backpack-rig/

Featherstone, Mike. 2009. "Ubiquitous Media: An Introduction." *Theory, Culture & Society* 26 (2–3): 1–22.

Flores, Arturo, and Serge Belongie. 2010. "Removing Pedestrians from Google Street View Images." In *IEEE Computer Society Conference on Computer Vision and Pattern Recognition Workshops* (CVPRW):53–58.

Gabrys, Jennifer. 2014. "Programming Environments: Environmentality and Citizen Sensing in the Smart City." *Environment and Planning D: Society and Space* 32 (1): 30–48.

Galloway, Anne. 2004. "Intimations of Everyday Life: Ubiquitous Computing and the City." *Cultural Studies* 18 (2–3): 384–408.

Gibson, James J. 2014. *The Ecological Approach to Visual Perception: Classic Edition*. New York: Psychology Press.

Graham, Stephen D.N. 2005. "Software-Sorted Geographies." *Progress in Human Geography* 29 (5): 562–80.

Greenfield, Adam. 2006. *Everyware: The Dawning Age of Ubiquitous Computing*. Berkeley, CA: New Riders.

Greenfield, Adam, and Mark Shepard. 2007. *Urban Computing and Its Discontents*. Situated Technologies Pamphlets 1. New York: The Architectural League of New York.

Hacking, Ian. 1990. *The Taming of Chance*. New York: Cambridge University Press.

Heidegger, Martin. 2008. *Being and Time*. Reprint edition. New York: Harper Perennial Modern Classics.

Innis, Harold Adams. 1951. *The Bias of Communication*. Toronto: University of Toronto Press.

Khosla, Aditya, Byoungkwon An, Joseph J. Lim, and Antonio Torralba. 2014. "Looking Beyond the Visible Scene." In *Proceedings of the IEEE Conference on Computer Vision and Pattern Recognition* (CVPR), 3710–3717. http://www.cv-foundation.org/openaccess/content_cvpr_2014/html/Khosla_Looking_Beyond_the_2014_CVPR_paper.html.

Kelly, Annalisa, and Hunter King. 2014. "Update Google Street View in New Orleans! ." *Blogspot*, Last modified May 3. http://nolastreetview.blogspot.com/.

Kinsley, Samuel. 2011. "Anticipating Ubiquitous Computing: Logics to Forecast Technological Futures." *Geoforum* 42 (2): 231–40.

Kittler, Friedrich A. 1996. "The City Is a Medium." *New Literary History* 27 (4): 717–29.

Lapenta, Francesco. 2011. "Geomedia: On Location-Based Media, the Changing Status of Collective Image Production and the Emergence of Social Navigation Systems." *Visual Studies* 26 (1): 14–24.

Macro Connections. 2014. "Place Pulse." *MIT Media Lab*. http://pulse.media.mit.edu/.

Malik, Suhail. 2005. "Information and Knowledge." *Theory, Culture & Society* 22 (1): 29–49.

Manovich, Lev. 1997. "Automation of Sight: From Photography to Computer Vision." *Manovich.net*. http://manovich.net/index.php/projects/automation-of-sight-from-photography-to-computer-vision

Massey, Doreen. 1993. "Power-Geometry and a Progressive Sense of Place." In *Mapping the Futures: Local Cultures, Global Change*, edited by Jon Bird, Barry Curtis, Tim Putnam, George Robertson, and Lisa Tickner, 60–70. New York: Routledge.

McClendon, Brian. 2010. "Explore the World with Street View, Now on All Seven Continents." *Google Lat Long*. September 30. http://google-latlong.blogspot.com/2010/09/explore-world-with-street-view-now-on-all.html

Naik, Nikhil, Jade Philipoom, Ramesh Raskar, and César Hidalgo. 2014. "Streetscore – Predicting the Perceived Safety of One Million Streetscapes." In *Proceedings of the 2014 IEEE Conference on Computer Vision and Pattern Recognition Workshops*, 793–799. CVPRW '14. Washington, DC: IEEE Computer Society. doi:10.1109/CVPRW.2014.121.

Nasar, Jack L. 1998. *The Evaluative Image of the City*. Thousand Oaks, CA: Sage.

Parks, Lisa, and James Schwoch, eds. 2012. *Down to Earth: Satellite Technologies, Industries, and Cultures*. New Brunswick, NJ: Rutgers University Press.

Prince, Simon. 2012. *Computer Vision: Models, Learning, and Inference*. New York: Cambridge University Press.

Quercia, Daniele, Neil O'Hare, and Henriette Cramer. 2014. "Aesthetic Capital: What Makes London Look Beautiful, Quiet, and Happy?" In *Proceedings of the ACM Conference on Computer Supported Cooperative Work*, 945–955.

Rakower, Lauren H. 2012. "Blurred Line: Zooming in on Google Street View and the Global Right to Privacy." *Brooklyn Journal of International Law* 37: 317–347.

Screen Media Daily. 2014. "CityBridge to Launch LinkNYC, Largest Urban Digital Ad Network." November 18. http://screenmediadaily.com/citybridge-to-launch-linknyc-largest-urban-digital-ad-network/.

Shepard, Mark. 2011. *Sentient City: Ubiquitous Computing, Architecture, and the Future of Urban Space*. New York: Architectural League of New York.

Singer, Natasha. 2012. "I.B.M. Takes 'Smarter Cities' Concept to Rio de Janeiro." *The New York Times*, March 3. http://www.nytimes.com/2012/03/04/business/ibm-takes-smarter-cities-concept-to-rio-de-janeiro.html.

Söderström, Ola, Till Paasche, and Francisco Klauser. 2014. "Smart Cities as Corporate Storytelling." *City* 18 (3): 307–320.

Sutko, Daniel M., and Adriana de Souza e Silva. 2011. "Location-Aware Mobile Media and Urban Sociability." *New Media & Society* 13 (5): 807–823.

Szeliski, Richard. 2010. *Computer Vision: Algorithms and Applications*. New York: Springer Science & Business Media.

Thatcher, Jim. 2013. "Avoiding the Ghetto through Hope and Fear: An Analysis of Immanent Technology Using Ideal Types." *GeoJournal* 78 (6): 967–980.

Thrift, Nigel. 2011. "Lifeworld Inc—and What to Do About It." *Environment and Planning D: Society and Space* 29 (1): 5–26.

Thrift, Nigel, and Shaun French. 2002. "The Automatic Production of Space." *Transactions of the Institute of British Geographers* 27 (3): 309–335.

United States Naval Observatory [USNO]. 2016. "Block II Satellite Information." March 9. ftp://tycho.usno.navy.mil/pub/gps/gpsb2.txt.

Weiser, Mark. 1991. "The Computer for the twenty-first Century." *Scientific American* 265 (3): 94–104.

White, Charlie. 2007. "Immersive Media Hiring Camera Drivers, for Google Streetview?" *Gizmodo*. July 27. http://gizmodo.com/283287/immersive-media-hiring-camera-drivers-for-google-streetview.

White House, Office of the Press Secretary. 2000. "Statement by the President Regarding the United States' Decision to Stop Degrading Global Positioning System Accuracy." *Office of the Press Secretary*. May 1. http://clinton4.nara.gov/WH/EOP/OSTP/html/0053_2.html.

Wilson, Jeffrey S., Cheryl M. Kelly, Mario Schootman. 2012. "Assessing the Built Environment Using Omnidirectional Imagery." *American Journal of Preventive Medicine* 42 (2): 193–199.

CHAPTER FIVE

Wearable Technology IN THE Production, Diffusion, AND Active Use OF Ubiquitous Knowledge

MARCO CENTORRINO AND SEBASTIANO NUCERA[1]

INTRODUCTION

Human history is a history of technology and mediations. The emergence of ever more sophisticated and functional technologies and related forms of mediation have created new relationships between real, virtual, and augmented experiences. Advances have favoured the creation of relational environments that extend beyond their intended design and application (Ingold 2004), which in turn has substantialized a different culture of interaction between individuals and contexts (e.g. Mazzoli 2011). The weaving of these contexts is, after language, the most powerful grammar at the base of interactions between individuals and their environments. We are now witnessing the creation of ecosystems steeped in higher-performing technology, though that technology is less visible.

Between the 1950s and the 1980's (Negroponte 1995), the idea of "ubiquity," which was already latent, became an object of study. Lifton and Paradiso (2009) define ubiquity as the possibility to merge real and virtual contexts. However, McLuhan (1964, 79) had previously suggested a predecessor to ubiquity, which he referred to as a form of "technology of explicitness" which enable a "translation of immediate sense experience into vocal symbols [so that] the entire world can be evoked and retrieved at any instant."

Nonetheless, the fading of boundaries between the body and technology, combined with the ubiquity of information flows today are not merely theoretical, or at least cannot be analyzed solely in these terms. This evolution has, in fact, been at the root of several different studies in areas such as online commerce (e.g. Black *et al.* 2010; McGuigan and Manzerolle 2015), education (e.g. Crompton 2016), the creation of relationships and social networks (e.g. Castells 2001; Jenkins 2006), information (e.g. Dvorak 2008; Jenkins 2006; Morcellini 2013), the daily use of technology (Hughes 2004; Kelly 2010), rehabilitative medicine (e.g. Zhu and Cahan 2016), gaming and entertainment (e.g. Foottit *et al.* 2016; Jackman 2015), and design and planning of objects (e.g. Norman 2005). Other research focuses specifically on preventive health and health monitoring (e.g., "Ubiquitous Health Monitoring"; see Hung, Chung, and Choy 2015).

This chapter is not merely an analysis of the management of knowledge flows; it is rather an attempt to understand how new technological interfaces (particularly wearable ones) restructure not only the access, production, and sharing of knowledge, but also recalibrate interactional spaces. However, this research asserts that ubiquitous processes occur not only in cultural heritage, but also in consumers (and producers) who are transported within media environments. The gradual shift from user-friendly devices to user-centerd data-sensitive contexts represents a further evolution of Marshal McLuhan's insights. The ideas of the "global village" and media as an extension of human bodies and senses (McLuhan [1964] 1994, 93, 252) describe a changing world in which people produce and share "applied knowledge…translated or carried across from one kind of material form into another" (80). In this sense, the theories of McLuhan are central to our work. Just as McLuhan noted, with respect to the early development of Gutenberg technologies that "could have created a new synthesis of written and oral education" (93), the ubiquitous system could also allow knowledge and skills to be shared without spatial or temporal barriers.

Within this chapter, we analyze the structures and use contexts of wearable technology. More precisely, we will look at how this subset of technology has affected, in terms of use and experience, the ways that knowledge is propagated, which is very different from the cultural cumulativity that we created and shared before the development of ubiquitous media (Tomasello 1999). Knowledge sharing is a process that allows one to materialize individual and collective memories (Stiegler 2012), creating a nascent sub-niche that preserves and shares knowledge through ubiquitous computing. These issues are particularly visible with wearable technologies.

The idea of "ubiquitous knowledge" is linked to two sources: a biological one (our body) and a cultural one (technology). In other words, the body becomes a medium and a platform, as Marcel Mauss foresaw ([1935] 2006, 75) when he wrote: "The body is man's first and most natural instrument. Or more accurately, not to speak of instruments, man's first and most natural technical object, and at the same time technical means, is his body." In McLuhan's work, this perspective is further developed; the body becomes technology and technology becomes the body. More recently, Greenfield (2006) argues:

> Of all the new frontiers opening up for computation, perhaps the most startling is that of the human body. As both a rich source of information in itself and the vehicle by which we experience the world, it was probably inevitable that sooner or later somebody would think to reconsider it as just another kind of networked resource.

In fact, we believe it is necessary to reassert this concept of corporeality that offers much for analysis, starting by overcoming reductionist interpretations that separate the biological from the symbolic (Balsamo 1995). Weiser's (1991) interaction paradigm of ubiquitous computing makes no separation between bodies, technology and the environment. On the contrary, Weiser argues that technology should be designed to integrate and blend in (and with) the physical world, since "the most profound technologies are those that disappear. They weave themselves into the fabric of everyday life until they are indistinguishable from it" (94). Within this study, we propose a series of arguments to support the idea that wearable technologies, by integrating seamlessly with bodies, are building a system of relationships in which the body is "co-opted" into the process of content creation (Nucera 2014; Viseu 2003).

FORMS OF SHARING AND ENJOYMENT IN DIGITAL CUMULATIVITY

Our ability to produce "cumulative culture", that is, the ability to reify, store, complement, and communicate social and environmental interactions (Tomasello 1999), results in the application of technologies to make up for a shortage or fulfill a need (Gehlen [1957] 1980; McLuhan [1964] 2013; Odling-Smee and Laland 2012). The American economist Brian Arthur (2009) differentiates between "technology" and "inventions," identifying in the latter entirely new creations lacking any material predecessors. Technology could not only be the result of combinations of other existing technologies, but also consists of tools used to create "opportunity niches," or more combinatorial possibilities with different user applications. Because of his focus on the combination of technologies, Arthur's position regarding the nature of technology seems particularly relevant to our discussion.

Although there is a process of accumulation of information and generation of knowledge at the base of cumulative culture, it is unreasonable to reduce the acquisition of information that takes place during social learning to a simple download of concepts. An interesting study by Ehn and Laland (2012) describes the dynamics that, in parallel with the process of social learning, allow individuals to refine and develop their social behavior, creating hybrids between cumulative culture and specific contexts. Subjective experiences and interactive learning shape the actions of individuals in a community (Lave and Wenger 1991). In this sense, the analysis conducted by Clay Shirky (2010) on the production of "cognitive surplus" becomes the basis for a "digital cumulativity," or a dynamic way of historicizing and manipulating the knowledge produced and shared within a digital media environment including wearable technologies. Communities (both actual and virtual) become places where information and knowledge are not only shared for the production of material and immaterial culture, but also where they are recombined, like grammatical elements, to achieve new forms of organizational and cultural production. In this sense, one of the most interesting examples is Wikipedia (Lih 2009), perhaps the most famous and successful project for the dissemination of knowledge that best reflects the words of Clay Shirky (2010, 29), who states:

> The cognitive surplus, newly forged from previously disconnected islands of time and talent, is just raw material. To get any value out of it, we have to make it mean or do things. We, collectively, aren't just the source of the surplus; we are also the people designing its use, by our participation and by the things we expect of one another as we wrestle together with our new connectedness.

The sharing of experiences in real and virtual environments, as well as the production of new cultural forms, are essential aspects for the scope of this study. If participation and active cooperation of and between users has made the creation of large amounts of knowledge possible, the challenge is to be able to take advantage of this knowledge. As Morcellini (2013) highlighted, with the increase of information flows, new criteria and strategies are necessary not only for the selection of content, but also for their organization and processing. It is not in fact reasonable to assume that increased information equals increased knowledge and, indeed, "the deprivation of knowledge has again become an open dispute, paradoxically marking the communication society as the most fragile from a socio-cultural point of view" (103, translated by the authors). In this sense, it becomes important to analyze not only the ways in which the information is structured within the web (Rosenfeld and Morville 2002), but also to understand how the information is provided (Morcellini 2013) and how this implements a corresponding process of cultural creativity such as through online collaboration (West and West 2009).

In this direction, we consider wearable technologies not only as a set of objects with a prescribed function, but also as the trigger for potentially very different uses beyond those prescribed. Costume and fashion studies' analyses on co-optations of clothing offer a model we can use to analyze wearable technologies. We propose the idea that the Touch-Wearable-Mobile technological system (TWMTS) has now reached operational levels that are amplified by the possibility of personally structuring space and time. TWMTS includes device, such as smartphones, smart glasses, smart watches, smart rings, and body sensors that are, just as Weiser predicted, becoming an integral part of our lives. For example, think of Google Maps, a service capable, based on our location, of suggesting the best route by incorporating feedback from other users or information on current traffic conditions. Aggregating user feedback is a very simple idea but it can greatly influence our choices. All in all, this process comprises a system of interconnected devices that are capable of not only accessing (and making available) digital cultural cumulativity or influencing our behavior, but also of predicting or anticipating the users' needs, just like in the most evolved home automation systems (Ojuroye, Russel, and Wilde 2016).

For this reason, the use of technology today cannot be analyzed as if it were simply the use of a tool. Current wearable technology is the most obvious example of how mobile technology is evolving beyond devices used for the transmission or storage of data, resulting in a thinning of the invisible line that divides the tool from its user (Clark 2003). More precisely, the levels of interactivity between users and technology are greatly amplified by new interfaces such as accelerometers and voice recognition (Siri, TellME, Cortana, Google Now). E-textiles (e.g., "LilyPad Arduino,"[2] an e-textile toolkit used in science education; Buechley *et al.* 2008), smart clothing (e.g., Solar Shirt by Pauline van Dongen[3]) and, more generally, wearable technology, have become essential tools for the production, propagation and use of "cognitive surplus" (Shirky 2010), a de-spatialized and distributed form of knowledge. The Smart Shirt, is only an accumulator of electric energy. But this is not a minor aspect. As McLuhan had already foreseen (1964, 58), "Under electric technology the entire business of man becomes learning and knowing." In this sense, research and investment on the creation of storage batteries has led to the first prototype of flexible batteries that can disappear into clothes. This would provide not only a continuous supply of electric energy but also never-before-seen ergonomy.

We share the idea of Joseph L. Dvorak (2007, 50), who suggests that we "should not view the user and the wearable as two separate entities that interact independently. Rather, there is an element of collaboration and even dependency between them." These new ubiquitary, experiential contexts therefore involve natural (the body) and cultural (technological) sources in dynamics that Adam Greenfield (2006) defines as the "everyware paradigm." This paradigm defines not just the current technological system, but also a profound and general transformation of cultural practices (Appadurai 1996) and daily routines (Silva 2010) that concern every aspect of life: from the preparation of food (Bell and Kaye 2002) to courtship practices (Whitty 2003).

NEW FORMS OF CO-CONSTRUCTED MIXED-REALITIES

In the preceding pages, we tried to highlight how technological evolution has produced structures and functions that embed users within a continuous process of recalibration. If the paradigm of "fashionology" (Rauschnabel *et al.* 2016) inscribes the clothing industry within classic sociological studies (e.g. Simmel [1904] 1957), then it is similarly necessary to analyze the "ubiquitous" within contexts of use that are (as described later) numerous and multifaceted. The many studies on augmented reality (e.g. Chang *et al.* 2014; Zimmerman, Land, and Jung 2016) offer a significant theoretical starting point for determining the ways in which individuals catalyze and accelerate mechanisms of incorporation and cognitive projection such as the use, representation, and sharing of "mental maps" (Lapenta 2012, 137). The network-context theorized by Shirky (2010) is not only the prelude to collaboration in knowledge creation, but also the first step towards cohabitation of spaces to be (re)mediated (Boccia Artieri 2009; *cf.* Bolter and Grusin 1999). The emergence of these spaces reflects Niche Construction Theory (NCT; see Kendal 2011) which helps explain the sensitive relationships between "knowledge" and "digital cumulativity" as in the case of collaborative writing (West and West 2009) and other expressions of digital connectivity (such as newsgroups, blogs, social networks, and photo/video-sharing communities).

The most apparent structure through which this "digital cumulativity" is conveyed is the World Wide Web. However, while it is correct to see the web as the synthetic structure through which we experience digital forms of "cultural heritage," it is also reasonable to state that such an answer seems decidedly partial and incomplete. The web is merely the structure that enables a refunctionalization of pervasive and wearable computing. The use and construction of experiential niches is the result of cooperative action that is part of, but at the same time transcends, the web.

We focus our attention now on one of the aspects which we believe deserves to be developed, and which is linked to the use of technology in environments for learning and knowledge dissemination. It is important to point this out because it is through this isomorphic relationship between technology and knowledge that co-constructed forms of "mixed-reality" are created (Lindgren *et al.* 2016; Pan *et al.* 2006). Forms such as augmented reality, with added context-user sensitive information, demonstrate the relationship between material (devices) and intangible cultural heritage (e.g. social practices), as happened in the democratization process of photographic technologies.

All the same, augmented reality is not an end point. In line with Arthur's (2009) intuitions, we can define augmented reality in terms of a "technological domain" where other technologies (or profiles) can insert themselves to (further) increase the field of application, creating "systems of devices and systems of systems" (Poslad 2009, 13). This aspect is highlighted in the description of two separate experiments conducted at museums. A first study by Chang *et al.* (2014) showed that the use of augmented reality tools made visitors pay more attention to artwork in museums and aided their understanding of it (Poslad 2009). For example, augmented reality allowed users to analyze, compare and interpret an artwork more thoroughly. As emphasized by the authors, the study also demonstrated that the devices used, in contrast to previous studies, allowed visitors to focus on the art rather than interacting with the devices. A study by Capuano *et al.* (2016) consisted of integrating augmented reality, semantic, and narrative models, and additional multimedia resources, creating a completely new and personalized museum experience based upon users' preferences and knowledge level (FIBAC Project). Their experiment is based on "cultural re-mediation theory," that is "the representation of one medium in another" (Bolter and Grusin 1999, 45), and shows that even within the theories regarding augmented reality, lines of thought can be both heterogeneous and complementary. In fact, while augmented reality has proven to be useful in education (Martín-Gutiérrez, Contero, and Alcañiz 2010) and has recently had great success in game applications (such as Pokémon Go), it struggles to establish itself in everyday life (Misra, Maheswaran, and Hashmi 2017).

This recalibration, which derives knowledge from behavioral forms that cement "swarm intelligence"—the collective behavior of decentralized, self-organized systems, whether natural or artificial (Callaghan 2016)—and "connective intelligence"—a concept inspired by Pierre Lévy's "collective intelligence" that describes the interaction of intelligences connected in a real project and in a connective environment (de Kerckhove 2001)—is a direct and obvious consequence of a different way of using (and interacting with) digital cumulativities. In these cumulativities, the individual remains entangled "in webs of meaning that he himself has spun" (Geertz 1973, 5).

TOWARDS A NEW PARADIGM OF "WEARABLE KNOWLEDGE"

The extension of our cognitive capacity through new technologies is a "breakthrough." The Touch-Wearable-Mobile paradigm encourages us, however, to provide a description of the actual uses of new technologies within structured educational contexts (e.g., the university classroom; Martín-Gutiérrez, Contero, and Alcañiz 2010) or informal contexts (e.g., in a museum; Sommerauer and Müller 2014). The idea of "Wearable Knowledge" refers to a range of considerations related to the concept of the "extension of sensitivity" (Montani 2014), meaning the ability to "augment" the perception of the environment around us, as was shown in the previously described experiment by Capuano and colleagues (2016). Similar concepts have been analyzed extensively in the cognitive sciences (Gallese and Lakoff 2005) and, more generally, in educational research (Chang and Li 2014; Crompton 2016; Lindgren *et al.* 2016; Pan *et al.* 2006). Bostrom and Sandberg (2009, 311) discuss the cognitive enhancement definable as "the amplification or extension of core capacities of the mind through improvement or augmentation of internal or external information processing systems." These aspects lead us to conclude our study by analyzing both the tools useful for "wearable knowledge" and the areas of application within which this paradigm finds its fullest expression today: smart glasses.

Among the best-known wearable devices in education are the wide range of smart glasses (for example Google Glass, Magic Leap, Microsoft Hololens). The diffusion of wearable technologies (101.9 million unit shipments in 2016; IDC 2016) reflects both the prospect of a different form of media consumption (Rauschnabel, Brem, and Ivens 2015) and the large number of user applications. Smart glasses and their use in smart learning environments demonstrate "wearable knowledge" and the digital and experiential cumulative effect that we have previously described. The technologies applied to learning or teaching have been particularly analyzed in educational science (e.g. Chen, Chang, and Wang 2008; Ogata *et al.* 2011). As evidenced by Lindgren and colleagues (2016, 176), "research has begun to demonstrate learning effects of embodied interactions with emerging technologies, particularly in STEM content areas." Through the example of the *gPhysics app*, Kuhn *et al.* (2015) measured wondering, cognitive load, and curiosity and show that the lack of familiarity with using Google Glass and limitations of the experimental paradigm can generate negative effects during the learning process. However, that study also shows that the use of Google Glass during the explanation and execution of a physical experiment improves students' performance and, in particular, their curiosity which, within educational contexts, becomes "a special feature of motivation" (*ibid.*, 3). It was particularly observed that some features of the smart glasses are especially useful in specific educational settings, not only in schools but also potentially in the industrial sector (Scavo, Wild, and Scott 2015).

Some consideration of smart glasses applications that go beyond the creation of Smart Learning Environments is required, however. The SMART Pivotheads of Microsoft Cognitive Services (2016), are an assistive technology which is capable of performing a real-time digital translation of the surrounding environment in the form of augmented realities that are not based on images. For example, they allow visually-impaired individuals to obtain information on the surrounding environment including the number of individuals present, their approximate age, physical characteristics, and a suggestion of the emotions they may be feeling at the time. Another possible application of this technology is the creation of virtual environments within which individuals who are physically distant work together to achieve a goal (Suh 2011). It is our belief, however, that models for the dissemination of knowledge based on augmented reality (rather than virtual reality) make up an educational framework with a greater (Schiller *et al.* 2014). A great amount of scientific evidence shows how immersive augmented settings enhance the educational experience in both adults (Crompton 2016) and children (Land and Zimmerman 2015; Zimmerman, Land, and Jung. 2016). The proposal recently suggested by Peña-Ayala and Cárdenas (2016) summarizes the ongoing restructuring within the education and training sectors, substantiating what the authors define as mobile, ubiquitous, and pervasive learning, or MUP-Learning. MUP-Learning is based on the ability to access knowledge: without physical constraints; which is adaptive; and relates to the degree of *wearability*. The key point, however, is certainly in the cultural trend, directed—as we have tried to argue—to more and more cumulative models of knowledge and learning that are based on ubiquitous technological artefacts.

CONCLUSION

In this chapter, we have highlighted how the dimension of wearability should not be studied as a simple technological or vestimentary evolution, but rather as a step towards "ubiquitous systems" in which the technologized body blends in with the environment, placing the user within an unexpected perceptual universe. Indeed, the causative relationship that binds social uses and ubiquitous dimensions is enabled by the use of mobile and wearable technologies. These technologies have helped to increase the propagation speed of, and access to, information flows in an ever-increasing number of distributed contexts. Following the digitization of knowledge, wearable technologies encourage us to rethink the relationships and mediations that are established within ubiquitous media ecosystems.

NOTES

1. Although the chapter is the outcome of a close collaboration, the first two paragraphs were written by Sebastiano Nucera and the last three by Marco Centorrino.
2. https://www.arduino.cc/en/Main/ArduinoBoardLilyPad
3. http://www.paulinevandongen.nl/project/wearable-solar-shirt/

REFERENCES

Appadurai, Arjun. 1996. *Modernity at Large: Cultural Dimensions of Globalization*. Minneapolis: University of Minnesota Press.
Arthur, W. Brian. 2009. *The Nature of Technology: What It Is and How It Evolves*. New York: Free Press.
Balsamo, Anne. 1995. "Forms of Technological Embodiment: Reading the Body in Contemporary Culture." In *Cyberspace/Cyberbodies/Cyberpunk: Cultures of Technological Embodiment*, edited by Mike Featherstone and Roger Burrows, 215–238. London: Sage.
Bell, Genevieve, and Joseph Kaye. 2002. "Designing Technology for Domestic Spaces: A Kitchen Manifesto." *Gastronomica: The Journal of Critical Food Studies* 2 (2), 46–62.
Black, Darren, Nils Jakob, Clemmensen, and Mikael B. Skov. 2010. "Pervasive Computing in the Supermarket: Designing a Context-Aware Shopping Trolley." *International Journal of Mobile Human Computer Interaction* 2 (3): 31–43.

Boccia Artieri, Giovanni. 2009. "Supernetwork: quando le vite sono connesse." In *Network Effect. Quando la Rete Diventa Pop* edited by Lella Mazzoli, 21–40. Torino: Codice.

Bolter, Jay David, and Richard Grusin. 1999. *Remediation. Understanding New Media.* Cambridge: MIT Press.

Bostrom, Nick, and Anders Sandberg. 2009. "Cognitive enhancement: Methods, Ethics, Regulatory Challenges." *Science and Engineering Ethics* 15 (3): 311–341.

Buechley, Leah, Mike Eisenberg, Jaime Catchen, and Ali Crockett. 2008. "The LilyPad Arduino: Using Computational Textiles to Investigate Engagement, Aesthetics, and Diversity in Computer Science Education." In *CHI 2008 Proceedings of the Twenty-Sixth Annual SIGCHI Conference on Human Factors in Computing Systems* 423–432.

Callaghan, Chris William. 2016. "Knowledge Management and Problem Solving in Real Time: The Role of Swarm Intelligence." *Interdisciplinary Journal of Information, Knowledge, and Management* 11 : 177–199.

Capuano, Nicola, Angelo Gaeta, Giuseppe Guarino, Sergio Miranda, and Stefania Tomasiello. 2016. "Enhancing Augmented Reality with Cognitive and Knowledge Perspectives: A Case Study in Museum Exhibitions." *Behaviour & Information Technology* 35 (11): 968–979.

Castells, Manuel. 2001. *The Internet Galaxy: Reflections on the Internet, Business and Society.* New York: Oxford University Press.

Chan, Marie, Daniel Estève, Jean-Yves Fourniols, Christophe Escriba, and Eric Campo. 2012. "Smart Wearable Systems: Current Status and Future Challenges." *Artificial Intelligence in Medicine* 56 (3): 137–156. doi:10.1016/j.artmed.2012.09.003.

Chang, Kuo-En, Chia-Tzu Chang, Huei-Tse Hou, Yao-Ting Sung, Huei-Lin Chao, and Cheng-Ming Lee. 2014. "Development and Behavioral Pattern Analysis of a Mobile Guide System with Augmented Reality for Painting Appreciation Instruction in an Art Museum." *Computers & Education* 71 (February): 185–197. doi:10.1016/j.compedu.2013.09.022.

Chang, Maiga, and Yanyan Li, eds. 2014. *Smart Learning Environments.* Cham: Springer International Publishing.

Chen, Gwo-Dong, Chih-Kai Chang, and Chin-Yeh Wang. 2008. "Ubiquitous Learning Website: Scaffold Learners by Mobile Devices with Information-aware Techniques." *Computers and Education* 50 (1): 77–90.

Clark, Andy. 2003. *Natural-born Cyborgs: Minds, Technologies, and the Future of Human Intelligence.* Oxford: Oxford University Press.

Crompton, Helen. 2016. "The Theory of Context-Aware Ubiquitous Learning and the Affordances of This Approach for Geometry Learners." In *Mobile Learning Design. Theories and Application*, edited by Daniel, Churchill, Jie, Lu, Thomas, K.F. Chiu, Bob, Fox, 303–314. Singapore: Springer International Publishing.

de Kerckhove, Derrick. 2001. *The Architecture of Intelligence.* Basel: Birkhäuser.

Dvorak, Joseph L. 2007. *Moving Wearables into the Mainstream: Taming the Borg.* New York: Springer Science & Business Media.

Ehn, Micael, and Kevin Laland. 2012. "Adaptive Strategies for Cumulative Cultural Learning." *Journal of Theoretical Biology* 301: 103–111.

Foottit, Jacques, Dave Brown, Stefan Marks and Andy M. Connor. 2016. "A Wearable Haptic Game Controller." *International Journal of Game Theory & Technology* 2 (1): 1–19.

Gallese, Vittorio, and George Lakoff. 2005. "The Brain's Concepts: The Role of the Sensory-Motor System in Conceptual Knowledge." *Cognitive Neuropsychology* 22 (3–4): 455–479.

Geertz, Clifford. 1973. *The Interpretation of Cultures: Selected Essays.* New York: Basic Books.

Gehlen, Arnold. (1957) 1980. *Man in the Age of Technology*. Translated by P. Liscomb. New York: Columbia University Press.

Giddens, Anthony. 1991. *Modernity and Self-Identity: Self and Society in the Late Modern Age*. Stanford: Stanford University Press.

Greenfield, Adam. 2006. *Everyware: The Dawning Age of Ubiquitous Computing*. Berkeley: New Riders.

He, Rongrui, Todd D. Day, Mahesh Krishnamurthi, Justin R. Sparks, Pier J. A. Sazio, Venkatraman Gopalan, and John V. Badding. 2013. "Silicon p-i-n Junction Fibers." *Advanced Materials* 25 (10): 1461–1467.

Hughes, Thomas P. 2004. *Human-Built World: How to Think About Technology and Culture*. Chicago: University of Chicago Press.

Hung, Kevin, Lee Chi Chung, and Sheung-On Choy. 2015. "Ubiquitous Health Monitoring: Integration of Wearable Sensors, Novel Sensing Techniques, and Body Sensor Networks." In *Mobile Health. A Technology Road Map*, edited by Sasan Adibi, 319–342. New York: Springer International Publishing.

Ingold, Tim. 2004. *Ecologia della Cultura*. Roma: Meltemi.

International Data Corporation (IDC). 2016. Worldwide Quarterly Wearable Device Tracker. Framingham, Massachusetts.

Jackman, Anna H. 2015. "3-D Cinema: Immersive Media Technology." *GeoJournal* 80 (6): 853–866.

Jenkins, Henry. 2006. *Convergence Culture: Where Old and New Media Collide*. New York: New York University Press.

Kelly, Kevin. 2010. *What Technology Wants*. New York: Penguin Group.

Kendal, Jeremy R. 2011. "Cultural Niche Construction and Human Learning Environments: Investigating Sociocultural Perspectives." *Biological Theory* 6 (3): 241–250.

Kuhn, Jochen, Paul Lukowicz, Michael Hirth, Andreas Poxrucker, Jens Weppner, and Junaid Younas. 2015. "gPhysics–Using Smart Glasses for Head-Centered, Context-Aware Learning in Physics Experiments". *IEEE Transactions on Learning Technologies*, 1–15.

Land, Susan M., and Heather Toomey Zimmerman. 2015. "Socio-Technical Dimensions of an Outdoor Mobile Learning Environment: A Three-Phase Design-Based Research Investigation." *Educational Technology Research and Development* 63 (2): 229–255.

Lapenta, Francesco. 2012. "Geomedia-Based Methods and Visual Research: Exploring the Theoretical and Methodological Tenets of the Localization and Visualisation of Mediated Social Relations with Direct Visualisations Techniques". In *Advances in Visual Methodology*, edited by Sarah Pink, 131–150. London: Sage.

Lave Jean, and Etienne Wenger. 1991. *Situated Learning: Legitimate Peripheral Participation*. Cambridge, UK: Cambridge University Press.

Lifton, Joshua, and Joseph A. Paradiso. 2009. "Dual Reality: Merging the Real and Virtual." In *International Conference on Facets of Virtual Environments*, edited by Fritz Lehmann-Grube and Jan Sablatnig, 12–28. Berlin Heidelberg: Springer International Publishing.

Lih, Andrew. 2009. *The Wikipedia Revolution: How a Bunch of Nobodies Created the World's Greatest Encyclopedia*. New York: Hyperion.

Lindgren, Robb, Michael Tscholl, Shuai Wang, and Emily Johnson. 2016. "Enhancing Learning and Engagement through Embodied Interaction within a Mixed Reality Simulation. *Computers & Education* 95: 174–187.

Lukowicz, Paul, Andreas Poxrucker, Jens Weppner, Benjamin Bischke, Jochen Kuhn, and Michael Hirth. 2015. "Glass-Physics: Using Google Glass to Support High School Physics Experiments". In *Proceedings of the 2015 ACM International Symposium on Wearable Computers* 151–154.

Martín-Gutiérrez, Jorge, Manuel Contero, and Mariano Alcañiz. 2010. "Evaluating the Usability of an Augmented Reality Based Educational Application". In *International Conference on Intelligent Tutoring Systems*, edited by Vincent Aleven, Judy Kay, and Jack Mostow, 296–306. Berlin Heidelberg: Springer International Publishing.

Mauss, Marcel. (1935) 2006. "Techniques of the Body." In *Techniques, Technology and Civilisation*, edited by Nathan Schlanger, 77–95. New York, Oxford: Berghahn Books/Durkheim Press.

Mazzoli, Lella. 2011. *L'impronta del Sociale. La Comunicazione fra Teorie e Tecnologie*. Milano: Franco Angeli.

McGuigan, Lee, and Vincent Manzerolle. 2015. "All the World's a Shopping Cart: Theorizing the Political Economy of Ubiquitous Media and Markets." *New Media & Society* 17 (11): 1830–1848.

McLuhan, Marshall. (1964) 1994. *Understanding Media: Extensions of Man*. Cambridge: MIT Press.

Microsoft Cognitive Services. 2016. "Wearable Technology Firm Is Helping People Who Are Visually Impaired See the World." *Microsoft.com*. Accessed September 15. https://customers.microsoft.com/en-US/story/wearable-technology-firm-is-helping-people-who-are-visually-impaired-see-the-world.

Misra, Sridipta, Muthucumaru Maheswaran, and Salman Hashmi. 2017. *Security Challenges and Approaches in Internet of Things*. Cham: Springer International Publishing.

Montani, Pietro. 2014. *Tecnologie della Sensibilità: Estetica e Immaginazione Interattiva*. Milano: Raffaello Cortina.

Morcellini, Mario. 2013. *Comunicazione e Media*. Milano: EGEA.

Negroponte, Nicholas. 1995. *Being Digital*. New York: Vintage Books.

Norman, Donald A. 2005. *Emotional Design: Why We Love (or Hate) Everyday Things*. New York: Basic Books.

Nucera, Sebastiano. 2014. *Corpi in-Tessuti. Evoluzioni e Mutamenti delle Pratiche Vestimentarie*, Roma: Aracne.

Odling-Smee, F. John, Kevin N. Laland, and Marcus W. Feldman. 2003. *Niche Construction. The Neglected Process in Evolution*. Princeton: Princeton University Press.

Ogata, Hiroaki, Mengmeng Li, Bin Hou, Noriko Uosaki, Moushir M. El-Bishouty, and Yoneo Yano. 2011. "SCROLL: Supporting to Share and Reuse Ubiquitous Learning Log in the Context of Language Learning." *Research and Practice in Technology Enhanced Learning* 6 (2): 69–82.

Ojuroye, Olivia, Torah Russel, and Adriana Wilde. 2016. "Smart Textiles for Smart Home Control and Enriching Future Wireless Sensor Network Data". In *Sensors for Everyday Life*, edited by Octavian Adrian Postolache, Subhas Chandra Mukhopadhyay, Krishanthi P. Jayasundera, and Akshya K. Swain, 159–183. Cham: Springer International Publishing.

Pan, Zhigeng, Adrian D. Cheok, Hongwei Yang, Jiejie Zhu, and Jiaoying Shi. 2006. "Virtual Reality and Mixed Reality for Virtual Learning Environments." *Computers & Graphics* 30 (1): 20–28.

Peña-Ayala, Alejandro, Leonor Cárdenas. 2016. "A Revision of the Literature Concerned with Mobile, Ubiquitous, and Pervasive Learning: A Survey." In *Mobile, Ubiquitous, and Pervasive Learning: Fundaments, Applications, and Trends*, edited by Alejandro Peña-Ayala, 55–100. Cham: Springer International Publishing.

Poslad, Stefan. 2009. *Ubiquitous Computing: Smart Devices, Smart Environments and Smart Interaction*. New York: Wiley.

Rauschnabel, Philipp A., Alexander Brem, and Bjoern S. Ivens. 2015. "Who Will Buy Smart Glasses? Empirical Results of Two Pre-Market-Entry Studies on the Role of Personality in Individual Awareness and Intended Adoption of Google Glass Wearables." *Computers in Human Behavior* 49: 635–647.

Rauschnabel, Philipp A., Daniel W. E. Hein, Jun He, Young K. Ro, Samir Rawashdeh, and Bryan Krulikowski. 2016. "Fashion or Technology? A Fashnology Perspective on the Perception and Adoption of Augmented Reality Smart Glasses." *i-com* 15 (2): 179–194.

Rosenfeld, Louis, and Peter Morville. 2002. *Information Architecture for the World Wide Web*. Sebastopol: O'Reilly.

Scavo, Giuseppe, Fridolin Wild, and Peter Scott. "The GhostHands UX: Telementoring with Hands-On Augmented Reality Instruction." In *Workshop Proceedings of the 11th International Conference on Intelligent Environments* edited by Davy Preuveneers, 236–243. Amsterdam: IOS Press.

Schiller, Shu Z., Brian E. Mennecke, Fiona Fui-Hoon Nah, and Andy Luse. 2014. "Institutional Boundaries and Trust of Virtual Teams in Collaborative Design: An Experimental Study in a Virtual World Environment". *Computers in Human Behavior* 35: 565–577.

Shirky, Clay. 2010. *Cognitive Surplus: Creativity and Generosity in a Connected Age*. New York: Penguin Press.

Silva, Elizabeth B. 2010. *Technology, Culture, Family: Influences on Home Life*. New York: Palgrave Macmillan.

Simmel, Georg. (1904) 1957, "Fashion." Reprinted in *The American Journal of Sociology* 62 (6): 541–558

Sommerauer, Peter, and Oliver Müller. 2014. "Augmented Reality in Informal Learning Environments: A Field Experiment in a Mathematics Exhibition." *Computers & Education* 79: 59–68.

Stiegler, Bernard. 2012. "Relational Ecology and the Digital Pharmakon." *Culture Machine* 13: 1–19.

Suh, Heejeon. 2011. "Collaborative Learning Models and Support Technologies in the Future Classroom." *International Journal for Educational Media and Technology* 5(1): 50–61.

Tomasello, Michael. 1999. *The Cultural Origins of Human Cognition*. Cambridge: Harvard University Press.

Viseu, Ana. 2003. "Simulation and Augmentation: Issues of Wearable Computers." *Ethics and Information Technology* 5 (1): 17–26.

Weiser, Mark. 1991. "The Computer for the 21st Century." *Scientific American* 265 (3): 94–104.

West, James A., and Margaret L. West. 2009. *Using Wikis for Online Collaboration: The Power of the Read-Write Web*. New York: John Wiley & Sons.

Whitty, Monica Therese. 2003. "Cyber-Flirting Playing at Love on the Internet." *Theory & Psychology* 13 (3): 339–357.

Zhu, Xinxin, and Amos Cahan. 2016. "Wearable Technologies and Telehealth in Care Management for Chronic Illness." In *Healthcare Information Management Systems*, edited by Charlotte A. Weaver, Marion J. Ball, George R. Kim, and Joan M. Kiel, 375–398. Cham: Springer International Publishing.

Zimmerman, Heather Toomey, Susan M. Land, and Yong Ju Jung. 2016. "Using Augmented Reality to Support Children's Situational Interest and Science Learning During Context-Sensitive Informal Mobile Learning." In *Mobile, Ubiquitous, and Pervasive Learning: Fundaments, Applications, and Trends*, edited by Alejandro Peña-Ayala, 101–119. Cham: Springer International Publishing.

PART THREE

Visualities

Ubiquitous Media and Visual Culture

CHAPTER SIX

Towards A New Visuality OF "Mobile Infography"

Examining Contemporary Visual Applications as New Ways of Seeing

ANA RITA MORAIS

> New technologies are not only amplifying the power of vision, they are also changing its nature (to include what was previously classified as invisible or unseeable) and its functions (making it a tool for the visual presentation of abstract data and concepts). (Robins 1996, 156)

INTRODUCTION: MOBILE CAMERA— TOWARDS A NEW VISUALITY

The contemporary smartphone camera emerges as a device which inaugurates a new paradigm in the modeling, production, appropriation, and consumption of visual images. If a decade ago we thought of camera-phones as personal and portable photographic media used to capture low-resolution stills, today our conception has evolved into a device that transforms information, augments reality, and extends the human sensory experience. Addressing *where* modern digital culture is located elicits a rather direct and uncontested response—it is both ubiquitously anywhere, and invisibly *everyware*. Blending the sensory extending capabilities of digital media technologies with the digital, coded world of information, urban space has become techno-synthetically produced (Drakopoulou 2013; McLuhan 1964)—and the mobile camera is a catalyst to this innovation.

Today, the constructed visualizations projected through the mobile camera lens pertain more to information than imagery, defining the proprietor with the designation of user or co-creator, rather than photographer. The innovative visual capabilities afforded by the software within the smartphone consequently have the power to alter how we perceive the device altogether. The mobile apparatus is eclipsed by the application as it facilitates and creates new kinds of vision, other ways of seeing, and alternative worlds of experience (Robins 1996, 57). In *Perspectives as Symbolic Form*, Erwin Panofsky (1991, 27) echoes Albrecht Dürer in conceiving that *perspective* signifies "seeing through," and, like the affordances of contemporary mobile visual technologies, users are promised a sense of immediacy and augmentation of information spaces (Bolter and Grusin 1999, 25). Surveying the range of smartphone apps that utilize the embedded camera illuminates a series of innovative perspectives and modes of engagement—one that sees users looking *through* the device, rather than *at* it.

In *Ready to Wear* (2013, 20), Isabel Pedersen asserts that there is nothing new about using a device that reads an aspect of the world that one normally cannot interpret; consider thermometers that translate exact temperatures, carbon monoxide alarms that perceive levels of poison undetectable by humans, and monitors that test blood for diabetic individuals who cannot sense their own glucose levels. In encountering these devices in the object world, we are extensively transformed by their structure; internally altered by the objects that leave their remnants and trace within us. This declaration is further underscored by our relationship to the software of the smartphone.

In the parlance of Marshall McLuhan (1964), Lev Manovich (2014, 80) asserts "software is the message," conceiving that it posits a new interface to our imagination, cultivating a collective language through which environments communicate, and an engine on which the world functions. When a technologically sophisticated smartphone camera is used to *take* a photograph, the process is not merely reflected by the union of optics and a photo-sensitive service that define outcomes, as is characteristic of conventional cameras. Rather, the device exhibits the intricacy of a processor that administers a series of digital functions, including analyzing image data, performing algorithmic changes, incorporating and layering other data spaces, and archiving image files (Chesher 2012, 98). In this manner, the smartphone shifts from an interpersonal communication device into a private, personal, and portable entity through which the user experiences and connects with the world. This posits a distinctive human-technology-world relation in the user, blurring the boundary between where the body ends, and where the technology begins.

In an effort to ground the concepts of mobile visual technology from novelty to ubiquity, the focus of this paper will be to define mobile photographic information, or what I term "mobile infography"—a portmanteau of information and photograph, enacted by the intersection of the mobile camera and software. Further, I hope that this definition will also speak to the value of these visual entities; *how* meaningful are these developments, and *what* is the real nature of their significance? I will begin with a focused definition of mobile infography, and will proceed into exploring the layers of this definition in taking up a series of visual apps as paradigms and prototypes for illustration. Where the first part of the paper speaks to contracting, and grounding the concept, the second focuses on the mobile interface, with particular attention to the mobile camera as a primary object of study, one that fosters an understanding of the ways in which these devices work collectively with bodies and objects.

DEFINING MOBILE INFORMATION PHOTOGRAPHY (OR "INFOGRAPHY")

Much of the literature on the camera-phone discusses its domestication into the new media landscape via modes of interpersonal communication and image sharing. A gap in the literature, however, is found in the intersection of these portable visual technologies into infospaces, creating what I have termed mobile infography. Contemporary visual mobile technologies are reflective of innovative information and communication technologies (ICTs) that are frequently delineated as "omnipresent" and "extensive" in computing, and simultaneously as "proliferating" and "embodied" in human-centered design (Bowers and Rodden 1993; Farman 2012; Graham *et al.* 2011; Grudin 1990). These definitions are germane to both the invisibility and ubiquity of mobile infography, recognizing that the highly converged smartphone is equivalently a computing, networking, and processing device.

Mobile infography ascends from the intersection between software and hardware. Where the software (the apps) produce the form, the hardware (the camera) dictates the content of what is produced. Revisiting Manovich's (2014) assertion that "software is the message" it is conceivable that mobile applications are the new interface to our imagination and the world; they are the form, and are distinct from the essence (the content) of what is being depicted. Parallel to the supremacy of form over content, and software over hardware, innovations in ubiquitous computing, everyware, and information visualization, alongside the capabilities of mobile and wireless technology, have encouraged the expansion of infospaces, and have subsequently broadened the informational possibilities presented to users as they experience and encounter lived space (Brewer and Dourish 2008; De Souza e Silva and Frith 2010; Greenfield 2006; Liao and Humphreys 2015; Manovich 2011; Rheingold 2002; Thrift and French 2002).

In what follows, I will account for the nascent definition of mobile infography. Fundamentally, it can be equated with the visual representation of information as projected through the mobile hardware of the camera, and subsequently translated via the software of the smartphone apps. I acknowledge that the nature of this definition is comprised of varying computing concepts; thus, I will borrow from information visualization, pervasive computing and everyware while contending the distinctive medium-specific variables that subsequently set mobile infography apart from these predecessors.

Information Visualization

It is difficult to characterize all forms of information visualization (infovis) into one comprehensive definition. At a fundamental level, it is agreeable that infovis is the rearrangement, or mapping between isolated data and visual representation. In an effort to trace the lineage of mobile infography I have mused on several relevant definitions of infovis. The first asserts that information visualization is "the communication of abstract data through the use of interactive visual interfaces" (Keim *et al.* 2006), and the second characterizes it as "the use of computer-supported, interactive, visual representations of abstract data to amplify cognition" (Card, Mackinlay, and Shneiderman 1999, 7). Both highlight the importance of the interface and the visual. Similarly, Manovich (2001, 2011) has described infovis as the transformation of quantified data, which is not visual, into a visual representation. Information visualization is thus a tool that assists individuals in collecting insight into data using graphics.

Where information visualization transforms raw data into visual forms, visual apps counter this process; they take images and subsequently convert or embed information within them. In this way, the images are rendered to communicate a designated and preconfigured mode of information—often *spoken* through the metadata of the immediate environment. It is in these unconventional and unanticipated uses and functions of the smartphone camera—and what those uses and functions mean—where we uncover a new visuality (Flichy 1995). This new visuality is one in which cameras are increasingly able to distinguish and interpret settings and the resulting visual content enables users to "do" things (Palmer 2012, 94).

Despite its contrasting outcomes to mobile infography, information visualization is crucial to the ways in which locative media employ the merging of both virtual and material spaces. One fundamental technological innovation that facilitates this organization and convergence of "real" and "virtual" is augmented reality (AR). AR apps present a particular style of software that produces a distinct form of mobile infography. Mediating the user's visual perception, AR applications use the smartphone's camera, GPS, gyroscope, accelerometer, and browser to overlay data onto an object or environment, through the device. Thus, AR is a container term for the use of data overlay on the real-time camera view of a location (Verhoeff 2012, 40). To further account for the link between information visualization and what I am defining as mobile infography, Jason Farman (2012, 14) discusses the innovative capabilities of AR apps. He notes:

By being able to point your mobile device at a store, monument, or geographic feature nearby and retrieve information on that object, users are able to engage and contribute to information through an interface that develops a sense of embodied proprioception in pervasive computing space.

Farman's discussion of embodiment is particularly relevant to the concept of augmented reality, which is also the product of ubiquitous computing. This notion of embodiment depends on what he acknowledges as "the cognitive unconscious" (27); our embodiment of new media and our sense of being-in-the-world are contingent on much of our surrounding environment *not* being noticed. We function as embodied beings in not observing or sensing everything. Thus, this delineation of mobile augmented reality and embodiment signals the second innovative computing concept that I will use to further define mobile infography—it is the product of *"pervasive computing" and "everyware."*

Pervasive Computing, Everyware and "Interfacelessness"

The shift from talking into the mobile phone, to navigating data functionalities is characteristic of what is commonly referred to as "pervasive computing." Where the communication landscape has typically rendered the cell phone a personal and privatizing entity, novel explorations of location-aware technologies challenge these assertions in affirming that smartphone interfaces now permit us to map our defined geographic coordinates, and access location-specific information. The data inscribed with site-specificity enables users to engage with both surroundings and individuals in innovative ways (de Souza e Silva and Frith 2012, i). Most relevant, however, is the nature of this relationship to place: domesticated mobile media are so enmeshed into the everyday that users are often rarely conscious of the extent of this integration.

The adhesion of data to location alters urban environments by modifying our once two-dimensional landscapes, towards "infospaces" replete with coded information. These infospaces can be exemplified through the content of the recordbreaking augmented reality app *Pokémon Go*. While the coded information, in this case the Pokémon themselves, are only decipherable to players (Pokémon trainers), the environment is replete with "invisible" information in the form of gameplay. Closely affiliated with applications that produce mobile infography, Howard Rheingold's (2002, 85) exploration of pervasive computing is defined through the design and innovation of sentient objects, "not because embedded chips can reason but because they sense, receive, store, and transmit information." As ubiquitous, global and highly accessible entities, mobile media are serving to facilitate a widespread understanding of the premise of pervasive computing. Adam Greenfield

(2006, 1) extends the margins of its definition further in his notion of "everyware." He explains:

> In everyware, the garment, the room and the street become sites of processing and mediation. Household objects from shower stalls to coffee pots are reimagined as places where facts about the world can be gathered, considered, and acted upon. And all of the familiar rituals of daily life—things as fundamental as the way we wake up in the morning, get to work, or shop for groceries—are remade as an intricate dance of *information* about ourselves, the state of the external world, and the options available to us at any given moment. (emphasis added)

In each of these scenarios presented by Greenfield, there are dominant informatics underscoring the seeming simplicity of the experience—and yet they never penetrate the surface of awareness. Rather, as Greenfield asserts, "things just work" (2). Engagements and interactions with everyware feel genuine, natural, spontaneous and human; individuals benefit from "the full power of information technology, without having to absorb the esoteric bodies of knowledge on which it depends" (2). This curious point of absorption is one of importance in defining mobile infography, and one that is reflected in pervasive computing and everyware. Through the interface users are able to navigate framed fragments of infospace without invasive and hectic modes of investigating. Instead, mobile infography is effectively characterized by the simultaneity of invisibility and ubiquity.

Reflecting this invisibility, Mark Weiser's (1994) influential essay "The World is Not a Desktop," offers insight into infography. Weiser's thesis can be easily digested—"a good tool is an invisible tool" (7). Arguing, "the most profound technologies are those that disappear," Weiser accounts for the capacity of these tools to enmesh themselves into the fabric of everyday life, until they are indistinguishable from it (*ibid.*). I equate this dematerializing nature of digital media with ubiquitous and pervasive computing, which often facilitates an environment in which the interface recedes into the backdrop of the everyday. Mobile infography extends this unconscious interaction; rather than focusing solely on the mobile device and our interactions with the interface, we simply act instinctively with our environment, and it responds accordingly (Farman 2012, 7).

Mobile visual apps such as *Layar*, *CamFind* and *PhotoMath*, (discussed in the second half of this chapter), are characterized as tiny, evocative, and innovative entities which are simultaneously challenging to our ontological outlook. To borrow from the phenomenological approach of Maurice Merleau-Ponty (1974), the structure of vision involves the dual location of subjectivity: the twofold experience of immersion and detachment. For Merleau-Ponty, visual experience is established through the correlation between these two ends: "when the spark is lit between sensing and sensible" (284). Through mobile vision, or the product of mobile infography, we animate, discover, respond to, pattern, and order the world; visibility is filled with signification (Robins 1996, 135).

Using my preliminary definition—one that is exclusive, and simultaneously a successor and product of information visualization, pervasive computing and everyware—I will shift my focus towards surveying the software that generates the digital artifacts of mobile infography.

EXPLAINING MOBILE INFOGRAPHY THROUGH APPS

Smartphones encompass an amalgamation of already established communication modes and interfaces that append themselves to the human body, and saturate the human sensorium. Echoing McLuhan's (1964) notable phrase that "media are extensions of the senses," the widespread popularity of mobile apps reinvents the conventional smartphone camera, and subsequently broadens the senses, primarily that of vision and memory. Rob Kitchin and Martin Dodge (2011, 4) reveal that while code is generally hidden, and invisible inside the hardware, it often produces visible and tangible effects in the world—the most critical of which I believe to be knowledge production. In what follows I will explore some of the applications that use unconventional visual methods as information tools, in an effort to substantiate my definition of mobile infography.

Google This Image: CamFind and Google Goggles

Mobile visual search engines allow users to query databases using images, rather than words—an option that has users balancing the benefits of communicating visually rather than lexically. Images then, are no longer merely visual signs, but rather afford new navigating possibilities. Applications like *CamFind* (Image Searcher, Inc.) and the now defunct *Google Goggles* use a series of techniques to help recognize and translate captured images. As the camera hovers in front of the object, the software functions to identify it using object recognition algorithms, which are then compared against counter images within its database. To further substantiate the search, the software tries to locate any visible text using optical character recognition (OCR), and employs the GPS function of the hardware to help filter location-specific content that might contribute to an understanding of the search query.

Musing on user-friendliness, CamFind boasts a comprehensive description of its app, stating: "With CamFind, understanding the world around you has never been easier. Simply take a picture of any object and CamFind uses mobile visual search technology to tell you what it is" (CamFind 2016). The software affords new ways of seeing that are distinct from the intrinsic capacity of human perception— one that is powered by an image recognition API known as CloudSight. When the image is taken, CamFind communicates with the CloudSight API and provides the user with relevant results. This extends CloudSight's mantra of "revolutionizing the way you interact with the world around you" (CloudSight 2016).

Reading objects, symbols, landscapes and images directly as information, both Goggles and CamFind are an expanded mobilization of what Félix Guattari (1995, 51) identifies as "a-signifying semiotics" (Chesher 2012). Chris Chesher (2012, 111) explains that smartphones have the capacity to

> [R]ead symbols and images directly as information, in addition to their conventional meanings as images. In classical signification, the signifier (the word "camera," or the image in a photograph) denotes a signified (the idea of a camera, or the impression of the photographed scene) through acts of interpretation.

When an app like CamFind interprets the title of a book through a photograph, an underlying process of a-signifying semiotics is actualized. This is reflective of the ways in which the smartphone camera effectively interprets the environment as if it were a digital passport of sorts. Under the guise of the app, images no longer function primarily as visual emblems. Rather, as Chesher notes, "they open up new existential territories of real time translation by recognizing distinctive shapes in the database, interpreting them according to the different image types, and connecting with Internet links" (*ibid.*).

Speaking to Guattari's concept, the translated mobile images operate as "point-signs," which on one hand belong to the semiotic order, and on the other mediate directly in a series of material machinic processes (Guattari 1995, 51). Further, Guattari notes that the "a-signifying semiotic" figures "don't simply secrete significations. They give out stop and start orders but above all activate the 'bring into being' of ontological Universes" (51). In connection with mobile infography, objects do not seamlessly emit metadata to the naked eye. Rather, when activated and held over the object, CamFind and Google Goggles translate the environment against their own databases, and subsequently provide information—*if* it is able to properly translate what is being viewed. These technical images then, are reflective of envisioned surfaces; they appear purely representational on the exterior, but are satiated with material and possibility beneath the visual (Flusser 2011, 33).

It is interesting to note the shortcomings of these applications; they fail to recognize unpopular images, brands and monuments alike. This re-conceptualizes some preconceived ideas of both information and importance. While my purpose is not to argue the capabilities of software to alter social power-dynamics, it is critical to assess the ways in which objects and space have the potential to be renegotiated through the intervention of digital technologies. This is actively exemplified in the nascent niche-market of concentrated visual search apps, relevant to particular themes and concepts. One examples of this includes Magnus, a searchable art identification app.

Self-dubbed as *Shazam* for the art world, *Magnus* is a New York-based smartphone art identification service with a mission to "democratize access to the art world" (Magnus 2016). The official webpage for the app notes that there are three main steps involved from the moment you snap a "photo" until the "magic" happens—a playful semantic choice. The app generates a digital fingerprint of the artwork as seen through the smartphone camera lens. In near-instantaneous time, Magnus algorithmically gathers data from its crowd-sourced database and designates the name of the artwork and artist, alongside relevant cost and historical information. While Magnus claims to have a success rate over 70%, it divulges that when results are not immediately returned, photos are "worked on" by the team—an interesting concept that posits humans and software in the same field.

There is a noteworthy connection between the digital nature of Magnus as software, and the materiality of the art world. In *Postphenomenology: Essays in the Postmodern Context*, Don Ihde (1993, 105) asserts "both art objects and technological objects—equipment—are 'thingly,' 'produced,' have ways of 'revealing' a world and belong in some way to the process called technē." In essence, then, the art object being photographed and the *Magnus* app are both emblematic of a mode of revealing—one is structured in information delivery, and the other acts as a means of creative expression. The camera and the object—in this case the art object—share a material commonality.

Translating the Everyday: From Words Lens to Google Translate

The aforementioned mobile visual search software flips image universes into informational universes; algorithms recognize attributes within the visualization against a database of graphics. In a similar way, the *Word Lens* (Quest Visual) app fuses lexis and graphic in the same arena, performing a series of sophisticated translations in the post-photography process. Rather than merely presenting captured images, the software generates translated text. On May 16, 2014, Google, Inc. acquired Quest Visual in order to merge the functionality of Word Lens into its translation service (Etherington 2014). The merger was completed half a year later, and the Google Translate app replaced Word Lens (Rosenbloom 2015).

To reiterate, mobile augmented reality is a container term for the use of data overlay on the real-time camera view of a location (Verhoeff 2012, 40). Employing AR, Google Translate employs the camera to identify foreign text with optical character recognition (OCR) and performs a near-instantaneous translation. Thus, the app helps to focus an otherwise foreign world; it was marketed as software that was indispensable when traveling abroad.

The translated words are displayed in the original context on the initial background, overlaying the primary text. The live transformation of the words onscreen sets the app apart from conventional translating tools. It is not inconceivable that the *Google Translate* app functions parallel to a foreign dictionary in the hands of a tourist. But it is important for the sake of defining mobile infography to look at what is new about new media, and in what ways an augmented reality translator differs from an analogue pocket dictionary.

The materiality of a dictionary affords a much different experience than using a real-time translating app like Google Translate. This gestures towards the notion that despite mimicking on many levels the same practice, the digital interface of the smartphone produces an altogether distinctive embodied experience (Farman 2012). Reiterating, Farman asserts that by investigating the media specificity of our engagement with cultural objects, "we can see that interfaces shape our embodied engagement with space and the ways we practice space as lived place" (44). This designation of embodied space deliberately extends Manovich's (2001, 25) division between media and new media:

> All existing media are translated into numerical data accessible for the computer. The result: graphics, moving images, sounds, shapes, and texts become computable, that is, simply sets of computer data. In short, media become new media.

Ultimately then, the "embodied content" of new media mobile software like Google Translate are non-transferable across media and situations; instead, as we are immersed, we give perspective to the information we engage with. In turn, this information both embeds itself, and characterizes our environment and our embodied engagement with space (Farman 2012, 42–44).

Yi-Fu Tuan (1977, 53) posits that tools and machines enlarge an individual's sense of space and spaciousness. In digital culture, and for the purpose of this investigation, smartphones and their respective apps are reflective of these designated tools. Sara Ahmed (2010, 31) explores the intersection between affect and objects, asserting that in order to be affected by something is to evaluate the *thing*; the appraisal is expressed in *how* bodies orient toward these artifacts. To give value to things is to shape what is near us. Further, Henri Lefebvre (1991, 37) muses that the "object" of interest must be expected to shift from "things in space" to the concrete "production of space." It is crucial to assert that smartphone software functions in the production of space only when the user is positioned as looking through the device—onto information spaces—rather than merely at it. This distinction can be exemplified in the overall success and efficacy of the app.

In order for an individual's experience of space to be effectively augmented, the technological entity must paradoxically vanish. Applicable to this software-hardware indivisibility paradigm are Martin Heidegger's (1962) theorizations of tools and equipment. Heidegger designates those entities that extend the hand, or in this case the eyes and mind as well, as "ready-to-hand" (99). While in use then, the tool is not distinguished by the way it performs, but rather echoes Ihde's (1990) notion of a "good" technology, which does not call attention to itself. The better the technology operates the more likely users are to be acclimatized to its functions. Thus, the goal here again is for technology to functionally disappear so that the user feels as though they are looking precisely at objects in their environment (Ihde 2008). This familiarity often causes users to lose sight of the technology's materiality—its *"thingness"*. Heidegger (1962, 99) reminds us that "the peculiarity of what is proximally ready-to-hand is that, in its readiness-to-hand, it must, as it were, withdraw in order to be ready-to-hand quite authentically." Ready-to-hand stands akin to Jay David Bolter and Richard Grusin's (1999, 23) notion of "immediacy," as it strives to make the interface "'natural' rather than arbitrary." Using augmented reality software to read and interpret information spaces posits an exceptional example for the concepts of ready-to-hand and immediacy. As the camera is engaged and the screen begins to present the transcribed content, the interface vanishes and the user is moved further into the information space.

Photomath: Show Your Work With AR

Photomath uses AR to read and solve mathematical problems in real-time, with the smartphone camera, billing it both the world's first (and smartest) camera calculator (Photomath 2016). In a brief "how-to" for the software, the creators note that when the app is active, it will automatically scan a mathematical expression, limiting the end-user's efforts. While we may not be in a rush to open up the blackbox (Latour 1999) of the conventional calculator, Photomath is impressive in its process-based focus—it allows users to map out the equations step by step. John Durham Peters (2003) posits that our instruments think with us, and in this way, the software gets full marks for adequately "showing its work," with the user.

The environment cultivated by users' interactions with smartphone technologies, particularly applications that use the smartphone camera, gesture towards a phenomenological encounter of hybrid space; one that is concurrently constituted out of the digital and material, or the virtual and the actual (Farman 2012, 78). Photomath interrogates this dichotomy of digital and material as the app translates equations from both texts and notebooks. Considering software then, we can measure its magnitude against the capacity to alter the conditions through which society, space, and time are produced. Where information was typically communicated, and received in time, software is now situating the focus on information retrieval in space. Manuel Castells (2000, 414) asserts that space is not a reflection of society—it is its expression. In other words, dataspace is not merely a photocopy or facet of culture, but is rather the essence of modern society.

Although Google Translate, Word Lens and Photomath respectively boast innovative and practical concepts, the majority of the discourse that surround them pertain to their shortcomings and failures. To revisit the notion of "ready-to-hand" and withdrawing, consider what happens when a smartphone user connects with a remote individual in a phone call; the interface of the phone typically recedes and the user is moved into the space of the conversation (Farman 2012, 29). If, however, the software fails, and Photomath crashes, or does not adequately decipher the mathematical expression (the font isn't clear, or the equation isn't supported), the sensory experience immediately shifts from the surrounding environment or textbook, to the cellular device, or in the parlance of Heidegger, "the equipment." The user will likely move the smartphone camera away from the equation, and then back towards it, attempting to troubleshoot and begin the decoding process anew. It is conceivable that the user may uncover a connection error or software malfunction. This process, for Heidegger, makes us incredibly conscious of the device, shifting the equipment from "ready-to-hand" to "present-at-hand". This ideological taken-for-grantedness is always already prominent with the voice and text capabilities of mobile media. It is conceivable that the properties of *infography* will further dichotomize this distinction between "ready-to-hand," and "present-to-hand" as applications fail and subsequently shift the interface into the foreground of infospace.

Reshaping and Extending The "Real": Layar

While the extension of the senses and information through mobile media is nothing new, the visual, interactive, and real-time nature of mobile infography, offers innovative means of experiencing, navigating, interpreting and enacting place (Graham, Zook, and Boulton 2012; Liao and Humphreys 2015). Applications like *Layar* exhibit the ways in which mobile media are capable of saturating environments with meaning, thus altering space by acknowledging it as a sense of place. For the purpose of this explanation, I am adopting Steve Harrison and Paul Dourish's (1996, 69) definition conceding that "space is the opportunity; place is the understood reality". In connection with mobile infography, space can be thought of as an abstract realm in which users, images and information coalesce. Place, on the other hand, is a socially constructed ideal that I argue may be fashioned by the influence of mobile infography. It is conceivable then, that mobile software *is* in fact "the message," as it offers users a new way of visualizing information, subsequently impacting their conceptions of space and place. This is the premise of augmented reality, and the crux of mobile infography.

In a pre-*Pokémon Go* era, Layar was once the world's most downloaded AR application; it accumulated nearly one million new downloads per month (Layar 2014). In activating the embedded smartphone camera, users intersect the unconventional realms of locative and visual media. By holding up the phone in a surrounding urban environment, users are capable of amassing information about events, locations, and advertisements at site-specific points of interest. Layar uses the information processed and collected by the smartphone users' position, and pairs it with content about the setting in its database (i.e. Wikipedia entries, social media sites, monuments, etc.). As a location-based search and discovery service the application mediates the user's experience of place and space by incorporating information directly into the landscape.

With Layar, performativity transforms viewing into making, and the city becomes a traversable "screenspace" (Verhoeff 2012) manipulated through the mediated perception of the camera feed and the user's haptic engagement with the device. At the intersection of code and software, the user's sense of place undergoes an even further construction—one that can be characterized as technological and mediatized in nature. This layered notion of structure is pertinent to the pervasive assertion that both spaces and places are never quite finalized, and are always in a state of *becoming* (Kitchin and Dodge 2011; Pred 1984; Relph 1976).

Technologies like Google Goggles, CamFind and Word Lens facilitate a thought-provoking body-tool relation that produces a specific phenomenological approach of "being-in-the-world." Layar on the other hand, presents an offshoot of phenomenology; undertaking the position of a technological entity that mediates a worldview for the user, it can be characterized as post-phenomenological. In transforming encounters and experiences of the world, users in turn become transformed by this process (Ihde 1990; Verbeek 2005; Ihde 2009; Wellner 2011). An example of post-phenomenology as applied to mobile infography would be the device that transforms the smartphone user's experience of the immediate environment, while being perceived as a prosthetic of the body. Echoing the aforementioned concept of looking through the device, rather than at it, the screen of the smartphone in AR browsing functions like a transparent window, framed by the flexible nature of the edges of the phone screen itself. This frame is transitory and adjustable by the designated user. What is relevant, however, is that AR browsing affords an intricate way of framing both "reality" and infography (Verhoeff 2012, 41).

Particularly relevant to both mobile AR and locative media are the ways in which data can be both retrieved and structured with site-specificity. Farman (2012, 39) asserts that this site-specificity "affords users a new window into the meaning of complex data and ideas." Linking back to the working definition of mobile infography, and the multifaceted computing concepts that I have employed for my own work, the transformation of intricate information into a wieldy and manageable visual layout is the ultimate objective of practitioners in related areas such as information visualization (*ibid.*). The aptitude of site-specificity to engage users with information in an embodied way has resulted in a growing interest in locating ways of revising our surrounding environments into information interfaces (43).

There is an interesting juxtaposition in the extension of information spaces, as all of the apps discussed do not elicit attention to the apps themselves—but rather to the translated spaces they cultivate: the scanned cultural monument identified in CamFind, the foreign restaurant menu viewed through Google Translate, the complex math equation solved in the classroom with PhotoMath, and the promotional film poster projected on a billboard with Layar. On a fundamental level, these software entities enable users to consume and produce information ubiquitously, while simultaneously cultivating the ability to experience space in novel ways.

FUTURE RESEARCH AND CONCLUDING REMARKS

Two decades ago, Kevin Robins (1996, 37) heralded the potentials of new vision technologies in expanding the range of photographic seeing "beyond seeing." While his proclamation was grounded in innovations of the remote sensing of microwave, infrared and short-wave radar imagery, the assertion can be actively substituted for information spaces, and infography.

The essence of mobile infography is analogous with the act of shining a flashlight down a dark hallway. Without the light, which stands in for the camera on the smartphone, everything is still situated in its place, you just can't see or perceive it fully. Aside from the practical examples featured in this chapter of the smartphone visual apps themselves, designating a pragmatic definition for mobile infography enables auxiliary inquires to be taken up as the field continues to expand. Some of these investigations might support uncovering the following: how is the camera embedded in the smartphone involved in remediating the ways we know, experience, feel about, and respond to the world; how do the resulting visualizations impact users' relationships with both phone interfaces and space; and in what ways do visualization practices inspire new ways of seeing with smartphone users?

It is evident that while mobile infography is in many ways not characterized by the notion of the "interfaceless interface," (Bolter and Grusin 1999) the images produced by the device are actualized with little effort by the user. The reverie of one day eliminating the interface—"the mind-machine information barrier"—is reflective of a desire to cultivate an ideal symbiosis between the technology and its user (Robins 1996, 48). The prominence of the concept of invisibility is rampant, both in the ready-to-hand smartphone, but also in the definitions of code/space (Kitchin and Dodge 2011) pervasive computing, everyware, and mobile infography. This inquiry has aimed to echo the efforts of contemporary technoliterary studies in seeking to establish frameworks to begin to understand the nature of intangible and covert media that are establishing a new layer to our mediated environments, and how this metadata is affecting our bodies, our human-technology relationship, and our phenomenal and ontological being (Gould 2014, 27).

On a fundamental level, this investigation contends that how one sees is just as relevant to what one sees. The power of software over hardware shifts the user into a position of looking through the mobile device, rather than at it. Defining mobile infography situates an innovative perspective of the nascent capabilities of visual media on conventional conceptions of information.

REFERENCES

Ahmed, Sara. 2010. "Happy Objects." In *The Affect Theory Reader*, edited by Melissa Gregg, and Gregory J. Seigworth, 29–51. Durham and London: Duke University Press.
Bolter, Jay David and Richard Grusin. 1999. *Remediation*. Cambridge, MA: MIT Press.
Bowers, John and Tom Rodden. 1993. "Exploring the Interface: Experiences of a CSCW Network." *Proceedings of the INTERACT '93 and CHI '93 Conference on Human Factors in Computing Systems, (CHI '93)*. New York.
Brewer, Johanna and Paul Dourish, P. 2008. "Storied Spaces: Cultural Accounts of Mobility, Technology, and Environmental Knowing." *International Journal of Human-Computer Studies* 66 (12): 963–76.
CamFind. 2016. "CamFind: Search the Physical World." *CamFind*, accessed 20 June 2017. http://camfindapp.com/.
Castells, Manuel. 2000. "Space of Flows." In *The Rise of The Network Society: Vol. 1: The Information Age: Economy, Society and Culture*, 407–459. Oxford: Blackwell Publishers.
Chesher, Chris. 2012. "Between Image and Information: The iPhone Camera in the History of Photography." In *Studying Mobile Media: Cultural Technologies, Mobile Communication, and the iPhone*, edited by Larissa Hjorth, Jean Burgess, and Ingrid Richardson, 98–117. New York: Routledge.
CloudSight. 2016. "Demo." *CloudSight*, accessed 20 June 2017. http://cloudsight.ai/api.
De Souza e Silva, Adriana, and Jordan Frith. 2012. *Mobile Interfaces in Public Spaces: Locational Privacy, Control and Urban Sociability*. New York: Routledge.
Drakopoulou, Sophia. 2013. "Pixels, Bits and Urban Space: Observing the Intersection of the Space of Information with Urban Space in Augmented Reality Smartphone Applications and Peripheral Vision Displays." *First Monday* 18 (11).
Etherington, Darrell. 2014. "Google Has Acquired Quest Visual, The Maker of Camera-Based Translation App Word Lens." *TechCrunch*, May 16, 2014. http://tcrn.ch/1lJ7F0f.
Farman, Jason. 2012. *Mobile Interface Theory: Embodied Space and Locative Media*. New York: Routledge.
Flichy, Patrice. 1995. *Dynamics of Modern Communication: The Shaping and Impact of New Communication Technologies*. London: Sage.
Flusser, Vilém. 2011. *Into the Universe of Technical Images*. Translated by Nancy Ann Roth. Minneapolis: University of Minnesota Press.
Gould, Amanda Starling. 2014. "Invisible Visualities: Augmented Reality Art and the Contemporary Media Ecology." *Convergence* 20 (1): 25–32.
Graham, Connor, Eric Laurier, Vincent O'Brien, and Mark Rouncefield. 2011. "New Visual Technologies: Shifting Boundaries, Shared Moments." *Visual Studies* 26 (2): 87–91.
Graham, Mark, Matthew Zook, and Andrew Boulton. 2012. "Augmented Reality in Urban Places: Contested Content and the Duplicity of Code." *Transactions of the Institute of British Geographers* 37 (4): 1–16.
Greenfield, Adam. 2006. *Everyware: The Dawning Age of Ubiquitous Computing*. Berkeley: New Riders Press.

Grudin, Jonathan. 1990. "The Computer Reaches Out: The Historical Continuity of Interface Design." *Proceedings of the SIGCHI Conference on Human Factors in Computing Systems (CHI '90).* New York: ACM.
Guattari, Félix. 1995. *Chaosmosis: An Ethico-Aesthetic Paradigm.* Sydney: Power Publications.
Harrison, Steve and Paul Dourish. 1996. "Re-place-ing Space: The Roles of Place and Space in Collaborative Systems." Proceedings of the 1996 ACM Conference on Computer Supported Co-operative Work, 1996 (CSCW '96). New York: ACM Press.
Heidegger, Martin. 1962. *Being and Time.* Oxford: Wiley-Blackwell.
Ihde, Don. 1990. *Technology and the Lifeworld: From Garden to Earth.* Bloomington and Indianapolis: Indiana University Press.
———. 1993. *Postphenomenology: Essays in the Postmodern Context.* Illinois: Northwestern University Press.
———. 2008. *Ironic Technics.* Copenhagen: Automatic Press Publishing.
———. 2009. *Postphenomenology and Technoscience: The Peking University Lectures.* Albany: State University of New York Press.
Keim, Daniel A, Florian Mansmann, Jörn Schneidewind, and Hartmut Ziegler. 2006. "Challenges in Visual Data Analysis." *Proceedings of Information Visualization (IEEE)* IV: 9–16.
Kitchin, Rob, and Martin Dodge. 2011. *Code/Space: Software and Everyday Life.* Cambridge, MA: MIT Press.
Latour, Bruno. 1999. *Pandora's Hope: Essays on the Reality of Science Studies.* Cambridge, MA: Harvard University Press.
Layar. 2014. "Layar's Industry Leadings Augmented Reality App Now Available on Google Glass." *Layar,* accessed 20 June 2017. https://www.layar.com/news/press-releases/layar-for-glass/.
Lefebvre, Henri. 1991. *The Production of Space.* Translated by Donald Nicholson-Smith. Malden, MA: Blackwell Publishers.
Liao, Tony, and Lee Humphreys. 2015. "Layar-ed Places: Using Mobile Augmented Reality to Tactically Reengage, Reproduce, and Reappropriate Public Space." *New Media & Society* (Online First Version, March 19): 1418–1435.
Magnus. 2016. "About." *Magnus,* accessed 20 June 2017. http://www.magnus.net/about/.
Manovich, Lev. 2001. *The Language of New Media.* Cambridge, MA: MIT Press.
———. 2011. "What is Visualisation?" *Visual Studies* 26 (1): 36–49.
———. 2014. "Software is the Message." *Journal of Visual Culture* 13 (1): 79–81.
McLuhan, Marshall. 1964. *Understanding Media: The Extensions of Man.* London: Routledge.
Merleau-Ponty, Maurice. 1974. "Eye and Mind." In *Phenomenology, Language and Sociology: Selected Essays of Maurice Merleau-Ponty,* edited by John O'Neill, 283–284. London: Heinemann.
Palmer, Daniel. 2012. "iPhone Photography: Mediating Visions of Social Space." In *Studying Mobile Media: Cultural Technologies, Mobile Communication, and the iPhone,* edited by Larissa Hjorth, Jean Burgess, and Ingrid Richardson, 85–97. New York: Routledge.
Panofsky, Erwin. 1991. *Perspective as Symbolic Form.* New York: Zone Books.
Pedersen, Isabel. 2013. *Ready to Wear: A Rhetoric of Wearable Computers and Reality-Shifting Media.* Anderson, SC: Parlor Press.
Peters, John Durham. 2003. "Space, Time, and Communication Theory." *Canadian Journal of Communication* 28 (4): 397–411.
PhotoMath. 2016. "PhotoMath." *PhotoMath,* accessed 20 June 2017. https://photomath.net/en/.
Pred, Allen R. 1984. "Place as Historically Contingent Process: Structuration and the Time-Geography of Becoming Places." *Annals of the Association of American Geographers* 74 (2): 279–297.

Relph, Edward. 1976. *Place and Placelessness*. London: Pion.
Rheingold, Howard. 2002. *Smart Mobs: The Next Social Revolution*. Cambridge, MA: Perseus Books.
Robins, Kevin. 1996. *Into the Image: Culture and Politics in the Field of Vision*. London: Routledge.
Rosenbloom, Stephanie. 2015. "Updates for Google Translate (Just Hold Up Your Phone)." *The New York Times*, January 14, 2015, http://nyti.ms/1zcDqrI.
Thrift, Nigel J., and Shaun French. 2002. "The Automatic Production of Space." *Transactions of the Institute of British Geographers* 27 (3): 309–325.
Tuan, Yi-Fu. 1977. *Space and Place: The Perspective of Experience*. Minneapolis: University of Minnesota.
Verbeek, Peter-Paul. 2005. *What Things Do: Philosophical Reflections on Technology, Agency and Design*. Philadelphia: Pennsylvania State University Press.
Verhoeff, Nanna. 2012. "Navigating Screenspace: Towards Performative Cartography." In *Moving Data: The iPhone and My Media*, edited by Pelle Snickars and Patrick Vonderau, 33–48. New York: Columbia University Press.
Wellner, Galit. 2011. "Wall-Window-Screen: How the Cell Phone Mediates a Worldview for Us." *Humanities and Technology Review* 30: 77–103.
Weiser, Mark. 1994. "The World is Not a Desktop." *Interactions* 1 (1): 7–8.

CHAPTER SEVEN

Entrepreneurial Journalism AND Ubiquitous Media

Considerations for Digital Labor

MAGGIE REID

INTRODUCTION

The ubiquity of digital media is a reality that must be confronted by journalists and news media organizations as they adapt to new consumption patterns and business models for media content. However, as unpaid media work becomes increasingly normalized, the idea that media is, or ought to be, "ubiquitous" is not without contention. This chapter seeks to problematize the uncritical celebration of media as ubiquitous (Tapscott & Williams, 2006) by focusing on the layers of unpaid labor that accompany digitization, neoliberalism and the reorganization of work as it pertains to the journalism field. While it is important to celebrate the decline of the stronghold of mass media organizations in the production of information, the labor environment that has ensued for journalists is one of precarity, risk and unpaid labor. I argue that this uncertain labor environment casts doubt on the idea that journalists necessarily have more autonomy in this context, while also focusing on the processes of commodification that accompany these changes.

By approaching ubiquitous media through a critical political economy approach, this chapter analyzes major shifts in the business, labor, and practice of news media creation in a digital context. I argue that immaterial labor that is undertaken by journalists operates both to create value for social media sites while also creating potential value for journalists themselves through brand development. This chapter will provide theoretical insight into the politics of ubiquitous media in the context of journalism work and the difficulties that emerge when media use and brand building are contextualized as labor, in an already precarious labor economy. I will further situate and relocate Dallas Smythe's audience commodity in brand-building professionalization practices for digital journalists. I argue not only that exploitation and alienation emerge from this environment but also that this context sets parameters for who can realistically pursue a career in journalism and in turn, how this might impact the field more broadly.

FROM MASS TO UBIQUITOUS MEDIA

This paper will approach ubiquitous media with the understanding that it not only refers to the increasing affordability and accessibility of digital technologies but how those conditions precipitate increased participation in the media system by individual content creators. Ubiquitous media also refers to the fact that media is now more mobile, flexible, and integrated in our daily lives. The idea that media is in fact ubiquitous in a digital context has important dimensions when considering what came before it. Preceded by the era of mass media where we often referred to it as "the media," given rising levels of concentration of power and ownership, the era of ubiquitous media carries much promise for decentralized media production and dispersal of informational power. As Featherstone (2009, 2) argues, "The media can no longer be considered to be a monolithic structure producing uniform media effects."

Instead, digitization has in many ways reduced barriers to entry, leading to the creation of new forms of content by individuals including blogging, citizen journalism, YouTube videos, and many other forms of user-generated content (UGC). This era has been praised by some scholars as representing a new era of cultural production from the bottom up, where people can become producers without having to go through traditional organizational channels (Bruns 2008; Jenkins 2006; Tapscott and Williams 2006). While the democratizing potentials of new technologies are surely important to consider, so are the implications this environment has on the labor that goes into that cultural production. This is particularly important to consider in the context of rises in precarious and unstable labor in the creative industries.

It has been argued that neoliberal policies and the proliferation of digital technologies have led to increased precarity for creative workers leading to a great deal of freelance or project based work, where risk is offset to individuals (Harvey 2006; Flew and Cunningham 2010; Neff 2012). A recent report on precarious work in Canada has indicated that over 40% of people that are employed in the creative and knowledge sectors are working in jobs with elements of precarity (Lewchuk et al. 2015). This has certainly become commonplace in the field of journalism. In this environment, individuals are increasingly engaging in self-branding for the purposes of establishing authenticity, credibility, and building social capital to ensure they have continued work in their field (Banet-Weiser 2012). In this sense, emerging journalists often must "pay for the chance to work" (Bousquet 2008, 63). This is another way of saying that this branding that must be employed is in fact work, and that this work is unpaid. There has been an increased focus as of late on the prevalence of unpaid work and the exploitation that occurs through unpaid internships (Cohen 2012; Corrigan 2015). Less attention, however, has been paid to online branding as "work" and how this may be understood in the context of the digital labor debates and understandings of autonomy, alienation and exploitation. To appreciate how this environment has been created, it is important to contextualize the forces that have given rise to changes in the production of news media and in turn, journalistic labor.

DIGITIZATION AND THE RISE OF ENTREPRENEURIAL JOURNALISM

There have been many structural changes to media organizations that have emerged through intensified media concentration and corporate convergence that have had major impacts on content creation as well as labor environments for journalism in Canada and internationally. Digitization has led to vast changes in the logic of media corporations as they strive to exploit the benefits of synergies while focusing on short-term profitability and maximizing audiences. This has undoubtedly influenced how journalistic content is produced, monetized, and consumed. This shift has led to what many would argue is a crisis in the news media industry, which is characterized by lower advertising revenue, dwindling subscriptions, and the need to regionalize, nationalize, and internationalize content to cut costs. Postmedia Network Canada Corporation's recent layoff of 90 journalists in early 2016 in efforts to regionalize and synergize operations (Watson 2016) is one example amongst many in the current Canadian media landscape that points to the increasing instability in the journalism profession. Fewer journalists are working within major media corporations as a result of digital convergence as journalism work may be adapted for multiple platforms. In addition, theorists have noted that intensified pressures to capture audiences has led to less investigative journalism and more entertainment style news (Cooper 2005; Skinner and Gasher 2005), enhancing the profit-based orientation of news media making.

On the other hand, the affordances of digital technologies and social networking sites (SNS) has led to the rise of "citizen journalism" and user-generated content (UGC), which has led many to question the future and utility of the journalism profession. Some have even argued that citizen journalism may fill in the gaps of the lost labor from massive layoffs (Shirky 2008). While it is true that media organizations often rely on citizen reporting and contributions when reporting the news (Compton and Benedetti 2010), this has implications not only for the labor of the profession but also for understandings of what it means to be a journalist and what it means to "do journalism." Can user-generated content really fill in the lost labor of investigative journalism? It is dangerous to instrumentalize UGC as something that can or should replace paid jobs as this could pose real threats to content, quality and veracity of journalistic output.

Given that the "crisis of journalism" in this environment has often been framed through declining revenues for news media organizations, unsurprisingly, the labor environment that has ensued is nothing short of precarious for those pursuing a career in the field, as internships and freelance work become normative. For those that are able to secure stable journalism work, their jobs have been expanded outside of information gathering and news reporting to include photography, editing, page production (Compton and Benedetti 2010) and more recently brand building and social media engagement, which severely alters the capacity of journalists to do actual "journalism work." As Cohen (2015b) argues, entrepreneurial journalism has been proposed as one potential solution to the crisis of journalism. The idea that journalists must be "savvy" and think like entrepreneurs to both build a brand and reach their audiences is becoming pervasive. While entrepreneurship in journalism is not a new phenomenon, disruptive digital technologies, the rise of neoliberalism, and the financial downturn have all been instrumental in bringing this term to the forefront of discussions on the future of journalism.

Entrepreneurial journalism is being adopted more and more as a pedagogical approach in some journalism schools in the US and Canada. Educators have argued that the move towards entrepreneurialism and a heavy focus on technical skills and innovation in journalism education detracts from the aims and functions of journalism's long established role in society and for democracy (Francoeur 2015; Levine, Benedetti and Gasher 2015) that has been defended by critical political economists. These arguments are counterbalanced by examinations of the tough realities in the marketplace and the expectation that graduates come equipped with particular sets of skills (Picard 2015; Shapiro 2015).

Scholars have long since argued that the hyper-commercialization of the media and the focus on short-term profits comes at the expense of "public service journalism." In other words, more and more market forces are determining and constraining media production and media products (See for example, Baker 2006; McChesney 2004; Herman and Chomsky 1988). In many ways, this speaks to the lack of autonomy of journalists working within mainstream media organizations to pursue content that may be in the public interest (Bourdieu 2005). These critiques were very much connected to the growing media concentration, corporate convergence and digitization that were increasingly rationalizing the production of news media in North America.

Now that there have been decades of decline in mainstream media audiences and the rise of digital technologies that have lowered the barriers to entry in creating media products, there has been a premature celebration by some scholars regarding the newfound autonomy of the journalism field or of journalists themselves. For Shirky (2008), the new media ecosystem means that long standing mainstream media institutions are weakened and this provides an opportunity to create content without the "filter of news media." Historically, journalism could be conceptualized as more of a one-way street, where journalists and editors decided what stories were "newsworthy" and the audience was somewhat separate from the production process. Now, audience desires are at the forefront of journalistic production, made easier by digital technologies, and this is celebrated as a form of democratizing the media. In many ways this can be understood as a shift towards a demand-based approach to journalism where journalists are to first consider audience desires, advertisers, etc. and which views the journalist's role as fulfilling a market function rather than that of a social good (Mensing and Ryfe 2013). The celebration of this democratization or "ubiquity" of news media production is both a critique of the paternalistic or top-down approach of old models for media production and viewed as a potential solution for the lost labor of journalists, who, amidst major layoffs, find it increasingly difficult to obtain secure work in the field. It is important to consider whether the increasing focus on audiences precipitates further commodification of news media, rather than a move away from it. Further, the relationship between the democratization of media technologies and the democratization of media production must be considered. Do journalists have more autonomy in this day and age? Also, how can we conceive of this "autonomy" in the context of the precarious labor conditions that accompany this environment?

The idea that journalists have more autonomy in the digital age is often touted by proponents of entrepreneurial journalism. The term "entrepreneurial journalism" (Cohen 2015b; Vos & Singer 2016) began emerging after the financial crisis in 2008. Unsurprisingly, the discussion surrounding entrepreneurial journalism in this context spoke to the need to innovate and find new business models to sustain journalism, considering the stagnation of old business models. At the heart of the search for innovative new models for news media was the journalist as an entrepreneur. In other words, if the jobs no longer exist, create them for yourselves. Struggles for stable work in the field can be repurposed as opportunities for those entering the field.

Cohen (2015b) situates the rise of entrepreneurial journalism within the rise of enterprise culture more broadly, which she attributes to the intensification of neoliberalism in the 1980s. This culture was particularly prominent in the cultural industries and very much reflects the decline in standard work; i.e., full-time work for a single employer with workplace benefits (Vosko 2010) and its replacement with non-standard work; i.e., precarious, part-time, contract, casual work with little to no workplace benefits. Journalists are increasingly engaging in self-branding and promoting to adapt to the precarious and "flexible" nature of the workforce (Hearn 2008). It is not just self-promotion that is often required of workers within digital media organizations but also pressures to promote their work and to increase circulation. Some are even paid based on how many people read their articles (Cohen 2015b).

It has certainly been recognized that so-called "personal brand journalism" (Wolff 2014) is replacing traditional career paths for journalists, where one completes a journalism program and attains employment at a large media organization. Increasingly journalists are required to gain notoriety before securing any paid work. According to Kuehn and Corrigan (2013) this is characterized through either writing for exposure or developing a social media following that can be leveraged into paid work. In this sense, entrepreneurial journalism is "a response to spreading precarity, a way to cope with job scarcity, declining wages, declining faith in the occupation, and journalists declining autonomy and control" (Cohen 2015b, 516). In this sense, the dismantling of mainstream media may not present increased autonomy for journalists after all, but rather an increased risk, personal responsibility, and unpaid labor time spent in order to secure paid opportunities.

THE AUDIENCE COMMODITY REVISITED: LEVERAGING AUDIENCES FOR FUTURE WORK

There have been many efforts by communications scholars to interpret participation in communicative activities online as a form of labor, more specifically referred to as digital labor. Theories of digital labor have often been grounded in a revitalization of Marxist theory in communication studies as well as a reinterpretation of Dallas Smythe's "audience commodity" in the digital age. Efforts have been made to conceptualize UGC and more broadly use of commercial SNSs as work. This notion has been widely contested, leading to what have been referred to as the "digital labor debates." At the heart of these debates is (1) whether such engagement may be considered "work" in the Marxian sense (i.e., a wage relationship) and (2) whether that relationship produces alienation and exploitation. This labor has been interpreted as distinct from wage labor relations as digital labor is often unpaid, invisible, and conceptualized as leisure. This frame is extremely important not only to apply to communicative activities that may be considered "leisure activities" but also to activities that may be deemed necessary for securing employment in a field like journalism.

The quote "When something online is free, you're not the customer, you're the product," uttered (but not coined) by Jonathan Zittrain, (Andrejevic 2014, 193) speaks poignantly to the invisibility of the mechanisms that are making a great deal of the activities that people engage in online "free." Given the seemingly free use of social media sites, web browsers, and search engines, there have been efforts to apply Dallas Smythe's concept of the audience commodity to the digital age, situating the activity and content that is generated by users as labor as it is what creates (surplus) value for these companies (Andrejevic 2014; Cohen 2011; Coté and Pybus, 2007; Fuchs and Sevignani 2013; Terranova 2000). This involves a shift in understandings of labor outside of the typical understanding of wage-labor relations to include activity that creates value, or immaterial labor (Hardt and Negri 2000). Smythe (2001) was concerned with the relationship between what he called the 'free lunch' or the media product and the advertising that enabled it to be free. The work of the audience was to do something of value to advertisers to be worth their asking price, making the "free lunch" a fiction of sorts as well as secondary to the selling of audiences to advertisers. What was being sold effectively then, was "audience power," the attention of audiences and for them to be responsive consumers to advertisements. In the digital age, uploading content, revealing information about personal preferences, and even simply liking things on social media sites like Facebook and Twitter, can be translated into advertising sales and social networking sites are dependent on this content to profit.

The relationship between the "free lunch" and advertising in the digital age is more complicated as the medium is far more malleable and customizable than it was with traditional mass media (Andrejevic 2014). There is a far greater ability to measure audiences in the digital medium because audiences themselves rather than major companies are the content producers. Christian Fuchs (2012, 702) maintains that "audience ratings no longer need to be approximated, but permanent surveillance of user activities and user content allows the definition of precisely defined consumer groups with specific interests." Active audiences have blurred the line between producers and consumers and have led to conceptualizing users as "prosumers" (Fuchs and Seivgnani 2013). The free lunch in this context may appear to some to be the "free" use of the social networking site, which resonates with Jhally and Livant's (1986) idea that television programs are the wages paid to audiences. However, Andrejevic (2014) argues that the free lunch in the digital age is not use but organization. By this he means that companies like Google and Facebook structure digital information spaces by tailoring searches and information that is presented to users as "natural" results. This, he argues, masks the economic imperatives of these companies. For example, Google would have different results for the same query to different users but their imperative is not to provide the "best results." Instead, "it's not what you need to know, it's what you want to know, what you're most likely to click" (Andrejevic 2014, 201).

This points to the increasing commodification of the informational spaces we inhabit, which may undermine some of the democratizing potentials that these spaces could facilitate given that users have a newfound producer role in this environment. This relates not only to searches but the types of ads that are aggregated for individuals in this context. Surveillance becomes a feedback loop through "behavioral advertising" that happens automatically when using social media. This has made it so ads can be tailored to specific individuals by using past behavior to determine advertising content (McStay 2011). It is not just about aggregating data about individuals but also learning about consumer behaviors and responses. In this sense, it is possible to create controlled environments to determine what search result or ad one is most likely to click on. Surveillance is used to both turn consumer wants into production as well as to manufacture consumer wants and needs (Manzerolle and Smeltzer 2011).

The structuring of informational spaces based on past behaviors works to give users "more of the same." This is also understood as a diagrammatic view of panoptic surveillance where surveillance becomes a 'predictive technique' (Elmer 2004; Manzerolle and Smeltzer, 2011). Braman (2006, 26) characterizes this as symbolic power, which "shapes the human behaviors by manipulating the material, social and symbolic worlds, via ideas, words and images." Elmer (2004, 49) argues that in this context consumers are "both rewarded with a pre-set familiar world of images and commodities and punished by having to work at finding different and unfamiliar commodities if they attempt to opt out." When one "opts in," this environment produces an affirmative culture where one's ideas are affirmed rather than challenged and expanded. This is problematic as it reveals how "informational power" that is produced through surveillance practices, impacts the exercise of symbolic power or the ability to influence information online on the basis of which decisions are made (Braman 2006).

The idea that the free lunch may be organization is extremely important for understanding how the field of journalism has changed over time. The ability to monitor what audiences are likely to click on has produced not only the further commodification of news media but of professional and citizen journalists themselves who must also build an audience and following online. Anderson (2011) argues that, increasingly, metrics are being used in newsrooms to make editorial decisions about what stories are likely to perform best, reinforcing the "culture of the click." In many ways, these norms are entering into the professionalization practices of emerging journalists, as journalists use commodified social networking sites to build their own following and brand that they can leverage into future work. In this sense, the value that the journalist can add to an organization through their social media following may be their ticket to paid work. The entrepreneurial journalists both works as an audience member and must perpetuate the culture of the click.

A tension within the digital labor debates surrounds whether it is fair to understand people's use of social networking sites as labor and whether that relationship is exploitative and leads to alienation. This requires moving beyond Marx's understanding of the traditional wage labor relationship to understand work in the neoliberal economy, where work and play time is further blurred and unpaid professional development activities are dubiously conceptualized as "work." Many scholars have also questioned whether these types of online activities produce exploitation given that there is an element of voluntarism involved in participation and a lack of explicit coercion or force (Arvidsson 2011; Caraway 2011; Hesmondhalgh 2010). Terranova (2004, 74) notably described 'free labor' as "simultaneously voluntarily given and unwanted, enjoyed and exploited." This sentiment is echoed in Andrejevic's (2009) earlier work on YouTube, where he finds it difficult to commensurate the autonomy that users may have with the commodification of the SNS.

Given this understanding of digital participation on social networking sites, it is necessary to rethink understandings of force and coercion. For many, the idea that there is any sort of explicit force to use Twitter is an unconvincing argument. For Marx, wage labor was coerced under threat of violence because if workers do not sell their labor power, they cannot afford the commodities they need for survival. With SNS there is no threat of violence. However, Fuchs (2012) would counter that by arguing that there is ideological coercion in the sense that, as SNS become more entrenched and companies possess a monopoly over communications, there are social disadvantages and exclusions for non-participation. Further, when extending the concept of coercion beyond day to day social media use, how "voluntary" can digital labor activities be when they are a requirement for entry into a field? Individuals who are engaging in online identity branding and content creation because they must build a following or gain exposure before securing paid work cannot be said to have the voluntariness that accompanies creating content for fun. Exploitation needs to be reconsidered given the reorientation of work under neoliberalism.

Hesmondhalgh (2010) argues that unpaid work may not be a problem in and of itself and is skeptical of the sweeping application of the designation to all aspects of our daily lives. However, he does maintain that we must understand how different forms of unpaid work may contribute to patterns of inequality—perhaps in the way that unpaid domestic labor does. This is already happening in the field of journalism where "women, people of colour, Aboriginal people, and working class people are drastically underrepresented" (Cohen 2015b, 526). This reality is exacerbated by the expectation that one work unpaid internships and be precariously employed in addition to engaging in unpaid online identity branding. The affordances of entering this field become that much greater as the layers of unpaid labor amass.

ALIENATION IN TIMES OF PRECARITY

Marx (1982) characterized alienation as a separation of control over the labor process, from the products one creates, and from other workers. The application of alienation to cultural work has been criticized as eliminating subjectivity (Caraway

2011; Hesmondhalgh 2010). Their critique goes back to Smythe's (1977, 6) idea of the audience commodity and his notion that "all non-sleeping time under capitalism is work time." The idea that capitalism subsumes all, and our activities exist in an umbrella under it, perpetuating it, may be reductionist and in some ways ignorant of struggles for change. On the other hand, Smythe's observation point in many ways to how the increasing commodification of our daily lives vis-à-vis communications technologies and SNS may extend into the seemingly autonomous realm of cultural work. Further, the increasing rationalization of the news media industry has huge impacts on the level of autonomy that journalists have in their practice.

Caraway (2011) and Hesmondhalgh (2010) also argue that it is problematic to assume that all creative work should be for a wage as opposed to some other reason such as self-actualization or fulfilment. Importantly, these are legitimate outcomes that can stem from creative work (Corrigan 2015). However, focusing on these rewards ignores the real losses to stable labor in the creative industries that have occurred over the last 30 years, particularly in the journalism field. These used to be jobs that existed, and it seems problematic to assume that a passionate body of citizens will fill the lost labor of journalism just because creative work bears the possibility of bringing a sense of internal satisfaction. If this argument were applied to other fields, it would surely not hold up. Given the degree of passion involved in the production of creative work, there are tendencies to treat creative works as ends in themselves or to exploit that passion to the detriment of creators, or against their own economic interests as companies profit from these creations. The labor involved in investigative journalism, for example, can take weeks, months and sometimes years to produce. This hard-hitting journalism is not likely to be replaced by unpaid citizens.

Workers in the journalism field may have some degree of autonomy, but in an increasingly rationalized and competitive industry, where do workers stand in relationship to those processes? Nikolas Rose (1999) and Gillian Ursell (2000) well articulate autonomy under neoliberalism by pointing to the processes of commodification and self-commodification that one must embark on to improve their chances of employment. One is autonomous in the sense that they are alone and individually responsible. If they are not successful, they only have themselves to blame. In many ways understanding media as ubiquitous parallels understandings of the ideal neo-liberal worker. The ideal neoliberal worker is flexible, adaptable, and mobile, blurring the lines between productive and leisure time. Cohen (2015b, 517) explains that the entrepreneurial journalist is:

> an enterprising individual who does not rely on traditional media organizations and who can chart her own path to success. She is an ideal neo-liberal worker: flexible, unattached, and adaptable. She embraces new technologies and 'innovative' practices to reinvent journalism as socially relevant, but also profitable. Well calibrated to market needs, the entrepreneurial journalist engages in perpetual self-commodification and self-marketing. Independent of any

audience, she builds an audience around her personal brand, develops, creates, and promotes content, and constantly hustles for work.

The entrepreneurial journalist participates not only in the commodification of news media, but also of themselves through online identity branding. These processes of commodification have been connected to many other aspects of digital labor, and as Manzerolle (2010) argues "the relative alienation and precarity of this category of workers is masked by the triumphalism of the prosumer." The question then becomes, do these levels of alienation and precarity shape the opportunities that are available to journalists, do they shape the types of content that journalists may pursue?

The idea that one must build a brand and sell that brand for future work means we are already speaking in the language of commodity exchanges. Cohen (2015b) argues that the competitiveness and pressures of being an entrepreneurial journalist entices journalists to create not what they want to write about, but what they can sell. In an environment where you bear all of the risk, it is unlikely that you will step outside of the bounds of industry expectations. The news media industry more than ever is beholden to audiences and quickly produced journalism. Precariously employed journalists are unlikely to pursue lengthy or investigative stories and this has a bearing on the role and capacity of news media more broadly.

IMPLICATIONS FOR THE FIELD OF JOURNALISM

Critical political economists have often focused on the role that journalism ought to play for a functioning democracy to exist and to hold those in positions of power to account. More attention must be paid to how the precarious state of media work and how the expectations for professionalization might hinder those visions from being realized. Deuze (2005) points out the traditional journalistic values, including the public service ideal, neutrality, credibility, autonomy, immediacy, and legitimacy are likely to be challenged by the introduction of social media into the daily lives of journalists. Research is already showing that social media use is not associated with traditional norms of objectivity and scrutiny (Hedman and Djerf-Pierre 2013). Journalists are being encouraged to adopt a market-oriented identity in their practice, whether that be as a freelancer or within the context of a media organization. This orientation narrows the aims and capacities of journalists to realize the promise of ubiquitous media and the role that journalism ought to play in society according to critical political economists.

It is important to consider what will happen to the field of journalism in the context of the reorganization of journalistic labor. We are certainly seeing more ideas being disseminated and perhaps more "journalists" than ever, but what about those who are trying to establish paid work in the field? The "culture of the click" and the increasingly metrics-based approach to news media leads us further in the direction of commodification of information. When journalists are required to work for free in order to work for money, this creates class barriers for who can pursue a career in journalism. The risk involved in this career path may lend itself to those who come from more privileged backgrounds and can "afford to work for free," at least for a time. This certainly has dire consequences for the type of media that is and has the potential to be produced.

It is important not to uncritically celebrate the newfound autonomy of creative workers and praise the digital age of collaboration and prosumption as some theorists have done. If these activities are not considered work, and freelancers are constantly struggling to find paid opportunities, this could present real losses to journalism itself as it becomes a less viable career option and livelihood. It is also problematic to deny contradictions and exceptions to the total commodification of creativity. What is clear, is that the work of journalism in fulfilling the role of a social good or that of a "watchdog," cannot be replaced by an army of enthusiastic citizen journalists or aspiring journalists working for free. There needs to be policy interventions to address this environment. Some of the most convincing solutions that have been proposed include a universal basic income or allowing freelance journalists to unionize (Cohen 2015b), which may set the wheels in motion to improve working conditions across the board. These solutions may even assist with providing journalists with more autonomy to pursue content that resembles a public good rather than a commodity. However, for any of these solutions to be realized, the activities of journalists who brand themselves online, build a following, promote and create content, and embrace the entrepreneurial spirit, needs to be recognized as work, despite its existence outside of typical wage-labor relations and the fact that it may bring some other kind of intrinsic reward.

REFERENCES

Anderson, Chris W. 2011. "Between creative and quantified audiences: Web metrics and changing patterns of newswork in local US newsrooms." *Journalism* 12 (5):550–566.

Andrejevic, Mark. 2009. "Exploiting YouTube: Contradictions of User-Generated Labor." In *The YouTube Reader*, edited by Pelle Snickars and Patrick Vonderau, 406–423. 2nd ed. Stockholm: National Library of Sweden.

———. 2014. "'Free Lunch' in the Digital Era : Organization Is the New Content." In *The Audience Commodity in a Digital Age: Revisiting a Critical Theory of Commercial Media*, edited by Lee McGuigan and Vincent Manzerolle, 192–206. New York: Peter Lang.

Arvidsson, Adam. 2011. "Ethics and Value in Customer Co-Production." *Marketing Theory* 11 (3): 261–278. doi:10.1177/1470593111408176.

Baker, C. Edwin. 2006. *Media Concentration and Democracy: Why Ownership Matters*. New York: Cambridge University Press.

Banet-Weiser, Sarah. 2012. *Authentic TM: The Politics of Ambivalence in a Brand Culture*. New York: New York University Press.

Bourdieu, Pierre. 2005. "The Political Field, the Social Science Field, and the Journalistic Field." In *Bourdieu and the Journalistic Field*, edited by Rodney Benson, 29–47. Cambridge; Malden, MA: Polity Press.

Bousquet, Marc. 2008. *How the University Works: Higher Education and the Low-Wage Nation*. New York: New York University Press.

Braman, Sandra. 2006. *Change of State Information, Policy, and Power*. Cambridge, MA: MIT Press.

Bruns, Axel. 2008. *Blogs, Wikipedia, Second Life, and Beyond: From Production to Produsage*. New York: Peter Lang.

Caraway, Brett. 2011. "Audience Labor in the New Media Environment: A Marxian Revisiting of the Audience Commodity." *Media, Culture & Society* 33 (5): 693–708. doi:10.1177/0163443711404463.

Cohen, Nicole S. 2012. "Cultural Work as a Site of Struggle: Freelancers and Exploitation." *tripleC: Communication, Capitalism & Critique. Open Access Journal for a Global Sustainable Information Society* 10 (2): 141–155.

———. 2015a. "From Pink Slips to Pink Slime: Transforming Media Labor in a Digital Age." *The Communication Review* 18 (2): 98–122. doi:10.1080/10714421.2015.1031996.

———. 2015b. "Entrepreneurial Journalism and the Precarious State of Media Work." *South Atlantic Quarterly* 114 (3): 513–533. doi:10.1215/00382876-3130723.

Compton, James R., and Paul Benedetti. 2010. "Labor, New Media and the Institutional Restructuring of Journalism." *Journalism Studies* 11 (4): 487–499. doi:10.1080/14616701003638350.

Cooper, Mark. 2005. "Hyper-Commercialism and the Media : The Threat to Journalism and Democratic Discourse." In *Converging Media, Diverging Politics: A Political Economy of News Media in the United States and Canada*, edited by David Skinner, James Robert Compton, and Mike Gasher, 117–144. Lanham, MD.: Lexington Books.

Corrigan, Thomas. 2015. "Media and Cultural Industries Internships: A Thematic Review and Digital Labor Parallels." *tripleC: Communication, Capitalism & Critique. Open Access Journal for a Global Sustainable Information Society* 13 (2): 336–350.

Coté, Mark, and Jennifer Pybus. 2007. "Learning to Immaterial Labor 2.0: Immaterial and Affective Labor: Explored." *Ephemera* 7 (1): 88–106.

Deuze, Mark. 2005. "What Is Journalism?: Professional Identity and Ideology of Journalists Reconsidered." *Journalism* 6 (4): 442–464. doi:10.1177/1464884905056815.

Elmer, Greg. 2004. *Profiling Machines: Mapping the Personal Information Economy*. Cambridge, MA: MIT Press.

Featherstone, Mike. 2009. "Ubiquitous Media: An Introduction." *Theory, Culture & Society* 26 (2–3): 1–22. doi:10.1177/0263276409103104.

Flew, Terry, and Stuart Cunningham. 2010. "Creative Industries after the First Decade of Debate." *The Information Society* 26 (2): 113–123. doi:10.1080/01972240903562753.

Francouer, Chantal. 2015. "A Foucauldian Foray into How Power Operates When Journalists and Public Relations Officers Meet." In *Toward 2020: New Directions in Journalism Education*, edited by Gene Allen, Stephanie Craft, Christopher Waddell, and Mary Lynn Young, 28–45. Toronto: Ryerson Journalism Research Centre. http://ryersonjournalism.ca/2014/11/18/toward-2020-new-directions-in-journalism-education- journal/.

Fuchs, Christian. 2016. "Dallas Smythe Today—the Audience Commodity, the Digital Labor Debate, Marxist Political Economy and Critical Theory. Prolegomena to a Digital Labor Theory of Value."

In *Marx and the Political Economy of the Media*, edited by Christian Fuchs and Vincent Mosco, 522–599. Leiden; Boston: Brill.

Fuchs, Christian, and Sebastian Sevignani. 2013. "What Is Digital Labor? What Is Digital Work? What's Their Difference? And Why Do These Questions Matter for Understanding Social Media?" *Triplec: Communication, Capitalism & Critique. Open Access Journal for a Global Sustainable Information Society* 11 (2): 237–293.

Hardt, Michael, and Antonio Negri. 2000. *Empire*. Cambridge, MA: Harvard University Press.

Harvey, David. 2006. *Neoliberalism: A Brief History*. Oxford: Oxford University Press.

Hearn, Alison. 2008. "'Meat, Mask, Burden': Probing the Contours of the Branded 'Self'." *Journal of Consumer Culture* 8 (2): 197–217. doi:10.1177/1469540508090086.

Hedman, Ulrika, and Monika Djerf-Pierre. 2013. "The Social Journalist." *Digital Journalism* 1 (3): 368–385. doi:10.1080/21670811.2013.776804.

Herman, Edward S, and Noam Chomsky. 1988. *Manufacturing Consent: The Political Economy of the Mass Media*. New York: Pantheon Books.

Hesmondhalgh, David. 2010. "User-Generated Content, Free Labor and the Cultural Industries: Digital Labor: Workers, Authors, Citizens." *Ephemera* 10 (3/4): 267–284.

Jenkins, Henry. 2006. *Convergence Culture: Where Old and New Media Collide*. New York, : New York University Press.

Jhally, Sut, and Bill Livant. 1986. "Watching as Working: The Valorization of Audience Consciousness." *Journal of Communication* 36 (3): 124–143. doi:10.1111/j.1460-2466.1986.tb01442.x.

Kuehn, Kathleen, and Thomas F. Corrigan. 2013. "Hope Labor: The Role of Employment Prospects in Online Social Production." *The Political Economy of Communication* 1 (1). http://www.polecom.org/index.php/polecom/article/view/9.

Levine, Meredith, Paul Benedetti, and Mike Gasher. 2015. "Selling Digital Dreams: 'Entrepreneurial Journalism,' the Decline of Public Service Reporting, and the Role of Journalism Education." In *Toward 2020: New Directions in Journalism Education*, edited by Gene Allen, Stephanie Craft, Christopher Waddell, and Mary Lynn Young, 82–110. Toronto: Ryerson Journalism Research Centre. http://ryersonjournalism.ca/2014/11/ 18/toward-2020-new-directions-in-journalism-education- journal/.

Lewchuk, Wayne, Michelynn Laflèche, Stephanie Procyk, Charlene Cook, Diane Dyson, Luin Goldring, Karen Lior, *et al*. 2015. *The Precarity Penalty: The Impact of Employment Precarity on Individuals, Households and Communities—and What to Do about It*. http://www.deslibris.ca/ID/246690.

Manzerolle, Vincent. 2010. "Mobilizing the Audience Commodity: Digital Labor in a Wireless World." *Ephemera: Theory & Politics in Organization* 10 (3/4): 455–469.

Manzerolle, Vincent, and Sandra Smeltzer. 2011. "Consumer Databases and the Commercial Mediation of Identity: A Medium Theory." *Surveillance & Society* 8 (3): 323–337.

Marx, Karl. 1982. *Economic and Philosophic Manuscript*. London: Lawrence & Wishart.

McChesney, Robert Waterman. 2004. *The Problem of the Media US Communication Politics in the Twenty-First Century*. New York: Monthly Review Press.

McStay, Andrew. 2010. "Profiling Phorm: An Autopoietic Approach to the Audience-as-Commodity." *Surveillance & Society* 8 (3): 310–322.

Mensing, Donica, and David Ryfe. 2013. "Blueprint for Change: From the Teaching Hospital to the Entrepreneurial Model of Journalism Education." Accessed March 26. http://www.academia.edu/3412374/Blueprint_for_Change_From_the_Teaching_Hospital_to_the_Entrepreneurial_Model_of_Journalism_Education.

Neff, Gina. 2012. *Venture Labor: Work and the Burden of Risk in Innovative Industries.* Cambridge, MA: MIT Press.

Picard, Robert G. 2015. "Deficient Tutelage: Challenges of Contemporary Journalism Education." In *Toward 2020: New Directions in Journalism Education*, edited by Gene Allen, Stephanie Craft, Christopher Waddell, and Mary Lynn Young, 4–10. Toronto: Ryerson Journalism Research Centre. http://ryersonjournalism.ca/2014/11/ 18/toward-2020-new-directions-in-journalism-education- journal/.

Rose, Nikolas S. 1999. *Powers of Freedom: Reframing Political Thought.* New York: Cambridge University.

Shapiro, Ivor. 2015. "To Turn or to Burn: Shifting the Paradigm for Journalism Education." In *Toward 2020: New Directions in Journalism Education*, edited by Gene Allen, Stephanie Craft, Christopher Waddell, and Mary Lynn Young, 11–27. Toronto: Ryerson Journalism Research Centre. http://ryersonjournalism.ca/2014/11/ 18/toward-2020-new-directions-in-journalism-education- journal/.

Shirky, Clay. 2008. *Here Comes Everybody: The Power of Organizing without Organizations.* New York: Penguin.

Skinner, David, and Mike Gasher. 2005. "So Much by so Few: Media Policy and Ownership in Canada." In *Converging Media, Diverging Politics: A Political Economy of News Media in the United States and Canada*, edited by David Skinner, James Robert Compton, and Mike Gasher, 51–76. Lanham, MD; Oxford, UK: Lexington Books.

Smythe, Dallas W. 1977. "Communications: Blindspot of Western Marxism." *CTheory* 1 (3): 1–27.

———. 2001. "On the Audience Commodity and Its Work." In *Media and Cultural Studies: Keyworks*, edited by Meenakshi Gigi Durham and Douglas M. Kellner, 253–279. Oxford: Blackwell.

Tapscott, Don, and Anthony D Williams. 2006. *Wikinomics: How Mass Collaboration Changes Everything.* New York: Portfolio.

Terranova, Tiziana. 2000. "Free Labor: Producing Culture for the Digital Economy." *Social Text* 18 (2 63): 33–58. doi:10.1215/01642472-18-2_63-33.

———. 2004. *Network Culture: Politics for the Information Age.* London; Ann Arbor, MI: Pluto Press. http://search.ebscohost.com/login.aspx?direct=true&scope=site&db=nlebk&db=nlabk &AN=167911.

Ursell, Gillian. 2000. "Television Production: Issues of Exploitation, Commodification and Subjectivity in UK Television Labour Markets." *Media, Culture & Society* 22 (6): 805–825. doi: 10.1177/0163443006006

Vos, Tim P., and Jane B. Singer. 2016. "Media Discourse about Entrepreneurial Journalism." *Journalism Practice* 10 (2): 143–159. doi:10.1080/17512786.2015.1124730.

Vosko, Leah F. 2010. *Managing the Margins: Gender, Citizenship, and the International Regulation of Precarious Employment.* Oxford: Oxford University Press.

Watson, H. G. 2016. "Postmedia Cuts 90 Jobs and Merges Newsrooms in Ottawa, Edmonton, Calgary and Vancouver." *J Source: The Canadian Journalism Project.* January 19. http://www.j-source.ca/ article/postmedia-begins-company-wide-layoffs-calls-newsroom-meetings.

Wolff, Michael. 2014. "Ezra Klein, Glenn Greenwald and the Odd Rise of Personal Brand Journalism." *The Guardian*, January 6, sec. Opinion. https://www.theguardian.com/commentisfree/2014/ jan/06/ezra-klein-leave-washington-post-personal-brand.

CHAPTER EIGHT

Youth Practices Online AND Offline

Ubiquitous Tools and Meaningful Contexts

PILAR LACASA, JULIÁN DE LA FUENTE, AND KATIUSKA MANZUR

INTRODUCTION[1]

In this chapter, we understand ubiquity as being linked to the concepts of presence, invisibility and support. From this standpoint, we examine the practices of children who use mobile devices to capture digital photos and video. Many consider photography and video, as well as devices such as mobile phones and tablets, to be ubiquitous in modern society (see, for example, Goggin 2011; Hand 2012; Medoff and Fink 2012). Based on the concepts of ubiquity (Weiser 1998) and the chronotope, which Bakhtin (1981) describes as a temporal and spatial backdrop, we seek to put forward a theoretical model that allows for the interpretation of these practices. We understand practices as activities, organized and widely enacted within particular cultures, which involve interaction with other people and material tools. The empirical data we discuss below comes from a two-year ethnographic study which aimed to analyze the online and offline practices of a young person using mobile devices. Children and adolescents make for interesting subjects in this regard because they anticipate or infer particular functions of technological tools which can often go unnoticed by adults.

While our general aim is to create a theoretical model to further develop the concept of ubiquitous practices, the specific goals of this paper are the following:

1. To analyze the practices of children when interacting with ubiquitous mobile devices in their daily lives;

2. To explore how those instruments mediate the interaction between online and offline environments;
3. To explain how these ubiquitous tools, used in specific contexts, allow for the construction of meaning through the processes involved in building digital micro-stories.

After presenting the main concepts supporting our theoretical model, we provide data using this theoretical framework to inform our interpretation. The conclusions will provide a reflection on how the concepts of ubiquity and the chronotope guide or inform adolescents' practices online and offline.

THEORETICAL MODEL

For the purposes of this chapter, we assume that technology becomes meaningful in relation to practices or, more precisely, that technology cannot be understood separate from practices (Díaz and Ekman 2011; Gitelman 2006). Figure 1 shows the elements of our proposed theoretical model, which integrates technological tools and the human practices in certain spatial and temporal contexts (Luria and Vygotsky [1930] 1992). We thus adopt a socio-cultural approach, looking beyond the individual to interpret these practices as a part of culture.

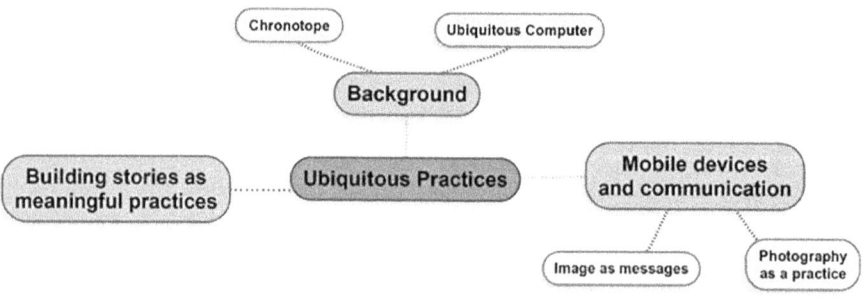

Figure 8.1. Theoretical model: Main concepts. Source: the authors.

In our study, we focus on cultural practices that relate, on one hand, to adolescents' use of mobile devices and, on the other, to the spatial-temporal context that gives meaning to particular practices. As we demonstrate below, the ideas of Mark Weiser and Mikhail Bakhtin, which are central to our theoretical framework, converge and supplement each other.

Background

Ubiquitous media and chronotopes both relate to the concepts of presence, invisibility and support, understood as help and scaffolding. They each provide the context for particular practices and should be understood in conjunction with each other even though they stem from different intellectual traditions. We will now look more closely at these two concepts, including recent developments.

Weiser (1996) argues that "Our computers should be like our childhood: an invisible foundation that is quickly forgotten but always with us, and effortlessly used throughout our lives." Invisible instruments are those which are not are at the upper level of our consciousness. These technologies disappear as people use them increasingly automatically. Weiser and Brown (1996) also speak about calm technology, which engages both "the centre and the periphery of our attention, and in fact moves back and forth between the two." The periphery is what goes unnoticed. Once the tool has been mastered using the main focus of our attention, it then shifts to the background. Ubiquity, as per this approach, does not require active attention; technologies disappear into the background and support particular practices. What matters is not technology itself, but its relationship with the people who use it. When a technology has shifted to the periphery of our attention, it is possible to focus on other targets, expanding our ability to undertake new practices (Carter 2013).

This idea resonates with the Bakhtinian idea of the chronotope. In describing the chronotope, Bakhtin argues that time and space are intrinsically connected; they constitute a whole. Bakhtin also made reference to the fact that chronotopes are not absolute, and there are relationships between them. No perspective is absolute; rather, perspectives are the product of particular temporal-spatial contexts. The third trait that Bakhtin attributed to the chronotope is that it is the framework that organizes social relationships. Bakhtin developed this concept by studying the ways of understanding the world found in literature (Bakhtin 1981; Morson and Emerson 1990). He argues that chronotopes give meaning to personal and group experiences: "Chronotopes…are the ground essential for the…representability of events. They are not contained in plots, but they make typical plots possible" (Morson and Emerson 1990).

Relating the contexts of human practices to a particular space and time, Bakhtin considers a chronotope to be an unconscious background, invisible at first glance. From his perspective, time and space are linked and form a whole that can only be separated abstractly. In short, space and time, interlinked in the concept of the chronotope, are an invisible context that supports practices and contributes to building the meaning of those practices (Hernan and Dade-Robertson 2016; Foth 2011).

Mobile Devices and Communication

We consider mobile devices and smartphones as ubiquitous because they are present and invisible, and they support people's practices (de Reuver, Nikou, and Bouwman 2016; Westlund and Bjur 2014). These technologies have transformed the ways in which people communicate and learn (Peña-Ayala 2016; Vanden Abeele 2016;). They have also generated a convergent world that creates new forms of space and time, as well as a new kind of audience (Nightingale 2011). boyd (2014) describes these developments in relation to the ways in which adolescents behave. The mobile technologies mentioned above are linked to certain practices, through which words, images, and sounds are shared through platforms that allow users to build and rebuild media content. We will describe the development multimodal discourses (Kress 2010; Rowsell 2013) supported by mobile devices, especially in relation to photography, in the section below.

Image as Message. Various authors have emphasized how images are conveyors of messages open to interpretation. Barthes (1981), for example, explores photography in his work *Camera Lucida*. He considers an image to be an act of communication with three elements: the photographer, the viewer, and the object (reference). He is also interested in the content of the messages, arguing that photographic images are an analogy of reality involving two types of messages, denotative and connotative.

- The denotative message is the analogic content, i.e., the scene, object or landscape. It is associated with description.
- The connotative message is concomitant with a certain interpretation of the image. It relates to aesthetics or ideology and is immersed in culture.

Sontag (2001) explores similar ideas but argues that photographs are valued because they provide information; photographers, however, alter and expand our notion of what deserves to be looked at and of what we have a right to observe. Sontag emphasizes the social perspective in the construction of meaning because it is spatially and temporally situated.

Recently, Kapidzic and Herring (2015) analyzed the self-image or self-branding that young people project on the Internet. From an ethnographic perspective, Miller *et al.* (2016) explore how people use social networks in different contexts around the world, particularly focusing on digital photography presented on Facebook. In their opinion, the content of social networking profiles is more important than the platform, and indeed it migrates from one platform to another, being transformed when it is interpreted in new and different contexts.

Photography as a Practice. Bourdieu and Boltanski (1990) view photography as a human practice linked to value systems which are dependent on particular social groups. In the context of digital photography, Hand (2012) also considers photography to be a ubiquitous practice. In his opinion, digital technologies have transformed the practices of "making, storing, distributing and displaying images" (4). Those practices are dependent on particular tools such as cameras integrated into smartphones (Gomez, Cruz, and Lehmuskallio 2016). The camera has become ubiquitous because it is something people carry on them, embedded in their smartphones, and which goes unnoticed. Not only have practices changed, but the symbolic value of photographs has changed, too, because photography is increasingly present and accessible in everyday life. As Hand (2012, 9) argues, "The ubiquitous presence of the camera changes what can be, and is, seen, recorded, discussed and remembered, making the visualization of public and private life bound up with relations of power, expertise, and authority."

Not only is the camera ubiquitous, but so is the content, i.e., the image, shared through the Internet. In order to understand this interpretation of ubiquity, one must go beyond the consideration of isolated images. Photography invades various domains of contemporary society. That is not simply to say that it has spread exponentially due to technological changes, but rather that its technical *and* social components have been transformed, and photography must thus be understood in new economic, social, political and cultural contexts (Elkins 2011).

To summarize, photography as a practice is not related only to the use of digital tools; its contexts have expanded and allowed it to become ubiquitous, and it has a particular meaning in the contexts where it is generated or interpreted.

Building Stories as a Cultural Practice

We will now look at how ubiquitous digital tools, present in specific times and spaces, relate to culture. Before we do so, it is important to clarify the concept of cultural practice. We assume the following definition, expressed in the context of historic-cultural psychology:

> Our definition starts by noting that practices are actions. The term 'practices' refers to what people do—that is, to matters that are open to observation by the researcher and by others in a social group. Thus, one of the appeals of attention to practices lies in their observability. However, what is open to observation is not behavior in the behaviorist sense but rather meaningful action, action that is situated in a context and open to interpretation. (Miller and Goodnow 1995, 6)

Practices, therefore, must be interpreted in the context of a culture, and are closely linked to daily activity and routine. They are immersed in and stem from social structures, where a set of social actors assign them a particular meaning. We will focus on the construction of stories as an example of a ubiquitous cultural practice in specific temporal-spatial contexts.

The work of Bakhtin (1981) once again helps us to explore the construction of stories, even if they are in the form of micro-blogs on the Internet. Microblogging is "the writing of short messages on the Web designed for self-reporting about what one is doing, thinking, or feeling at any moment" (Barton and Lee 2013, 38). The author, the characters, the narrator, and space/time are all dimensions that need to be considered. All of them are developed in Bakhtin's work:

- The author is present through the characters; he or she controls them and gives them an identity.
- Often, the narrator provides unity. Originality may be linked to the way in which the elements are combined.
- The space and the time of the narrative; the chronotope. Space supports the action, and time is present through the plot.

METHOD

We will now present a study we undertook in Spain with children and adolescents, mostly throughout 2014 and 2015. We designed workshops in cooperation with teachers and institutional coordinators from particular communities. Members of the research team worked as observers.

This research is part of a broader project, based on an ethnographic perspective (Pink *et al.* 2015, 3) and a case study (Yin [1984] 2009). That is, we adopt an inductive approach, in which the design of the study evolves due to both the role of theory as well as the researcher's own involvement. We focus on the processes of human activities, not just on their products. The project examines adolescents' activities within the framework of a mobile culture, including practices which involve constructing meaning (Goggin and Hjorth 2014).

Participants

This particular study, which began in October 2014, focuses on a girl, who we will refer to as Nadia, who is 10 years of age as of 2016. We have tracked her presence on the internet and also held informal interviews with her. Nadia had an iPod when she first attended our workshops, but she did not have an online presence or social media profiles. She now has an iPhone 5S. Following her attendance at one of our workshop, Nadia opened an Instagram account, which is currently private, meaning only her followers can view it. She has more than 150 followers and follows around the same number of people herself. More recently, she has become a regular user of *Musical.ly*, a social network that allows users to create and share short videos.[2] On this social network she has 173 followers, she follows 41 users and has given 1,795 likes. We must highlight that Nadia is the third of four sisters and the older two, who are currently 12 and 15 years old, are very active on online networks.

We explore Nadia's relationships with photography and video as ubiquitous phenomena in online and offline contexts of her everyday life. The decision to focus on a single subject through a case study is justified as her social practices allow us to reflect in depth on the proposed theoretical concepts. We will show how particular activities can be understood as practices, mediated by ubiquitous tools, which support the construction of meaning.

Context

From October 2014, Nadia attended three educational workshops organized by the research team in an informal context and one in her school environment. These workshops seek to facilitate online and offline interactions, mediated by digital technology, to develop young people's digital literacy (Lacasa, de la Fuente, and Martín-Garrido 2016). They are organized in community scenarios both in and outside of schools. The participants are children and young people aged between 8 and 14. The workshops last approximately three hours.

We used social network apps, particularly Instagram and Vine. Our contact with young people at the workshops allowed us to closely follow the activities some of them engaged in, including Nadia. The data collected using ethnographic techniques came from several sources: (a) audio and video recording from the workshops, (b) Nadia's online and offline multimodal productions, stored on her mobile devices (c) formal and informal interviews conducted twice a month since 2014, and (d) the researchers' summaries.

Analysis

We adhered to the following principles and guidelines, inspired by the theoretical approach outlined above, when carrying out the analysis. First, we adopted the general frameworks of visual ethnography (Pink 2013) and cultural anthropology (Horst and Miller 2012) when interpreting Nadia's practices; second, we analyzed these practices in specific spatial and temporal contexts; third, these practices were understood in relation to those people who are present in Nadia's social environment, i.e., family, schoolmates, friends and also the research team; finally, the qualitative analysis seeks to reveal the process through which her participation in online and offline communities is influenced.

RESULTS

Ubiquitous Mobile Devices and the Chronotope: Practices in Context

The data we are going to discuss in this section came from one of the workshops Nadia attended which was organized by the research team to facilitate the development of literacy skills related to digital technology. We define this literacy as the ability to manage the communicative possibilities created by a digital mobile instrument (Jenkins, Ford, and Green. 2013). As such, we are much more interested in how people approach digital tools than in the technological instruments themselves. These workshops are activities oriented to develop digital literacies encouraging a conscious use of multimodal discourses in communicative online and offline scenarios (Lacasa, de la Fuente, and Martín-Garrido 2016). During the workshop conversations, the researchers and other participants drew the girl's attention to online audiences who are often far away. With support from the researcher, Nadia began to understand that mobile phones and tablets are tools to create specific messages or stories, and a way to say something to someone that she may not know personally.

Figure 8.2 shows various scenes from the workshop. These spaces and times are reflected in three specific examples included in Figure 8.2. We can see three situations, organized by three chronotopes. First is a large group situation, dominated by computers, and organized, perhaps, according to a school-style pattern. In the second, children were working in small groups, which also favored activity in pairs. In the third, children worked by themselves to develop digital literacies. In this case, time and space are intrinsically connected.

We will look at a particular situation in which a certain space and time shaped social interactions between the participants, another feature of Bakhtin's chronotope. The small group scenario that appears in Figure 8.2 shows how the researcher helped to generate an idea of an audience. She wanted to show the children that a photograph is indeed a form of communication. The researcher took advantage of a resource in the physical space where the workshop took place. It was an open space with corners that allow for different types of activities. In this case, a trip around the world was used as a theme; children took pictures to tell other people, audiences far away, that they were astronauts traveling around the world.

Each of the three situations appearing in Figure 8.2 makes sense in relation to each other. The large group situation, which took place at the beginning and at the end of the workshop, generated shared goals, which are further defined in small groups, where the strategies to achieve them are generated. Thus, the large group is what gave meaning to the small group activities, as well as to Nadia's individual productions.

Figure 8.2. Multiple spaces and times. Scenarios at the workshop. Source: the authors.

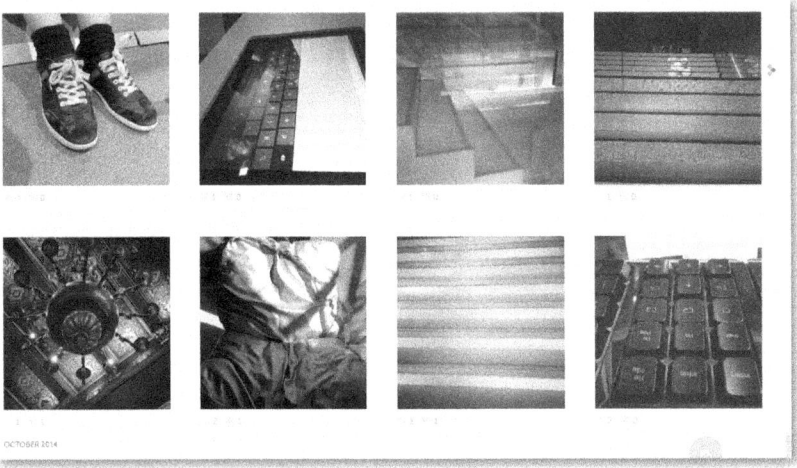

Figure 8.3. Nadia's first posts on Instagram, 2014 10 04. Source: pictures courtesy of the participant.

Figure 8.3 shows the photographs taken by Nadia in this context and published on Instagram. She published eight photos, but she took 44. All of her published photos feature close-up photography, supplying information on certain details of the situation. Only two are mid-ground shots that show people's activities during the workshop. The contents of the photographs show participants' personal details such as their sneakers or backpack; aspects related to the computer, which she shows through images of the keyboard; and, finally, some aspects of the physical space. It is important to observe that her photos focus not only on technology as an instrument, but that she also highlights geometric shapes and textures. For example, she uses the same perspective on the stairs and the keyboard.

The factors mentioned above in relation to the images included in Figure 8.3 can also be interpreted in relation to the last of the traits that Bakhtin attributes to the chronotope, i.e., a framework that organizes social relationships. Space and time define the context, and material instruments—in this case digital cameras—also form part of the context. Nadia used the camera based on her goal: to communicate information from a specific situation that would make sense to others in other contexts in which the messages are received.

Practices on a Social Network

The concept of practice is particularly important when it comes to inspiring the design of devices based on the experience of the user, in this case children. We will examine the practices related to participation in a social network such as Instagram, and the evolution of these practices over time. Nadia, one month after attending the workshop, began to use this social network with the support of her older sister. She opened a private account which remains very active. For her, Instagram became primarily a personal communication tool; by observing the content of her photographs, we can see a world that becomes increasingly personal, a channel for self-assertion that is made clear even by observing the photographs that she has removed from the account.

Figure 8.4 shows two snapshots of the account taken a year apart. The differences between these two moments in time can be interpreted in terms of the concepts of ubiquity and the chronotope, bearing in mind once again the traits of these two concepts, which now take on meaning as we observe how the girl's practices evolve over time.

Figure 8.4. Nadia on Instagram: Changes over time. Source: pictures courtesy of the participant.

First, we can refer to ubiquitous practices associated with multiple dimensions of time and space, because the images show different contexts and situations that have been transformed, including the transformation of the images that provide a general overview of the Instagram account. We can speak of ubiquity because Nadia was not conscious of her evolution; when asked, she simply said that she preferred it this way. Neither was she aware of her strategies when she participated in the network; in other words, she used Instagram as an instrument without being fully aware of how this software support her practices (Weiser 1998).

Second, the sharing of images allows users to participate in a community, but also reveals users' values. We speak of ubiquity because the software she uses supports the way she presents new values, as demonstrated by the content of the photographs that she published, even as she does not appear to be aware of this. For example, in 2016 she stopped participating in two fandom communities and she eliminated all productions associated to them: one was One Direction, a music group which is popular among adolescents and which her sister followed, and the other was another media phenomena that interested her personally: *Frozen*, the Disney film, which was popular in 2014 when she opened her account.

Finally, social practices in spatial and temporal contexts have consequences that relate to the choice of photographs for publication. Nadia seeks to present places and contexts relevant to her everyday life, which are increasingly evident in her photos, and these photos also reveal something about her. For example, the number of likes correlates to the self-image that she wants to project. Although Nadia has a private account it is clear that she is present in a public domain; at least she is forced to consciously construct a public self-image.

Ubiquitous Photography

We will interpret the pictures that are stored in Nadia's phone based on the concept of ubiquitous photography, which entails both digital technology and related practices (Hand 2012). An initial examination of the unpublished content reveals a significant distinction. First, there are screenshots which clearly show that the iPhone is being used to access social networks. Second, there are photographs that Nadia considers valuable, as she is either the photographer or the object of the photo, showing that the pictures have been taken with her mobile phone by someone helping her. Examples of each of these situations are provided in Figures 8.5 and 8.6.

Barthes' (1981) contributions are relevant to both examples. He places photography in a communicative context, and differentiates between the photographer, the object and the viewer. Digital photography transforms the relationships between these three elements. The opportunities opened up for continuous transformation allow us to refer, once again, to the concept of ubiquity. Images can be transformed with varying degrees of control in multiple spatial-temporal contexts, and new meanings can be constructed.

Figure 8.5 shows, using screenshots from Nadia's mobile phone, three different practices used in digital photography which we consider to be ubiquitous and related to particular spatial-temporal contexts. They are ubiquitous because she uses tools that allow her to manipulate the images in the way described by Weiser (1996), who describes the invisible foundation of activities which are quickly forgotten but always with us. In other words, these social supporting activities are both present and invisible. In the image on left, Nadia uses apps to create a remix, in which original images are rebuilt by combining them with other previously existing images. In this case, Nadia includes an image of a camera. The central screenshot shows SMS messages and contains a keyboard that has been transformed from its original format. She has also shared an Instagram screenshot showing one of the singers from the band One Direction. In all of these cases we can refer to photography as ubiquitous because the instrument is less important than its function, and the tool itself goes unnoticed (Bourdieu and Nice 1980). The use of tools may or may not imply a conscious control of them.

YOUTH PRACTICES ONLINE AND OFFLINE | 155

Figure 8.5. Photography from the mobile phone screen. Source: pictures courtesy of the participant.

Figure 8.6 shows another type of photographic content. These are three images of Nadia, all of which seek to achieve aesthetic effects. All these images have been processed using mobile apps, with different degrees of complexity. She plays with filters and overlays to achieve her desired aesthetic effect. In this case, ubiquity relates to the storage of these photographs as digital images on a mobile phone, ready to be published and transformed at any time and in any place. In this case, we believe the concept of ubiquity is relevant because Nadia usually transforms images with a low degree of consciousness, a process which in analog photography would be much more complicated and conscious.

Figure 8.6. Artistic effects. Source: pictures courtesy of the participant.

Ubiquity and Micro-Stories as Practices

So far, we have looked at photography as an instrument associated with particular youth practices. We will now discuss how other practices can be supported by video, offering new possibilities for expression and communication. We will focus on another social network, *Musical.ly*, which is accessed through an app developed in 2014. Users create videos which are backed by soundtracks that may or may not be included in the app. They can use different recording speeds and apply various filters and effects. It is also possible to remix content posted by other users, and these remixes can even be displayed as good examples in the app. Users can also collaborate to produce videos together. The availability of soundtracks invites users to perform activities which are comparable to karaoke. We will use a production by Nadia as an example to analyze the opportunities stemming from these kinds of tools and their design.

Figure 8.7 includes a set of frames from a production by Nadia. The song she chooses is *The Hard Knock Life*[3] from the Broadway musical *Annie*. The songs from the musical are popular on YouTube and Nadia knows them. Nadia reconstructed her everyday reality in her video production. Like the performers in the musical, she related the song to her own daily life. The video features her cleaning the house, doing some reading and writing activities, and asserting herself r own through the use of exaggerated gestures.

Figure 8.7. It's the Hard Knock Life. Nadia on *Musical.ly*. Source: pictures courtesy of the participant.

We must interpret these images in relation to the concepts of ubiquitous media and the chronotope. On the one hand, we focus on the digital tools used for producing the micro-stories. They are present and transformed everywhere, because the girl carries not only her iPhone but also her personal pictures and videos. Working with the same application, which is present in multiple contexts, makes the practice and the final production ubiquitous. On the other hand, we need to consider the idea of chronotope, i.e., a specific sociohistorical context, as an invisible foundation that supports stories and contributes to building shared meanings.

We will now explore the elements of this micro-story that may influence the design of new products considered as ubiquitous media. First, this app allows the user to practice narrative construction by providing elements and features that support the process. The times and spaces in the narrative are multiple. The micro-story is recorded in a particular everyday context, though it was inspired by content found on the Internet (i.e., the song). In this case, the narrator is present through the lyrics of the song, and the song is the text that guides the activity of the character.

Second, recording within the app, by using the functions of the iPhone, allows the user to connect with other people and also to share personal or group creations with them. Therefore, the media production is expressive and communicative, immersed in the context of the social network.

Third, multimodal narratives are built, which are considered to be narratives in which multiple discursive elements compose the story. In short, these elements have meaning together, as a whole, because the app facilitates the potential for ubiquitous creative processes.

Fourth, the stories develop from people's online and offline daily lives. The lines separating these two worlds are increasingly blurred. The Internet allows for specific ways of being in the world and of representing the self in the world. We have already pointed out, for example, how the online world provides resources in the form of content that can be reused and repurposed in new contexts and contribute to the development of a self-image.

CONCLUSION

The goal of this paper was to propose a theoretical model to analyze children's and adolescents' practices in an environment characterized by ubiquitous media (Weiser 1991) and located in multiple spatial-temporal contexts or chronotopes (Bakhtin 1981), which constitute the background upon which social meaning is constructed. As we have attempted to demonstrate in the case study above, the concept of ubiquity is linked to the traits of presence, invisibility and support.

The main results stemming from the interpretations proposed could guide the design process for ubiquitous mobile devices, taking into account the way in which they are present in the everyday lives of young people. These conclusions are organized in relation to the proposed objectives.

Our first objective was to analyze adolescents' relationships with smart and ubiquitous mobile devices in the context of their daily lives. Our main conclusion is that they are beginning to be used unconsciously because they are increasingly present in their environment. In addition, these instruments make sense within particular spatial-temporal contexts or chronotopes.

This use, however, does not imply that young people are able to fully harness the possibilities of the instrument in online and offline environments by themselves. Nadia's attendance at the workshop and the conversations we had with her over time show that she was participating in collective endeavors. The need for collaboration to use ubiquitous media could be linked to the opportunities they offer as tools for representing the world; this is similar to what happened in the past with other technologies, such as writing. These abilities are learned by participating in collaborative social and cultural activities as demonstrated in our case study above.

Our second goal was to explore how ubiquitous tools enable participation in social networks in multiple contexts that imply the use of multimodal language. Mobile devices are communication technologies that extend people's creative abilities in online and offline environments. They simplify processes of representation that were much more complicated when using analog technology. Participation through media production is not only about young people using these digital media properly, but also about them creating through the use of new discourses and language, and sharing their creations in collaborative environments where they can be accessed alongside other people's creations.

We saw how Nadia harnessed the potential of photography as a form of expression and representation of the world, taking materials from the Internet and placing them in new contexts, projecting onto them new meanings which disclose personal and group values. Remix processes are of particular importance here. This is what happens, for example, when she takes the images that are present in fan communities, and begins to use them with the help of her older sister. Nadia becomes an active participant who creates and shares her own productions and those of other people on the Internet, demonstrating how the Internet has become a means of self-expression and communication.

Our third objective was to explore how ubiquitous tools, present in particular spatial and temporal contexts, allow for the construction of meaning through the building of digital micro-stories. Creating stories has been placed at the very root of meaning construction processes (Bruner 2002), which is why we believe it is necessary to explore how ubiquitous media help young people interpret the world. In this case, the ability to remix what others have created has generated specific ways of constructing meaning through micro-stories.

The way Nadia uses Musical.ly should be understood not as an absolute, since this app could be replaced by another at any time. What is important here are the possibilities that it opens up for participation, and the skills Nadia puts into practice. This case study shows how she uses the many possibilities offered by technology, much of the time in collaborative situations. Her digital media projects show how she put three new skills into practice: (a) skills related to the representation of the world; for example, the performance of the song from *Annie* in which she plays the main character, inspired by a YouTube production and supported using songs and sounds from the Internet; (b) the use of multimedia content and tools, where the combination of image and sound allows for the construction of new meanings resulting in new multimodal discourses; and (c) the related technical skills required to select frames, edit them and combine them.

NOTES

1. We would like to thank the Spanish Ministry of Education and the University of Alcalá for their support in writing this paper. Thank you so much also to the girl involved in the case study for her participation and co-operation during the study, and to her family.
2. Instagram: https://www.instagram.com/ and Musicaly.ly: http://musical.ly
3. YouTube video http://bit.ly/2cQ8eXA. Lyrics http://bit.ly/2cGy93j

REFERENCES

Bakhtin, Mikhail M. 1981. *The Dialogic Imagination: Four Essays*. Edited by Michael Holquist. Austin: University of Texas Press.
Barthes, Roland. 1981. *Camera Lucida: Reflections on Photography*. 1st American ed. New York: Hill and Wang.
Barton, David, and Carman Lee. 2013. *Language Online: Investigating Digital Texts and Practices*. Milton Park, Abingdon, Oxon: Routledge.
Bourdieu, Pierre, and Luc Boltanski. 1990. *Photography: A Middle-Brow Art*. Cambridge: Polity Press.
Bourdieu, Pierre, and Richard Nice. 1980. "The Aristocracy of Culture." *Media, Culture & Society* 2 (3): 225–254. doi: 10.1177/016344378000200303.
boyd, danah. 2014. *It's Complicated: The Social Lives of Networked Teens*. New Haven: Yale University Press.
Bruner, Jerome. 2002. *Making Stories. Law, Literature, Life*. Cambridge, MA & London, UK: Harvard University Press.
Carter, Michael J. 2013. "The Hermeneutics of Frames and Framing: An Examination of the Media's Construction of Reality." *SAGE Open* 3 (2): 1–12. doi: 10.1177/2158244013487915.
de Reuver, Mark, Shahrokh Nikou, and Harry Bouwman. 2016. "Domestication of Smartphones and Mobile Applications: A Quantitative Mixed-Method Study." *Mobile Media & Communication* 4 (3): 347–370. doi: 10.1177/2050157916649989.

Díaz, Lily, and Ulrik Ekman. 2011. "Introduction to Mobile Ubiquity in Public and Private Spaces." *Digital Creativity* 22 (3): 127–133. doi: 10.1080/14626268.2011.606819.

Elkins, James. 2011. *What Photography Is*. New York: Routledge.

Foth, Marcus. 2011. *From Social Butterfly to Engaged Citizen: Urban Informatics, Social Media, Ubiquitous Computing, and Mobile Technology to Support Citizen Engagement*. Cambridge, MA: MIT Press.

Gitelman, Lisa. 2006. *Always Already New: Media, History and the Data of Culture*. Cambridge, MA: MIT Press.

Goggin, Gerard, and Larissa Hjorth. 2014. *The Routledge Companion to Mobile Media*. London: Routledge.

Goggin, Gerard. 2011. "Ubiquitous Apps: Politics of Openness in Global Mobile Cultures." *Digital Creativity* 22 (3): 148–159. doi: 10.1080/14626268.2011.603733.

Gomez Cruz, Edgar, and Asko Lehmuskallio, eds. 2016. "Digital Photography and Everyday Life: Empirical Studies on Material Visual Practices." In *Routledge Studies in European Communication Research and Education*. London; New York: Routledge.

Hand, Martin. 2012. *Ubiquitous Photography, Digital Media and Society Series*. Cambridge, UK; Malden, MA: Polity Press.

Hernan, Luis, and Martyn Dade-Robertson. 2016. "Atmospheres of Digital Technology: Wireless Spectres and Ghosts Outside The Machine." *Digital Creativity* 27 (3): 214–233. doi: 10.1080/14626268.2016.1210647.

Horst, Heather A., and Daniel Miller. 2012. *Digital Anthropology*. English ed. London; New York: Berg.

Jenkins, Henry, Sam Ford, and Joshua Green. 2013. *Spreadable Media: Creating Value and Meaning in a Networked Culture, Postmillennial Pop*. New York: New York University Press.

Kapidzic, Sanja, and Susan C Herring. 2015. "Race, Gender, and Self-Presentation in Teen Profile Photographs." *New Media & Society* 17 (6): 958–976. doi: 10.1177/1461444813520301.

Kress, Gunther R. 2010. *Multimodality: A Social Semiotic Approach to Contemporary Communication*. London; New York: Routledge.

Lacasa, Pilar, Julián de la Fuente, and Beatriz Martín-Garrido, eds. 2016. *Social Networks and Adolescents*. Madrid: iTunes: Apple Store (iBook). http://apple.co/1QIjYpL

Lurija, Aleksandr Romanovič, Lev Semenovič Vygotskij, and Evelyn Rossiter. 1992. *Ape, Primitive Man, and Child: Essays in the History of Human Behaviour*. New York: Harvester Wheatsheaf.

Medoff, Norman J., and Edward J. Fink. 2012. *Portable Video: News and Field Production*. 6th ed. Waltham, MA: Focal Press.

Miller, Daniel, Elisabetta Costa, Nell Haynes, Tom McDonald, Razvan Nicolescu, Jolynna Sinanan, Juliano Spyer, Shriram Venkatraman, and Xinyuan Wang. 2016. *How the World Changed Social Media*. London: UCL Press.

Miller, Peggy J., and Jacqueline J. Goodnow. 1995. "Cultural Practices: Toward an Integration of Culture and Development." In *Cultural Practices as Contexts for Development*, edited by Jacqueline J. Goodnow, Peggy J. Miller and Frank Kessel, 5–16. San Francisco: Jossey-Bass.

Morson, Gary Saul, and Caryl Emerson. 1990. *Mikhail Bakhtin. Creation of Prosaics*. Stanford, CA: Stanford University Press.

Nightingale, Virginia. 2011. "Introduction." In *The Handbook of Media Audiences*, edited by Virginia Nightingale, 1–18. Malden: Wiley-Blackwell.

Peña-Ayala, Alejandro. 2016. "Mobile, Ubiquitous, and Pervasive Learning: Fundaments, Applications, and Trends." In *Advances in Intelligent Systems and Computing* Volume 406. Cham: Springer.

Pink, Sarah, Heather Horst, John Postill, Larissa Hjorth, Tania Lewis, and Jo Tacchi. 2015. *Digital Ethnography: Principles and Practice*. 1st ed. Thousand Oaks, CA: Sage Publication.

Pink, Sarah. 2013. *Doing Visual Ethnography*. 3rd ed. Thousand Oaks, CA: Sage Publications.
Rowsell, Jennifer. 2013. *Working with Multimodality: Rethinking Literacy in a Digital Age*. London; New York: Routledge.
Sontag, Susan. 2001. *On Photography*. 1st Picadore USA ed. New York: Picador USA; Farrar, Straus and Giroux.
Vanden Abeele, Mariek M. P. 2016. "Mobile Youth Culture: A Conceptual Development." *Mobile Media & Communication* 4 (1): 85–101. doi: 10.1177/2050157915601455.
Weiser, Mark. 1991. "The Computer for the Twenty-First Century." *Scientific American*. 265: 94–104. doi: 10.1038/scientificamerican0991-94.
Weiser, Mark. 1996. "Ubiquitous Computing." *Ubiq.com*. March 17. http://www.ubiq.com/hypertext/weiser/UbiHome.html.
Weiser, Mark. 1998. "The Invisible Interface: Increasing the Power of the Environment Through Calm Technology." In *Proceedings of the First International Workshop on Cooperative Buildings, Integrating Information, Organization, and Architecture*, 1–1. CoBuild '98. London, UK, UK: Springer-Verlag. http://dl.acm.org/citation.cfm?id=645968.758439.
Weiser, Mark, and John Seely Brown. 1996. "The Coming Age of Calm Technology." *Ubiq.com* October 5. http://www.ubiq.com/hypertext/weiser/acmfuture2endnote.htm.
Westlund, Oscar, and Jakob Bjur. 2014. "Media Life of the Young." *Young* 22 (1): 21–41. doi: 10.1177/1103308813512934.
Yin, R. K. 2009/1984. *Case Study Research. Design and Methods*. 4th ed. Los Angeles: Sage.

CHAPTER NINE

Everywhere AND Nowhere, Simultaneously

Theorizing the Ubiquitous, Immaterial, Post-Digital Photograph

KRIS BELDEN-ADAMS

Walter Benjamin wrote about the revolutionary impact that photography's ubiquitous circulation had upon human consciousness, and upon previously stable conceptions of time and space. To those ends, he defined the term "aura"—a quality possessed by an "original" material image—as a "strange weave of time and space; the unique appearance of a distance, however close at hand" (Benjamin 1977, 49). Benjamin's reception-oriented account of photographic reproductions suggested that an object's aura is essentially and necessarily related to a viewer's experience with that object in its unique, physical, *original,* temporal-and-spatial context. Reproduced images, he noted, carried images across multiple spaces and times, made them ubiquitous as both practice and product, and replaced the aura with easy access, familiarity, contingency, and invitations for viewers to weave new contexts and multiple meanings for images.

Although Benjamin was writing about issues of originality and the sensory effects of photographically induced visual stimulation in the 1920s and 1930s, his ideas are particularly relevant to the state of the medium in today's Post-Digital age, as digitization and photography's diverse social practices have become normalized and entrenched in our sensorium so much that their effects may be studied, theorized, and perhaps even quantified. Despite its potentially misleading name, Post-Digital discourses do not announce the end of digital media or a divorce from its analog roots. For photography, the Post-Digital age has become almost entirely uncontroversial and has been accepted as a state of being, as smartphones enable users to share their digital images online with a global audience almost as quickly as they are made, often with the push of a single "share" button. While the voracity and instantaneity of digital image exchange exceeds the ubiquity that Benjamin witnessed, such photographs are no less "shocking" to the human visual sensorium (Hand 2012, 4–8; Rubinstein and Sluis 2008, 9). N. Katherine Hayles (2012, 2) has noted that "web interactions," in particular, are "extraordinarily effective in re-training (or more accurately, repurposing) our neural circuitry, so that the changes are not only psychological but physical as well." Post-Digital studies enable us to take a closer look at how our consumption and processing of visual representations are shaped by digital media. This essay offers such an examination of the embodied effects of digital social media photographs with reference not only to Benjamin's observations, but also to many contemporary commentators who have argued that the acts of photographing, looking, and sharing images have become performative reflexes in an age in which "we will photograph everything and look at nothing" (Malik 2016).

Digital vernacular photographs such as "selfies" present an opportunity to re-examine Benjamin's prescient theories of visual conditioning and viewer-based reception. But they also resist his analogy of the aura. Aura may be considered only as the privileged, singular "exposure" contact between a subject and a camera's light-sensitive receptors. Yet social media photographs, such as selfies, call for a re-evaluation of the photographic aura's singularity. The selfie, for instance, lacks a reception-based connection to any original space/time/singular presence or aura. Instead, it inhabits an ephemeral nexus as a digital facsimile available for recirculation on the ephemeral walls of social media sites—which make unstable semi-public archives and lend themselves to open use and even parody. In digital vernacular images, Benjamin's fear that photographic reproduction would, in effect, obliterate the material specificity of the aura finds apparent fruition. But as noted by scholars such as Geoffrey Batchen (2001, 146–162), since William Henry Fox Talbot's invention of the negative, photography always has had a complicated relationship to originality and to the conception of a singular aura. Photography—and its vernacular practices, in particular—presents a challenge to histories of the medium that privilege one-of-a-kind masterworks by "master artists."

This chapter explores those ideas prompted by Benjamin's writings on photographic ubiquity, and proposes that digital photography both benefits from Benjamin's conflicted insights about auratic time/space, visual ubiquity, reception theory, and originality—yet challenges these ideas in ways that helps reveal new paths for Post-Digital humanities scholarship on vernacular social media photography. Specifically, it will be argued that the aura has much to add to our discourses on digital social media photography if considered as a fluid attribute of: (1) the photograph's subject, (2) the context of its viewing, and (3) conditioning viewers' habits of consuming digital images.

SELFIES: A WELL-VISITED FRONTIER

While on a six-hour-and-28-minute spacewalk on September 5, 2012, Japanese astronaut and flight engineer Akihiko ("Aki") Hoshide took a photograph of himself from the International Space Station (ISS) (Figure 9.1). Hoshide is surrounded by the pitch-black depths of outer space, which is broken only by the Sun on the left side of the picture plane. His out-reaching arms, the camera, a robotic arm of the International Space Station, and the Earth are reflected in the spherical surface of his helmet visor. Hoshide was hardly the first astronaut to take a selfie from outer space. At least 11 predecessor astronauts made self-portraits while in space: Mike Collins and Edwin ("Buzz") Aldrin (1966), Neil Armstrong and Pete Conrad (1969), Ed Mitchell (1971), Donald Pettit (2003), Stephen Robinson (2005), Joe Tanner (2006), Mike Fossum (2006, 2011), and Scott Parazynski and Clay Anderson (2007) (Meeker 2015; NASA, 2016). Of these, five of the photographs were made in the post-2004, social media era of Facebook, MySpace, and Flickr, and if shared on such websites, would retroactively fit the definition of the "selfie" established by Oxford Dictionaries (Oxford Dictionaries, 2013) in 2013: "[A selfie is a] photograph that one has taken of oneself, typically one taken with a smartphone or webcam and uploaded to a social media website." Selfies typically are made at arm's length (although this distance may be extended by using a "selfie-stick"), using the built-in cell phone camera with an insistently-rectangular aspect ratio. Given the typical close proximity of the camera to the subject, the focus of such images is the self-conscious staging of oneself for a social media forum audience of friends, relatives, and/or acquaintances. Selfies are made to be shared with a public audience of social media followers. They offer intimate, close-up views for an audience whose personal relationships with the subject may or may not be that close.

Beyond these attributes, the selfie has no set conventional composition, setting, color palette, or pose (although the "duckface," head tilt, and distortive downward-facing, chin-diminishing camera-angle quickly became selfie tropes) (Belden-Adams 2017; Manovich 2014, 2017; Oxford Dictionaries 2013). Space selfies such as Hoshide's frequently utilize helmet reflections to show not only the astronaut, but more of their impressive setting and the act of the spacewalk itself. (Hoshide's colleague, Indian-American astronaut Sunita Williams, also appears in the reflection of Hoshide's helmet visor.) Digital astronaut selfies fall into a sub-category of this vernacular photographic practice called the "extreme selfie," i.e., a digital, social-media-circulated self-portrait made in a locale that is highly inaccessible for personal-safety reasons, or to which access is severely restricted (Colbert 2013). In this extreme selfie, Hoshide provides proof of his status as one of 88 astronauts to date who have resided on the ISS since its completion 15 years ago. Moreover, in explanation on Twitter of the impetus to make this selfie, Canadian astronaut Chris Hadfield (2013) wrote: "During a spacewalk you are constantly assaulted with the majesty of where you are, and what is happening. Distracting workplace." Space selfies become a way to vicariously experience outer space in an accessible way, while also echoing the common motivations for making tourist selfies: to provide proof of presence in a particular desirable location, and to lend the viewer visual evidence of its majestic, unusual, and/or enviable vistas.

Figure 9.1. Akihiko ("Aki") Hoshide, *Space Selfie, International Space Station Imagery: ISS032-E-025258*, Sept. 5, 2012. Courtesy, National Aeronautics and Space Administration (Public Domain).

THE "AURA" AS SINGULAR, SUBJECT-BASED TEMPORAL/SPATIAL "WEAVE"

Hoshide's selfie engages Benjamin's ideas about the aura as an attribute unique to the subject, stilled in its unique, inseparable "weave" of space (in both senses of the word) and time. Specifically, Hoshide positions himself in the vast blackness of outer space, with the Sun shining into the camera's lens from the viewer's left and the International Space Station's armatures and the Earth reflected in the distorted spherical form of his helmet visor. Also visible in the reflection is the camera itself, a Nikon D3S, which is held by Hoshide's outstretched, space-suited arms. The sun—without atmosphere to diffuse its light—the Earth, the ISS, and camera collectively certify his presence in this particular place, at a specific brief window of time during his Sept. 5, 2012 spacewalk, as the sun bathed the entire face of the Earth in enough light to produce an image that appears on Hoshide's visor. To make this image, Hoshide anticipated the sun's movements to ensure just the right light and position to create the mirrored glare of a reflected image. (If not positioned correctly, Hoshide's face—and no reflections—would be visible instead.) The sun—as well as the reflected images of Earth, the ISS, and colleague Williams—add spatial and implied temporal specificity to the moment captured in Hoshide's selfie. The image then encapsulates Benjamin's unique, specific "aura" of the unique "weave," or combination of time and space that brought Hoshide in contact with the frozen duration of time that we see, from this particular view of outer space.

Hoshide here bears witness to the auratic awe of his original encounter with floating weightlessly in outer space and freezes it to be shared it with viewers who most likely never will enjoy such a view first-hand. Heretofore, a vast global viewing public may access a frozen moment of that experience (even it is someone else's) through photography. Nonetheless, the unique momentary aura of contact between the light that reflected off of the subjects in Hoshide's selfie are unique from other temporal/spatial weaves. In his 1931 essay "Little History of Photography," Benjamin (1999) defined the term "aura" as a "strange weave of space and time: the unique appearance or semblance of distance, no matter how close it may be" (Benjamin, 1931, 518). This interaction between humanity and outer space represents a monumental feat of exploration and scientific advance that impregnates this frozen moment with a greater gravity of achievement than visible in almost any other selfie.

Benjamin argued that an object's aura is essentially and necessarily related to that object's unique relationship to a particular, original temporal and spatial context:

> In even the most perfect reproduction, *one* thing is lacking: the here and now of the work of art—its unique existence in a particular place. It is this unique existence—and nothing else—that bears the mark of history to which the work has been subject. This history includes changes to the physical structure of the work over time, together with any changes in ownership....The here and now of the original underlies the concept of its authenticity. (Benjamin, 2002b)

A prerequisite to an artwork's/object's authenticity, Benjamin argued, is its persisting connection to its original position within both time and space. For instance, as one looks at Hoshide's awe-inspiring selfie in outer space, viewers may wish to impossibly recapture the aura that that exposure time and place held for the astronaut. But the viewer only can access so much of Hoshide's original experience vicariously.

THE "AURA" AS MULTIFARIOUS, VIEWER-BASED TIME AND SPACE

According to the Oxford Dictionary's definition, selfies necessarily reside on the ephemeral walls of social media sites. Selfies such as Hoshide's were created in the anticipation of online circulation in social media. One important thing set Hoshide's self-portrait apart from those of his 11 precursor astronaut/photographers: his selfie went "viral." The medical term "viral" has been applied to online communications to express the rapidity and "infectiousness" with which digital images and ideas may circulate in social discourses. Photographs such as Hoshide's do not necessarily actively solicit their virality (although certain distribution of images can help make that more likely). Hoshide's image instead was not the agent of action, but the subject of others' actions and recontextualizations. What may have begun as an image celebrating one man's awe with, and presence in, outer space, quickly became an online sensation (Pocklington, 2013). For a selfie such as Hoshide's to become viral, Paul Frosh (2015, 1608) suggests, "It requires, among other things, that these viewers have been adequately socialized through having seen, taken, or heard tell of selfies." This is to say, such images were a part of a visual, online, social media vernacular by the time NASA and other sources shared and recontextualized Hoshide's selfie. It entered a reception field in which social media not only enabled easy posting and sharing of such photographs, but users also had embraced the selfie as a relatively new genre of photography.

The earliest account of Hoshide's selfie first appeared on National Aeronautics and Space Administration's (NASA) "International Space Station" webpage on the day of the spacewalk (Sept. 5, 2012) and was released into the public domain (NASA, 2012). This is not unusual. Social media photographs are shared and recirculated almost as quickly as they are made and therefore have the capacity to span the globe with rapidity, ease, and near-immediacy. The selfie was picked up and posted by a meme-creation site, KnowYourMeme, a website that advertises itself as "a website dedicated to documenting Internet phenomena: viral videos, image macros, catchphrases, web celebs, and more," on the same day it was posted. KnowYourMeme viewers were invited to recreate the image accompanied by their own text (*Reflection* 2012). The online science-news site Gizmodo posted the image two days later (Horn 2012). After appearing on the NASA site and on KnowYourMeme, it was shared globally by hundreds of blogs, social media, and photography-sharing pages (such as StumbleUpon, Imgur, Tumblr, Reddit, Flickr, Facebook, MySpace, Twitter, and Instagram), and gained its own Wikipedia page on Sept. 14, 2012 (Photo-iss032e0252528, 2012). On Sept. 18, 2012, NASA anointed it "Astronomy Picture of the Day." The selfie was then featured as one of the "Farthest Reaching Selfies" on National Geographic's website, and promptly was featured on news sites including the Associated Press, *Wired* magazine, *Esquire*, *Vogue*, *The Japan Times*, and *Business Insider* (National Geographic 2013; Wired 2013). The image, and its repackaged parodies, was also quickly shared by countless other viewers—including Hoshide himself, as well as by colleague Hadfield—on Facebook, Twitter, Tumblr, Instagram, and various other social media sites. It was celebrated at the top of many selfie lists of 2013—the same year that the word "selfie" was sanctified by the Oxford Dictionaries as the Word of the Year (Oxford Dictionaries 2013). Parodies of the space selfie proliferated in the three years following his spacewalk, but have become less popular four years later. Viral images thus have a life span of several years in the public eye after their "infectious" spread begins. But like many fads, the attention they capture peaks and subsides (Blakeley 2011; Knibbs 2013).

Mass-distribution of photographic reproductions, Benjamin suggests, enables the potential for multiple, simultaneous presences of a photograph across many spaces and times. This effectively obliterates the singularity of the aura. For instance, as John Berger (1977, 19–34) notes in his analysis of Benjamin's essays, the experience of seeing an artwork by Leonardo da Vinci in person was transformed after the advent of mechanical reproduction. The various reproductions, parodies, and recontextualizations of the *Mona Lisa* (c. 1503–1506) within contemporary visual culture have made it difficult for viewers to access the painting's original aura—its authenticity, its authority as an object, and its mystery, Benjamin argues. Instead of being an affect-laden masterwork by one of art history's Renaissance master artists, the *Mona Lisa*'s affect has been numbed and the image has been reframed as an enduring icon for the idea of "art" within Western visual culture. Photographic reproduction also has allowed the *Mona Lisa* and other reproduced subjects to circulate far removed from the time and space in which they originally were embedded, so that they may be discussed and experienced vicariously, albeit through a lens colored by its reproduced parodies (as Miss Piggy, Monica Lewinsky, punk rockers, body builders, etc.), memes, products (postcards, cookie jars, watches, mugs, toilet paper, ties, socks, t-shirts, etc.), and effigies (sculpted from Cheetos, burned toast, screenprints, etc.) (Mona Lisa Parodies—Google Search 2016). Indeed, viewers become numb to the intended beauty and mystery of the *Mona Lisa* because its reproductions have circulated virally in popular culture for decades. Instead, viewing the *Mona Lisa* in person becomes less about experiencing the artwork itself and all about the ritual of photographing it as an "art tourist," as evidenced by the recent popularity of taking selfies with the painting (Guthrie 2014; Mona Lisa Selfies—Google Search 2016).

Hoshide's selfies led almost instantaneously to a proliferation of viewer-created "memes." In memes, users add brief bits of text to narrate images, such as Hoshide's selfie (Shifman 2013, 18). Many viewers who made memes joked about the ridiculousness of their tolerance for airline turbulence (compared to that of space travel), they celebrated Hoshide's as a selfie that humbles almost all other extreme selfies, some suggested that Hoshide was practicing his "duckface" under his reflective helmet visor, and many viewers made fun of what they saw as the mundane, insignificant settings of conventional selfies and/or travel self-portraits—in comparison to Hoshide's humbling subject matter. Interestingly, viewers reacted to Hoshide's selfie by making fun of themselves and of the conventions of the selfie itself—such as the "duckface" pose, its use to document travel, and the lackluster occasions in which it is often used. This is to say, memes are one way by which viewers recontextualize photographs to make them about themselves and their worlds, rather than about the subject—which the first part of this paper explored in an analysis of Benjamin's work on the subject-based "aura." Incidentally, many scholars recently have argued that selfies are manifestations of vanity and self-focus, and some have suggested that this tendency emerged as a response to a new era of interactive, user-centered media (Senft and Baym 2015, 1589; Sorokowski *et al.* 2015, 123–127). As Raúl Rodríguez-Ferrándiz (2016, 228) has argued, Benjamin even "foresaw the concept of 'mass narcissism' as an effect of technical reproducibility." In contrast, the viewer-based aura occurs in countless spaces and times, and is intensely personal, individualized, and subjective. These multiple, simultaneous presences of a photograph such as Hoshide's occupy many viewers' spaces and times, worldwide. Moreover, the remaking and recontextualizing of photographs as memes adds layers of narrativity that multiply an image's connotations dramatically. The image's ubiquity and cultural saturation are magnified as viewers assume partial authorship. Virality effectively obliterates the singularity of the aura and give it a personal, subjective plurality.

"Original" vintage printed versions of selfies have no privileged place in this digital, immaterial image-sharing economy. By definition, if a self-portrait is not shared on social media, it is not a selfie. Instead, selfies inhabit an ephemeral nexus as digital facsimiles that multiply until viewers' interest in sharing them fades. They also intrinsically challenge notions of "originality" by virtue of being photographs. The medium's relationship to a privileged, singular original image almost always has been a point of contention. Since 1841, when William Henry Fox Talbot announced the invention of his calotype process, photographers could make multiple prints from a single negative. As Batchen has pointed out, our current histories of photography have failed to account for the multiple possible interpretations of a single negative that were part of the working process of practitioners such as Ansel

Adams (Batchen 2001, 146–162). Through an analysis of the impact of Corbis's ownership of the digital reproduction rights of single "preferred" prints of Adams's work (which excluded Adams's multiple interpretations of negatives), Batchen (2001, 152–154) suggests that:

> [P]hotography is produced within and as an economy that Jacques Derrida calls *différance*; any particular photographic image is "never present in and of itself," but "is inscribed in a chain or in a system within which is refers to other [images], by means of the systematic play of differences."

The aura of the subject is contingent upon the agencies of interpretation and reinterpretation by the photographer. Any one photograph's aura of authenticity as "the" preferred version (or, "vintage print") vanishes. In its place, the photograph's reproducibility, in Corbis founder Bill Gates's esteem, "is likely to increase rather than diminish reverence for the real art and encourage more people to get out to museums and gallery" (*ibid.*, 154). By Gates's logic, digital reproductions of Leonardo da Vinci's *Mona Lisa*, for example, encourage viewers to see the original, creating a new sort of "cult value" for the painting that is akin to "art tourism." Incidentally, throngs of tourists regularly visit the Louvre and enter the da Vinci gallery, only to turn their backs to the *Mona Lisa* and take selfies with the famous painting. This trend began after rappers Eminem and P. Diddy both took selfies in front of the painting in 2010 (Heritage 2013). As of Sept. 30, 2016, a search for "Mona Lisa selfie" on Google gleaned 755,000 results (Mona Lisa Selfie–Google Search 2016).

Benjamin argued that experiences with reproductions of the *Mona Lisa* lack the authenticity of an "original encounter" with the painting because the desire to see the artwork was shaped by impressions formed by the viewer during previous encounters with the image. Selfies, other digitally-circulated social media images and their mutated memes and parodies raise important questions about the status—or even, the relevance—of distinctions between the original and the copy in the digital image-making, image-circulating economy. But they also give us cause to pause and consider Benjamin's writings about the potentially revolutionary impact of photographic ubiquity. Social media mass-circulated images have the potential to enter and influence public consciousness, just like their print-based precursors. Benjamin suggested that the power of widespread image circulation therefore has the capacity to "redeem" the "lost aura," but his writings are unclear about exactly *how* a state of plurality and viewer-determined, reception-based might restore the sanctity of an image's singularity—if indeed it can (Benjamin, 2003, 267).

THE "AURA" AND SENSORY PERCEPTION, CONDITIONING

To Benjamin, perceptions of both time and space in an age of the mechanical reproduction of images were intrinsically subjective and mutable: "Just as the entire mode of existence of human collectives changes over long historical periods, so too does their mode of perception" (Benjamin 2002b, 104). Benjamin's comments that theorize analog photographic reproduction prove useful for the task of describing the sensory impact of image ubiquity and instantaneous global communication during the digital age. As an object, a digital photograph, including the selfie, enables time's release from any one, privileged, original auratic reception-based, space/time matrix to the possibility of inhabiting many, simultaneously. This unprecedented degree of ubiquity affects and conditions habits of consuming visual imagery such as photographs.

For Benjamin, time is at once subjectively experienced and objectively expressed—even if perhaps, problematically and inadequately. His skepticism about the possibility of articulating time with any degree of objective precision first appears in a discussion of photography's relationship to time in 1922. In it, he refers to "earthly time," and suggests that it varies from images made by a photographer's apparatus. Benjamin's writings convey his personal struggle with the polar tendencies of subjectivity and objectivity by insisting upon centering temporality and its expression within the modern observer. In his notes for *The Arcades Project* (1927–1940), Benjamin mentions a few of a myriad of ways in which temporality may be experienced by specific modern observers:

> Rather than pass the time, one must invite it in. To pass the time (to kill time, expel it): the gambler. Time spills from every pore—To store time as a battery stores energy: the flâneur. Finally, the third type: he who waits. He takes in the time and renders it up in altered form—that of expectation. (Benjamin 2002a, 107)

Benjamin argues that these typological characters, who all presumably share human biological sensorial capacities—the "gambler," "flâneur," and those who "wait"—experience and exemplify the differential use of time, despite capitalist industrial modernity's efforts to institutionalize time's rigid, standardized measurement and mathematical description. The human sensorium's perceptions of time, Benjamin writes, have suffered great "trauma or shock" at a time during which the speed of life accelerated dramatically as a result of the explosive growth of the passenger railroad, telegraph, telephone, radio, and automobile industries—which each forever altered previous conceptions, or "weaves," of space and time. Benjamin here defiantly insists that time exists because of, and is defined by, the observer, not by the capitalist industrial system of modernity. A newfound awareness of time's intensified effects, Benjamin writes, is innately biological: "In the spleen, time becomes palpable: the minutes cover a man like snowflakes" (Benjamin and Zohn 1968, 184). Benjamin's observations about the bodily effects of time's rapidly changing perceptions and experiences in the modern age remain centered in the individual. To Benjamin, time's experience and the trauma it inflicts are innately personal, variable and subjective. They mark the very definition of the age of industrial modernity.

Digital vernacular photography, in comparison, is a fittingly immaterial form for exploring the fluctuating conditions of time and space in an age of digital modernity, a time in which all previously held "solid" conceptions of material time and space have been thrown into contention in an unprecedented manner by near-instantaneous communication on social media. In the Post-Digital age, photography's digitization and its diversity of social practices have become normalized to such a degree that we may now historicize them—and study the effects of ubiquity upon the human sensorium. Roy Ascott (2013, 191–192) suggests that a Post-Digital critical lens may "go behind the image to a second state of semantic fluidity, and open-ended semiosis." Several scholars have written accounts of the psychological and physical effects of living in the digital age. Hayles (2012, 3) has suggested that the human cognition shaped by digital mediation is also physical and mental:

> The more one works with digital technologies, the more one comes to appreciate the capacity of networked and programmable machines to carry out sophisticated cognitive tasks, and the more the keyboard comes to seem an extension of one's thoughts rather than an external device on which one types. Embodiment then takes the form of extended cognition, in which human agency and thought are enmeshed within larger networks that extend beyond the desktop computer into the environment.

Specifically, the making of cell phone photographs is performative, physical, and relational. Photographers extend their camera-holding hands and arms into the space, press a button, and capture a "touch" of the world. Shooting and sharing digital images on social media sites, Mette Sandbye (2012, 97) suggests, is a very different approach to making photography to preserve the past: "Today photography is predominantly a social, everyday activity rather than a memory-embalming one, creating presence, relational situations, and communication." To make a selfie, thus, is a way of connecting socially, of conveying presence and maintaining relationships. The selfie engages this economy of social habitude in which the "personal" becomes the "public" and potentially the viral. This digital vernacular photographic practice depends on the extension of human life into the virtual cyber-realm of social media engagement for its potency. The selfie represents a self-consciously staged version of the self as "avatar," or, *as it wants to be seen* by a massive public global network. To viewers, Hoshide reveals himself to be both adventurer, pioneer, among very few people who get to travel to outer space and—despite the "bookworm" stereotype that his engineering skills might otherwise suggest—he is a man who is hip to the latest social media trends. But no matter how much information Hoshide tried to give his viewers, their interpretations of his selfie can vary, as they are products of their unique experiences in their own positions in space/time.

Habits of viewing in the Post-Digital age undeniably are shaped by digital mediation. A diversity of social practices has become normalized and entrenched in our sensorium to such a degree that their effects may be studied, theorized, and perhaps even quantified. Hayles has argued that the human sensorium's embodiment of the habits and patterns of cognition of the digital age are not necessarily the realization of a Benjaminian "shock" or "trauma," but merely are different from those with which viewers engaged before, in a print-based economy of visual consumption. Hayles (2012, 10) suggests that humans and technics have merely coevolved together.

Indeed, the sensorium that is conditioned by digital media, most of these scholars agree, is a complex one. Most digital media are best engaged instantaneously, by skimming, scanning and consuming visual material quickly. Consumers are accustomed to having an often-overwhelming wellspring of information from sources of varying reliability available, and may personalize data—such as photographs—for our variegated needs or desires, such as memes, composite or montaged photographs, adding personal messages to frame a post or a repost of someone else's image, etc. Historian Roger Chartier (2003, 110) suggests that Benjamin's writing on the aura was, in fact, prompted by his concerns over the "erasure of distinction between the creator and the public," which was based on the addition of opinion columns written by readers as a feature in daily newspapers. Likewise, the digital photographic image provides such a viewer-centered, user-driven, participatory experience in which the viewer is an active text-creator/re-creator, rather than a passive consumer of visual information.

Recent studies have suggested that the shift from passive audience members to actively engaged viewers of visual data has been assimilated differently, according to when which each generation was introduced to digital mediation, and how adeptly they assimilated its tools into their routines. As Mary Meeker (2016) states in her report on Internet-culture trends, a key difference between Generation X (which encountered the Internet as young adults) and Generation Z (which used the Internet extensively from a young age) is that the latter consumes the world in images, rather than words, and regularly uses Snapchat, Facebook, and Instagram to post personal updates using photographs. The effects of digital conditioning have made this younger group savvy consumers of visual culture who see hundreds—perhaps thousands—of images a day, at a quick glance. While Hoshide's selfie celebrates its unique purview in outer space, many social media photographs do not. Instead, they celebrate the self in often more banal settings of everyday life. Such photographs share the appearance of a good meal, a day spent with friends, pets, children, and another day at school or work. This has prompted some photographers and curators to dismay for the loss of the medium's former importance. For instance, Craig Richards quipped that "People take photographs because they can, not because they should" (Brown 2013). As rapid visual consumption is rewarded, the slower, deliberate, contemplative viewing and connoisseurship of photographs have declined, along with deeper analysis of visual culture—and possibly also, the possibility of an auratic, transcendent experience viewing a masterwork of art history like the *Mona Lisa*.

But again, Benjamin's writings argue the potential of mechanical reproduction to create a human appetite for information and images could lead to the loss of the aura. In an essay that is almost eerily prescient of the digital age, he writes of the "social basis" of this phenomenon:

> [T]he desire of the present-day masses to 'get closer' to things spatially and humanly, and their equally passionate concern for overcoming each thing's uniqueness by assimilating it as a reproduction....The stripping of the veil from the object, the destruction of the aura, is the signature of a perception whose "sense for sameness in the world" has so increased that, by means of reproduction, it extracts sameness even from what is unique. (Benjamin 2003 255–256; 174 [Italics are Benjamin's emphasis])

This "getting closer, spatially and humanly," for Benjamin, meant busy streets, assembly lines, and a dizzying array of visual stimuli on the streets of the modern city. But it also brought easier access to goods and services and increasingly networked communication and transportation. As Benjamin laments the declining occurrence of experiencing the unique, superior, original object in an age of copies, he also implicitly grieves for the loss of an immersive, contemplative viewing of such a preferred work of art (*ibid.*). In today's world, Benjamin's sentiments perhaps raise questions about "slow" vs. "fast" viewing. In the book *Thinking, Fast and Slow*, economist Daniel Kahneman (2011) suggests that instinctively, our brains react to stimuli in two ways, as "fast, instinctive and emotional," or "slower, more deliberative, and more logical." Fast thinking leads to "automatic" behaviors of habit, bred by "frequency," that are "emotional, stereotypic," and driven by the subconscious. The reflexive performance of snapping photographs of everyday things—including the self—in various locales, perhaps, can be seen as such an "automatic" behavior. Kahneman juxtaposes this set of stimuli-processing reactions with "slow, effortful, logical, calculating, conscious" behaviors, which are prompted by a lack of frequency (2011). Kahneman's comments on cognitive processing certainly are akin Benjamin's thoughts on the aura, which likewise imply that a preferred, superior degree of immersive contemplation that viewers ought to experience in the presence of an original artwork has been lost in an age of photographic ubiquity.

CONCLUSION

Although most of his essays were written in the late 1920s and 1930s for an audience of his own contemporaries, Benjamin's writings on photographic ubiquity and the human sensorium present apt springboards for analyzing various dimensions of digital social media photographs such as selfies. Hoshide's selfie, in essence, is comprised of a collection of light from that fraction-of-a-second, carefully planned exposure duration. Moreover, it was inspired by the wonder of being among the very few human beings who have gone to outer space and experienced the transcendent awe of viewing Earth from afar, while floating weightlessly during a spacewalk space near the International Space Station. The image was immediately shared, recirculated, and virally circulated from NASA's sites to more than 16,700,000 social media, news, meme-generating, and fan websites. Its immense dissemination far surpassed that which Benjamin would have anticipated. Nonetheless, his writings on the viewer-based effects of mechanical reproduction elucidate the varying and seemingly endless variations of reception contexts. Guided by Benjamin's ideas about the "aura," a closer look at the online reception of Hoshide's selfie suggests that the viewer-based "aura" (which Benjamin actually may have considered the *destruction* of the singularity of the "aura") occurs in countless spaces and times, and is intensely personal, individualized and subjective. Multiple, simultaneous presences of a photograph such as Hoshide's occupy many viewers' spaces and times, worldwide.

Finally, Benjamin's writing about the manner by which his own age faced changes (including mechanical reproduction) that reconstructed the formerly stable postulates of time and space has offered a model for reflecting on the Post-Digital age. Viewers' habits of consuming images have been shaped by online media. Younger generations that lived their entire lives with access to the Internet and social media have become conditioned to process a glut of available information from a variety of sources quickly, and to look to visual images, rather than text, for information. These trends in cognitive processing and viewing habits mark a significant shift from a material, contemplative, and textual culture to the emergence—and increased prominence—of a virtual, interactive, quick-processing, digital, and visually communicative one. This paradigm shift transforms habits of consuming photography, which in turn changes the form and conventions in which the medium manifests itself—and continues to do so. As these trends in human cognition become more pronounced in the decades and generations to come, Benjamin's concerns about interactive media and the potential "loss" of immersive contemplation provide a useful touchstone for contextualizing these changes, and perhaps ultimately, better understanding and defining them as part of a more complex sensory experience in the Post-Digital world.

REFERENCES

Ascott, Roy. 2013. "Behind the Image and Beyond." *Technoetic Arts* 11 (3): 191–92. doi:10.1386/tear.11.3.191_7.

Batchen, Geoffrey. 2001. "Photogenics." In *Each Wild Idea: Writing, Photography, History*, 146–62. Cambridge, MA: MIT Press.

Belden-Adams, Kris. 2017. "Locating the 'Selfie' within Photography's History—and Beyond." In *#Selfie – Imag(in)ing the Self in Digital Media*, edited by Sabine Wirth, Jens Ruchatz, and Julia Eckel, forthcoming. Leuven, Belgium: Leuven University Press. http://www.academia.edu/9621088/_SELFIE__Imag_in_ing_the_Self_in_Digital_Media.

Benjamin, Walter. 1977. "Walter Benjamin's 'Short History of Photography' [1931]." Translated by Phil Patton. *Artforum* 15.

———. 1999. "Little History of Photography [1931]." In *Selected Writings. Volume 2, 1927–1934*, 507–530. Cambridge, MA: Belknap Press of Harvard University Press.

———. 2002a. *The Arcades Project.* Translated by Howard Eiland and Kevin McLaughlin. Cambridge, MA: Harvard University Press.

———. 2002b. "The Work of Art in the Age of Mechanical Reproduction (Second Version, 1935)." In *Walter Benjamin: Selected Writings. Vol. 3,* edited by Howard Eiland and Michael William Jennings, translated by Edmund Jephcott. Cambridge, MA; London: The Belknap Press of Harvard University Press.

———. 2003. "The Work of Art in an Age of Its Technological Reproducibility" (Fourth Version, 1936–1939)." In *Selected Writings Volume 4, 1938–1940*, edited by Howard Eiland and Michael W Jennings, 251–83. Cambridge, MA: Belknap Press of Harvard Univ. Press.

Benjamin, Walter. 2003. *The Arcades Project*. Cambridge, MA: Belknap Press of Harvard University Press

Benjamin, Walter. 1968. *Illuminations*. New York: Harcourt, Brace & World.

Berger, John. 1977. *Ways of Seeing: Based on the BBC Television Series with John Berger*. London: Penguin Books.

Blakeley, Kiri. 2011. "Why Does Something Go Viral?" *Forbes*. September 6. http://www.forbes.com/sites/kiriblakeley/2011/09/06/why-does-something-go-viral/.

Brown, Ian. 2013. "Humanity Takes Millions of Photos Every Day. Why Are Most so Forgettable?" *The Globe and Mail*. June 21. http://www.theglobeandmail.com/life/humanity-takes-millions-of-photos-every-day-why-are-most-so-forgettable/article12754086/.

Chartier, Roger. 2003. "From Mechanical Reproduction to Electronic Representation." In *Mapping Benjamin: The Work of Art in the Digital Age*, edited by Hans Ulrich Gumbrecht and Michael Marrinan, 110. Stanford, CA: Stanford University Press.

Colbert, Annie. 2013. "14 Extreme Selfies That Push Duck Face off a Cliff." *Mashable*. September 19. http://mashable.com/2013/09/19/extreme-selfies/.

Frosh, Paul. 2015. "The Gestural Image: The Selfie, Photography Theory, and Kinesthetic Sociability." *International Journal of Communication* 9: 22.

Guthrie, Bruce. 2014. "The Mona Lisa Agrees—Enough with the Selfies!" *The New Daily*. July 11. http://thenewdaily.com.au/life/tech/2014/07/11/bruce-guthrie-selfie-mona-lisa/.

Hadfield, Chris. 2013. "Good Morning! Some Selfies Are More Thought-Provoking than Others. Amazing What You Can See in the Reflection.pic.twitter.com/Z39tadWK1W." Twitter. *@Cmdr_Hadfield*. September 30. https://twitter.com/Cmdr_Hadfield/status/384703312341114880/photo/1?ref_src=twsrc%5Etfw.

Hand, Martin. 2012. *Ubiquitous Photography*. Cambridge: Polity Press.
Hayles, N. Katherine. 2012. *How We Think: Digital Media and Contemporary Technogenesis*. Chicago, IL: The University of Chicago Press.
Heritage, Stuart. 2013. "Selfies: The Dos and Don'ts of the Word of the Year." *The Guardian*, November 19, sec. Technology. https://www.theguardian.com/technology/shortcuts/2013/nov/19/selfies-dos-donts-oed-word-of-the-year.
Horn, Leslie. 2012. "Astronauts Using DSLRs…In Spaaaaaaaace!" *Gizmodo*. September 7. http://gizmodo.com/5941368/astronauts-using-dslrs-in-spaaaaaaaace.
Kahneman, Daniel. 2011. *Thinking, Fast and Slow*. New York: Farrar, Straus and Giroux.
Knibbs, Kate. 2013. "Achieving Viral: Here's the Secret Sauce behind Images That Win the Internet." *Digital Trends*. September 27. http://www.digitaltrends.com/social-media/what-makes-a-viral-image/.
Malik, Om. 2016. "In the Future, We Will Photograph Everything and Look at Nothing." *The New Yorker*, April 4. http://www.newyorker.com/business/currency/in-the-future-we-will-photograph-everything-and-look-at-nothing.
Manovich, Lev. 2016. "Selfiecity." *Selfiecity*. Accessed October 28. http://www.selfiecity.net/#theory.
———. 2017. "Selfiecity." In *#Selfie – Imag(in)ing the Self in Digital Media*, edited by Sabine Wirth, Jens Ruchatz, and Julia Eckel, forthcoming. Leuven, Belgium: Leuven University Press. http://www.academia.edu/9621088/_SELFIE_-_Imag_in_ing_the_Self_in_Digital_Media.
Meeker, Elizabeth. 2015. "Best Ever Astronaut 'Selfies.'" December 23. http://www.universetoday.com/105234/best-ever-astronaut-selfies/.
Meeker, Mary. 2016. "2016 Internet Trends Report." Presented at the Code Conference, June 1. http://www.kpcb.com/internet-trends.
"Mona Lisa Parodies—Google Search." 2017. Accessed March 30. https://www.google.com/search?q=mona+lisa+parodies&client=opera&hs=yv6&source=lnms&tbm=isch&sa=X&ved=0ahUKEwik k5Hh8L7PAhWBMyYKHXSGDsQQ_AUICCgB&biw=2085&bih=1013&dpr=0.67.
"Mona Lisa Selfie—Google Search." 2016. Accessed September 30. https://www.google.com/search?newwindow=1&client=opera&biw=1920&bih=612&tbm=isch&sa=1&q=Mona+Lisa+Selfie&oq=Mona+Lisa+Selfie&gs_l=img.3..0l6j0i5i30k1j0i8i30k1l3.46570.46570.0.47106.1.1.0.0.0.0.183.183.0j1.1.0....0...1c.1.64.img..0.1.182.QiMFbWy0ZQY.
NASA. 2012. *ISS-32 American EVA b3 Aki Hoshide.jpg*. Photograph. http://spaceflight.nasa.gov/gallery/images/station/crew-32/html/iss032e025258.html. https://commons.wikimedia.org/wiki/File:ISS-32_American_EVA_b3_Aki_Hoshide.jpg.
National Geographic Society. 2013. "Exploring the Farthest Reaches." *National Geographic*. March 27. https://web-beta.archive.org/web/20130404024057/http://www.nationalgeographic.com/125/exploring-farthest-reaches/.
Oxford Dictionaries. 2013. "The Oxford Dictionaries Word of the Year 2013." *OxfordWords Blog*. November 18. http://blog.oxforddictionaries.com/press-releases/oxford-dictionaries-word-of-the-year-2013/.
———. 2017. "Viral – Definition of Viral in English." *Oxford Dictionaries | English*. Accessed March 30. https://en.oxforddictionaries.com/definition/viral.
"Photo-iss032e025258." 2012. September 5. https://spaceflight.nasa.gov/gallery/images/station/crew-32/html/iss032e025258.html.
Pocklington, Rebecca. 2013. "Best selfie ever? Astronaut becomes viral sensation with his picture in space." *The Mirror*, Last Modified 18 November 2013, accessed 20 June 2017. http://www.mirror.co.uk/news/weird-news/best-selfie-ever-astronaut-becomes-2804912.

"Reflection of ISS Astronaut in a Helmet." 2012. *Know Your Meme.* September 5. http://knowyourmeme.com/photos/563259-selfie.

Rodríguez-Ferrándiz, Raúl. 2016. "Benjamin, BitTorrent, Bootlegs: Auratic Piracy Cultures?" In *PHOTOMEDIATIONS: A Reader.*, edited by Kamila Kuc and Joanna Zylinska, 227–250. London: Open Humanities Press.

Rubinstein, Daniel, and Katrina Sluis. 2008. "A Life More Photographic." *Photographies* 1 (1): 9–28. doi:10.1080/17540760701785842.

Sandbye, Mette. 2012. "It Has Not Been—It Is. The Signaletic Transformation of Photography." *Journal of Aesthetics & Culture* 4 (1): 18159. doi:10.3402/jac.v4i0.18159.

Senft, Theresa M., and Nancy K. Baym. 2015. "Selfies Introduction ~ What Does the Selfie Say? Investigating a Global Phenomenon." *International Journal of Communication* 9 (May): 1588–1606.

Shifman, Limor. 2013. *Memes in Digital Culture.* Cambridge, MA: MIT Press.

Sorokowski, P., A. Sorokowska, A. Oleszkiewicz, T. Frackowiak, A. Huk, and K. Pisanski. 2015. "Selfie Posting Behaviors Are Associated with Narcissism among Men." *Personality and Individual Differences* 85 (October): 123–27. doi:10.1016/j.paid.2015.05.004.

Tetsutaro Saijo. 2013. "水口哲也が案内する業界未来図：ゲームの未来を読み解くキーワ [The Age of Global Gaming]." *WIRED.jp.* January 5. http://wired.jp/2013/01/05/the_age_of_global_gaming_10_keywords/.

PART FOUR

Economies

Critical Political Economy Perspectives

CHAPTER TEN

Ubiquitous Media AND Monopolies OF Knowledge

The Approach of Harold Innis[1]

EDWARD COMOR

Harold Adams Innis (1894–1952) began his career as a political economist and economic historian but beginning in the 1930s he turned his attention more to questions concerning culture, media, and civilizational survival. Known today mainly for his "staples theory" of development and what came to be called "medium theory," in retrospect, Innis charted the foundations of a broadly conceptualized dialectical materialist analysis of ubiquitous media. It is in relation to this that Innis forged a concept that is particularly germane to the subject of this book: what he called monopolies of knowledge.[2]

Ubiquitous media, for Innis, are developed and used as means of organizing and sustaining power-laden social relations. More than the presence of a pervasive technology (in a contemporary context smartphones and automobiles, for example), in addressing ubiquity Innis was referencing media (broadly defined to include institutions, organizations, and technologies[3]) that constitute means of producing and reproducing a given socio-economic order.[4] Innis, having analyzed over four thousand years of history, found that the predominance or ubiquity of some media in a given place and time reflects and affects—they *mediate*—that society's power relations in complex and often contradictory ways.

In this chapter, Innis' approach to ubiquitous media will be outlined. It will focus on how and why such media influence taken-for-granted thinking in a given place and time. To explain, the concept "monopoly of knowledge" is applied to two ubiquitous media of Innis' time: the price system and printing. In the first section, some background concerning the bases of his interest in media and monopolies of knowledge is provided. In the second, what might be called Innis' approach to ubiquitous media is presented and this, in the third section, is demonstrated through the examples of the price system and printing. In the penultimate section, his approach is loosely applied to the contemporary ubiquity of digital communications technologies. Finally, in the chapter's conclusion, key parts of the argument presented will be summarized and Innis' admonition against those treating such an approach as some kind of prognosticative template is underlined.

As I explain in what follows, the ubiquity of a medium or complex of media generally facilitates status quo relations and thinking but, in so doing, it also tends to ossify or "bias" that culture's capacities in relation to knowledge. Ubiquity or monopolization thus implies problems and these can impel alternative developments involving, prospectively (but not inevitably), a re-casting of the monopolies of knowledge. For Innis, ubiquity reflects, shapes, and yields conditions that are contradictory for both dominant interests and, in most cases, even those who oppose them.

CONCEPTUAL BACKGROUND

In the Preface of his book *Political Economy in the Modern State*, Innis (1946) references the apprehensions expressed by Socrates concerning writing and its implications for memory: through their use of "written characters" learners "will be hearers of many things and have learned nothing; they will appear to be omniscient and will generally know nothing; they will be tiresome company, having the show of wisdom without the reality." In the same paragraph, Innis relates this warning to the printing press and radio, stating that they also "have enormously increased the difficulties of thought" (Innis 1946, vii).

Here and elsewhere Innis recognizes the Promethean paradox of humanity's mastery over nature: the advance of science and technology, essential as they are to civilizational advance, also imply the shackling of the intellect. Indeed, for him, a turning point for Western civilization was the invention of the printing press. With the ubiquity of the printed word, mechanized ways of thinking flourished. Modern printing technologies and their commercial and political applications mediated a certain inter-subjective mentality that was decidedly unreflexive (i.e., an absence of critical self–awareness). This, from Innis' perspective, reflected and furthered the capacity to manage, administer, and control—to apply power—on an unprecedented scale. Unreflexive and present-minded norms of thinking thus were both consciously promoted (especially through advertising, the price system, and mass democracy) and structured into the relations of daily life.

Innis, in the mid-1940s, drawing from the classical dialectic between power (or force) and knowledge (or intelligence), points to the growing predominance of power over knowledge with technologies, organizations, and institutions mediating their (prospectively tragic) imbalance. The struggle between power and knowledge is, for Innis, universal in the history of civilization while the specific implications of such institutional, organizational, and technological media are not. To underline this, in addition to Prometheus, Innis references the myth of Minerva.[5]

Innis begins his first dedicated historical analysis of the role played by communications in civilizational history (in his paper "Minerva's Owl") as follows: "Minerva's owl begins its flight in the gathering dusk not only from classical Greece but in turn from Alexandria, from Rome, from Constantinople, from the republican cities of Italy, from France, from Holland, and from Germany" (Innis 1951, 5). Minerva is the goddess who embodies force and wisdom. Derived from Athena, she represents the dynamic tension between power and knowledge. Her owl—a bird of prey—scavenges marginal cultures seeking the materials and ideas needed to sustain and reproduce. Rather than just looting or emulation, knowledge can be developed in creative ways with the support of power, and power, in turn, is regenerated through living forms of knowledge ("living" knowledge refers to forms developed and used to be thoughtful and creative while "dead" forms are crafted and applied to administer and control).[6] When and where this balance takes place, civilization can adapt in the face of crises.[7] However, when power dominates and its agents do not understand their long-term need for living knowledge, collapse beckons (Watson 2006, 306–312).

The owl—once an extension of Minerva's wisdom—provides Innis with a metaphor for the status and treatment of knowledge in the twentieth century. Scholars and other intellectuals now are subservient; they furnish the powerful—primarily the state and corporations—with tools and techniques needed to administer and control. The powerful perpetuate themselves but, under these imbalanced conditions, the creative capacities that knowledge and wisdom entail are eradicated.

More than just a resource to help his contemporaries assess their political-cultural conditions with some perspective, Innis, more ambitiously, drew on such mythologies and the histories of ancient empires as means of assessing what shapes the parameters of cultural capacities. What he referenced as "the Greek tradition" (1946, 65) was, arguably, the fulcrum of this perspective.

Before the invention of the Greek alphabet, communication through writing in the Near East was inaccessible to all but a small number of mostly religious elites whose mastery over an esoteric and thus sacred language separated them and the media they monopolized from the vernacular. Their diffusion of knowledge to others mostly involved rituals and ecstatic modes of learning. In Greece, the oral tradition—reliant on myth, song, poetry, and performance—was itself similarly limiting (a limitation to rational thinking that Plato, for one, criticized). Writing using a phonetic alphabet, however, enabled people to counterbalance the dominance of their ears and an ecstatic education to instead use their eyes through script. Emotive rituals now could be complimented or countered through a widely accessible communications system removed from the spoken word. As such, the individual's ordering of his/her own ideas (and thus sense of individualism) was significantly advanced (Watson 2006, 370).

In terms of the dialectic between power and knowledge, this and many other examples demonstrate the complexity in Innis' work—a complexity that is almost certainly purposeful. References to power and knowledge invite readers to actively engage their intellectual capacities and Innis, in keeping with this method of presentation, refused to champion some form of media determinism. As he puts it in the first paragraph of *The Bias of Communication* (1951), the papers in that book are an attempt to answer the question "Why do we attend to the things to which we attend?" Innis then tells us that "They do not answer the question but are reflections stimulated by a consideration of it. They emphasize the importance of communication in determining 'things to which we attend' and suggest also that changes in communication will follow changes in 'the things to which we attend'" (xliii).

Here Innis states that changes in communication follow changes in the things to which we attend. Innis' concept of bias clearly is not about the inherent conceptual and sensual orientations inscribed through media; bias, instead, is a heuristic tool used to assess the historical determinants shaping power-knowledge dialectics. Rather than a master concept applied to find *the* truth, bias is applied as a means of investigating why dominant truths are conceptualized as they are. In fact, bias served an almost secondary role for Innis—secondary and supportive to his more general concerns regarding power relations and what he termed "monopolies of knowledge."

INNIS' APPROACH TO UBIQUITOUS MEDIA

Through monopolies of knowledge we find what is, in essence, Innis' approach to ubiquitous media. For him, space and time are the two fundamental indices of human existence, not just organizationally but also in terms of perception and understanding. The need to comprehend and control both is, for him, a profound and complex endeavor not least because they are the subjects of ongoing change. "The concepts of time and space," he writes, "must be made *relative and elastic* and the attention given by the social scientist to problems of space should be paralleled by attention to problems of time" (Innis 1946, 34. Emphases added).

Controlling or monopolizing knowledge—control over both the information available and how it is interpreted—prospectively takes place through predominant and, certainly, ubiquitous media.[8] Media, in effect, enable not only a dominant way of organizing society, they also facilitate appropriate or common sense ways of thinking. There is, in fact, a link between the development or presence of ubiquitous media and such monopolies but it is not a direct causal relationship. Moreover, the use of a ubiquitous medium does not itself yield a monopoly of knowledge, but in its absence, the capacity to develop and sustain such a monopoly is questionable.

For Innis, media are the relational environments through which human interactions take place. They reflect and influence biases. Biases, generally, constitute our conceptual capacities—the parameters in which information and experience are processed into what is knowable. Simply put, how a medium is structured—whether it is writing, the price system, a bureaucracy, or the Internet—influences how people using it think. Ultimately, the materialization of such biases through social structures and a society's inter-subjectivities constitute the framework for what is thinkable and imaginable.[9]

Over the long course of civilizational history, Innis tells us that empires come and go alongside their capacity (or incapacity) to sustain and control political economic activities. In this *longue durée* analysis, ubiquitous media constitute crucial intellectual and structural nodal points through which social-economic relations are established and extended over time and space. The development and maintenance of an empire thus involves the capacity to recognize and respond to the endogenous and exogenous problems that such mediated conditions entail. Media are developed, entrenched, or reformed in response. Successful empires can do this while others fall into crises.

Informing this historical pattern was, to repeat, a dialectic that Innis was familiar with in part through his encounters with the work of classicists—that between power and knowledge. Power (involving coercive mechanisms and force) needs knowledge (often in the hands of specialists and elites) that can be applied to organization and administration. Those in commanding positions (particularly political, economic, and military leaders) tend to focus on such dimensions to the neglect of more reflexive and critical forms of knowledge (knowledge usually produced by intellectuals, artists, and even political dissenters). In other words, those in power occupying the centre or core are compelled to dominate the intellectual and political margins. The core, however, needs what the margins produce—from wealth to creative thinking—in order to (at least in the long term) reproduce itself. Power's necessary dominance over knowledge thus constitutes a threat to itself.

Power tends to dominate knowledge—promoting and using what Innis would refer to as "dead" forms of knowledge—yet power also needs another kind of knowledge—"living" knowledge—in order to successfully respond to the (inevitable) problems facing the system or empire. In sum, living (self-reflective, creative, critical) forms of knowledge are needed as a resource for thinking differently; to, in effect, counterbalance the tendency towards a monopolization of knowledge. As Innis (1951, 34) recognizes (and warns) in *The Bias of Communication*,

> The use of a medium of communication over a long period will to some extent determine the character of knowledge to be communicated and suggest that its pervasive influence will eventually create a civilization in which life and flexibility will become exceedingly difficult to maintain.

A sustainable society, empire, or civilization thus must possess the capacity to resist its own biases and ossification. This capacity is not (simplistically) the outcome of some kind of liberal tolerance of marginal groups who wish to communicate and express themselves (i.e., outcomes of, in a contemporary context, access to the Internet and entrenched civil and speech rights). Such human rights, while theoretically desirable, are not directly equated, in Innis, with the capacity to think reflexively and produce living forms of knowledge.[10] Nor is this capacity seen to be an inevitable outcome of an individual's or group's marginalized status. Instead, Innis recognizes that *a monopoly of knowledge can engulf not just elites but also a society's most exploited and intellectually radical elements.*

With this and the overarching power-knowledge dialectic in mind, we can read one of Innis' most widely cited passages with some precision. In *Empire and Communications*, he outlines his oft-quoted theory of technology and time/space bias:

> The concepts of time and space *reflect* the significance of media to civilization. Media that *emphasize* time are those that are durable in character, such as parchment, clay, and stone.... Media that *emphasize* space are *apt* to be less durable and light in character, such as papyrus and paper. The latter are *suited to* wide areas in administration and trade....Materials that emphasize time *favour* decentralization and hierarchical types of institutions, while those that *emphasize* space *favour* centralization and systems of government less hierarchical in character. Large-scale political organizations such as empires must be considered from the standpoint of two dimensions, those of space and time. *Empires persist by overcoming the bias of media which overemphasizes either dimension.* They have *tended* to flourish under conditions in which civilization *reflects* the influence of more than one medium, and in which the bias of one medium towards decentralization is *offset* by the bias of another medium towards centralization. (Innis 1950, 5. Emphases added)

The reader will note that Innis, in relating media to an empire's control over space or time, stresses how their characteristics emphasize propensities, not concrete necessities, and that they entail tendencies rather than determining factors. Media, in other words, imply the structuring of capacities—the parameters of what is possible or impossible, imaginable or unimaginable. Spatial or temporal biases emerge from the use of technological, organizational, and institutional mediators in the pursuit and administration of (or resistance to) power. The predominance of particular mediators in a given place and time reflects and tends to perpetuate general biases. These biases are shaped by and, in turn, shape the formation of particular ways or systems of thinking and, more abstractly, monopolies of knowledge.

In most of his writings Innis uses the concept of a monopoly of knowledge liberally. In "Minerva's Owl," for example, he writes that

> I have attempted to suggest that Western civilization has been profoundly influenced by communication and that marked changes in communications have had important implica-

tions…I have attempted to trace the implications of the media of communication for the character of knowledge and to suggest that a monopoly or an oligopoly of knowledge is built up to the point that equilibrium is disturbed. (Innis 1951: 3)

In just this paper, Innis lists an array of influential technologies (most directly clay, the stylus, cuneiform script, papyrus, the brush, hieroglyphics and hieratic writing, the pen, the alphabet, parchment, paper, printing, the printing press, celluloid, and radio) in what can be read as an overview of the rise and fall of monopolies of knowledge. Also, Innis addresses the development and implications of many dozens of other media—technologies, organizations, and institutions. For example, the ancient development of the horse and chariot facilitated the unity of city states primarily through the use of force but also through the corporal awareness of Rome's power that this military technology entailed. The use of coins after 700 BCE provided for both the flexible development of market systems and the capacity to further abstractify the nature of human relationships. The development of libraries and museums enabled both the conservation and utilization of the past. The Roman contract clarified obligations and reduced the costly need for public ceremony. The rise of monasticism provided the Roman Catholic Church with agents who reproduced (selections of) written knowledge while also promoting faith and the bible throughout Europe. The rise of commerce involved institutions that encouraged exchange, individualism, and order. Advertising promoted aspects of existing reality and stimulated new and more abstract realities. In these and many other examples, institutions, organizations, and technologies are developed, applied, or modified to mediate capacities concerning power and knowledge. They extend existing relations and open up potentials for their disruption.

THE PRICE SYSTEM AND PRINTING

Let us now be more specific on how the concept "monopoly of knowledge" is related to Innis' analyses of ubiquitous media. In this section, I do this through a brief consideration of two relatively contemporary examples: the price system and printing.

The price system is the predominant means of valuing what people exchange using monetary representations—representations that, by the twentieth century, constituted a dominant means of understanding economic relations and policy-making. Innis began his critique of the price system by demonstrating the inaccurate and even delusional aspects of its use. What had been a relatively rational measurement of human preferences in relation to resources became the central mechanism through which imbalances in (or a disequilibrium between) desires and capabilities were understood and worked out. Innis thus critiques more than just the price system's influence in capitalist development; he also assesses its implications in modern thought.

The price system is a predominant institution providing unprecedentedly complex economic relations with both their grease and glue. As such it mediates and fundamentally influences human thought through its concrete applications and in how it is used to organize abstract relations and ideas. Assessing its impact, Innis traces the price system's development from the efforts of European states to administer mercantilist activities involving the importation of gold and silver to subsequent developments in the construction of classical political economy to its use as a means of managing (and legitimizing) political economic relations promoted by powerful vested interests. Thus, through its pervasive use, the favored calculations or valuations of merchants, industrialists, bankers, accountants, state administrators, and others (such as advertisers and modern corporations) came to take precedence as reified ways of thinking.

A monopoly of knowledge thus can be structured through the ubiquitous use of such a medium. More than this, however, Innis was disturbed by how such monopolies became entrenched in ways of thinking that are largely unperceived and self-perpetuating. In the case of the price system, through its material and intellectual pervasiveness, it became a means through which its own faux neutrality was reproduced and applied in everything from the calculations used to declare war to the costs and benefits of staying in a marriage. The price system, according to Innis, has even limited our capacity to imagine the future by funneling our community and personal values through a prism of monetary and mathematical calculations. "The successful politician," writes Innis (1946, 165), "is precluded from policies which indicate class or self-interest but he is successful in so far as he succeeds in enlisting the support of the price system."

The ubiquity of the price system and its largely unspoken advantages for some interests over others enables its perpetuation and encloses both expert and common sense thinking in an invisible cage that delimits the boundaries of reality. For example, given the price system's institutionalization in the seventeenth century in response to the vast influx of gold from the new world, he writes that "It would be interesting to speculate on the history of economic thought if England had been an important producer of precious metals and not an importer and an exporter" (*ibid.*, 146). The price system, while initially counter-balancing the irrationalities of religion, subsequently perpetuated biases that enabled control while, in so doing, it also framed the parameters of creativity.[11]

The price system's "dangers," writes Innis (*ibid.*, ix), "follow obsession and intolerance to a philosophical interest and skepticism." It is in this context—the tendency of "dead" forms of knowledge to overwhelm the "living"—that Innis assesses the first half of the twentieth century in a way that emphasizes the extraordinary implications of such intellectual mechanisms:

The outbreak of irrationality, which in the early part of the twentieth century became evident in the increasing interest in psychology following the steadying effects of commerce in the nineteenth century, is the tragedy of our time. The rationalizing potentialities of the price system and its importance in developing powers of calculation in the individual have failed to prevent a major collapse. It has been argued that man as a biological phenomenon has been unable to sustain the excessive demands of rationalism evident in the mathematics of the price system and of technology. (Innis 1946: 98–99)

As for another ubiquitous medium—printing—Innis stresses its importance in terms of what he calls the mechanization of knowledge. Rapid economic growth, particularly dating from industrialization in the nineteenth century, and the related rise of democracy and public opinion (mostly through literacy and the commercial press) entailed the development of media (institutions, organizations, and technologies) enabling growth and control over workers/consumers/citizens. This complex of developments directly implied the ubiquitous availability and use of printed forms of communication.

With wood pulp replacing rags as the raw material for newsprint, and with a train of print technology developments (driven most overtly by the demands of advertisers), mass market journalism flourished by the end of the nineteenth century. Changes in other areas of publishing emerged also; changes molded, perhaps most significantly, through the growing power of voters and consumers. What was called "the new journalism"—the penny press being an extreme form—was facilitated by (and itself influenced) broader and deeper cultural developments. In this history, through his understanding of center-margin relations and the power-knowledge dialectic, Innis saw media being used in a paradoxical way: power seemingly was being decentralized through democracy and the rising influence of public opinion but these also constituted means of controlling polities and markets. The demands of the working class, for example, were funneled through mediators (such as advertising-sponsored newspapers) that both fragmented intellectual capacities and incorporated dissent through another institutional development—mass consumption.

In this process, journalistic and other writing standards were debased. But also in the context of these changes, some news organizations turned away from "spuriousness" and, instead, promoted "accuracy and truth," especially as the former was not in keeping with the newspaper's emerging role as the medium of their advertisers supposed truthfulness (Innis 1946, 27–28). Nevertheless, in seeking to accommodate mass readerships on behalf of capitalist interests, and in light of the growing competition facing the press with more sensually-engaging media such as cinema and radio, newspapers and other printed communications came to demonstrate an antipathy to "the deep intensity of thought" (Babe and Comor 2018, n.p.; Sir Walter Scott, quoted in Innis 1946, 30).

Printing, as a technology developed in conjunction with (and in support of) other influential developments, promulgated a general interest in current events, accessible explanations, and seeing-is-believing standards of "truth" (the latter typically involving images and statistics). The development of mass education, for example, involved the state-sponsored rise of textbook publishing. Beyond its political and nationalistic implications, Innis (*ibid.*, 100) argues that the textbook "has become…a powerful instrument for the closing of men's minds" due to, among other things, "its emphasis on memory and its systematic checking of new ideas" through indexes and their re-publication as updated editions. "Biases," Innis continues, "become entrenched in textbooks which represent monopolies of the publishing trade and resist the power of thought."[12]

Textbooks enabled power (through the state) to manage the dissemination of knowledge and, in so doing, particular forms of knowledge were perpetuated. Even Canada's universities were compelled to conform. They were (and still are), after all, publicly funded. As such, research and teaching activities—particularly in the context of a present-minded and price system dominated culture—have to be substantiated in terms of their demonstrable (as opposed to abstract and long-term) contributions. As with the newspaper, in the university the timeliness of knowledge and its relevancy to contemporary (and often fashionable) concerns became increasingly valued. Both journalism and academia actively perpetuated this shift and the volume, subject matter, and quality of publications reflected this directly.

The ubiquity of printing enabled an explosion of information and knowledge in largely debased and vernacular forms and the qualitative dimensions of knowledge were, in effect, flattened.[13] Partially in response to this (and enabled by the unprecedented availability of print technology), specializations flourished. More than just advertising and its immediate gratification priorities had come to dominate cultural norms and intellectual pursuits.

The upshot, for Innis, has been the mechanization (and deadening) of knowledge and, through this, some disturbing developments. Indeed, Innis characterized the nineteenth century as a period of relative rationalism while, in light of the changes mediated through the price system, industrialized printing, and other ubiquitous media, the twentieth was characterized by an irrationalism yielding "a century of war" (*ibid.*, 55; Babe and Comor 2018, n.p.). Publications addressing increasingly isolated fields and sub-fields revealed, for him, a lack of perspective that is both spatial (as with cross-at-your-own-peril boundaries of expertise) and temporal (especially in terms of the present-mindedness that most specializations imply).[14]

The unprecedented availability of information and the precision afforded by print technologies constituted something very different from a democratization of knowledge and the foundations for a more thoughtful society. Academic knowledge, for one thing, was being produced and thought about in more functional, instrumental, and exacting terms, rather than in terms of its value as a means of reflection, critique, and even collective understanding. "Knowledge," Innis observes, instead "has been divided to the extent that it is apparently hopeless to expect a common point of view" (Innis 1951, 190). According to Innis (1946, 126):

> The rapid growth of bureaucracies recruited from highly specialized social sciences has brought the rapid growth of ecclesiasticism and the rapid decline of scepticism. Democracies are becoming people who cannot understand, run by people buttressed and protected by the ramparts of research....[In the words of Locke] 'The greater part cannot learn and therefore they must believe.'

The mechanization and mass consumption of printed communications propagated, through both form and content, the value of the new, the practical, and the intellectually manageable. This, for Innis, constituted a fundamental contradiction. Industrial scale printing enabled and embodied a pernicious compounding of the short-term and unreflexive thinking that had become lauded as an inherently democratic and thus unimpeachable right. But in the absence of even those on the political and intellectual margins (for example, many workers as well as artists and intellectuals concentrating on mostly "living" forms of knowledge) having the capacity to recognize this decline of thoughtfulness, the ahistorical (if not suicidal) drumbeat of "progress" continued. More than this, Innis viewed the rapid development of efficient and more "perfect" methods of communication to be compounding this mostly invisible crisis. Beyond the many specializations these afford, the power to produce and circulate sounds and images portraying "reality" would mediate even more time-neglecting forms of knowledge. Power (Minerva), in effect, was treating knowledge (her owl) as a pet rather than a means of enlightenment and survival (Watson 2006, 309). The "enormous capacity" of Western civilization "to loot," writes Innis (*ibid.*, 102), particularly through the ubiquity of increasingly realistic mediations, "has left little opportunity for consideration of the problems which follow the exhaustion of [cultural and intellectual] material to be looted."

TOWARDS AN INNISIAN APPROACH TO UBIQUITOUS DIGITAL MEDIA

To summarize, the ubiquity of a medium facilitates or provides the capacity for the emergence or entrenchment of some form of monopoly of knowledge. While the medium itself does not determine this monopolization, the ways in which a medium structures, or enables the production and communication of some kinds of information over others and some ways of thinking in relation to others are its most germane implications. The price system and printing demonstrate this and so too might an Innisian analysis of digital communications technologies.

As with other ubiquitous media, Innis certainly would assess digital technologies in the context of a complex of political economic and cultural dynamics and in relation to other influential mediators. Monopolies of knowledge, such as the mechanistic, specialized, organizational, administrative forms of knowledge dominating much of the twentieth century (and related biases concerning spatial control to the neglect of time), are neither automatically perpetuated nor transformed by the wide scale introduction of such a medium. Moreover, as an historicist, Innis would argue that we cannot fully comprehend the implications of any emergent technology, organization, or institution until time gives us the perspective needed to make such an assessment.

Having said this, however, following his efforts to comprehend the uses and implications of the predominant media of his time, we can at least begin an Innisian analysis of ubiquitous digital media by recognizing them to have been built within (and in response to) the parameters of existing media (broadly defined) and the general dynamics driving (and the capacities framing) their development. The price system, for example, was and remains an institutionalized means of organizing and facilitating economic (and other) activities in ways that are constitutive of a particular political economic order and the values and vested interests it supports. Likewise, printing enables some powerful interests to maintain or extend their control over a society's wealth and common sense thinking involving the capacity to shape public opinion through education, advertising, and the allocation of or specialized control over such resources. Viewed historically, the ubiquity of these media has been and remains a reflection of their enormous usefulness and flexibilities especially (but not exclusively) as nodal points of power among both status quo and competing interests. If for no other reason, ubiquitous media become ubiquitous because they are handy to vested interests. The consequences of their use, however, are not always predictable as the dynamics and factors shaping history are too complex.

For Innis, history provides us with the potential to assess the present with some perspective, enabling us to identify general tendencies and patterns that we might apply to contemporary developments. For one thing, established cultural and economic capacities and dynamics shape the structuring of emergent media while older media are compelled to change in response to the demands mediated by the successful new ones. The owners, editors, and writers of newspapers and books, for example, in their responses to radio and cinema, modified their products in order to be more attractive and accessible (mostly through simplifications, sensationalism, photography, color printing, comics, etc.). Today, in light of the "obvious" advantages of online forms of journalism, most newsprint versions are deemed to be a waste of time (and money)—especially for advertisers—and the book, through its many digitized iterations, is becoming a hybrid vehicle crafted to engage consumers even more sensually (as opposed to intellectually) than it had in the past. Through this technological "progress"—involving the book's "democratization" and "liberation" from publishers—the value of concentration, reflection, and long-term considerations (not to mention the prestige of the author and the written word itself) likely are being further marginalized.[15] As Innis (1951, 82–83) observed, such spatially biased developments—i.e., the unprecedented reach and accessibility of online publications—make it "increasingly difficult to achieve continuity or to ask for a consideration of the future."

Part of this annihilation of time involves, for Innis, an understanding of the pressures facing people in our time—given that "time is money" and "money is time" (George Gissing quoted in Innis 1951, 83)—and that new media enable us to live more of our lives without having to engage in the difficult and time-consuming task of critical/self-reflexive thought. Representations of reality—like assumptions that "Truth" is the outcome of scientific and mathematical applications—have been perfected through digital technologies. However, as Innis quotes Geoffrey Scott, "It is…the last sign of an artificial civilisation when Nature takes the place of art" (Scott quoted in Innis 1951: 193). What Innis means by this becomes apparent in the following excerpt from his essay "A Plea for Time":

> The effects of new media of communication evident in the outbreak of the Second World War were intensified during the progress of the war. They were used by the armed forces in the immediate prosecution of the war and in propaganda both at home and against the enemy. In Germany moving pictures of battles were taken and shown in theatres almost immediately afterwards. The German people were given an impression of realism which compelled them to believe in the superiority of German arms; realism became not only most convincing but also with the collapse of the German front most disastrous. In some sense *the problem of the German people is the problem of Western civilization. As modern developments in communication have made for greater realism they have made for greater possibilities of delusion.* (Innis 1951: 81–82. Emphases added)

In the absence of an innate capacity to recognize that information and experience are not themselves objective realities, the technological mastery of media presents the individual and the mass public with little room for interpretation (i.e., nature over art). In this observation, Innis harkens back to the concerns that Plato says were expressed by Socrates with the advent of the Greek alphabet and writing (as quoted earlier). To repeat, as Innis (1946, vii) quotes Socrates in *Phaedrus*, with writing, people will convey "the show of wisdom without the reality."

In a world mediated, regulated, and governed through mostly unquestioned representations (prices as values; printed words as truths; digital technologies mimicking concrete experiences), ways of thinking that entail little or no reflection (let alone historical or philosophical perspective) are normalized. Thoughts, let alone actionable concerns, about society's long-term duration thus become further marginalized; they are deemed to be a waste of time and money, especially in a political economy and culture that perpetually lacks the former and values, more than anything else, the latter.

An Innisian analysis, furthermore, would recognize that digital technologies reflect and extend capitalism's (and, more generally, power's) emphasis on timeliness and efficiency in decision-making and, indeed, daily life itself.[16] As with Innis' recognition that biases tend to be self-perpetuating, this closing off of reflexive thinking in effect undercuts critiques concerning the monopoly of mechanized knowledge. In a cultural environment stressing individualism and efficiency and in the absence of time-consuming reflexive capacities, all kinds of digitally-mediated communications are embraced as the priorities and values they facilitate are both pervasive and seemingly obvious.

Innis, of course, assessing contemporary developments through his historical perspective and historicist epistemology, underlined that such media-facilitated monopolies of knowledge are inherently contradictory. Power appears to be served as Minerva's owl has been all but caged. Amidst splintering attention spans and fashion-induced moments of dissent, powerful vested interests (including, when organized, the citizens of liberal democracies) tend to focus their energies on management and control rather than conceptualizing (let alone forging) radically different ways of thinking. More generally, this neglect of time—particularly the value of understanding history, the time required to reflect, and the imagination and creativity needed to think about alternatives—compels the Innisian analyst to consider contemporary developments involving digital technologies to be far less liberating than many assume them to be. Here we would do well to recall the myth of Prometheus.

From Innis' study of history—a study driven in part by his quest to develop an alternate (relatively unbiased) perspective—he tells us that the margins of any political economic system and culture have the greatest capacity to resist, particularly given their removal from the full force of the core's framing dynamics and mediated realities.[17] In their struggles with the core (or political economic empire) they may be compelled to adapt dominant media in light of their own needs and interests. This, for Innis, is not necessarily the basis for revolution but, instead, it constitutes an important means of countering monopolies of knowledge. To use his preferred language, marginal demands may constitute part of a system's unused capacities and, thus, new ways of thinking may emerge as a result of center-margin tensions and dynamics.

As Innis' work reveals, however, imperial centers draw from or directly loot the economic and cultural resources of their margins as they are primary sources for ideas and innovation. The systemic drives associated with capitalism compel new means of control, new bases for resistance and, indeed, the potential for cultural vibrancy. But in our contemporary context, through the price system and other ubiquitous media (including digital technologies used to educate, advertise, market, and "stay connected all the time"), Innis' concerns about spatial control, the mechanization of knowledge, and an immediate future of misunderstanding and instability appear to be warranted.

CONCLUSIONS

Under the conditions of their contemporary use, digitally mediated communications provide instantaneous knowledge. Their seeing-is-believing qualities facilitate what Innis might call the delusion of certainty. Specializations are perpetuated and publics gravitate towards the less time-consuming and intellectually supportive views of like-minded others. Arrogance and narcissism deepen as truths are pontificated based on not much more than experientially-informed reckonings and prejudices. The reach and perfection of digital communications likely would prompt Innis to reiterate his statement that:

> Enormous improvements in communication have made understanding more difficult. Even science, mathematics, and music as the last refuge of the Western mind have come under the spell of the mechanized vernacular. Commercialism has required the creation of new monopolies in language and new difficulties in understanding. (Innis 1951, 31)

Innis also observes that the introduction a new medium tends to "check the bias of the first [and dominant medium] and to create conditions suited to the growth of empire" (Innis 1950, 169). In other words, there is a tendency for power to adjust its course as a result of the counterbalance to its monopoly of knowledge that may emerge through the use of a new (and perhaps ubiquitous) medium. Barring complete collapse—a development that in the twentieth century he associated with another, now atomic/nuclear, world war—Innis, however, does not anticipate anything remotely revolutionary.

Perhaps today's rapid development of ubiquitous digital media constitutes this very occurrence: digital media somehow constituting a check and counterbalance to print (or, as McLuhan put it, the dominance of typographical man). Certainly, other ubiquitous media—such as the price system—are not directly threatened by digitization. However, a goal of this chapter has been to point out that such general tendencies are, for Innis, not laws of history. There is no, to borrow from some Marxists, immanent dialectic at work (except, arguably, the trans-historical dialectic between power and knowledge). Innis' dialectical materialism is, instead, historically conditional in that Innis resisted what he criticized others for following: ossified schools of thought generating mechanized forms of knowledge.

Nevertheless, from an Innisian perspective, the transition to digital media seems to constitute the widening and deepening of pre-existing conditions more than the mediation of a new period of cultural vibrancy. Certainly something new is taking shape but, most likely, this is unfolding through an entrenched monopoly of knowledge and, therefore, the dawning of a more reactionary political culture—"reactionary" on the part of not just the right and left but the center also.

What Innis provides analysts conducting research on the subject of ubiquitous media is an approach that compels us to focus on the structural and intellectual capacities at hand, the complex dynamics and mediations at play, and the generally unseen tensions and contradictions that may be at work. Innis' understanding of ubiquitous media is slippery and complicated and, thus, prone to simplifications bordering on assessments akin to some kind of media determinism. In this chapter, following Watson (2006), I have argued that the most productive link to Innis' concerns is not some straightforward analysis of media bias but, instead, it is to relate ubiquitous media to monopolies of knowledge and, more broadly, the dialectic between power and knowledge.

In monopolies of knowledge, assumptions about the truth fatally supersede "the *search* for truth" (Innis 1946, 126. Emphasis added). In pursuing questions concerning the development and implications of ubiquitous media, Innis would underline this very point as both a guide and a warning.[18]

NOTES

1. This chapter was written while preparing, with co-editor Robert Babe, the re-publication of Innis's *Political Economy in the Modern State* (Toronto: University of Toronto Press, 2018). Through that project he played an important role in the intellectual development of what I present herein, and I recognize that portions of this chapter echo parts of our work for that book. I also acknowledge the assistance of Vincent Manzerolle for his thoughtful input during the chapter's development. Finally, I am compelled to dedicate this chapter to the late Professor Ian Parker. His influence on my understanding of Innis's work has been immeasurable.
2. Although I have found no direct (let alone sustained) use of the term "ubiquitous media" in Innis' work, in what follows I hope to demonstrate his interest in the subject.
3. Institutions, in Innis' works, refer to both formal institutions (such as the Church) and the more socio-economic (such as the price system). Organizations generally reference headquartered collectivities such as banks, political parties, or universities. Technologies, it should be noted, also imply techniques (his references to print, for instance, involve abilities related to literacy).
4. For Marx, the commodity form (conceptualized as an institution) might be said to mediate such contemporary relations while, for Innis, what he called the price system was central in similar (but more limited) ways.
5. Later in his career, during the 1940s, Innis came to appreciate Greek mythology as an ideal-type form of knowledge in that it embodied both the vibrancy of orality (particularly at the time of Plato, at the dawn of writing) in conjunction with its capacity to communicate ontologically objective truths concerning shared conditions. Alexander John Watson (2006, 301) suggests that Innis' critique of monopolies of knowledge drew from similar themes found in Greek mythology.
6. Innis' understanding of power developed from a political economy-based relational and structural conceptualization (as in his earlier research on Canadian economic history) into an approach char-

acterized by a complex of relations in which power/force and knowledge/intelligence constitute dialectically interdependent capacities.
7. According to Innis, "The success of organized force is dependent on an effective combination of the oral tradition and the vernacular in public opinion with technology and science." (Innis 1951, 5).
8. Although Innis never used the term ubiquitous to describe an institution, organization, or technology, the engaged reader can discern quantitative and qualitative differences between media that are predominant and those that are ubiquitous at a given place and time. In his six years of dedicated writing on media and communications (1946–1952), various media such as radio, the automobile, and roads had become predominant while the price system, print capitalism, and the state were ubiquitous.
9. Of course, the material properties of media foundationally shape the capacities of such structures.
10. On democracy as practiced in the mid-twentieth century, quoting François Guizot, Innis writes that "It readily sacrifices the past and the future to what is supposed to be the interest of the present" (Innis 1946: 95).
11. In Marx, something very similar can be seen in the predominance of the commodity form and its profound implications in social relations. Its ubiquity—more abstract and defining than Innis' concerns about the price system—mediate concrete/living relations through the predominance of abstractions.
12. On the other hand, "Abolition of standard texts in favour of the publication of a wide variety of books increases the cost of education to the publishers, the state, and the purchaser of books, but it tends to break down broad stereotypes" (Innis 1946, 162).
13. The first two chapters of Innis' (1946) *Political Economy in the Modern State*, for example, explore and demonstrate this theme through the history of the newspaper in the United States and Britain and the modern press in England.
14. On this second point, as the interests and exclusionary vocabularies of specialists develop, their work becomes less accessible to others and, as such, their primary readership are similarly specialized administrators, scholars, and bureaucrats.
15. It is in this cultural context that pension fund investments and insurance issues are worth losing sleep over but seemingly abstract concerns involving, for example, ecological survival or the proliferation of nuclear weapons are, for most, mere "issues."
16. More generally, as classical political economists (most notably, Marx) first recognized, capitalism is a historically unique form of production (and reproduction) entailing, through legal and other modes of abstractification, a *systemic drive* to expand the accumulation of capital and, in the process, shorten the timeframes of all kinds of social relations.
17. Through his direct and indirect references to center-margin and core-periphery relations, Innis alludes to a range of structural and cultural conditions that, to repeat, elaborate classical power-knowledge dialectics. His use of space-time dialectics in his later writings is an obvious example (both alluding to tensions and contradictions involving the capacity to control and think reflexively). Implicit in this ever-mediating dynamic is the complexity of hegemonic power, entailing both coercive and consensual capacities.
18. Indeed, in the first paragraph of his Preface to *Political Economy in the Modern State*, Innis writes that "The volume is intended as a guide and as a warning" (1946, vii).

REFERENCES

Babe, Robert E. and Edward A. Comor. 2018. "Editors' Chapter Introductions." In *Political Economy in the Modern State*, edited by Robert E. Babe and Edward A. Comor, n.p. Toronto: University of Toronto Press.

Innis, Harold A. 1946. *Political Economy in the Modern State*. Toronto: The Ryerson Press.

———. 1950. *Empire and Communications*. London: Oxford University Press.

———. 1951. *The Bias of Communication*. Toronto: University of Toronto Press.

Watson, A. John. 2006. *Marginal Man: The Dark Vision of Harold Innis*. University of Toronto Press.

CHAPTER ELEVEN

THE Mediated Experiences OF Our Everyday/Everynight Lives

Notes From a Case Study on Digital Labor

SUSAN BRYANT

Canadian feminist sociologist Dorothy Smith (1999) has argued compellingly for a political economy of the everyday and everynight worlds as a means of highlighting the limitations of mainstream critical analyses of social relations. Her primary focus in making this argument has been to accentuate the need for increased attention to *women's* standpoints and experiences when carrying out research; not only should women become generators of knowledge but women's experiences needed to be brought within the frame of the research gaze. Smith's concept of the everyday and everynight as a focus of analysis has also been foundational to the development of an institutional ethnographic approach that enables researchers to consider experiences outside what she calls the "ruling relations" (Smith 1999, 31; see also Campbell and Gregor 2008; Smith 1987, 1990).

Smith's (1999) approach has included a wider range of experiences within the focus of social research, as well as more nuanced and in-depth methods that take as central activities or experiences that may have previously been considered too banal or mundane to be worthy of researchers' consideration. Her institutional ethnography asks ethnographic questions about everyday life, but sets the insights gained within the larger political economic context in order to make the personal, the everyday, a key aspect of social analysis. Smith's political economy is therefore more holistic both in terms of considering all of the hours of individuals' lives, and in terms of including categories of people (as well as activities) previously excluded from traditional social science research.

Smith's attention to the everyday and everynight experiences of subjects seems all the more relevant within the context of our contemporary media world, given that the ways in which most digital technologies have been adopted have involved a permeation of almost every moment of our everyday and everynight lives and experiences. In this chapter, I take up Smith's approach in general terms, and employ it to demonstrate the need to understand contemporary digital culture in not only a critical, but also a more holistic manner. This approach is used as the basis for an analysis of the experiences of a group of undergraduate teaching assistants (TAs) working with an online writing course at a Canadian university—online courses being one expression of our digital age that relies more and more on ubiquitous media, with students accessing and working on the course through their laptops and/or smartphones. In particular, the study explored the experiences of these undergraduate TAs with respect to the overall sense of connection or disconnection that they felt with/from the students they were responsible for (and also with/from others, including their fellow TAs and the course instructors). The study also explored the ways in which ubiquitous media offered opportunities for and/or challenges to the achievement of a positive paid work experience for these Teaching Assistants.

As I will demonstrate, the study revealed three key findings with regard to the TAs' experiences of their digital labor. First, the TAs' overall experience of the work, for the most part, was one in which they felt they were working on their own, and that the limitations of online communication negatively affected the degree to which they viewed their work experience as positive. Second, in terms of work-related satisfaction, they derived considerable fulfillment from knowing that they were helping students with their learning. Third, they explained that being able to meet the students' expectations often meant that they had to be almost constantly available, with no division between their paid and unpaid time.

"ALONE TOGETHER" IN THEIR EVERYDAY/EVERYNIGHT EXPERIENCES?

Sherry Turkle (2011) asserts that in the contemporary environment of being connected 24 hours a day, individuals are "tethered" to their digital devices and end up being in touch with a potentially limitless number of other people, yet fundamentally disconnected and lonely much of the time. She examines the cultural shifts to spending time "with" people we care about more and more through mediated means which enable us to make others "pauseable" and notes that "we have found ways of spending more time with [people] in which we hardly give them any attention at all" (2001, 264). Turkle makes the point that those who have immersed themselves in digital media as a key way of maintaining their relationships with others are "always on," always together, yet ultimately alone (Turkle 2011). This concern is discussed below in terms of the TAs' experiences with feeling digitally connected and yet isolated in their work in many respects.

Turkle also offers an analysis of the implications of ubiquitous media for the issue of the so-called "work-life balance" that is much discussed in our era. She argues that:

> Technology ties us up as it promises to free us up. Connectivity technologies once promised to give us more time. But as the cell phone and smartphone eroded the boundaries between work and leisure, all the time in the world was not enough. Even when we are not 'at work,' we experience ourselves as 'on call'; pressed, we want to edit out complexity and 'cut to the chase.' (13)

This blurring of the presumed line between work and leisure is, of course, a phenomenon with which women have long been familiar. A key contribution made by Dorothy Smith to our thinking about women's experiences was to highlight the fact that political economic analysis needed to be widened to include around-the-clock experiences and social relations. Such a shift would shine analytical light on women's political and material conditions, in particular, and allow for a widening of the lens of political economy to include those often outside of its formal focus, outside of the "relations of ruling" (Smith 1999). Implicit in Smith's arguments, and highlighted by numerous other feminists, is the artificiality of the dichotomy between paid and unpaid labor and between the so-called private realm of the household and the so-called public realm of paid work and other aspects of society (see, for example, Bergeron 2016; Garey and Hansen 2011; Hochschild 1989, 1997, 2011; Waring 2004). As feminist economist Marilyn Waring (2004) has so eloquently and compellingly argued, the long uncounted, unacknowledged, and unpaid (and often 'round the clock) labor of women around the world has historically been key to the operation of the formal global economy—a fact which therefore makes untenable the idea of home and work as separate. Interestingly, in the era of ubiquitous media, almost everyone—regardless of gender—is experiencing the permeation of their paid work lives into what they might have previously considered personal or private time. It is therefore very timely to revisit Dorothy Smith's arguments about the need for political economic analysis that looks at the everyday and the everynight, and to consider how women's (as well as men's) lives are being affected by the ways we are embracing ubiquitous technologies.

To suggest that using Smith's (1999) notion of a political economy of the everyday/everynight to better analyze the experiences of both men and women is absolutely *not* to diminish the importance of ongoing gendered analyses. Judy Wajcman (2008, 2015) has argued that long-standing gendered relations with respect to family responsibilities, as one example, need to be carefully assessed when analyzing the types of changes we are seeing within digital culture. We can extend Smith's political economy of the everyday/everynight to examine the experiences of all involved with ubiquitous media, but nonetheless retain a critical, gendered analysis within that assessment. Indeed, we need to be cognizant of the fact that women and girls have in some studies been found to have less leisure time per day (see Bittman and Wajcman 2000; Wajcman 2015; Waring 2004), but that even more important is the finding that even when men's and women's leisure time is comparable in number of hours, the time is qualitatively different. That is, men's leisure time tends to be in longer blocks of time and free of disruptions, while women's is in shorter blocks and tends to be interrupted or punctuated by other activities (Erikson 2011; Hochschild 1997; Wajcman 2015). As Judy Wajcman (2015, 81) argues: "The fragmentary character of women's leisure changes its quality. Interrupted leisure, snatched between work and self-care activities, is less restorative than unbroken leisure." Moreover, Wajcman has argued that the increasing permeability between so-called work and so-called leisure/private life brought about by the use of digital media —what she calls "the incessant pinging of phone, text and email messages" (81)—may have differential outcomes for men and women, whereby women, not surprisingly, may find that it increases their levels of stress and sense of an acceleration of the pace of life (2008, 2015). That is, because their lives have perhaps long involved constant multi-tasking, the addition of digital intrusions only adds to the list of things to be attended to at once (*ibid.*).

Moreover, as ubiquitous media experiences require of us a more holistic analysis of individuals' overall life experiences—without compartmentalizing the so-called public and private—we may also find that men now have less separation of their paid activities from their leisure (see Ladner 2008; Menzies 2011; Wajcman 2015). They now face many disruptions coming at them via digital devices, both related to their paid work and their social/personal lives, and they may be having to multi-task more and more. We must remember that it is not progress for men to now be facing some of the same challenges women have long faced, and even more pressingly, that a gendered analysis is still of utmost importance. This is so since despite their subversive and/or alternative possibilities, technologies have historically had a tendency to be taken up in everyday life in ways that reinforce dominant social relations including those related to gender (Wajcman 2004, 2009).

Sherry Turkle's concerns about contemporary ways of communicating and what they might mean for everyday experiences are also relevant for considering the practice of working in an online course—particularly when the majority of the teaching assistants in the study at hand were part of the generation that Turkle hones in on because they have grown up "tethered" (Turkle 2011, 171). If there are indeed potential limitations associated with new communication media, how might these also present challenges for particular types of online work? This study sought to understand the degree to which the mediated means of communication, which were by far the dominant form of interaction between TAs and students, shaped the experiences of working as a TA in the online course being studied. The study participants were asked about their feelings of connection and/or disconnection in their paid work role, how these feelings related to the overall quality of the experience, and how they organized their time in terms of the permeation of their paid work into their leisure/personal time.

Analyses of digital media's role in the changing landscape of paid work experiences are numerous (see, for example, Freeman 2009; Huws 2012, 2014; McKercher and Mosco 2008, 2010; Menzies 2005; Shade 2014; Wajcman 2008), but some of the concepts related to immaterial labor and, in particular the idea of "affective labor," seem especially helpful for this analysis. The types of work that involve highly intellectual and informationalized tasks have been identified as making up at least one version of what Lazzarato (1996) calls "immaterial labour." Within what has been called the post-Fordist era of immaterial labor, we have seen an increase in precariousness along with expectations of more mobility. At the same time, the distinctions between leisure and paid work time seem to have become more and more blurred (see Lazzarato 1996; Negri and Hardt 2000). Moreover, the notion of *affective labor*, in which "education, attitude, character, and 'prosocial' behavior [are] the primary skills employees need" (Hardt and Negri 2004, 108), seems to apply especially well to the work conducted by the undergraduate teaching assistants. That is, the work falls into the category of immaterial labor by its very nature—intellectual and informationalized—and also requires a high degree of affective sophistication in order to carry it out well. Moreover, it is indeed a form of "guiding" and "helping" work, as can be seen by both the job description and by the fact that the undergraduate students who applied for these positions often specifically articulated their desire to have a job that involved supporting and helping their peers in a course setting. They are indeed front-line workers of the university—they are the primary, and perhaps only, individuals interacting with students in a huge online course.

Assessing the experiences with this type of highly mediated, affective work for this group of young adults was the focus of the research. It is worth noting that less than 25 per cent of the respondents were men, and that this is representative of the typical gender split amongst the TAs in the course. While only one study does not indicate whether or not the affective labor involved in the TA position generally appeals more to women, the gendering of the role in the study at hand means that it was more often women than men who were vulnerable to the permeation of this paid work throughout their everyday and everynight lives.

Given the fact that immaterial labor, and perhaps especially affective labor, often results in the collapse of time/space boundaries between paid work and personal or leisure life, Smith's (1999) political economy of the everyday/everynight is a particularly appropriate approach to my research questions. Since the primary means of communication between students and TAs in the course being studied was email and a course website, the dividing line between being 'at work' and "not at work"—particularly given the dominance of smart phone use which enables ubiquitous digital access—seems potentially non-existent. Moreover, since institutional ethnography seeks to consider the experiences outside of the "ruling relations" (Smith 1999; see also Campbell and Gregor 2008), the approach is appropriate because the TAs worked for an academic institution, but both the men and the women were outside the relations of power in terms of either the university administration or the professorial level of workers involved in designing and delivering the course. These front-line workers were absolutely integral to the delivery of the course; indeed, the course, as it was offered—to over 2,000 students at a time—would simply not have been possible without their labor. And yet, these workers had very little input into the structures and systems within which they work.

(PRIMARILY) ONLINE TEACHING ASSISTANTS

During the semester in which the study was carried out, there were 51 undergraduate teaching assistants working with the large online writing course that was required of all undergraduate arts, humanities, and social science students at a medium-sized Canadian university. Approximately 2,200 students take the course, and this was the case in the winter semester in which the research was carried out. The goal of the course was for students to take two semesters of writing instruction (including grammar review, basic research and information assessment techniques, and academic writing with peer review activities) which was intended to help them improve their writing and therefore improve their chances of success in their subsequent years of study.

Most students took the two courses during their first undergraduate year and those that achieved very high marks in the course and demonstrated a high level of leadership and communication skills were considered to work as paid undergraduate TAs in the course, usually in their third or fourth years of study. They were provided with a one-day training session as well as ongoing individual mentoring by a more experienced TA. Each TA was assigned to a sub-section of the class, and their work involved answering questions by email, posting assignment guidance and reminders online, and assisting with the grading of students' work through an online platform. They also held one face-to-face office hour per week, and helped proctor the in-person exam in the course. Sign-in sheets used in the TAs' office showed over several semesters that the face-to-face office hours held by TAs were seldom used by the students. Students seemed to prefer to ask a question by email rather than attend an office hour to get help or feedback, as is discussed below in the findings section.

In order to provide full anonymity, and because they were already working in an online environment, an online questionnaire (through Fluid Surveys) was deemed the most effective way to reach the course TAs. Teaching assistants were invited to participate in the study by means of an announcement on the course website. The survey contained 16 questions, with the majority of them being open-ended in order to allow the TAs to elaborate on their experiences in as much detail as they wished. Table 11.1 presents some of the details related to the survey responses.

Table 11.1. The Survey

Total number of TAs working in course that semester	51
Fully completed surveys submitted	27
Survey response rate	52.9
Women who submitted a complete survey	21
Men who submitted a complete survey	6

The responses were analyzed question by question, searching for patterns in the data as well as with a view to identifying anomalies or atypical replies and experiences (see Berger 2013; Bryman, Bell, and Teevan 2012; Denzin and Lincoln 2011; Kirby, Greaves, and Reid 2006; Van den Hoonaard 2012). The respondents were very generous with their answers to the mainly open-ended questions, providing considerable detail in their completion of the survey.

THE FINDINGS—(DIS?)CONNECTED EVERY DAY AND EVERY NIGHT

Of the 27 respondents, all but one teaching assistant was between the ages of 18 and 25, with the final individual indicating that s/he was between 26 and 34 years of age. This outcome was consistent not only with the general demographics of the TA ranks of the course, but also with the general undergraduate demographic of most universities. When asked how many semesters they had worked as TAs with the course, the mean number of semesters worked was 3.5. In analyzing the responses, I have been careful to consider the responses to each segment of the survey as a whole, but also to reconsider the comments according to the level of experience the TA had with the course, in order to assess any differences that may exist.

The research was intended to understand how the Teaching Assistants' managed their time during their everyday/everynight lives. The TA contract was for 100 hours over the course of the semester, with the work being relatively evenly distributed throughout the semester; given that there were almost weekly assignments in the course, even the grading work remained steady overall. Therefore, the 12-week semester resulted in approximately eight hours of TA work per week. As individuals who were also full-time students, TAs needed to be organized and judicious with their use of time. This fact was exacerbated by the fact that 21 of the 27 responded that they also had other paid work in addition to the TA position. The mean number of hours worked in addition to their TA activities was 12.8 hours, with the range being between 3 and 30 hours per week.

When asked about fitting the TA work into their regular day, and how they managed the flow of communication from students as well as their grading work, the replies were very similar across the respondent group. The following three statements are representative of the TA group:

> Since a lot of work consisted of opening and answering emails, I would do this whenever I had free time. I would do this once I woke up, I would do it in between classes when I had access to a computer, I would do it once I came home, and again before bed. I was very mindful of checking email a lot when being a TA. It would be scattered throughout the day, I never set time aside just for email. For marking, I would try to do it during a certain block of time.

> I tried to respond to students' emails as quickly as I could (I would get email notifications on my phone, so that was convenient for responding to students' questions). I would usually finish my TA marking after I finished my regular school work, which meant marking into the wee hours.

> Since I would receive students' emails on my phone throughout the day, I would answer them right then and there so they wouldn't have to wait all day for a response. As for marking, I usually did it at the end of the night, after I finished my own homework.

As can be seen from this subset of responses, the TAs tended to set aside blocks of time to complete grading work—often late at night, after their own homework was completed—but the task of replying to student emails was something they viewed as part of the overall flow of their days and nights. Despite the fact that the explicit expectations set out in the course's TA training were simply that they should answer emails at least once every 24 hours, and this only between Monday and Friday, the sense that they felt they should not keep students waiting for a reply—at all—came up again and again in the TAs' responses.

The findings related to the responses to emails from students seem in line with what we have observed with respect to the acceleration of expectations in reply time in the digital age—what Judy Wajcman (2008), amongst others, has referred to as the acceleration of the pace of life. The tendency for students to leave their work, and therefore their questions, to the last minute exacerbated the sense of urgency surrounding some of the emails that the TAs received. However, the sense that one must respond immediately to each and every message right away seems likely to have been all the more internalized by a generation of workers who have grown up in the era of ubiquitous media. Since the TAs were, for the most part, of the same generation as the students to whom they were replying, the expectation of an immediate reply on the part of the student emailing was met with a corresponding, immediate reply from the teaching assistant. Indeed, both the student and the TA were what Turkle (2011) would refer to as "tethered" to their digital connections.

I should note that there was clearly a type of self-selection that resulted in highly successful, motivated, and conscientious students becoming interested in this type of immaterial, affective labor, and this might also explain them being so responsive with regard to emails. However, what seems even more noteworthy from the findings of this research is not merely that these were very keen and caring immaterial laborers, but how unquestioningly they accepted that their paid work would permeate every hour and minute of their lives. The political economy of the everyday and everynight experience has shifted—every moment of one's day or night has the potential to be appropriated in this ubiquitous media context. It would certainly be possible to set aside specific times during the day or night that would be dedicated to answering emails, in the same manner that most of the TAs reported carving out particular times in their schedules to do their grading. However, the TAs, for the most part, seemed to consciously choose to respond to email on an ongoing basis, with this aspect of the work woven into their everyday/everynight lived experiences. It is interesting to note that the majority of the TAs in this study were women, and therefore likely more vulnerable in terms of the types of stress to which Wajcman (2008, 2015) refers.

In addition to asking the TAs about their patterns of work, I also asked them a number of questions related to their experiences of working with students primarily in a mediated context. When asked if there were challenges to answering students' questions via email, and whether the medium presented any opportunities not available when meeting students in person, TAs' comments included the following:

> Email is not as efficient as explaining to the students in person. You cannot observe facial expressions and they cannot ask you questions during an explanation. It is difficult to see if they fully understand or not.

> It is hard to answer student questions via email because many students have trouble articulating what their actual question is. As well, students are more bold when they are unhappy with a grade since they can't see their TA face to face. It does present opportunities because questions can be answered sometimes in a five minute email where a meeting would be more lengthy.

> Email allows me to think over my wording and check with my professor or Head TA when I am uncertain of something. However, I find that email often comes across terse. It can be difficult to tell if a student has understood an explanation…

> Without a face put to the name, I think a lot of students don't really see their TAs as teachers or mentors. Many students would make appointments to meet with TAs and never show up, most likely because they don't think of us as a physical person....It's very frustrating.

Most of the TAs saw both opportunities and challenges in using email as the primary means of communicating with students in the course. As shown in the TAs' comments, the fact that students were able to receive a very quick response to their questions was seen as a very positive element of the medium. In addition, many of the TAs, as seen above, noted that the asynchronous nature of email gave them time to formulate a well-written and accurate reply to a student's question. They didn't feel put on the spot or rushed in terms of the reply they provided. This was especially important to many of them since the course is a writing course and the TAs knew the importance of modelling good writing in their emails to students.

On the other hand, almost all of the TAs offered comments on what they saw as the challenges of communicating with students via email. As seen in the illustrative quotes provided above, the TAs were very concerned about the quality of the communication, indeed the *teaching*, when using email rather than a face-to-face meeting. Sometimes this revolved around the problem of students not explaining their question very well, and other times it related to the barriers to being able to tell if the student had understood the reply. Long and detailed questions requiring an involved reply were considered especially unsuited to email interactions. Concerns were also raised about the difficulty of establishing a personal connection, with students not having put a face to the name, and vice versa. At best, this might mean that hesitant or shy students would be willing to ask a question they would not otherwise have asked. However, at the other end of the spectrum, TAs reported finding students' emails to be terse, or even rude at times, which they believed the student would not likely have been in a face-to-face discussion.

What is particularly noteworthy about the TAs' comments is the degree of *affective* labor (Hardt and Negri 2004) that was being taken on by these young front-line workers. The Teaching Assistants had a keen desire to mentor their students within the course and they reported spending considerable time and effort to make sure that their students received the help and support they needed in the potentially alienating format of an online, first-year course. This type of labor goes above and beyond just replying to emails in a perfunctory manner—the TAs cared about their students, wanted them to do well in the course, and put a lot of themselves into their interactions with them. However, using email as the primary means of communicating much of the instruction and support meant that this was a somewhat complicated and even contradictory process.

The contradictions in these interactions and relationships lay in the TAs' overall acceptance of the drawbacks of email conversations in exchange for the widespread view that the benefits—convenience, speed, efficiency—outweigh the problems.

The perspective on ubiquitous media that sees particular values related to efficiency, speed, and convenience as almost always worth the trade-offs is a pervasive one within our culture, and this study reveals that the TAs (and the students) have internalized these ways of employing email communication within the context of the course. Yet, the limitations to what can be "delivered" via email in terms of teaching and learning are also substantial, based on the TAs' comments. It seems that the TAs were pleased to be able to provide such rapid and efficient responses to the students, but were nonetheless frustrated that they often had to work harder at their affective labor in order to do a good job in terms of supporting students effectively, with sometimes mixed results, by their own estimation. It should be noted that the type of emotional work performed by the TAs falls very much within the scope of Smith's political economy approach—affective labor is one aspect of social relations that often falls outside the focus when research is not inclusive of everyday/everynight experiences, those experiences outside the "relations of ruling" (Smith 1999).

As noted already, each TA was required to hold one hour of office time each week, and when asked if they would have preferred to meet with students in person to answer questions or to respond to student needs by email, the results were resoundingly in favor of the in-person option for anything but simple questions. The following are a sample of the types of comments provided:

> I prefer to help students in person because I feel that students do not read or comprehend their emails and/or feedback on their assignments; therefore, they continue making the same mistakes. Through my experience, I find that if a student comes in for help, they will understand how to correct their mistakes....

> I prefer to meet during office hours. I find that students seem to have more questions than they initially think; these questions tend to be asked only when the student is engaged with the TA and the subject matter is laid out for both the TA and the student to see simultaneously.

> Throughout the semester, I did not have any students visit me during my office hours. I wish they would have because I genuinely wanted them to do well in the class, and it would have stopped them from committing the same errors over and over again in their writing. Both are fine for me. My preference would be during office hours for complicated issues or complex questions.

The challenges related to mediated communication when working in an instructional role were made very clear from these comments. As Sherry Turkle (2015) has recently argued, there are good reasons to be concerned that in the era of ubiquitous media we are losing our ability to have meaningful conversations with one another. We tend to favor the brief, often pausable types of interactions that digital media afford us, and if at all possible we no longer choose face-to-face conversations, with all of their messiness and unpredictability. She notes that younger people are more and more hesitant to speak on the phone, let alone face to face with someone, if there is the option to digitally message instead (Turkle 2015). This tendency can be seen in the fact that so few of the course's students chose to see their teaching assistant during office hours, even when their questions were more complex than could be effectively handled by email; digital communication was preferred almost every time over a face-to-face meeting—despite the lowered effectiveness of their learning opportunities.

Moreover, the challenges for the TAs to doing a good job in terms of instruction within the mediated context were coupled with the overall issues related to disconnection that came with the course environment more generally. Concerns related to a sense of disconnection were even more pronounced in the comments TAs made when asked if they felt like they were part of a team in their role within the course. Head teaching assistants and instructors were only an email away, and many respondents explained that they felt some connection to those individuals (mostly through their email contact with them). A number of TAs also responded that they felt part of a larger "project" in that the course had such a large number of students who could benefit from improving their writing skills, and they enjoyed contributing to its success. However, the responses the teaching assistants provided also reveal a somewhat isolating work experience at some levels. A sample of the related comments helps bear out this concern:

> For the most part the work can be completed independently and from a remote location, which makes it difficult to enforce a team atmosphere.
>
> Other than at orientation, I feel like the team is the Head TA and myself. I rarely communicate with TAs in my section unless they are in the office at the same time as me.
>
> There are times when I feel like I am a part of a team (orientation, office hour, proctoring), but I think that because most of the time I am working alone, I tend to feel like an individual doing an individual's job.
>
> I do since there are other people you can contact and speak to, but in a way we barely see each other so it feels less like a team.

When asked more generally about what they saw as the opportunities and challenges related to working as TAs in this online course, the responses tended to summarize some of what has already been brought to the fore. One of the most often mentioned advantages or opportunities of the job was the flexibility to work when it suited their schedule, and even to work other jobs off-campus as well. As students themselves, the TA work could be arranged to a considerable extent around other commitments, and this was mentioned over and over again. TA work in the course was also described as "challenging, yet rewarding," and an experience that "makes one empathetic to the needs of the students."

In terms of challenges to the job, generally, the comments focused repeatedly on the "lack of face-to-face contact with the students" and on feeling "like I am always on call as a TA, especially since I have email on my phone." The latter comment highlights the tension between the positive aspects of flexibility mentioned by these workers and the drawbacks of being "always on." Additionally, not meeting the students face to face, and having a hard time "engaging your students" were seen as challenges to the mediated course environment as well.

CONCLUSIONS: UBIQUITOUS MEDIA, CONNECTION, AND FLEXIBILITY

The tensions associated with the nature of this type of immaterial labor are numerous; issues of connection/disconnection and flexibility/constancy were key aspects of their experiences. Two of the respondents' comments about the overall experience of working in the course sum up many of the findings quite comprehensively:

> I think [the course] reflects, to some degree, something I've experienced with other online communication, where absence and constant presence happen at the same time. Because it's conducted for my students, I'm always 'there' in their minds and need to respond immediately. Even though we don't need to respond after 5:00 p.m. on Fridays, it becomes a job that is never gone and can't be put down at any time, because someone could always contact you. Despite that, because it's conducted online, I'm also always absent from the students, and it's difficult to foster good will or any connection between us that shows I care and want to help them.

> Electronic communication can be great; but there certainly are limitations. I think that students should continue to be reminded that for many issues, going to see their TA is the best option by far. I know most students don't seem to take advantage of this opportunity, probably because emails are quicker and easier for them. I have had lots of students email me about something, and I have asked them to come and see me either during my office hours or during a scheduled appointment; I would estimate that 10% actually end up coming to see me. In one sense, I wonder if students rely a bit too much on emails, neglecting to make the in-person contact that would truly allow them to overcome their difficulties and succeed in the course.

Ubiquitous media is indeed being engaged with in ways that have implications for our experiences of our everyday and everynight lives. The example of front-line immaterial laborers in an online course provides insights into the kinds of things we should be continuing to analyze. The TAs are part of an ever-increasing number of digital laborers whose work is primarily online and therefore potentially making demands of them around the clock. As the permeation of our paid and unpaid lives becomes more and more intense, we need to consider individuals' experiences more holistically. It becomes impossible to analyze paid work experiences in isolation from other activities, and vice versa. This may be even more the case when we consider that many aspects of immaterial labor now include an affective component, which may be even more difficult to shut out during our personal time. Furthermore, one of the troubling aspects of the findings of this study is the degree to which ubiquitousness, for lack of a better term, has been normalized and internalized, making it all the more difficult to continue to develop critical lines of interrogation and analysis. This is certainly the case for young adults, but it may also be a serious concern for all ages.

Dorothy Smith's (1999) focus on the political economy of the everyday/everynight should continue to remind us that we need to understand individuals' experiences in a holistic way, one that considers practices outside of the 'relations of ruling' and/or the formal economy. The feminist approach that makes clear the artificiality of the dichotomy between so-called public and private life may seem in some ways to have come into its own with the permeation of all aspects of our lives by ubiquitous media. However, this development—the widening of the analytical gaze to include the so-called public and private, at least in some respects—comes along with increasing complexity and contradictions related to digital media. Indeed, men may be facing some new challenges in terms of the blurring of boundaries between paid work and leisure, and Smith's enduring feminist arguments certainly should be used to keep assessing the on-going and/or new ways in which women may be facing complex challenges with respect to demands on their time as well as the related stressors.

Additionally, as Sherry Turkle (2011, 2015) has argued, despite being more connected through our devices there are important changes potentially at play in terms of how we relate to one another which demand on-going critical attention to the issues of presence and absence that are mentioned by one of the respondents above. If paid work is to be rewarding and meaningful, consideration needs to be given to the challenges related to an ever-increasing reliance on mediated communication. Furthermore, if our lived experience, day and night, is to also include the ability to genuinely "be" with others (Turkle 2015) as well as to enjoy meaningful leisure time, attention needs to be paid to the decisions made about how ubiquitous media is adopted and employed.

Finally, beyond their desire to help students, one of the key reasons why the TAs in the study responded favorably about their experiences was because of the flexibility it offered them. They could mold their TA work around their own studies and, for some, they could have other employment off-campus as well. Convenience and flexibility are good reasons to make use of ubiquitous media to a variety of ends, and the technologies could allow us better control over our everyday/everynight experiences. However, what the TAs' comments reflected is that there is a tendency to equate this type of flexibility, especially the ability to answer messages on a smartphone, with constancy. Yet, it would be possible to use our devices to afford flexibility without necessarily attending to them constantly. If we continue to fail to understand this distinction, as Sherry Turkle (2011) has argued: all the time in the world—everyday and everynight—will not be enough.

REFERENCES

Berger, Arthur A., 2013. *Media and Communication Research Methods: An Introduction to Qualitative and Quantitative Approaches.* Thousand Oaks, CA: Sage.
Bergeron, Suzanne, 2016. "Formal, Informal, and Care Economies." In *The Oxford Handbook of Feminist Theory*, edited by Lisa Disch and Mary Hawkesworth, 179–296. Oxford: Oxford University Press.
Bittman, Michael, and Judy Wajcman, 2000. "The Rush Hour: The Character of Leisure Time and Gender Equity" *Social Forces*, 79 (1): 165–195.
Bryman, Alan, Edward Bell, and James J. Teevan, 2012. *Social Research Methods,* 3rd Canadian ed. Toronto: Oxford University Press.
Campbell, Marie and Frances Gregor, 2008. *Mapping Social Relations: A Primer in Doing Institutional Ethnography.* Toronto: University of Toronto Press.
Denzin, Norman K., and Yvonne S. Lincoln, 2011. "The Discipline and Practice of Qualitative Research." In *The Sage Handbook of Qualitative Research,* 4th ed., edited by Norman K. Denzin and Yvonne S. Lincoln, 1–20. Thousand Oaks, CA: Sage.
Erikson, Rebecca J. 2011. "Emotional Carework, Gender, and the Division of Household Labor." In *At the Heart of Work and Family: Engaging the Ideas of Arlie Hochschild*, edited by Anita Ilta Garey and Karen V. Hansen, 61–73. New Brunswick, NJ: Rutgers University Press.
Freeman, John, 2009. *The Tyranny of E-Mail: The Four-Thousand-Year Journey to Your Inbox.* New York: Scribner.
Garey, Anita I., and Karen V. Hansen, eds. 2011. *At the Heart of Work and Family: Engaging the Ideas of Arlie Hochschild.* New Brunswick, NJ: Rutgers University Press.
Hardt, Michael, and Antonio Negri. 2004. *Multitude: War and Democracy in the Age of Empire.* New York: Penguin Press.
Hochschild, Arlie. 1989. *The Second Shift: Working Parents and the Revolution at Home.* New York: Viking.
———. 1997. *The Time Bind: When Work Becomes Home and Home Becomes Work.* New York: Metropolitan Books.
———. 2011. "Inside the Clockwork of Male Careers." In *At the Heart of Work and Family: Engaging the Ideas of Arlie Hochschild*, edited by Anita Ilta Garey and Karen V. Hansen, 17–29. New Brunswick, NJ: Rutgers University Press.
Huws, Ursula. 2012. "The Reproduction of Difference: Gender and the Global Division of Labor." *Work Organisation, Labor and Globalization*, 6 (1): 1–10.
———. 2014. *Labor in the Global Digital Economy: The Cybertariat Comes of Age.* New York: Monthly Review Press.
Kirby, Sandra L., Lorraine Greaves, and Colleen Reid. 2006. *Experience, Research, Social Change: Methods Beyond the Mainstream,* 2nd ed. Peterborough: Broadview Press.

Ladner, Sam, 2008. "Laptops in the Living Room: Mobile Technologies and the Divide Between Work and Private Time among Interactive Agency Workers" *Canadian Journal of Communication* 33 (3): 465–489.

Lazzarato, Maurizio. 1996. "Immaterial Labor" *Radical Thought in Italy: A Potential Politics*, edited by Paolo Virno and Michael Hardt, 133–147. Minneapolis, Minnesota: University of Minnesota Press.

McKercher, Catherine, and Vincent Mosco. 2008. *Knowledge Workers in the Information Society*. Lanham, MD: Lexington.

McKercher, Catherine, and Vincent Mosco. 2010. "Getting the Message: Communications Workers and Global Value Chains" *Work Organisation, Labor and Globalization* 4 (2): 1–9.

Menzies, Heather. 2011. *No Time: Stress and the Crisis of Modern Life*. Vancouver: Douglas and McIntyre.

Negri, Antonio, and Michael Hardt. 2000. *Empire*. Cambridge, MA: Harvard University Press.

Shade, Leslie Regan. 2014. "Give Us Bread, But Give Us Roses: Gender and Labor in the Digital Economy." *International Journal of Media and Cultural Politics* 10 (2): 129–144.

Smith, Dorothy. 1987. *The Everyday World as Problematic: A Feminist Sociology*. Toronto: University of Toronto Press.

———. 1990. *Texts, Facts and Feminity: Exploring the Relations of Ruling*. London: Routledge.

———. 1999. *Writing the Social: Critique, Theory, and Investigation*. Toronto: University of Toronto Press.

Turkle, Sherry. 2011. *Alone Together: Why We Expect More from Technology and Less from Each Other*. New York: Basic Books.

———. 2015. *Reclaiming Conversation: The Power of Talk in a Digital Age*. New York: Penguin Press.

Van den Hoonaard, Deborah K. 2012. *Qualitative Research in Action: A Canadian Primer*. Toronto: Oxford University Press.

Wajcman, Judy. 2004. *TechnoFeminism*. Cambridge, UK: Polity.

———. 2008. "Life in the Fast Lane? Towards a Sociology of Technology and Time." *The British Journal of Sociology* 8 (1): 59–77.

———. 2009. "Feminist Theories of Technology." *Cambridge Journal of Economics* 34: 143–152.

———. 2015. *Pressed for Time: The Acceleration of Life in Digital Capitalism*. Chicago: University of Chicago Press.

Waring, Marilyn. 2004. *Counting for Nothing: What Men Value and What Women are Worth*, 2nd ed. Toronto: University of Toronto Press.

PART FIVE

Localities and Communities

Spaces, Places, and Time

CHAPTER TWELVE

Push Narratives

Ubiquitous Mobile News and Participatory Local Media in Himalayan India

JACQUELINE H. FEWKES AND ABDUL NASIR KHAN

Standing in Kargil, a border town in north India, the landscape may seem like a glimpse of a movie set for a remote location. Snow-capped Himalayan mountains are marked only occasionally by twisting cliff-side roads, and tower over a busy mountain town made of predominantly mud-brick architecture. Water rushes through glacier-fed rivers, and villagers living nearby engage in the hard work of high altitude agriculture on steep terraced hills. Yet those familiar with the region will know that behind this seemingly peaceful scene lies a complex political history of contested borders between India and Pakistan, and within the town of Kargil lives a diverse multi-lingual and multi-ethnic population that reflects the rich history of the region as part of the Central-South Asian branch of the Silk Route.

While the landscape of this town is certainly arresting, it is its mediascape that has captured our interest; Kargil is home to a thriving local media industry that includes a number of different local channels that have been created to serve local media interests. This local media success story in Kargil depends in large part on access to contemporary technologies and varied media platforms to make possible the establishment of traditional local television stations in the highly competitive global mediascape. The local media of Kargil are not simply local cable channels; these are media institutions that make use of multiple screen technologies to engage media viewers as active media participants. In addition to television channels, Kargili local media disseminate programming through webcasts, online streaming video, and more recently, mobile apps such as WhatsApp (a cross-platform mobile messaging app that allows users to join groups through which they can exchange messages—including images, video, and audio content) anywhere in the world. The variety of media shapes viewership, allowing viewers in developing regions such as Kargil to access information with technological flexibility; for example, even if television is not working and the Internet is "down," mobile apps provide important alternatives.

In this chapter, we will briefly discuss a few theoretical perspectives that could be applied to this case study—globalization, media convergence, and ubiquitous media—and consider what it means to use these terms, based on the types of issues commonly addressed through the use of each theoretical lens. In the Kargil case study we have found that the concept of ubiquitous media is a theoretical tool that allows us to simultaneously focus on both technologies and user experiences as central issues of interest, without privileging one over the other. Discussion through the lens of ubiquitous media demonstrates how we can understand local media as part of broader media issues, and suggests new avenues of inquiry in cultural studies of media.

THE MEDIA SETTING—BACKGROUND AND METHODS

The research featured in this chapter is part of a larger project on the role and technologies of local media in Kargil, a small town in the region of Ladakh, the most northern part of Jammu and Kashmir State of India. The Kargil district—within which the town of Kargil is located—borders with Pakistan on its northwest edge. It is situated at just over 8,700 feet above sea level, and for six months of every year the region is cut off from the rest of India because of the cold and snow on the main highways. While Kargil is thus a fairly remote region in India due to its geographic location in the Himalayan mountains, the town is a well-populated urban area; the population of Kargil district in 2011 was 119,307 (Gov. of India, 2011).

Due to its importance in colonial politics and historical trade, the region obtained local communication facilities well before many other parts of Himalayan Central and South Asia; the first post office in Ladakh was opened in 1875 and the first telegraph office near Kargil opened in 1882 (Fewkes 2009, 85–86). Most of the communication facilities at this time were only available for elites such as colonial representatives, wealthy traders, and—in a few cases, such as ownership of the first radio in Ladakh—missionaries (Lone 2013, 114). The Government of India provided the area's first regional media to a public audience in 1971 by opening a radio station. Even this station did not at first provide universal access to media, as the broadcasts were only available to those select members of the community who could afford a radio (Morup 2002, 7).

The region provides a challenge to media studies, as no previous studies have been published specifically about media in the Kargil region. In spite of this, Census of India data on regional technology ownership provides a fascinating picture of the local mediascape. According to the 2011 Census of India there has been significant recent growth in access to communications technologies in the region. In 2001 a little over 3,000 Kargili households had television, by 2011 that number had jumped to just over 8,000 (Gov. of India, 2011). In spite of this Kargil is still ranked lowest in numbers of television ownership compared to other districts of Jammu and Kashmir State, and among the lowest among all the districts in India (*ibid.*). Kargil is also last in the state rankings in terms of telephone, radio, and computer ownership. The low numbers for district ownership across categories of communications technologies suggest that the low numbers of television ownership is thus part of a larger trend of lower screen culture access. This relationship is supported by the similarity in recent growth of ownership of these other media technologies. While in 2001 there were reportedly no households in the Kargil district that owned a computer, by 2011 there were 1,005 (*ibid.*). Similarly, in 2001 data on telephone ownership there were a recorded 897 households in Kargil with some type of telephone; by 2011 that number had increased to 10,562 (*ibid.*). While fascinating, these numbers leave many questions for researchers interested in studying media culture in the region. The data available for ownership of telephones, for example, does not distinguish between types of telephones such as landlines or cellphones, and within the last category, the types of cellphones. While many Kargilis may have smartphones that can access videos, a majority of the counted telephones may be landlines or older cell phones that are only used for making calls. It is therefore difficult to discern how much the very high growth in telephone ownership has influenced Kargili screen culture, however overall the Census of India data clearly demonstrates that media access has grown rapidly in Kargil district in recent years.

While there is no specific published data available for the numbers of people watching local Kargili programs, or for the number of different devices each individual uses to watch these programs, local channel owners claim in interview that approximately 20,000 people in Kargil are watching their programs on television screens, while global online viewing has a viewership of perhaps 100,000. These numbers are quite small when we compare them to other media audiences; to put them into perspective we should consider the following numbers. Twenty thousand regional viewers in 8,000 households with televisions suggests that, on average, there are 2.5 viewers of local channels per household with television. In contrast there were an estimated 116.4 million households in the United States with televisions in 2015, and the combined viewership of the top three channels (NBC, CBS, ABC) was 23,871,000, meaning that (for the purposes of comparison) .205

viewers per household with a television on average watch these national channels (Mitchell and Holcomb 2016; Nielsen Media Research 2016).

Local television stations in Kargil exist within a national mediascape. Indian local television began in the 1990s, with the widespread and rapid construction of small local cable television distribution networks before public policy for cable television was formulated, allowing for unregulated growth (McDowell 1997, 161). The growth of small channels in India during this time period was unprecedented. There were only 150 local cable channels in whole country in the 1980s, however by the 1990s there were over 12,000 channels, and by the time of regulation in 1995 there were an estimated 100,000 local channels in India (Sinclair 2005). Cable gave operators a fairly easy and relatively inexpensive (compared to satellite) way of showing their own programs. Not all of these channels were what we might call a "local channel", however, as many did not broadcast any locally made or regionally specific programs (*ibid.*). Cable operators purchased the rights from the distributors to show programming from national and international channels, or show their own content. Today a number of "local" television stations in India are also a part of larger corporate or political structures; the commercial ownership of these stations affects media policies and messages (Thomas 2014). Of course, this broadcasting of other content on a local community television channels is not specific to the Indian media context (e.g. Baltruschat 2004), and the focal point of a station, its aims and intent in addition to content, can also distinguish between local channels and local stations.

Based on this understanding of local media—as channels that are controlled within a region, are developed to reflect regional interests, and that contain novel content specific to the region—there are three local stations of interest in Kargil: *Kargil Today*, *Al Noor News Ladakh*, and *S TV Ladakh*[1]. These three stations were the focus of this study.

All three stations are independent broadcasters that are headquartered in Kargil and produce their programs in Kargil itself. Al Noor ("The Light") News Ladakh— also called Al Noor News Network—was started in March 5, 2009 and was the first private news-broadcasting channel of Ladakh. The second, Kargil Today, was started on December 31, 2012, and the third, S TV Ladakh, started in 2014.

The stations offer similar contents, with some variation. Al Noor was started with an intention to provide "infotainment" and also to function as media awareness forum for the people of Kargil; the station produces and telecasts news, talk shows, advertisements, and documentaries. Their programs are produced in multiple languages, including Urdu, Hindi, Purig, and Shina. Kargil Today produces and telecasts the same type of programs in Urdu, Hindi, English, and Purig. S TV produces and telecasts news, current affairs, and advertisements. A majority of the programs on S TV are done in Hindi and Urdu but the station has recently started using the Ladakhi, Balti, Purig and Shina languages too. While recognized as local stations due to their interests, goals, production settings, use of local languages, and broadcast contents, all three stations have founding owners with experience in media outside of the region, and formal training in communications.

In this chapter, we focus on one aspect of a larger study on the role of local media in Kargil, in which we employed a variety of methods, including interviews, media content analysis, a survey, and text analysis. The interviews were conducted with the owners of local television stations, as well as employees who work at the stations, through telephone and e-mails.[2] The survey was conducted online with television viewers living in different parts of India.

During this research, several different sources discussed how Kargili local television stations have adopted and transformed various media platforms for their own purposes, prompting an interest in the relationship between the role of local media and use of multiple technological platforms to disseminate that media. Thus we began to look carefully at the various media platforms used by these stations. The owner/director of S TV reported, for example, that in addition to their cable channel they share news through YouTube and mobile apps; he estimates that while around 10,000 people watched the S TV shows through cable in Kargil, many more people watch online or follow on their phones. Al Noor and Kargil Today programming is also available on the Internet through mobile apps, social networks, and YouTube. The viewers on these media platforms extend outside the local region covered by local cable broadcasting, and therefore in order to better understand the role of local Kargili media we therefore began to ask larger theoretical questions about media globalization, convergence, and ubiquitous media.

APPLYING A THEORETICAL LENS: GLOBALIZATION, MEDIA CONVERGENCE, AND UBIQUITOUS MEDIA

The concepts of media globalization and media convergence are relevant to consider in this study in relation to, and perhaps even in contrast to, the notion of ubiquitous media. While in the 1990s globalization became a hotly contested phenomenon in many disciplines, the conceptual focus of the term has been rendered diffuse by the sheer popularity of the term; media found in multiple geographic locations is frequently labeled as "global" both in popular and academic writing. While some writers discuss global media as a cultural phenomenon (e.g. as in the case of Appadurai, discussed below), in many other cases little attention is paid to the claim beyond that of scale and mechanics of globalization. Globalization has become a largely descriptive term, rather than an analytical lens or explanatory model, for most authors.

Globalization in the contemporary world is frequently defined as a set of transnational power relations, practices, and technologies that have shaped the modern world (e.g. Schirato and Webb 2003). Tony Schirato and Jen Webb ask readers to challenge the values assumed to be associated with this set of relations, practices, and technologies; they consider the contradictions between common concepts of globalization as creating equal media access and opportunities, and an observed flow of research, development, science, and technology that is confined to selected sites and nodes of the capitalist network (*ibid.*). Thus critics of globalization claim the term is simply a cover-up for more specific transnational forces, such as the strengthening of capitalism and imperialism in more areas of the world (Durham and Kellner 2006). In the Ladakhi case, a focus on the concept of globalization can help to highlight two issues: the scope of local media's impact—particularly its movement across national borders—and the ways in which Kargili local stations depend on non-local technologies that are controlled by institutions in other parts of the world.

Considering scope raises the question of how we can discuss media as local when it has a global audience and dissemination. Arjun Appadurai's (1990) "mediascape" offers a conceptual place in which to situate such simultaneously global/local media. Appadurai not only considers the technologies of media that are globally shared, but also "the images of the world created by these media" (9). The mediascape, in creating narratives about the global, produces "strips of reality" (299). This perspective on media globalization thus emphasizes the perspectives that result from the global dissemination of news, regardless of the scale of that dissemination. As Faye Ginsburg (1994, 366 points out, the use of the concept of mediascapes allows for "situated analyses that take account of the interdependence of media practices with the local, national, and transnational circumstances that surround them." Thus Appadurai's mediascape suggests understanding local media as part of a larger dialogue with the forces of globalization, rather than as special exceptions to globalization, while still emphasizing the ways in which local media is specific to its context of production. The focus on narratives produced by global media trends allows for a focus on viewership—for example, prompting questions in the Kargili case about the ways in the community participates in global media arenas—but rarely leads research focused on technological trends and their implications.

Studies that focus on the technologies of media globalization tend to emphasize the dichotomy between local and global roles, and lead to questions about power relations within this dichotomy, as the global media industries produce a hegemonic medium from corporations that are controlled by a handful of people and have unlimited power (Schirato and Webb 2003). This dichotomy has significant implications; the owners of Kargili stations localize global technologies in ways that serve their media purposes and at least temporarily level the playing ground, but are still dependent on the global technology conglomerates that run the platforms that they use. The technologies of global media are a form of power; if, for example, companies such as Facebook and YouTube were to drastically change their policies, the local Kargil stations could lose their access points to the international viewers. While media localization is therefore possible—seemingly made possible by global technologies—it can also be blocked by the same. This is why there is a general call in media globalization studies for "continuing analyses of power relations, global capital, and the role of subaltern/minority peoples in the emergence of new media processes and products" (Wilson and Peterson 2002, 455). This conceptual approach, while prompting significant questions about media globalization, continues to center the analytical focal point on media production and distribution practices, without necessitating a more holistic understanding of media processes such as consumption, replication, and reinterpretation.

A focus primarily on the technologies of global dissemination also suggests consideration of the notion of media convergence. Henry Jenkins (2006) describes media convergence as a combination of multiple media activities, and the movement of contents on different media platforms. Kathleen Oswald and Jeremy Packer (2011) write that today the media is defined by these different platforms; media success is no longer about keeping a viewer on one transmission, now viewers are being kept busy through multiple screens at different times and in different spaces. All these screens—televisions, computers, tablets, mobile phones—work in concert to connect consumers to their information (*ibid.*). Others have observed users should know that mobile and portable technologies are a component of a bigger network made up of all the interoperable devices that can relay groups of information from one place to another; a cell phone is no longer just a mobile device for talking but becomes a tool for all-round transformation of social practices (Sawchuk, Crow, and Longford 2010). Similarly Jenkins (2006) observes that media convergence involves numerous media companies cooperating with each other, and media consumers, who are moving between different media platforms to find the content they want. Theories of media convergence that promote an understanding of how media is defined by its simultaneous transmission on multiple screens are therefore useful, and may sound like a study of ubiquitous media. Yet media convergence studies offer a generally—although not exclusively—media-centric approach to study of this phenomenon. A media convergence approach to the study of local media in Kargil would suggest a focus on the technologies of dissemination, and the companies that control these technologies. From this perspective the production of local news would very little to do with Kargil as a local region, or even its national context in India majority as a majority of the media technologies are controlled in other countries.

For these reasons Jenkins argues that media convergence should not be seen as simply a technological process that brings together different media functions into the same device (*ibid.*). The consumer plays a significant role in circulation of the media contents from different media systems, and therefore how media crosses between different national borders. Convergence should be looked at as a shift in culture, in which consumers are inspired to find out new information and to make connections with diverse forms of media content that is continuously changing (*ibid.*). This concept is significant for discussing the adoption of new communications technologies—for example, in the Kargil case, the adoption of mobile apps for local news—that are used by the Kargili stations to increase access to local television news programs in unique new ways. This can be achieved through a focus on ubiquitous media, a theoretical perspective that encourages consideration of both media technologies and consumer perspectives by focusing on the experience of interacting with multiple media platforms.

UBIQUITOUS MEDIA

The concept of ubiquitous media allows for an examination of the experience of using such media, to examine what it means that viewers of multiple screens are kept busy through varying activities—viewing, searching, chatting, posting, etc.—situated in different times and spaces. From its earliest iterations, the concept of ubiquitous technologies has been used to theorize the relationships between these screens—or whatever multiple technologies are employed—and recognize that these relationships create new linkages both through the ways in which individuals may relate to them, and in relation to each other.

Barton, Goddi, and Spasojevic (2003, 1) offered an early definition of the concept in 2003, writing:

> Our term for this research area is 'ubimedia,' a concatenation of 'ubiquitous computing', and 'physically-linked hypermedia.' We note that the structure of media is evolving from standalone media objects (photographs, audio tracks, books) to collections of semantically related media objects connected by hyperlinks. These hyperlinks may bridge digital and physical objects as well, thus the term 'physically-linked hypermedia.'

The hyperlinks in this understanding of ubiquitous media give rise to new possibilities inherent in the arrangement of technologies, rather than simply in the technologies themselves.

As Mike Featherstone (2009) points out in the introduction to *Ubiquitous Media*, these systems of integrated mobile and non-mobile technologies have given users a "greater capacity for switching modes, enhanced flexibility and integration," and these new patterns of usage lead to conceptualizing ways of interacting with technologies that are not centered around notions of an external top-down media power (*ibid.*, 2). This is certainly true in the Kargili case, where mobile app users have become active participants in the news dissemination process, often guiding local stations' content choices.

Thus although ubiquitous media is found across platforms, the cross-platform nature of ubiquitous media is not its only conceptual offering. Ubiquitous media related questions about interactions with technologies and their presence in daily lives provide a compelling analytical focus through which to better understand contemporary media. This presence has four unique features that are worth considering in the Kargili context. These are that the study of media ubiquity: requires methodological focus on the holistic contexts in which is occurs; is a sensory experience; provides a framework through which to reconcile seemingly disparate elements within a media system; and has cultural implications that extend beyond any defined community of users.

UBIQUITY, CONTEXT, AND METHODOLOGICAL CONSIDERATIONS

Ubiquitous media necessarily has a history; by recognizing its insertion into the daily lives of users we recognize that there must first be a context for the action of insertion. A focus on ubiquitous media, therefore, requires considering producers' agency in choosing this form of media over other media technologies. In the study of ubiquitous media we are thus prompted to ask questions about context—how, when, for what reasons, and what are some of the possibilities inherent in this media arrangement.

Following this this line of reasoning we begin to ask questions about the regional origins of local Internet and social media roles. Many expectations about access to mobile technologies in developing regions are challenged by these questions. While we might expect that Kargil, a remote Himalayan area with poor Internet connections and limited electricity access, would have a lower rate for the likeliness of using Internet than in other parts of India, our survey showed us that actual technologies patterns were the reverse—in spite of the challenges to accessing online media, informants in the region were more likely report getting their news online than those in New Delhi, the heavily populated urban capital of India. Media ubiquity is about access, and the possibilities of access, in users' lives; access is shaped in part by the linkages between diverse devices. In the Kargil region, media technology usage is linked in part by their relations to electric networks. Electricity in the region is often provided only for a few hours a day, rather than continuously for 24 hours, and households are on a rotation to receive power on certain days at certain hours. It is therefore near impossible to watch television any time you want, or even regularly at a set time to access a scheduled program. Internet access allows people to access the news according to their own schedules, and chargeable devices such as smart phones mean that viewers are not restricted by electricity availability. The mobile Internet is cheap, easy to use, and can be accessed anywhere; as in the Kargil news case Internet use sends news to people continuously through apps. In spite of this position of relative privilege within media networks, however, the disadvantage of using mobile Internet for streaming audio-visual materials in Kargil is that both computers and mobile devices in the region rarely stream video effectively because of slow and intermittent Internet connections.

This context of media arrangements—the ways in which technologies relate to each other—helps to better understand the movement towards mobile apps usership in the Kargili media context. Our informants explained that Kargili local channels began posting news segments on YouTube in 2011, and a survey of the shows produced through this medium between 2011 and 2015 indicates that online streaming viewership of Kargili local news first increased, then peaked in 2013, and began to decline in 2014. This decline coincided with the growth of the use of the mobile app WhatsApp, suggesting that although the two technologies coexist in Kargili mediascapes today, their coexistence has boundaries that need to be examined more carefully to understand the relationships between these technologies.

UBIQUITOUS MEDIA AS A SENSORY EXPERIENCE

Ubiquitous media is not inert, and it is not experienced passively; it engages user senses. Consideration of ubiquitous media as a sensory experience can help to explain how the Kargili local station's use of WhatsApp as a media tool for news dissemination has become so popular. All three local television stations in Kargil now use WhatsApp to send subscribers news and information, and as mentioned earlier, the app has become one of the most popular mediums for distributing news among their viewership. One of the most basic uses of WhatsApp for Kargili media purposes is to quickly notify people of breaking news.

The immediacy of the app, that it sends you a notification directly to your phone as a "push" message, makes it well suited to these types of alerts, and the physical sensations (e.g. sound and vibration) of mobile alerts inserts the media into the user's environment. While WhatsApp is particularly well suited for disseminating breaking news, it matures as a technological tool when used to bring together diverse forms of media—text, video, pictures, reader commentary—in one place, as seen below, in order to offer participants access to a developing narrative.

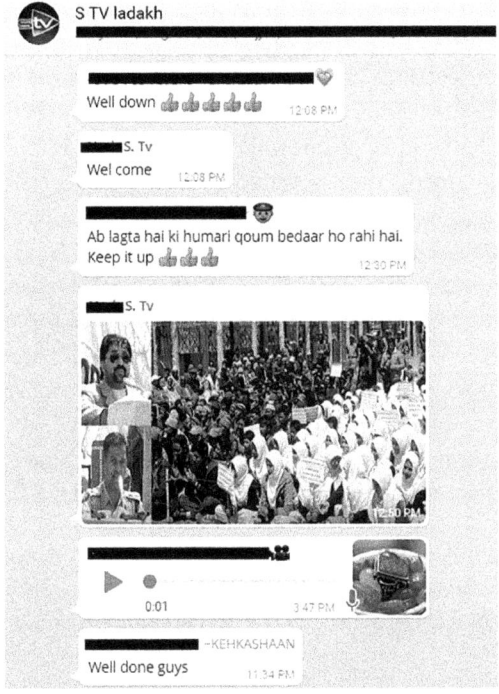

Figure 12.1. Anti-corruption campaign discussion, with photo, text, and video commentary (S TV Ladakh 2015. WhatsApp message to author, October 2). The phonetically spelled Urdu comment reads, "It looks like now our community is awakening."

The contents of the screenshot in Figure 12.1 demonstrate how the many different features of the app can work together to provide a holistic and interactive media environment. That interactive media environment quickly becomes ubiquitous to the user's daily experience after subscribing to the stations' WhatsApp groups. Upon joining one of these groups the media user will immediately begin receiving twenty to thirty messages a day; the mobile app frequently rings or vibrates with news stories, group members' comments, and posts from other sources. On busy news days the increase in media output is palpable, with a non-stop flow of messages that makes the user's cellphone beep, buzz, flash, or otherwise alert the user that news is available. The constant activity and immediacy of these posts—including the "push" message design that allows you to access media even when your phone is not in an active mode—helps to create a very personal interaction with the news, as it inserts itself into the user's day.

This palpable presence of Kargili stations has a significant impact on users. The experience of accessing Kargili local stations becomes participatory, and its regular presence in their lives through alerts is as meaningful to users as the contents of the posts. Many studies of local media assume that participants engage with local media because they produce content specific to the region (e.g. Higgins 1999; King and Mele 1999; Meadows 2009; Roy 2008; Sinclair 2005). Local channels are indeed an excellent source of information for viewers interested in a particular region. In this Kargili media case, however, accessing the regionally specific content as information is only part of the reason for media popularity. Surveyed media participants frequently claimed that they conceptualized local media as a form of regional advocacy—explaining for example that it could be used to bring regional issues to the attention of politicians—and "belonging" to the media was a way to signify engagement in community interests. Sensory media experiences that physically engage the users of mobile apps allows Kargilis to incorporates local media consumption into their lived experience, existing in the "real" or "on-ground" world (as opposed to that online). As Kargili users frequently interact with their regional identity through devices, participation in ubiquitous media becomes a symbolic act of situatedness.

UBIQUITOUS MEDIA AND DISPARATE ELEMENTS

In creating new sensory experiences, ubiquitous media not only shape humans' interactions with the world around them, but also reconfigure the very notions of humanness. N. Katherine Hayles' (2009) work suggests that the "binary divide between active, communicative humans and passive, silent, fixed objects no longer works" once we recognize that ubiquitous media such as RFIDs (radio frequency identification devices) may autonomously gather and utilize information about their environments (Featherstone 2009, 4, on Hayles 2009). As with Appadurai's notion of the mediascape, the concept of ubiquitous media encourages us to consider media perspectives that break down boundaries of conventional dichotomies such as local/global; ubiquitous media studies take this deconstruction process further to suggest that these boundaries disintegrate at even more fundamental levels, such as individual/technology. As discussed earlier, we might consider the sensory experience of constant mobile updates to integrate the media narrative into an individual's daily life, making it a part of the individual's identity rather than a separate media technology.

In ubiquitous media the line between media producers and consumers is similarly erased. Anne Allison's (2009) discussion of Japanese "cool" consumerism of linked technologies— arranged around commercial characters such as Pokémon and Hello Kitty—suggests that this form of media ubiquity is a central part of the contemporary Japanese youth scene; access to communications technologies, a shift to immaterial labor, and the economic flexibility of this generation enables consumers to be creators of games and other leisure commodities. The use of WhatsApp in Kargili media networks similarly creates instances where consumers become producers, a significant media movement. Initial Kargili media posts on WhatsApp mirror traditional media, offering local news stories written by the station employees, and including formal media photographs, audio, and/or videos. Through the use of the mobile app, however, group members—those who would traditionally have a more passive role as media viewers—often comment with additional text, photos, and videos of their own to transform these stories. Group members also post both local and non-local news that they find of interest, directly influencing the range of topics offered by Kargili local media. While the local stations monitor the discussions and sometimes warn group members to keep discussion civil, conflicts in the comments can yield very interesting discussions about news and the media. Group members may challenge co-members choice of content, for example requesting that others do not post graphic photos or unreliable news.

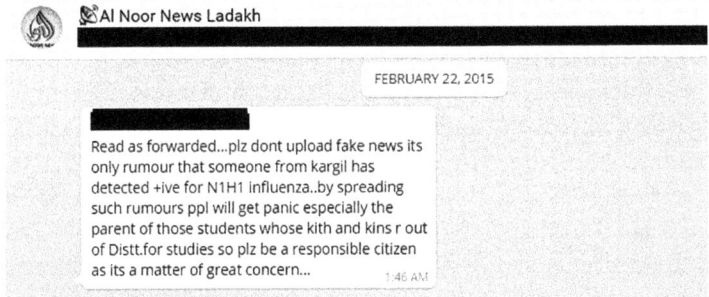

Figure 12.2. A comment on news that other group members found was not reliable, a WhatsApp screenshot from Al Noor News Ladakh 2015 (Al Noor News Ladakh. 2015. WhatsApp message to author, February 22).

The screenshot in Figure 12.2 is a response to a member who had previously posted an unreliable story in Al Noor News Ladakh group. This story—a fabricated tale about a Kargili person being diagnosed with "N1H1 influenza"—provoked a strongly negative reaction from other members, who castigated the original poster for posting it without verifying the story. Commentators like the one above specifically remind the person posting the news about the potential viewers, the impact news had on others, and the responsibility of citizens to think of the impact of news on others. Use of WhatsApp—and the ubiquity of the media that allows for constant interactions between members throughout the day—therefore gives participants the chance to express ideas about, and be critical about, unethical media practices. This ability for both media members and the public to provide commentary on media choices, to create a media metanarrative and contribute to what has in the past been a professional discursive arena, contributes to the deconstruction of differentiation between media producers and consumers.

This blurred line between media roles is not an incidental outcome, but a central paradigm upholding the ubiquity of Kargili local media; the formal media structures actually enforce active user participation in the WhatsApp groups as an expected component of group membership. We discovered this after being temporarily removed from one Kargili station's WhatsApp group after a few months of observing the group. When asked about the removal the group administrator, a station employee, replied: "your [*sic*] one of the silent members in this group. So I revised some silent members without any notice."

Similarly, the dichotomy between local/global can be investigated through this conceptual approach; ubiquitous media studies suggest we must pay attention to how disparate forms of media are woven together, providing a ways of making sense of media that crosses genres and combines various screens, such as one of the most popular Kargili news videos on YouTube, called "Kareena & Saif Kargil Visit, By Hosain Ibn Khalo". This short (under three minute) news video about Bollywood stars visiting Kargil blends national fictional narratives with regional news, set to a soundtrack from a local album playing as background music. Viewed 2640 times on YouTube, the video is the single most popular YouTube video produced by local Kargili stations.

The "screens" combined through ubiquity may be technological, stylistic, and/or ones of scale. Local and global boundaries are erased through these hybrid programs. Kargil Today and Al Noor News Ladakh have both produced a number of short documentaries that focus on local issues, and do so emulating the news documentary style seen on Al Jazeera. Thus they present locally oriented programs such as *Aawam ke Aawaz* [*Voice of the People*] (Al Noor News Ladakh 2015a) that are fundamentally shaped by transnational media styles.

Small Kargili news studios frequently use green screens in newer videos to create alternative landscapes in the media, particularly landscapes linked to famous cities or companies in other parts of the world such as New York's Times Square or the Al Jazeera studio. These images present interesting questions about why the Kargili stations would like to create visual connections between their media and the places/organizations used on the green screen.

The interrelations of ubiquitous media disorder dichotomies such as individuals/technologies, producers/consumers, and global/local. Thus while ubiquitous media studies encourage researchers to consider the ways in which different technologies cohere, as does the theoretical perspective of media convergence, the perspective also suggests a pressing need to understand how disparate media elements coexist, to examine the seeming disintegration, discords, and fragments of media experiences as meaningful components of a more complex media narrative.

THE CULTURAL IMPLICATIONS OF UBIQUITOUS MEDIA

Researching ubiquitous media requires a serious consideration of the new forms of expression that arise from the interconnections between media technologies and experiences of users within in these systems.

In the Kargil case study this would encourage researchers to explore, for example, how Kargili local identity may be growing in new directions. In interviews a number of our informants suggested that some of the largest audiences for Kargili local media are located outside of Kargil itself, pointing out several patterns of regional migration that would affect viewership locations, such as that 80% of Kargili students go for higher education outside of Kargil. These diasporic communities access local media as a way of staying connected to their hometown, and they have an active presence in the media forums outside of the local cable channel media. Diasporic participation in local media prompts recognition that labeling the media as "local" does not require a measurement of "Kargiliness" or pinpointing geographic locations of activity, but rather suggests a more fluid notion of cultural identity, and allows for examination of the new forms that arise within ubiquitous media.

As Kargili local media becomes a site for cultural growth, the patterns of language use signify some of these changes. Kargili local media uses local languages—a traditional component of local media (e.g. Sinclair 2005)—but in utilizing multiple technologies the media mixes these languages in new ways.

Kargil is a culturally diverse and multilingual region, within which languages such as Balti, English, Hindi, Kashmiri, Ladakhi, Shina, Urdu, and Purig are all commonly used. While some of these languages are closely related, others are based in different language families and utilize different alphabets. It is a challenge to reflect this wide-ranging multilingual environment in a media context, but content analysis of the language use patterns in Kargili local media suggests that the regional media does not simply replicate regional language patterns, they have instead has created new patterns of use. The media technologies and training of formal media producers shape many linguistic choices for the channels' broadcasts; for example, due to technological constraints such as the availability of fonts, video titling is most frequently presented in Urdu, Hindi, and/or English. The channels most frequently post news in English in the mobile apps and social media, for similar reasons. Textual language patterns in Kargili media thus create new linguistic patterns within the community, one that does not simply reflect the frequency of use of these languages in the Kargili community. These linguistic patterns are then responded to in the participatory media, such as social media and mobile apps, where consumer/producers may replicate the formal media's language use patterns, or indirectly—and even directly at times—challenge those patterns.

CONCLUSIONS

We have used the concept of ubiquitous media to consider some aspects of the diverse user experiences of Kargili local television station programming across multiple media platforms, with a particular focus on media access through multiple platforms that are not traditionally thought to be a part of local media, such as streaming video and the mobile communication apps. The use of these technologies complicates traditional understandings of media roles; through online streaming local news broadcasts can become a global product, mobile apps with a social media component transform news consumers into communities of news commentators, and mobile media becomes an experience fully integrated into users' daily lives. The complexity of Kargil's local mediascape thus requires new ways of analyzing media in order to fully understand how multiple media technologies shape local media user experiences and the types of media narratives that are made possible by these experiences.

Interpreting the mediascape through the analytical lens of ubiquitous media has fostered a better understanding of the contexts of media development. The ubiquitous nature of this media creates new forms of interactive local media narratives, as the use of mobile apps, with alerts and push messages, inserts media into users' daily lives as a sensory experience. WhatsApp stories unfold rapidly, with constant updates from multiple sources and user comments. Stories are broken up into short segments that create a narrative arc, becoming ubiquitous though continuous push notifications on a mobile device. The media format on WhatsApp thus combines the multiple perspectives of a talk show and the narrative approach of a documentary with the urgency of breaking news, into a text based media presence integrated into users' daily lives.

The use of multiple media platforms, such as cable television and YouTube videos, and the styles that cross platforms within this media, allow local stations to combine global television styles with community interests in ways that blur the line between local/global interests, while simultaneously challenging producer/consumer and individual/technology dichotomies as well.

The very concept of culture is shaped by a consideration of ubiquitous media, not only providing media participants with a meaningful assemblage of the aforementioned fragments, but also actively fostering new possibilities in terms of cultural identity. The idea that ubiquitous media can "grow" new forms of culture is conceptually appealing, providing a fresh perspective on the ways in which ubiquitous media arenas contribute to understandings of culture as a dynamic process.

NOTES

1. These are not the only local stations in Kargil; there are also two other stations in Kargil run by religious organizations. The latter two stations are, however, special interest media outlets with limited content and are therefore not included in this research.
2. Interview data in this article is provided anonymously to protect the privacy of individuals when necessary; some non-essential but identifying information may also have been changed for this reason

REFERENCES

Al Noor News Ladakh. 2014. *(Face to Face Talk with) "Thupten Tsewang" ency*. https://www.youtube.com/watch?v=qihQB4WhOl4.
———. 2015a. *Aawam Ke Aawaz: Sharchey Village Boycott Comming Assembly Elections*. https://www.youtube.com/watch?v=76S4aEZ17eI.
Appadurai, Arjun. 1990. "Disbuncture and Difference in the Global Cultural Economy." *Theory, Culture & Society* 7 (2): 295–310. doi:10.1177/026327690007002017.
Baltruschat, Doris. 2004. "Television and Canada's Aboriginal Communities." *Canadian Journal of Communication* 29 (1). http://www.cjc-online.ca/index.php/journal/article/view/1403.
Barton, John, Patrick Goddi, and Mirjana Spasojevic. 2003. "Creating and Experiencing Ubimedia." Technical report HPL-2003-38. Palo Alto, CA: HP Labs. http://www.hpl.hp.com/techreports/2003/HPL-2003-38.html.
Durham, Meenakshi Gigi, and Douglas Kellner. 2006. *Media and Cultural Studies: Keyworks*. Malden, MA: Blackwell.
Fewkes, Jacqueline H. 2009. *Trade and Contemporary Society along the Silk Road: An Ethno-History of Ladakh*. Abingdon, Oxon: Routledge.
Ginsburg, Faye. 1994. "Embedded Aesthetics: Creating a Discursive Space for Indigenous Media." *Cultural Anthropology* 9 (3): 365–382. doi:10.1525/can.1994.9.3.02a00080.
Government of India. 2011. "Census of India." Accessed December 1, 2014. http://www.censusindia.gov.in/DigitalLibrary/Archive_home.aspx.
Higgins, John W. 1999. "Community Television and the Vision of Media Literacy, Social Action, and Empowerment." *Journal of Broadcasting & Electronic Media* 43 (4): 624–644. doi:10.1080/08838159909364513.
Jenkins, Henry. 2006. *Convergence Culture: Where Old and New Media Collide*. New York: New York University Press.
Kargil Today. 2013. *KT Drass Winter Story*. https://www.youtube.com/watch?v=z2P-7TML2kc.
———. 2015. *KT News Headlines, Hosain Ibn Khalo, New Year 2015*. https://www.youtube.com/watch?v=XlHrfXgUbVA.
King, Donna L., and Christopher Mele. 1999. "Making Public Access Television: Community Participation, Media Literacy and the Public Sphere." *Journal of Broadcasting & Electronic Media* 43 (4): 603–623. doi:10.1080/08838159909364512.
Lone, Mudasir Ahmad. 2013. "Ladakh: Society, People and Place: A Sociological Outlook." *Acme International Journal of Multidisciplinary Research* 1 (5): 112–119.
McDowell, Stephen D. 1997. "Globalization and Policy Choice: Television and Audiovisual Services Policies in India." *Media, Culture & Society* 19 (2): 151–172. doi:10.1177/016344397019002002.

Meadows, Michael. 2009. "Electronic Dreaming Tracks: Indigenous Community Broadcasting in Australia." *Development in Practice* 19 (4–5): 514–24. doi:10.1080/09614520902866363.

Mitchell, Amy, and Jesse Holcomb. 2016. "State of the News Media 2016." *Pew Research Center's Journalism Project*. June 15. http://www.journalism.org/2016/06/15/state-of-the-news-media-2016/.

Morup, Tsering. 2002. "Leh Radio Station Gutted in Devastating Fire." *International Association for Ladakh Studies (IALS)*.

Nielsen Media Research. 2016. "Nielsen Estimates 118.4 Million TV Homes in the U.S. for the 2016–17 TV Season." *Neilsen*, Last Modified 26 August 2016. http://www.nielsen.com/us/en/insights/news/2016/nielsen-estimates-118-4-million-tv-homes-in-the-us--for-the-2016-17-season.html.

Oswald, Kathleen, and Jeremy Packer. 2011. "Flow and Mobile Media." In *Communication Matters: Materialist Approaches to Media, Mobility and Networks*, edited by Jeremy Packer and Stephen B. Crofts Wiley, 276–287. New York: Routledge.

Roy, Abhijit. 2008. "Bringing up TV: Popular Culture and the Developmental Modern in India." *South Asian Popular Culture* 6 (1): 29–43. doi:10.1080/14746680701878539.

Sawchuk, Kim, Barbara A Crow, and Michael Longford. 2010. "Introduction." In *The Wireless Spectrum: The Politics, Practices, and Poetics of Mobile Media*, edited by Kim Sawchuk, Barbara A Crow, and Michael Longford, 1–13. Toronto, Ontario: University of Toronto Press. http://www.deslibris.ca/ID/433750.

Shirato, Tony, and Jenn Webb. 2003. *Understanding Globalization*. London: Sage Publications. http://www.myilibrary.com?id=36905.

Sinclair, John. 2005. "Globalization and Grassroots: Local Cable Television Operators and Their Household Subscribers in India." *Media Asia* 32 (2): 69–77. doi:10.1080/01296612.2005.11726776.

Thomas, Pradip. 2014. "Communication & Global Power Shifts: The Ambivalent State and the Media in India: Between Corporate Compulsions and the Public Interest." *International Journal of Communication* 8: 466–482.

Wilson, Samuel M., and Leighton C. Peterson. 2002. "The Anthropology of Online Communities." *Annual Review of Anthropology* 31 (1): 449–67. doi:10.1146/annurev.anthro.31.040402.085436.

CHAPTER THIRTEEN

Towards Journalism Everywhere

The New Opportunities and Challenges of Real-Time News Streams in Finland

TURO USKALI

INTRODUCTION[1]

In early May, 2016 the World Wildlife Fund (WWF) set up a web camera on a cliff on the shore of Finland's largest body of fresh water, Lake Saimaa. The foot of the cliff is known to be a good location to see the Saimaa ringed seals, an endangered species which live only in this particular lake system. Few Finns had, prior to this webcast, ever seen a Saimaa ringed seal in the wild.

Most of the time, the live video-feed showed no activity on the rocks at the foot of the cliff. Nevertheless, soon after the webcast started, a Saimaa ringed seal, later called Pullervo, did choose the location as his sunbathing spot. Aside from a couple visits from a female called Siiri, the web-stream was relatively uneventful. However, during the month of May 2016, Finns viewed the Pullervo live-video stream over two million times for an average of 28 minutes (*Helsingin Sanomat* 2016). In sum, the WWF's live-webcasting proved to be a surprisingly popular form of entertainment for the 5.5 million Finns.

Similar live webcasts focusing on wildlife, especially nesting eagles or other big birds, have been available since 2009, when live-mobile-video services such as Bambuser, Livestream, and U-Stream started. The initial offerings were intermittent. Now new actors in the industry, like Animal Planet, regularly produce live webcasts of a variety of animals, from cats and dogs to pandas and penguins. Thus, it may be argued, live animal streams helped to prepare audiences for viewing lengthy, real-time, always-on, always-accessible video streams.

In a similar vein, Nordic national public broadcasters, like the Norway's NRK, have started to test live video marathons. The first episode of NRK's "Slow-TV" series, in 2009, was a recording of a train journey that lasted 7 hours and 16 minutes. The audience was approximately 1.2 million people. Other similar ventures have included a channel boat trip in 2012 (12 hours), a coastal cruise in 2013 (379 hours of live production over seven weeks), and a national knitting night in 2013 (13 hours). This phenomenon can be referred to as "ubiquitous communication," real-time information streams or pulses which can be produced and consumed by almost everyone, anywhere, via Internet connections.

Relatedly, "ubiquitous journalism"[2] refers to real-time news streams and pulses which can be produced and consumed by almost everyone anywhere via Internet live-streaming links. Ubiquitous journalism may also be called "journalism everywhere." Consequently, the concept of news production in the era of "journalism everywhere" and social media may need to be redefined because potentially anyone can now produce news. News is no longer defined by news organizations based on their news criteria (see for example Galtung and Ruge 1965), but also by society. For example, hyperlocal events in our neighborhoods, work-related new information, or new family matters can be defined as news to us.

Critically speaking, the live-feeds of WWF, Animal Planet, or NRK were not journalism, which can be defined as critically examined factual information about timely topics that are new to the audience or, in other words, news (See, for example, McQuail 2013, 1–4). Journalism also includes other genres such as features, interviews and documentaries. This chapter argues that live-streaming does not necessarily qualify as a journalistic product, even when produced by a news organization. For this to qualify as journalism, there needs to be at least some kind of journalistic element, commentary, voice over or contextualization. In order to understand the need for these new concepts, "ubiquitous communication" and "ubiquitous journalism" and what makes them distinct from traditional journalism, we present a short historical overview.

FROM NEWS TICKERS TO LIVE SPORT EVENTS

The news business has always benefited from speed. The first news agencies were created in France, Great Britain, Germany and the United States (Read 1992). Initially, horses, ships and railways set the pace of news production and dissemination. Later, the telegraph revolutionized communication and also offered fresh bulletins to the nineteenth century news (primarily newspaper) business. The tickers (telegraphic printing apparatuses), a modern version of which appears beneath some television newscasts, were first used in 1891 by the New York Stock Exchange and could be defined as one of the first "real-time news media" (Ojala and Uskali 2007).

In journalism, sports have often been at the forefront of live coverage. An early example occurred in 1911, when a Kansas-Missouri American football game was simulated mechanically, almost in real-time, by the *Lawrence Daily Journal-World* with the help of the telegraph and the representation of the gridiron that had been built in front of the newspaper's office:

> The ball was arranged so that it could be turned and shown by the colors whether it was Kansas' ball or Missouri's ball. Every minute that vast crowd kept its eyes on the ball, and how they cheered when it neared the goal line.—There was a leased wire run from Rollins field and there was no relaying, no waiting at St. Louis, or Kansas City. At the key there was W. C. Fountaine, of the Western Union, and never has a man at the key handled a wire service in the manner that Fountaine did. His copy was accurate, it was speedy, and he took it so that there was no delay in getting the story to the outside field. (Ljworld.com 2016)

Later during the interwar and post-WWII years, radio (1920's) and television (1950's) revolutionized live broadcasting of sporting events. Nowadays live sports broadcasting occurs 24/7 and media agreements can be calculated in billions of dollars. The Olympic Games, football (soccer), American football, basketball, baseball, tennis, golf, rugby, cricket, and even ice hockey are all prestigious live sports events (for more detail see WIPO 2016).

Television news has specialized in live broadcasting and breaking news since its inception, as exemplified by the first moon landing in 1969. Later, the Cable News Network (CNN) revolutionized the television news business by creating the very first 24/7 news channel during the 1980s which, as Tunstall (2008) argues, was made possible by new and cheaper satellite technology. Other broadcasters have followed the model and today many international and major national broadcasters are able to use the 24/7 news cycle model in every major breaking news situation. As Emily Bell (2016) argues: "Our news ecosystem has changed more dramatically in the past five years than perhaps at any time in the past five hundred." Journalism needs to constantly adopt and adapt new technologies in order to stay relevant.

THE SOCIAL MEDIA EFFECT ON UBIQUITOUS JOURNALISM

"Ubiquitous journalism" is closely linked to the concept of citizen journalism (Gillmor 1994; Jarvis 2006; Rosen 1999). In hindsight, citizen journalism was initially, and certainly before the invention of social media services, a mainly theoretical construction without many successful practical or long-lasting implications. For example, Maher (2005) provocatively claims that "citizen journalism is dead." He argues that citizen journalism had three weaknesses: ethics, economics, and epistemology (see also: Outing 2005). Maher was almost prophetic as Dan Gillmor's much-hyped commercial citizen journalism venture *Bayosphere* lasted less than a year (April 2005–January 2006) (see Johnson 2006) and Jay Rosen's online collaborative journalism experiment *Assignment Zero* lasted for just 12 weeks in early 2007 (Howe 2007).

There are however numerous examples in the twenty-first century of citizens taking advantage of digital technologies to initiate and participate in breaking news. The earliest examples relate to the Indian Ocean earthquake and tsunami in 2004 and the London bombings in 2005. In both cases, mobile technologies and telecommunications infrastructure still restricted the quick sending of the still images of digital cameras, but in the latter case, mobile phones were used by citizens for sending images to the newsrooms (Uskali 2007, 198–200). The notion of "journalism everywhere" in the early 2000s was not yet compatible with live video streaming.

The emergence of social media would have a profound influence on "journalism everywhere." According to Nancy K. Baym (2015) the term "social media" first appeared around 2004, when the Internet was still primarily funded by The United States' National Science Foundation. Interestingly, all commercial activity was still banned before 1994. According to Fuchs (2014, 48) most of social media technologies originated prior to Tim O'Reilly coining the concept of Web 2.0 in 2005.

We use the term social media to refer to "forms of electronic communication (as Web sites for social networking and microblogging) through which users create online communities to share information, ideas, personal messages, and other content (as videos)" (Merriam-Webster 2016). However, Fuchs (2014, 6) emphasizes "social media is a complex term with multi-layered meanings." A frequently asked question about social media is 'what is *social* about social media?' (boyd 2015; Couldry 2015; Fuchs 2014; Papacharissi 2015; Van Dijck 2013). Since each and every medium offers some social aspects for communication, it could be argued that "all media is social." The rise of social media including blogging, micro-blogging and social networking has brought about new ways of disseminating the news. In this way, social media is also "spreadable media" and "an expression of participatory culture" as Jenkins, Ford, and Green (2013) have suggested. Van Dijck (2013) even argues that we should replace the term "social media" with "connective media."

Blogging, and especially live-blogging, are used in some early forms of ubiquitous journalism. Thurman and Walters (2013, 83) define live-blogging as a "single blog post on a specific topic to which time-stamped content is progressively added for a finite period—anywhere between half an hour and 24 hours." They state that *The Guardian* started to use live blogging in 1999. Initially, for about eight years, live-blogging was mainly used for live sport reporting. The London bombings in July 2005 were a turning point in live-blogging, especially in the UK. After that, live blogs evolved as a popular daily component of many UK news sites; they were also increasingly used to cover serious breaking news events. In 2012, The Guardian's live blogs were getting 300% more views and 233% more visitors than conventional online articles on the same subject (*ibid.*, 85).

The development and innovations in the UK's newsrooms, from the BBC to newspapers and news agencies like Reuters, have always been closely watched and also copied by many news organizations around the world. Blogging went mainstream in the Nordic countries in 2005–2010. One interesting example is the Finnish Business Weekly *Talouselämä*, which for years had a special financial crisis live-blog. Several journalists regularly updated it, but one can argue that it was not technically a live blog, at least when using Thurman and Walters' definition which limits the use of the live-blog to only 24 hours.

Since its launch in 2006, the micro-blogging service Twitter has also been used in many local and global breaking news events (Beckers and Harder 2016; Vis 2013). Indeed, Twitter is already a common tool for journalists around the world and is replacing live-blogging to an extent, or at least having the effect of reducing the number of live-blogs. This was the case, for example, with the real-time reporting of the mass murderer Anders Behrink Breivik's court hearings in Oslo by the Finnish newspaper *Helsingin Sanomat's* Scandinavian correspondent (Kauhanen 2012). Since 2009, *Helsingin Sanomat* has used Twitter regularly in news events by inserting thematic hashtags. The newspaper had, by November 2016, gained impressive Twitter statistics with over 40,000 tweets and almost 200,000 followers.

Many sports journalists turned to Twitter during the London 2012 Olympics in a trend that was also strong in the Rio 2016 Olympics. In both Olympic Games, many broadcasters such as the BBC, also offered plenty of live webcasts of events—in London about ten, and in Rio over 30 at one time, including journalistic voice-overs.

The emergence of low cost smartphones offering HD quality cameras and mobile Internet connections has enabled anyone to be a potential citizen journalist. As Manuel Castells (2009) claims, this is the era of "mass self-communication." Facebook's personalized and algorithmic based "news stream" has arguably been one of the most successful ubiquitous communication paradigms, so far with over two billion users. However, an increased dependency on social media platforms can profoundly influence the future of news organizations:

Journalism is a small subsidiary activity of the main business of social platforms, but one of central interest to citizens. The Internet and the social Web enable journalists to do powerful work, while at the same time helping to make the business of publishing journalism an uneconomic venture. (Bell 2016). What has happened already, according to Bell, is that news publishers have lost control over distribution, and increased the power of social media companies.

THE FINNISH MEDIA SYSTEM AS A TEST BED

In this section, I will present some additional findings about "journalism everywhere" in the Finnish media system. First, some explanations: why bother to focus on the Finnish media landscape and its 5.5 million inhabitants? Hallin and Mancini (2004) consider Finland, along with other Nordic countries, as belonging to the Democratic Corporatist model of media systems. First, the countries that have adopted this model share historical similarities, such as the early development of a mass-circulation press, a strong party press, and relatively strong state-owned public broadcasting companies. Second, in the context of the contemporary media landscape, the Nordic countries seem to still have high newspaper circulations, independent public broadcasting companies and a strong journalistic professionalism.

Beginning in 2016, Nordic journalism educators have started to emphasize the special Nordic model. Hovden Nygren, and Zilliacus-Tikkanen (2016, 15) consider how "the many similarities of their educational and media systems, and relative lack of language barriers, means that Nordic journalism teachers have very often looked across the Nordic borders for useful models and inspiration for their own programmes."

In particular, the high quality of Finland's basic national education system offers solid ground for media professionals to tackle the new communication challenges and opportunities.[3] It is also worth emphasizing that Nordic countries are very often at the top of the lists of the most technologically advanced societies. This is especially due to their strong history in mobile technology and the influence of companies like Nokia and Ericsson. For example, Finland was in fifth place in 2016 in the Global Innovation rankings, following Switzerland, Sweden, the UK, and the US (Dutta *et al.* 2016). These conditions in combination indicate that Finland is well positioned to be a test bed for current and future communication modes, such as Twitter's live mobile video service, Periscope, which includes real-time chat.

Periscope entered the news scene in Finland in 2015. As is often the case with innovative services, early users experimented with it. The first example is from *Helsingin Sanomat*, when a photographer used Periscope at rival pro- and anti-immigration demonstrations in Lahti (central Finland) in October 2015. The reporter went to these two rival demonstrations, which took place in close proximity, and using voice-over, commented on what he saw and experienced.

Another example is from February 2016, when *Keskisuomalainen*, a central Finland newspaper, used Periscope at an annual student festivities event. There was no voice-over with this broadcast and the camera stayed in one place the entire time. This lack of movement resulted in some critical remarks by the viewers in the Periscope broadcast chat stream as they wanted new camera perspectives, more information, and also more active participation by the photographer from *Keskisuomalainen*. There was no reaction to these critiques. Also, many amusing but incorrect comments were published in the chat stream. One false claim was that every time the local ice hockey team JYP won, there were street celebrations.[4] *Keskisuomalainen*'s Periscope broadcast appears to have been a one-off. Furthermore, based on the definition outlined above, this live stream was not journalism, but ubiquitous communication because it did not involve any journalism elements (such as criticism).

Facebook Live, the popular social network's live video option, is the newest tool for ubiquitous communication and journalism, and became available to all Facebook users in Finland in February-March 2016. Some prominent US news organizations, like *the Washington Post*, are aiming to be more "visual and visceral" (Ciobanu 2016) on Facebook Live and avoid talking heads. In other words, the reporters need to go out of the newsrooms more for Facebook Live. This video option was prominently visible during the US Presidential elections in autumn 2016, when many Facebook Live sessions were broadcast. They first appeared on MTV3, the commercial TV broadcaster owned by the Swedish media company Bonnier, and *Helsingin Sanomat*.

After the US elections, Facebook Live has maintained its position as the leading social media live video platform in Finland. Based on the observations by the author of this chapter, almost every day there are many Facebook Live sessions by various Finnish news organizations. The themes vary from entertainment to morning news programs and foreign news.[5] After the adoption of Facebook Live by the Finnish news media, the use of Periscope for the same outlets has diminished. It seems that ubiquitous journalism favors the social media platforms that can offer the largest audience, and right now that is clearly Facebook.

In addition to Periscope and Facebook Live, which offer new opportunities for ubiquitous journalism and communication, new devices like camera drones and smartwatches are also available to journalists. Camera drones in particular are often mentioned as suitable new tools for breaking news events and, especially, for crisis reporting. Video recordings, shot with camera drones, first appeared in the news media in 2011 in connection with the riots in Warsaw and the Occupy Wall Street movement. In Finland, all the major news organizations have used camera drones for journalistic purposes in recent years. The majority of camera drone news footage has been about social unrest (demonstrations) and natural disasters (floods) and also for environmental and investigative reporting (Lauk, *et al.*, 2016).

Still, to date, none of the Finnish news organizations have used camera drones to provide live video connections. This is due to the technical limitations of camera drones, and the risk assessments of the journalists' organizations. For example, according to interviews most of the regional newspapers in Finland have not yet even invested in drones, but used freelancers. (Lauk, Uskali, and Kuutti 2016.) Nevertheless, the latest drones are capable of sending live video streams in flight and with 4K quality. In the near future, this technology could be a game changer, especially in live breaking news situations.

The adoption of smartwatches for journalistic purposes has been quite slow in Finland, with the key problems being that, initially, smartwatches were too expensive, and because the first generation of smartwatches still needed smartphones in order to be used. Only one evening newspaper *Ilta-Sanomat* has customized a special app for smartwatches. Research indicates users of smartwatch news apps in Finland are still only numbered in the thousands (Uskali and Hirvinen 2016). Smartwatches are, however, effective in breaking news situations and also in delivering financial and sports news (*ibid.*). The hyped promotion of computer wearables, especially smartwatches, seemed to be cooling during 2016. According to IDC (2016), the smartwatch market declined over 50% in the third quarter of 2016.

Still, news streams accessed via smartwatches could be one possible scenario for the future of "journalism everywhere"; another is Virtual Reality/Augmented Reality, which was greatly hyped in 2016 (Nordrum 2016). Furthermore, automated journalism, also known as robot journalism, which refers to content creation and publishing based on algorithms, could offer new interesting openings for ubiquitous journalism (Diakopoulos and Koliska, 2016).

CONCLUSIONS

With the development of ubiquitous computing, smartphones, social media, and the automation of communication and wireless Internet connections, new real-time data streams are already a reality. This chapter has been an attempt to introduce and justify new concepts of ubiquitous communication, and ubiquitous journalism (also "journalism everywhere") to media, journalism, and communication research. Ubiquitous journalism was defined as real-time news streams and pulses, which can be produced and consumed by almost everyone, everywhere via Internet connections. In a similar vein, ubiquitous communication refers to real-time information streams or pulses, but lacking in journalistic commentary.

The evolution of ubiquitous communication and journalism can be seen in the case of Finland. Not only are news organizations constantly testing new applications like Periscope or Facebook Live, but also NGOs like the World Wildlife Fund can offer live-streaming hits like Pullervo, the Saimaa ringed seal.

The trend towards ubiquitous journalism everywhere is not without problems. Ubiquitous journalism has its risks, especially for sending unverified and false information, as seen in the case of the *Keskisuomalainen* Periscope broadcast mentioned above. Therefore, criticism, fact-checking and verifying sources should be included in the practices of ubiquitous journalism. The need for this quality control was already in evidence during the US presidential elections, when Facebook shared more fake news rather than real news (Isaac 2016).

Finally, ubiquitous communication and journalism seem to favor social media platforms that can safeguard the largest audiences. Camera drones, smartwatches, virtual reality and automated journalism may offer new opportunities for the future of journalism everywhere. Therefore, future research on ubiquitous communication and journalism should focus on these emerging areas of innovations.

NOTES

1. I thank the ViSmedia project (http://vismedia.org/) at the University of Bergen, Norway for supporting this research, and Derettens (www.derettens-english-language-editing.com) for proofreading the manuscript.
2. The term ubiquitous journalism was first used by the Georgia Institute of Technology for a seminar in January 2008, but the term was not yet defined properly. (See Stenger 2008)
3. The OECD's Pisa rankings compare the test results of 15 year olds in countries and regional education systems, and for some time Finland has produced the best achieving pupils. (OECD/Pisa, 2016).
4. Initially, Periscope only provided storage and viewing capacity for the first 24 hours. A change of policy by Periscope has enabled users to have the choice of longer storing and have viewing capacity for longer periods.
5. For a directory of all Facebook Live broadcasts: https://www.facebook.com/livemap/.

REFERENCES

"Animal Planet Live – Animal Planet L!VE." 2016. *Animal Planet Live – Animal Planet L!VE.* Accessed August 30. http://www.apl.tv/.
Baym, Nancy K. 2015. "Social Media and the Struggle for Society." *Social Media + Society* 1 (1). doi:10.1177/2056305115580477.
Beckers, Kathleen, and Raymond A. Harder. 2016. "'Twitter Just Exploded.'" *Digital Journalism* 4 (7): 910–920. doi:10.1080/21670811.2016.1161493.
Bell, Emily. 2016. Facebook is eating the world. Columbia Journalism Review. March 7, https://www.cjr.org/analysis/facebook_and_media.php.
boyd, danah. 2015. "Social Media: A Phenomenon to Be Analyzed." *Social Media + Society* 1 (1). doi:10.1177/2056305115580148.
Castells, Manuel. 2013. *Communication Power.* Oxford: Oxford University Press.
Ciobanu, Madalina. 2016. "The Washington Post Sees Opportunities for 'Slow TV' on Facebook Live." 2016. August 26. https://www.journalism.co.uk/news/the-washington-post-sees-opportunities-for-slow-tv-on-facebook-live/s2/a668468/.
Couldry, Nick. 2015. "Social Media: Human Life." *Social Media + Society* 1 (1). doi:10.1177/2056305115580336.
Diakopoulos, Nicholas, and Michael Koliska. 2016. "Algorithmic Transparency in the News Media." *Digital Journalism* (July): 1–20. doi:10.1080/21670811.2016.1208053.
Dijck, José Van. 2013. *The Culture of Connectivity: A Critical History of Social Media.* New York: Oxford University Press.

Dutta, Soumitra, Bruno Lanvin, and Sacha Wunsch-Vincent. 2016. *The Global Innovation Index 2016: Winning with Global Innovation*. http://www.wipo.int/edocs/pubdocs/en/wipo_pub_gii_2016.pdf.

Galtung, Johan, and Mari Holmboe Ruge. 1965. "The Structure of Foreign News: The Presentation of the Congo, Cuba and Cyprus Crises in Four Norwegian Newspapers." *Journal of Peace Research* 2 (1): 64–90. doi:10.1177/002234336500200104.

Gillmor, Dan. 1997. *We the Media: Grassroots Journalism by the People, for the People*. Beijing; Sebastopol, CA: O'Reilly Media.

Hallin, Daniel C, and Paolo Mancini. 2004. *Comparing Media Systems: Three Models of Media and Politics*.

Hovden, Jan Fredrik, Gunnar Nygren, and Henrika Zilliacus-Tikkanen. 2016. *Becoming a Journalist: Journalism Education in the Nordic Countries*. Gothenburg: Nordicom.

Howe, Jeff. 2007. "Did Assignment Zero Fail? A Look Back, and Lessons Learned." *Wired*. July 16. http://archive.wired.com/techbiz/media/news/2007/07/assignment_zero_final?currentPage=all,%20 17.11.2016.

International Data Corporation. 2016. "Smartwatch Market Declines 51.6% in the Third Quarter as Platforms and Vendors Realign, IDC Finds." www.idc.com. October 24. http://www.idc.com/getdoc.jsp?containerId=prUS41875116.

Isaac, Mike. 2016. "Facebook Considering Ways to Combat Fake News, Mark Zuckerberg Says." *The New York Times*, November 19. https://www.nytimes.com/2016/11/20/business/media/facebook-considering-ways-to-combat-fake-news-mark-zuckerberg-says.html.

Jarvis, Jeff. 2006. "Networked Journalism." *BuzzMachine*. July 5. http://buzzmachine.com/2006/07/05/networked-journalism/.

Jenkins, Henry, Sam Ford, and Joshua Green. 2013. *Spreadable Media: Creating Value and Meaning in a Networked Culture*. New York: New York University Press.

Johnson, Miki. 2006. "'Citizens Media' Pioneer Dan Gillmor Leaving Bayosphere." *Editor & Publisher*, January 25. http://www.editorandpublisher.com/news/citizens-media-pioneer-dan-gillmor-leaving-bayosphere/.

Kauhanen, Anna-Liina. 2012. (@AL_Kauhanen) | Twitter." 2012. *Twitter*. Accessed March 31, 2017 https://twitter.com/AL_Kauhanen.

Kokko, Tuomas. 2016. "WWF:n Norppalive Päättyi – Lähetystä Katsottiin Yli Kaksi Miljoonaa Kertaa [WWF's Saimaa Ringed Seal Live Ended—Webcasts Were Watched over Two Million Times]." *Helsingin Sanomat*, June 2. http://www.hs.fi/kotimaa/art-2000002904303.html?share=bb01258f3816f0c41d5a5788f339a862.

Lauk, Epp, Turo Uskali, Heikki Kuutti, and Helena Hirvinen. 2016. "Drone Journalism. The Newest Global Test of Press Freedom." In *Freedom of Expression and Media in Transition: Studies and Reflections in the Digital Age*, edited by Ulla Carlsson, 117–125. Göteborg: NORDICOM.

Lauk, Epp, Turo Uskali, Heikki Kuutti, , and Pertti Snellman. 2016. *Droonijournalismi : kauko-ohjattavien kamerakopterien toimituskäyttö [Drone journalism. The use of remotely-piloted camera drones in journalism]*. Jyväskylä: Jyväskylän yliopisto, viestintätieteiden laitos. https://jyx.jyu.fi/dspace/handle/123456789/51821.

Lawrence Daily Journal-World for Nov. 27. 2011. "100 Years Ago: Football Fans Enjoy Mechanized Reproduction of KU-MU Game." November 27. http://www2.ljworld.com/news/2011/nov/27/100-years-ago-football-fans-enjoy-mechanized-repro/?print.

Maher, Vincent. 2005. "Citizen Journalism Is Dead." *New Media Lab*.

McQuail, Denis. 2013. *Journalism and Society*. London: Sage.

Merriam-Webster. 2016. "Definition of SOCIAL MEDIA." November 21. https://www.merriam-webster.com/dictionary/social+media.

Nordrum, Amy. 2016. "The Fuzzy Future of Virtual Reality and Augmented Reality." *IEEE Spectrum: Technology, Engineering, and Science News*. November 15. http://spectrum.ieee.org/tech-talk/consumer-electronics/gadgets/can-you-see-it-the-future-of-virtual-and-augmented-reality.

OECD/PISA. 2016. https://www.oecd.org/pisa/, 30.8.2016.

Ojala, Jari, and Turo Uskali. 2007. "Any Weak Signals?: The New York Times and the Stock Market Crashes of 1929, 1987 and 2000." In *Information Flows: New Approaches in the Historical Study of Business Information*, edited by Leos Müller and Jari Ojala, 103–136. Helsinki: SKS, Finnish Literature Society.

Outing, Steve. 2005. "'Citizen Journalism Is Dead!'...." *Poynter*. August 5. http://www.poynter.org/2005/citizen-journalism-is-dead/70502/.

Papacharissi, Zizi. 2015. "We Have Always Been Social." *Social Media + Society* 1 (1). doi:10.1177/2056305115581185.

Read, Donald. 1992. *The Power of News the History of Reuters, 1849–1989*. Oxford: Oxford University Press.

Rosen, Jay. 1999. *What Are Journalists For?* New Haven, CT: Yale University Press.

Stenger, Brad. 2008. "Ubiquitous Journalism Panel." presented at the Journalism 3G: The Future of Technology in the Field: A symposium on computation + journalism, Georgia Institute of Technology, Atlanta, GA, January 9. http://web.archive.org/web/20160414022626/http://www.computational-journalism.com/symposium/2008/01/09/ubiquitous-journalism-panel/.

Thurman, Neil, and Anna Walters. 2013. "Live Blogging–digital Journalism's Pivotal Platform?" *Digital Journalism* 1 (1): 82–101. doi:10.1080/21670811.2012.714935.

Tunstall, Jeremy. 2008. *The Media Were American: US Mass Media in Decline*. New York: Oxford University Press.

Uskali, Turo. 2007. "Ulkomaanuutisten Uusi Maailma [the New World of Foreign Reporting]." Tampere: Vastapaino. http://vastapaino.fi/kirjat/ulkomaanuutisten-uusi-maailma/.

Uskali, Turo, and Helena Hirvinen. 2016. *Uutisia ranteessa?: älykellojen soveltuvuus journalismiin. Loppuraportti [News in the wrist? The use of smartwatches in journalism]*. Jyväskylä: Jyväskylän yliopisto, viestintätieteiden laitos. https://jyx.jyu.fi/dspace/handle/123456789/52230.

Vis, Farida. 2013. "Twitter as a Reporting Tool for Breaking News." *Digital Journalism* 1 (1): 27–47. doi:10.1080/21670811.2012.741316.

WIPO. 2016. "Broadcasting & Media Rights in Sport." http://www.wipo.int/ip-sport/en/broadcasting.html.

PART SIX

Surveillances

Privacy, Surveillance, and Ubiquitous Media

CHAPTER FOURTEEN

"Framelessness," OR THE Cultural Logic OF Big Data

MARK ANDREJEVIC

INTRODUCTION

Everywhere the figure of the frame is in crisis. The boundaries that once limited information collection and use have transformed alongside with the very forms of representation that we rely on to reproduce our reality for us. Total information collection and virtual reality go hand-in-hand. Both aspire to the digital reduplication of reality. The spatial boundaries that once differentiated spaces of work, leisure, and domesticity from one another have been reconfigured along with those that separated fact from fiction. The wager of this chapter is that these developments are related.

Once upon a time, in the 1990s or thereabouts, the Internet was figured as a unique place (a "cyberspace") we might enter into, complete with a new set of affordances: virtuality, interactivity, connectivity. In recent years, however, this vision of a distinct information space has overflowed the bounds of the screen, spilling out into the world formerly known as real life ("RL"). The contemporary technological imaginary collapses cyberspace into physical space, virtuality into reality—which perhaps explains the resurgent fascination with virtual reality and augmented reality. As the physical world—what cyberpunk authors once described as "meatspace"— becomes increasingly interactive, it takes on some of the characteristics of online spaces. In practice, this means providing the physical world with an interactive digital overlay: a prospect sometimes described as ubiquitous computing or, alternatively, the Internet of Things. We find traces of this overlay cropping up all around us in various guises, devised by a range of corporate players. Amazon Go stores, for example, anticipate a world in which stores track individual users as they move through the aisles, using cameras, Wi-Fi networks, microphones, and a range of other sensors to monitor and analyze every movement in detail. Just as Web browsers can track the actions of individual users in order to identify, customize, and predict, so-called "smart" spaces promise increasingly comprehensive forms of data collection and responsiveness. Since we always are in physical space, and only sometimes inhabit "virtual" space, the possibilities for information collection become increasingly comprehensive as interactivity colonizes our lived environment. We might describe ubiquitous computing or the "Internet of things" more generally as environmental interactivity, so long as we understand this primarily as a passive form of interactivity: we are monitored as we act—a fact that redoubles our actions in the form of interactions that are recorded by the monitoring interface.

As in the case of online spaces, however, we are largely unaware of the extent to which we are being monitored in our newly smartened spaces. Consider for example, Amazon.com's desperate ploy to avoid having to divulge just how much information its digital assistant, Echo, collects about those who interact with it. Amazon at first refused to comply with a search warrant asking for voice recordings captured by Echo that were related to a murder investigation in Arkansas, arguing that Alexa, the voice of the company's assistive artificial intelligence, has First Amendment protection. Paradoxically appealing to the user's right to privacy, the company argued that, "The responses may contain expressive material, such as a podcast, an audiobook, or music requested by the user. Second, the response itself constitutes Amazon's First Amendment-protected speech" (Fox-Brewster 2017). The absurdity of Amazon's defense indicates the urgency with which it seeks to avoid divulging just how much information Echo collects as it sits in homes across the country with its electronic ears perked.

Echo bookends the era of electronic mass media inaugurated by the rise of radio and the consequent penetration of speakers into the home. In the early days of radio regulation, there was much concern about the intrusion of an agent of commerce into the domestic sphere: it was one thing to bring music and news into the intimate sphere of the bourgeois home, and something else altogether to pipe in the brash voice of commerce. As Secretary of Commerce in 1921, future president Herbert Hoover found it "inconceivable that we should allow so great a possibility for service to be drowned in advertising chatter" (Marchand 1986, 89). However, as events unfolded, the inconceivable has rapidly become so conceivable that now we are invited not just to pipe ads into our homes, but also to send our own information back the same way. If mass society relied on mass advertising, mass customized society relies on comprehensive data collection. The radio is a one-to-many medium, whereas Alexa is also a many-to-one medium, completing the de-differentiation of the domestic sphere from the realms of marketing and consumption. It should thus come as no surprise that Amazon is at the forefront of the rapid delivery technology that enables consumers to shop without leaving the comfort of home, even going to the length of patenting a flying warehouse that would allow near-instantaneous delivery of products to homes in cities that it hovers over (Newitz 2016). High-speed consumption, it turns out, relies on the same logics of verticality that are coming to characterize warfare and communication (thanks to the figure of the drone, which is being used to deliver both wireless Internet access and lethal missiles). The smart home does double and triple duty as both shopping mall and market research laboratory. Each act of consumption is redoubled in the form of a data point. But these points exist in an expanding ecosystem of information facilitated by interactive spaces: Alexa will know not only what consumers order on Amazon.com, but what music they were listening to when they ordered, at what time of day, what they were searching for online, and so on. As the technology develops, the limits to data collection fall away, yielding the prospect of what might be described as a fully monitored and recorded life. This prospect reconfigures the differentiated forms of monitoring associated with the spaces of the industrial era, when the workplace was the exclusive site of employer monitoring and the marketplace was the defined site of commercial eavesdropping and information collection. Just as the spaces of monitoring have converged, so too have its functions: the fully monitored life is a resource for market and police, as well as employers and educators. The scope of monitoring expands alongside the functions enabled by smart objects. If a smart refrigerator can purchase milk for us when the carton runs low, it can also share our eating habits with marketers, educators, health professionals, and police, depending on who has access to the data.

In this respect, perhaps the most apt description of the coming phase of interactivity is ubiquity. The frame that delimited when and where information collection would take place is giving way. If, once upon a time, physical space dictated the type of monitoring that took place within it, the rise of digital technology has dramatically transformed the situation by creating monitored digital enclosures without walls. In the pre-digital era, a shopping mall could track customers using closed circuit television. Employers could monitor workers visually, but not once the workers were out of sight (on the road delivering packages, for example). Now sprawling electro-magnetic enclosures allow employers to track and communicate with geographically dispersed employees. Cell phone companies can track which billboard their users are likely to have seen based on the data they collect about subscribers' movements throughout the course of the day. Even brick and mortar stores can learn where their consumers have shopped previously, just as Web sites learn from embedded "cookies" what previous sites users have visited.

Just as the frame of physical walls has given way to overarching digital enclosures (created by everything from Wi-Fi networks to GPS satellites, cellphone towers, and, of course, signal-carrying drones) so too have the distinctions between the uses of different types of data blurred. Your online browsing data can be used by advertisers and the NSA alike. Thanks to the advent of speculative forms of data mining, information about your consumption preferences might also be useful to employers, health care providers, and marketers. The frames that defined what data might be collected and how it might be used have been removed. Consider, for example, the finding by an employee screening company that the most robust predictor of future employee success is which browser job applicants use when they apply for work (*Economist* 2013). The choice of browser might be outside the frame that encompassed the traditional information used to evaluate employees (experience, education, qualifications, etc.)—but it allegedly has useful predictive value. The unfettered use of data drives up its speculative value, which helps explain the regulatory shift under the Trump administration toward allowing Internet service providers (ISPs) to sell users' information without having to get their permission (Wheeler 2017).

The crisis of the frame is readily discernible in the realm of representation—which is not as far from that of surveillance as we might at first imagine. Consider the developments in digital imagery that promise to dispense with the limit of the frame: virtual reality, augmented reality, and 360-degree cameras. The goal is to free the image from the frame that has shaped and constricted it—in part to fulfill the promise of total information capture and to overcome the biases of partiality and selectivity. Relatedly, in the realm of data collection, spies and marketers envision the prospect of data collection without limits: that is, with no built-in or logical restriction on the range, depth, and functions of monitoring. The goal, as one intelligence official put it, is to "collect everything and hold on to it forever" (Sledge 2013)—which is perhaps one working definition of a contemporary aspiration to framelessness. Comprehensive data capture is also the goal of the recreation of entire spaces in the virtual realm and thus of an emerging aesthetic of framelessness. If you want to reproduce a space in its entirety, you need to collect all the information about it you can. When it comes to data capture, the so-called Internet of Things promises always-on, networked convenience, anticipating an era of frameless information collection.

For example, the rise of in-home virtual assistants (including Amazon's Echo, Google Home, and LG's Hub Robot) herald an area of constant connectivity—not just between people, but between users and the objects that comprise their built environment. Such devices capture everything that is said all the time—and thus an expanding array of information about tastes, preferences, desires, needs, and patterns of life. In principle, there is no limit on the range of information to be captured.

These developments in the realms of data collection and representation—two sides of the same process—align themselves with the destabilization of other, related concepts of the frame, including those from sociology and psychoanalysis. The anthropologist Gregory Bateson (1972) describes the frame as a crucial form of meta-communication about messages that indicate how they are to be interpreted. He proposes the example of animals at play nipping one another. In order to ensure that the nip is not taken as a sign of aggression or threat, the animals must have an understanding about the action itself: a frame that designates what might otherwise be a warning or a threat as a form of play. We might say something similar about sarcasm: it is the frame that indicates to the listener that what one says is not to be taken seriously. The need for a frame becomes apparent when the frame itself breaks down—that is, when I have to tell you "I'm just kidding." By contrast, when the frame is functioning, the message carries with it its own instructions for interpretation. As Maher (2001) puts it, "Bateson…stressed that framing implies sender–organized relationships among elements in a message, which reminds the receiver, 'these messages are mutually relevant and the messages outside the frame may be ignored'" (in Reese et. al. 2001, 86). In the media realm, we see media frames break down when, for example, a satirical article from *The Onion* is picked up by another media outlet as an actual news story.

Media studies has taken up the notion of the frame to describe the process whereby media gatekeepers decide what counts as news and how a particular story is crafted according to unstated biases and preconceptions. The media critic Todd Gitlin (1980) describes media frames as, "persistent patterns of cognition, interpretation, and presentation, of selection, emphasis, and exclusion, by which symbol-handlers routinely organize discourse, whether verbal or visual" (7). In concrete terms, the frame refers to the set of priorities that shapes a story and its eventual interpretation: will a story about an industrial strike, for example, focus on the hardships to which workers are subjected or on the inconvenience of the strike for consumers? Will news about the elimination of regulations emphasize the negative impact on the environment or the benefits to industry? The answers to these questions typically depend upon the established context wherein readers or viewers interact with news outlets. Conservative viewers reading articles in conservative outlets expect a certain type of framing—and the same goes for progressive news outlets and their audiences.

By contrast, the convention of objectivity works to dissimulate the existence of a frame by implying that the selection of facts and their presentation in a story takes place neutrally: that the world is being presented simply "as it is." As Walter Cronkite used to say after his newscast (but before the advent of journalistic reflexivity), "and that's the way it is." Clearly, it's not that way anymore. The current consensus of the savvy audience echoes Todd Gitlin's (*ibid.*) assertion that some form of framing is inevitable: "for organizational reasons alone, frames are unavoidable, and journalism is organized to regulate their production." It is worth signaling in advance of the coming argument that the promise of frameless representation is to present the world in its entirety through the capture of *everything*—and thus to rehabilitate the standard of a particular version of objectivity. Virtual reality journalists, for example, envision the possibility of recreating an event in its entirety so that it can be experienced "as if you are there"—so that the representation becomes (virtually) indistinguishable from the event itself. The promise is to recreate the feeling of immediacy—of being *there*. As virtual reality journalism pioneer Nonny De La Pena puts it,

> If you were walking home and you saw somebody get hit by a bicycle, you would have a very different visual feeling about standing there than if you told your friends about it that night. They'd hear your story and then go 'Oh,' but they wouldn't have the visual feeling of your whole body being on the scene. That's the difference with these whole body experiences, when you can walk around and you can be in the middle of it. (Garling 2015)

In this form of representation, the frame is no longer in the text—which is meant to be indistinguishable from or coextensive with reality (and thus not selective)—but in the viewer. Then the question becomes, how can the viewer become unframed: or rather, what type of viewer can match the framelessness of the representation? One answer might be a viewer that is non-selective, that is able to process all the available information without leaving any out—clearly a non-human "viewer."

We might describe the contemporary media moment—and its characteristic attitude of skeptical savviness regarding the contrivance of representation—as one that implicitly embraces the ideal of framelessness (and its associated aesthetic of immersion). To put it somewhat differently, the driving force behind the contemporary critique of representation is that it falls short of framelessness: representations are always necessarily selective, biased, and therefore subject to debate, correction, and disbelief. This is the message of the charge of "fake news" mobilized by the political right in the contemporary media landscape: not that all news is patently untrue, but that it is always incomplete, subject to further forms of explication and contextualization in ways that deprive it of any real evidentiary purchase. We might say something similar with regard to the seemingly most straightforward of images: for example, the notorious Trump/Obama inauguration crowd comparison photos (Wallace, Yourish, and Griggs 2017). On the political right, these images led to much online debunking of "fake news," with headlines like, "More Fake News: Media Contrived Photos to Diminish Trump's Inauguration Crowd" (*The Great Recession Blog* 2017) At issue, among the less fanatical conspiracy theorists, was the timing and the framing of the shot (the more fanatical ones got into the realm of manipulated images). Similar efforts were expended to reframe the alleged communications between the Trump administration officials and Russian operatives. When Trump supporters describe information about his campaign's contacts with the Russians as "fake news" they most likely do not mean that these discussions never took place, but that they are being incorrectly framed as objectionable, when they were, in actuality (a) a normal and acceptable form of diplomacy and/or (b) a desirable disruption of the status quo that reveals Trump to be a dynamic innovator.

It is notable that the charge of fake news, which originated as a way of describing demonstrably untrue stories circulated by right wing media outlets and their audiences, was so easily taken up and repurposed by the political right. Originally used as a term for stories like the false claims that the Pope had endorsed Donald Trump or that Hillary Clinton was running a satanic child-sex ring out of a pizza parlor in Washington, DC, fake news rapidly became a rallying cry on the right to debunk any negative story about Donald Trump—even those that were demonstrably true (such as the story about contacts between Gen. Michael Flynn and a Russian official that led to Flynn's eventual resignation as National Security Advisor) (Haberman et al. 2017). In other words, there is a significant distinction between the use of "fake news" by partisans on the left and on the right: the former use it to resuscitate a "reality principle" while the latter use it to dispense with one altogether. The ease with which the right has taken over the term is perhaps a function of the long-established critique of truth and objectivity originally mobilized by the political left. Activists and progressives have played a crucial role (along with critical theorists) in describing the ways in which established political truths are caught up in relations of power and domination. They have pointed out the perspectival character of truth and knowledge and how this tends to serve the interests of entrenched political and economic powers. They provided an important and necessary critique of Walter Cronkite's "and that's the way it was." However, they also provided the inspiration and some of the tools for a reactionary right-wing critique that seeks not to challenge entrenched forms of power and domination, but to insulate these from the truths that threaten them. The reactionary goal is to take any sting out of the attempt to "speak truth to power." The incunabulum of the Trump era has been an exercise in the futile purchase of truth upon entrenched power: the journalistic trash-heap is piled high with stories that sought to be Trump's undoing (including the *Access Hollywood* tape, the Trump University fraud case, and so on).

To consider the role that the ideal of framelessness plays in the cry of "fake news," we might return to the notion of frame analysis (Goffman 1974). A well-developed tradition in communication studies, frame analysis seeks to trace the boundary that determines what remains excluded from the frame whereby a particular event or debate is interpreted or recounted. Much media criticism has been devoted to tracing the dimensions of the media frame—and, importantly, to noting how framing serves particular interests and political agendas. At the same time, framing analysis carries with it the vertigo of the infinite regress: what frames do the frame analysts bring to bear (and through what frame are these frames-behind-the-frame to be approached)? We are relearning why Hegel (2010) dubbed the infinite regress a "bad" form of infinity. As critique turns back upon itself, it becomes increasingly reactionary. This progression is a familiar one: the recognition of the necessary existence of a frame is mobilized as a delegitimizing tool that can be directed against any possible narrative account—which is *always necessarily partial* (because of its frame).

The frame—although most familiar to us as a visual metaphor—translates readily into the register of narrative: as in the case of media frames and framing devices. Telling a story means, by definition, knowing what to leave out. So do theorizing, categorizing, and thinking abstractly. In his parable on memory, Jorge Luis Borges (1970) introduces the character of Funes, whose memory is so comprehensive (or exhaustive) that for him to remember a day takes a full day. This is the goal of the complete database (and of virtual reality): to reconstruct a moment in its entirety—but to do it faster than the speed of human cognition so as to avoid the pitfalls of Funes. His superhuman memory was the result of an accident—a fall from a horse—and it left him both enhanced and impaired. The parable's narrator, a childhood acquaintance of Funes, observes, "I suspect, however, that he was not very capable of thought. To think is to forget differences, generalize, make abstractions" (115). It is also to tell stories—to selectively organize details of one's world in ways that make sense out of it rather than simply reiterating it wholesale. There would be no way to narratively reconstruct for someone else Funes's experiences (they are as infinite as time is sub-dividable). The only way to convey these experiences would be through immersion in Fune's world, a form of mind-melding or thought sharing of the sort envisioned in science fiction (as in the movie *Strange Days*, which features a device that records experiences so that they can be shared from one mind to another). In a similar vein, Facebook founder Mark Zuckerberg anticipates that virtual reality technology will become a medium for direct, language-free sharing of experiences: "I think you're going to be able to capture a thought. What you're thinking or feeling, in its kind of ideal and perfect form in your head and be able to share that with the world in a format where they can get that" (Dewey 2016).

The model of experience here is a familiar, classically liberal, Lockean one: that language is an extraneous add-on: a hopelessly inadequate translator of the primary thought of individuals, rather than a medium that helps give shape to our thoughts, enabling them to unfold. The fantasy of such a conception of thought is the surpassing of language entirely—and, not incidentally, the obliteration of the social and its irreducible otherness. The direct melding of experience will overcome the distinctness of individual subjects in a "singularity" of shared consciousness, while simultaneously devaluing that most social of formations: language. Thus, the hallmark of the complementary developments of big data and the rise of conspiracy theory in mainstream politics is a re-characterization of the defining feature of narrative—its incompleteness—as its *flaw*. We might say something similar of the fate of theory, whose abstraction is increasingly portrayed these days, despite its productivity, as simply reductionist—and it is this move that underwrites both the critique of theory and the political inertness of this critique. The story of everything, oddly, has nothing to tell us.

THE FATE OF NARRATIVE

The move toward framelessness, then, aligns itself with a version of post-narrativity, insofar as the goal is to leave nothing out (to collect everything and hold on to it forever). Put somewhat differently, we might describe framelessness as a theory of non-omission insofar as the goal is to collapse representation into presentation: to say to the viewer "You Are There," as Walter Cronkite dubbed the series that recreated historical events in the form of live news shows. Consider, for example, the advertising copy for a device called *LifeLogger*, that allows people to videotape their lives continuously: "Did you know that we humans can only statistically remember around 0.001% of our lives? If that shocks you, and you wish you could recall more, LifeLogger Technologies has you covered" (Tech Research Team 2015). We see, once again, the function—this time of memory—recast as its flaw: the alleged problem is that memory (like narrative) is selective: it picks and chooses events as it charts the movement of our lives through time. Of course, LifeLogger has its own flaw—it is a point-of-view camera, which means that it subjectivizes the viewing gaze, rather than capturing the entirety of surrounding reality. At the very least, the promise of comprehensive memory would require a 360-degree camera, although, of course, this would remain anchored to a particular subject and the movement of this subject through space and time. The real but impossible goal would be a form of information capture that replicated the view from nowhere/everywhere (i.e., one that is not linked to a particular perspective or point-of-view). Such forms of information capture cannot be visual in the perspectival sense of replicating the position of a particular viewer—nor can they be absorbed by an individual viewer, who is necessarily perspectivally constrained. Iconic representations, such as pre-perspectival paintings, for example, might be described as views from "nowhere"—insofar as they are not constrained to a particular viewpoint. At the same time, they remain enframed—they are selective, and they are not designed to capture existing reality.

How then to conceptualize a representation that seeks to replicate a 3-D space but from an unrestricted perspective (not tied to a locatable viewer)? If we were to imagine the form such "presentations" might take—they might be something along the lines of 4-D virtual reality models (encompassing both space and time) that replicate a world in its entirety. Such simulations might be viewed perspectivally—by a specific viewer, but, prior to the intervention of the viewer, they would notionally encompass all possible perspectives.

The collection of enough information to produce such representations would be comprehensive and exhaustive: a network of sensors that made it possible to reproduce the physical world in its entirety. We can already discern data collection strategies that move in this direction, combining as much information as possible across space and time, such as the development of "smart dust" sensors that, "float in the air throughout the entire city and track movement, biometric indicators, temperature change, and chemical composition of everything in their city" (Rowinski 2013). Such devices provide information that—taken to the limit—allow for the recreation of an entire space in real time, tracking shifts and movements as they emerge and dissipate.

Nevertheless, the ideal goal of reproducing reality in its entirety remains an unattainable one. Virtual reality falls irrevocably short. Sensors remain limited in their scope even as the range of possible dimensions for sensing continues to expand (haptic, olfactory, infrared, affective, etc.). And yet, in the face of the impasse of incompleteness and its critics (who long for what?—the end of uncertainty, history, individuality, subjectivity?), the impetus toward framelessness remains strong. This impetus marks the locus of a refusal: the refusal to engage with the contradictions of the critique of framing, subjectivity, and narrative—and the unsurpassable horizon these categories represent for finite beings.

Unsurprisingly, then, the impetus toward framelessness coincides with aspirations of immortality, spawning futurist Ray Kurzweil's fantasy of the singularity (Kurzweil 2005): a moment at which human and machine merge, presumably just in time to make sense of all the data that has accumulated in the interim. As virtual reality pioneer Jaron Lanier (2014) put it, in his sardonic take on the fantasies he helped to fuel: "What most outsiders have failed to grasp is that the rise to power of 'net-based monopolies coincides with a new sort of religion based on becoming immortal" (326). From the perspective of the singularity, the view from nowhere becomes possible, but the price is the obliteration of the subject whose perspective posed the accursed limits to knowledge and comprehension.

There is a seemingly democratic cast to the fantasy of framelessness, insofar as it envisions the prospect of total inclusion: the notion that every type of information (and the entities that generate it) matters. Such has been the import of some recent development in "new materialism" inspired by Bruno Latour's (2005) "parliament of things" in which certain rights are assigned to non-human objects: all those that participate in the construction of our shared reality. The work of Jane Bennett (2009) pushes further in this direction, envisioning a cascade of descriptions without end: the causes of a power outage include not just human actions (the deregulation of the energy grid and resulting manipulations of the power supply), but the physical properties of electricity—and the materials used to transmit it, along presumably, with the complete histories of their development and implementation. What Derrida (1979) described as the cascade of "extrinsic empiricals" is enfolded into the infinitely expanding frame of such accounts. However, for Derrida, framelessness is ruled out: deconstruction is, after all, a narrative art. Thus, Derrida cautions: "Deconstruction must neither reframe nor fantasize the pure and simple absence of the frame" (33).

Derrida's residue of Kantian self-restraint (the reminder to acknowledge our limitations as finite beings) may have logical force, but it does not necessarily have practical purchase. The rise of so-called post-truth politics (Fallows 2012) and "fake news" demonstrate the conservative force of post-frame deconstruction. There is a disconcerting deflation of what Slavoj Žižek (1999) calls symbolic efficacy in the era of the paradoxically nicknamed "truthers" who resolutely cling to a growing number of conspiracy theories— while simultaneously embracing a savvy skepticism that consigns even the most damning of established factual accounts to irrelevance. This is the conjunction that must be accounted for in the era of Trump: the combined performance of skepticism ("the mainstream media seeks to tangle us in its tissue of lies") with blind faith in gut instinct ("We know his goal is to make America great again—it's on his hat") (Frizell 2015). These are the two faces of the contemporary information environment: the generalization of suspicion punctuated by the selective suspension of disbelief.

Another way to approach this combination is through the juxtaposition of the ideal of framelessness with the frisson of conspiracy theory: on the one hand the goal of an exhaustive and definitive representation (the full truth), on the other an inexhaustible proliferation of irresolvable and indeterminate rival accounts (an over-determined set of incompatible, underlying truths). These approaches are two sides of the same deadlock of narrative, marked by the impossibility of its completeness (since language is always a stand-in for a missing referent that it can never capture). As Hegel (Hegel and Miller 1998) famously put it, it's impossible to "say" the object to which one refers: "if they wanted to say it, then this is impossible, because the sensuous This that is meant cannot be reached by language" (226). This incompleteness is also language's condition of possibility. In the Borges fable, Funes engages in the impossible experiment of trying to invent a language that would have a distinct word for every sensuous particular: to turn everything into a proper noun. He was thwarted by the fact that each particular exists in time so that a different word would be needed not only for every leaf on a tree, but for each leaf at every moment. As the narrator puts it, "he was disturbed by the fact that a dog at three-fourteen (seen in profile) should have the same name as the dog at three-fifteen (seen from the front)" (Borges 1970, 113). A language contrived to capture all sensuous particularity would not be a language at all, but simply a re-creation of reality—which we would then have to find some way to talk about. It is telling that the fantasy of the CEO of one of the largest data collection companies in the world, Facebook, is to eventually replace language with direct experience. As Zuckerberg put it in his reflections on the future of virtual reality, "having the ability, the raw ability over time, to be able to share a pure thought or feeling—in the way that you want, and give you control over that —50 years from now, that might not be a crazy thing to think about" (Dewey 2016).

THE GAP OF DESIRE

The goal of direct transmission of thought discounts the role that language plays in the formation of our thoughts and experiences. In this respect, it asserts the primacy of the pre-social and the pre-linguistic, anticipating the collapse of the realm of the social (a collapse that has become so characteristic of the contemporary politics of anti-social individualism: think of the Internet billionaires who are busy building reinforced bunkers in anticipation of society's demise) (Osnos 2017). The prospect of framelessness envisions a series of collapses of the gaps that characterize both language and the subject. Perhaps the foundational gap in question is that between culture and biology—the realm that is formative of human sexuality proper, according to psychoanalytic theory. The attempt to overcome this gap comes as no surprise, given its link to human finitude and its concomitant forms of desire. There are a number of claims built into this observation, so it is worth working through some of the connections between them. The target of framelessness is a perceived *lack*—and lack is at the basis of subjectivity (and thus language and discourse), so, it should come as no surprise at this point that the target of framelessness becomes the subject itself (and language!). In logical terms the condition of the existence of a distinct and unique subject is finitude (the stirrings of the subject emerge when an individual realizes that it is, literally, "not-all"—that it is distinct from its surrounding world, dependent on it, but unable to control it). In psychoanalytic terms, the subject comes into being through its relation to desire/lack as mediated by language. This is the core of the Lacanian (Lacan and Fink 2002) conception of the relationship between language and the subject: that whereas individual entities have needs, these turn into desire proper only when they enter the medium of language—that is when they are expressed (and are therefore addressed to an "other"). In the Lacanian formulation, desire is the surplus of demand (the articulated need) over need. Desire is thus driven by the transposition of need into the social register of language. Need is the motor of desire, but desire is not reducible to need: no need, no desire. Need, is, in this context, biological, and thus caught up in the logic of physical reproduction and then, through the medium of language, in the process of societal reproduction—it bridges these two, but not in a fixed manner. That is, desire cannot be fully reduced to an underlying need. In this sense, a psychoanalytic approach challenges the forms of biological reductionism that seek to explain social behaviors or attributes in purely biological or evolutionary terms. As the Lacanian philosopher Alenka Zupančič (2008) puts it in her discussion of the Freudian approach to sexuality, "it can neither be completely separated from biological, organic needs and functions (since it originates within their realm, it starts off by inhabiting them), nor can it be simply reduced to them" (11).

The further point is that there is no such thing as desire proper in non-social, a-linguistic beings. The notion of a machine language can be somewhat deceiving in this context, for it suggests that robots, computers, or drones have language in the same way that humans do. The psychoanalytic point is that machine-readable language is something of a misnomer. Machines don't have needs in the way that biological entities do; they do not pose demands in the way that linguistic ones do. They do not straddle the realms of biology and culture the way linguistic subjects do. The logic of both lack and surplus is absent from machine language. The code of the machine is purely operational—it does not refer to an absent referent, but collapses the signifier into the signified: this is the logic of code and of the operational image/symbol.

A simpler way to make this point is to pose the difference between content and metadata. When Google tells us that we needn't worry about our privacy because no humans read our Gmail messages, they are catering to our notion of the other's desire: they want to tell us that we don't need to worry about how other *people* might see us or what they make of our communications with others—that is to say, we don't need to worry about the desire of some "other" (only, of course about the desire of the big Other that Google has become!). When machines read our emails, they don't read for content, but for the patterns they can glean through the combination of the words in these messages with a range of other variables (time, date, addressee, subsequent clicks, etc.). Such machines seek to operationalize our words—to determine what combination of words mediates between two states: such as not clicking on an ad, and clicking on it. What we might mean by those words beyond their operational value is immaterial (and inaccessible to non-subjects, in any case). As MIT's Alex Pentland (2012) puts it in his paean to data mining: "the power of Big Data is that it is information about people's behavior instead of information about their beliefs." In the end, it's not even information about people's desires or demands—but about the predictability of their responses. What might it mean to create a machine that would read and *understand*, say, Wordsworth's "Intimations of Immortality" (trailing clouds of data…)? Even more importantly, what might it mean to create a machine that might *want* to do so? All of which is to suggest, that in an era when we are invited to imagine our future convergence with our computers, psychoanalytic theory has an important role to play in reminding us of the biological underpinnings of subjectivity.

Another way to approach the connection between biology and subjectivity is to consider the fate of desire in a context of framelessness. The goal of total information capture is the perfection of prediction and the pre-emption of desire. In the realm of consumption, this logic manifests itself in the form of the womblike promise of addressing needs before they arise. The automation of commerce envisions the fulfillment of the marketer's umbilical promise to "know what you want before you want it" (and to deliver it in real time). In the realms of policing and security, the promise of total information awareness is similar: to intervene and modulate the environment before a subject knows that it wants to do harm. As Ben Anderson

(2011) states in his discussion of counter-insurgency, the goal is to intervene before a member of the population converts to insurgent status:

> Because popular support is never definitively achieved, attempts to produce and harness it must be continuous. They must also *extend throughout life without limit* because *everything* has the potential to initiate the becoming (counter)insurgent of the population and thus the formation of new enemies. (224, emphases added)

This process of total information capture and total environmental control is pre-disciplinary, it does not require the process of subjectification, but envisions intervention at another level—one that short circuits subjective forms of control and decision making. Such developments help explain the resurgent interest in affect—not just in theory-land, but also in cognitive neuroscience.

Affect dispenses with the frame of the subject—whereas desire is coextensive with this frame. Affective modulations are pre-subjective, extra-individual, and non-cognitive. By contrast, the psychoanalytic understanding of desire is rooted in subjectivity, language, and thus, necessarily a frame. As Slavoj Žižek (1997) puts it in his discussion of what he describes as the object cause of desire ("object *petit a*"), this object, "is not what we desire, what we are after, but rather that which sets our desire in motion, in the sense of the formal frame which confers consistency on our desire...[T]he cause of desire is nothing other than this formal frame of consistency" (39). The linking of subjectivity to partiality and thus incompleteness is a familiar trope in the critique of narrative accounts: such and such an account can't be "objective" because something is left out of the picture—precisely the subjective investment (desire) of the person who framed the account.

At both ends of the process, then, the logic of framelessness anticipates the collapse of the subject: through its pre-emption on the one hand, and its surpassing on the other. To process all possible information requires a frameless perspective—the view from nowhere—and is anticipated by an emerging aesthetics of framelessness, although this is admittedly developed with an eye to a human observer. Taken to its limit, the aesthetics of framelessness pushes in the direction of non-human observation. The destiny of virtual reality, from an instrumental perspective, is what Trevor Paglen (2014), following Harun Farocki, describes as the rise of the "operational image" (1). Such an image is no longer intended for a viewing subject: "Meat-eyes are far too inefficient to see what's going on anyway. Nowadays operational images are overwhelmingly invisible" (2). Data visualization techniques can never keep up with the huge amount and array of information that is being stockpiled—and to what end? The fantasy of perfect pre-emption envisioned by total information awareness is one of the elimination of risk, decision-making, and desire: an operational perfection in the service of what Freud (1961) described as, "the most universal endeavor of all living substance—namely to return to the quiescence of the inorganic world" (56).

REFERENCES

Anderson, Ben. 2011. "Facing the Future Enemy: US Counterinsurgency Doctrine and the Pre-Insurgent." *Theory, Culture & Society* 28 (7–8): 216–240.
Bateson, Gregory. 1972. *Steps to an Ecology of Mind: Collected Essays in Anthropology, Psychiatry, Evolution, and Epistemology.* Chicago: University of Chicago Press.
Bennett, Jane. 2009. *Vibrant Matter: A Political Ecology of Things.* Durham, NC: Duke University Press.
Borges, Jorge Luis. 1970. *Labyrinths: Selected Stories and Other Writings.* Translated by James E. Irby and Anthony Kerrigan. London: Penguin Books.
Derrida, Jacques, and Craig Owens. 1979. "The Parergon." *October* 9: 3–41.
Dewey, Caitlin. 2016. "Here Are Mark Zuckerberg's Full Remarks about How Much He'd Like to (Literally!) Read Your Thoughts." *The Washington Post*, June 14. https://www.washingtonpost.com/news/the-intersect/wp/2016/06/14/here-are-mark-zuckerbergs-full-remarks-about-how-much-hed-like-to-literally-read-your-thoughts/?utm_term=.b94fcb6547d5.
Fallows, James. 2012. "Bit by Bit It Takes Shape: Media Evolution for the 'Post-Truth' Age." *The Atlantic*, August 29. https://www.theatlantic.com/politics/archive/2012/08/bit-by-bit-it-takes-shape-media-evolution-for-the-post-truth-age/261741/.
Freud, Sigmund. 1961. *Beyond the Pleasure Principle* Vol. 840. New York: WW Norton.
Frizell, Sam. 2015. "Donald Trump Supporters Vent Frustration in Frank Luntz Focus Group." *Time.Com.* August 25. http://time.com/4009413/donald-trump-focus-group-frank-luntz/.
Garling, Caleb. 2015. "Virtual Reality, Empathy and the Next Journalism." *Wired*, November. https://www.wired.com/brandlab/2015/11/nonny-de-la-pena-virtual-reality-empathy-and-the-next-journalism/.
Gitlin, Todd. 1980. *The Whole World is Watching: Mass Media in the Making & Unmaking of the New Left.* Cambridge: University of California Press.
Goffman, Erving. 1974. *Frame Analysis: An Essay on the Organization of Experience.* Cambridge: Harvard University Press.
Haberman, Maggie, Matthew Rosenberg, Matt Apuzzo, and Glenn Thrush. 2017. "Michael Flynn Resigns as National Security Adviser." *The New York Times.* Last modified February 13, 2017. https://www.nytimes.com/2017/02/13/us/politics/donald-trump-national-security-adviser-michael-flynn.html.
Haggith, David. 2017. "More Fake News: Media Contrived Photos to Diminish Trump's Inauguration Crowd." *The Great Recession Blog.* Last modified January 26, accessed March 20. http://thegreatrecession.info/blog/trump-inauguration-photos-rigged/.
Hegel, Georg Wilhelm Friedrich. 1998. *Phenomenology of Spirit.* Translated by A.V. Miller. Oxford: Oxford University Press.
———. 2010. *The Science of Logic.* Translated by George Di Giovanni. Cambridge: Cambridge University Press.
Kurzweil, Ray. 2005. *The Singularity is Near: When Humans Transcend Biology.* London: Penguin.
Lacan, Jacques. 2002. *Écrits: A Selection.* Translated by Bruce Fink. New York: WW Norton.
Lanier, Jaron. 2014. *Who Owns the Future?* New York: Simon and Schuster.
Latour, Bruno. 2005. *From Realpolitik to Dingpolitik. Making Things Public: Atmospheres of Democracy.* Cambridge: MIT Press.
Marchand, Roland. 1986. *Advertising the American Dream: Making Way for Modernity, 1920–1940* Vol. 53. Berkeley: University of California Press.

Newitz, Annalee. 2016. "Amazon's Demented Plans for Its Warehouse Blimp with Drone Fleet." *Ars Technica*, December 29. https://arstechnica.com/information-technology/2016/12/amazons-demented-plans-for-its-warehouse-blimp-with-drone-fleet/.

Osnos, Evan. 2017. "Doomsday Prep for the Super-Rich." *The New Yorker*, January 30. http://www.newyorker.com/magazine/2017/01/30/doomsday-prep-for-the-super-rich.

Paglen, Trevor. 2014. "Operational Images." *E-Flux*, no. 59 (November). http://www.e-flux.com/journal/59/61130/operational-images/.

Pentland, Sandy. 2012. "Reinventing Society in the Wake of Big Data: A Conversation with Sandy Pentland." August 30. https://www.edge.org/conversation/alex_sandy_pentland-reinventing-society-in-the-wake-of-big-data.

Reese, Stephen D., Oscar H. Gandy, Jr., and August E. Grant, eds. 2001. *Framing Public Life: Perspectives on Media and Our Understanding of the Social World*. Mahwah, NJ: Erlbaum.

The Economist. 2013. "Robot Recruiters," April 6. http://www.economist.com/news/business/21575820-how-software-helps-firms-hire-workers-more-efficiently-robot-recruiters.

Rowinski, Dan. 2013. "Connected Air: Smart dust Is the Future of the Quantified World." *ReadWrite*, November 14. http://readwrite.com/2013/11/14/what-is-smartdust-what-is-smartdust-used-for/.

Seipel, Brooke. 2016. "Trump: I 'Know Things That Other People Don't Know' about Hacking." *The Hill*, December 31. http://thehill.com/blogs/blog-briefing-room/news/312335-trump-i-know-things-about-hacking-that-other-people-dont.

Sledge, Matt. 2013. "CIA's Gus Hunt on Big Data: We 'Try to Collect Everything and Hang on to It Forever.'" *Huffington Post*, March 20. http://www.huffingtonpost.com/2013/03/20/cia-gus-hunt-big-data_n_2917842.html.

Tavernise, Sabrina. 2016. "As Fake News Spreads Lies, More Readers Shrug at the Truth." *The New York Times*, December 6. https://www.nytimes.com/2016/12/06/us/fake-news-partisan-republican-democrat.html.

Tech Research Team. 2015. "Got a Bad Memory? This Company Has You Covered." *Wall Street Daily*. Last modified August 29, accessed March 20, 2017. https://www.wallstreetdaily.com/2015/08/29/lifelogger-logg-wearable-tech/.

Thomas Fox-Brewster (2017). "The Little Black Book of Billionaire Secrets." *Forbes Magazine*, February 23. Retrieved online March 20, 2017 at: https://www.forbes.com/sites/thomasbrewster/2017/02/23/amazon-echo-alexa-murder-trial-first-amendment-rights/#61a9c0c55d81.

TIME Staff. 2017. "Read President Trump's Interview with TIME on Truth and Falsehoods." *TIME Magazine*. Last modified March 23, accessed March 29. http://time.com/4710456/donald-trump-time-interview-truth-falsehood/.

Wallace, Tim, Karen Yourish, and Troy Griggs. 2017. "Trump's Inauguration vs. Obama's: Comparing the Crowds." *The New York Times*. Last modified January 20, 2017. https://www.nytimes.com/interactive/2017/01/20/us/politics/trump-inauguration-crowd.html.

Wheeler, Tom. 2017. "How the Republicans Sold Your Privacy to Internet Providers." *The New York Times*. Last modified March 29, accessed March 29. https://www.nytimes.com/2017/03/29/opinion/how-the-republicans-sold-your-privacy-to-internet-providers.html.

Žižek, Slavoj. 1997. *The Plague of Fantasies*. London: Verso.

Žižek, Slavoj. 1999. *The Ticklish Subject*. London: Verso.

Zupančič, Alenka. 2008. *Why psychoanalysis? Three interventions*, Vol. 2, Aarhus, Denmark: Aarhus Universitetsforlag Press.

CHAPTER FIFTEEN

THE Relationship Between Ubiquitous Media AND Surveillance OF Dissent From THE Civil Rights Movement TO Black Lives Matter

SARAH HARNEY

Activists have frequently made use of technology as a tactical way to expand the reach of their communications and influence diverse publics. For example, "transistor radios allowed Cuban guerilla fighters to transmit from the Sierra Maestra, television coverage transformed the riots in Selma, Alabama into a national event, and e-mail accounts allowed Zapatistas in Chiapas to launch global communiques" (Bonilla and Rosa 2015, 7). Following this trend, digital media have become an integral component of contemporary social movements. From the Anti-Globalization movement, to Occupy Wall Street, and #BlackLivesMatter, digital media have figured prominently. Although digital media reduce the transactional cost for political activism, they also introduce several risks, such as the potential for surveillance. Yet surveillance of dissent is not a new phenomenon. One of the most well-documented examples of this is COINTELPRO (Counter Intelligence Program),[1] which was implemented by the FBI and designed to "disrupt and neutralize individuals deemed to be threats to domestic security" (Boykoff 2007, 46). COINTELPRO targeted a number of social movements occurring in the 1960s, with its most notable targets being the Black Panther Party, and Martin Luther King. This begs the question, what makes contemporary digital media surveillance of activists different than that of the past? Although surveillance of dissent is not new, the setting in which it is taking place, as well as the technologies used have drastically changed.

To examine what makes contemporary surveillance of social movements distinct, this chapter looks back to the Civil Rights movement in order to contextualize present day surveillance of the Black Lives Matter movement. Two questions are raised in this chapter: How can we conceptualize the effects of both past and contemporary surveillance of social movements? And, how has ubiquitous media changed how surveillance of social movements occurs? To help answer these questions, this study will draw upon the theory of biopower as described by Michel Foucault, as well as the concept of the surveillant assemblage, proposed by Haggerty and Ericson. Foucault's concept of biopower provides a framework for theorizing the effects of surveillance on both past and contemporary social movements. Meanwhile, Haggerty and Ericson's (2007) theory of the "surveillant assemblage" helps to illustrate how contemporary surveillance systems differ from those of the past. They argue that we are witnessing a "convergence of what were once discrete surveillance systems" (*ibid.*, 104).

This study argues that the intent, effect, and even some tactics of both past and contemporary forms of surveillance of social movements have similarities. What makes contemporary surveillance different is its ubiquity. The ease and technological capacity of digital surveillance allows for police to widen the net that they cast, monitoring routine activities of an increasingly large number of activists. Digital surveillance methods have the capability to bring together data collected from diverse systems, resulting in a more wide-ranging picture of social movement actors and activities. The larger implication of ubiquitous surveillance is that it increases the ability of police to monitor and preemptively disrupt social movement activities, while making it progressively difficult for activists to completely subvert surveillance.

SURVEILLANCE AND THE CIVIL RIGHTS MOVEMENT

Before discussing surveillance of the Civil Rights movement, I will contextualize these events by explaining the protest policing approach used during this time. It is important to note that protest policing can encompass a wide array of tactics. For example, these tactics can encompass both repression and suppression; "repression is violent, while suppression, a broader term, also encompasses other, subtler modes of silencing opposition" (Boykoff 2007, 11). Surveillance has developed alongside other policing tactics, enabling and informing both repressive and suppressive methods. The 1960s was a volatile time for protest policing in the United States, and was largely characterized by the escalated force approach[2] (McPhail, Schweingruber, and McCarthy 1998).

During the 1960s, the US engaged in both direct violence against, and surveillance of, civil rights activists. In response to the rise of various social movements during this time, from "1956 to 1971, the FBI enacted a program known as COINTELPRO that was designed to disrupt and neutralize groups that were deemed to be threats to national security" (Boykoff 2007, 46). Because of Supreme Court rulings that protected the right to peaceful protest, the FBI could not outright arrest participants in these social movements as they saw fit. The FBI instead sought to "disrupt organizing efforts by spreading distrust and factionalism among members of targeted organizations,[3] discouraging nonmembers from supporting activist efforts, and preventing movements from accessing resources" (Hoerl and Ortiz 2015, 594).

To achieve the aims of COINTELPRO, a number of protest policing tactics were used, but the overall purpose was always to preemptively neutralize a perceived threat. One of the most prominent examples of the aforementioned tactics involved what the FBI called "black nationalist-hate groups." A large portion (almost 80%) of COINTELPRO's operations were targeted against such groups, which included the Black Panther Party and civil rights activists (Boykoff 2007). In 1966, two black students attending Merritt College in Oakland, California (Huey P. Newtown and Bobby Seal), founded the Black Panther Party (*ibid.*). When they established the organization, Newton and Seal identified their primary objective as "promoting the achievement of all of our human rights, including the right to defend ourselves against any threat to the achievement of those rights" (Roman 2016, 8). Membership expanded quickly, and the party grew to "4,000 members and 33 chapters within its first 4 years" (Brame and Shriver 2013, 501). By the late 1960's, the Black Panther Party had become an influential social movement in the US. Due to this as well as the Black Panther Party's emphasis on revolutionary politics and armed self-defense, they quickly drew the attention of the US government and its intelligence networks (Boykoff 2007).

Under COINTELPRO, the Black Panther Party was subject to a number of protest policing tactics such as direct violence, and subtler forms of suppression which included surveillance (*ibid.*). In his study on political repression of the Baltimore chapter of the Black Panther Party, Jeffries (2002) found that legal repression, covert repression, and violent repression of the party was common. He found that under the umbrella of legal repression,[4] harassment laws had been employed at least twenty times throughout the chapter's existence (*ibid.*, 77). Meanwhile, the party had been subject to about 15 incidents of covert repression, and an excessive amount of violent oppression (Bennett 2010). Covert repression included surveillance and use of informants to disrupt social movement activities, while violent repression encompassed any sort of physical assault used to frighten or harm movement members (*ibid.*).

One of the most well-known examples of state-sanctioned violence enacted against the Black Panthers occurred on December 4, 1969 when Black Panther Party (BPP) leaders Fred Hampton and Mark Clark were killed after Chicago

Police raided their apartment (Boykoff 2007). The FBI's role in this raid was long suspected, but confirmed after COINTELPRO documents were stolen from the Pennsylvania FBI office in 1971 by unknown activists and made public (Bennett 2010). One document obtained from this raid linked BPP informant, William O'Neal,[5] as well as the FBI, to the incident. The document was of a floor plan of Fred Hampton's apartment that had been hand drawn by William O'Neal (Bennett 2010). The document had been given to the officer that led the raid, and following the raid, it was documented that William O'Neal had received a special bonus from the FBI as a thank you for providing them with the diagram (Bennett 2010). In this case, on the ground surveillance conducted by William O'Neal played a key role in enabling direct violence against the Black Panther Party.

Information gathering played a significant role in efforts to suppress the Black Panther Party. The above example demonstrates that although the information-gathering practices used were not always technologically advanced, information sharing between local and national levels of policing was widespread and played a large role in suppression of the movement. Brame and Shriver (2013, 506) conducted an analysis of FBI files "spanning nearly 8 years, from 1968 to 1976, to examine the relationship between national and local FBI forces to repress Black Panther Party activity, focusing on FBI files maintained on the Winston-Salem[6] chapter of the party." Their study found that information gathering was important in how both local and national policing of the movement occurred. Information was usually collected to "forewarn law enforcement agencies of planned activities, to gather evidence for possible preemptive prosecutions under an anti-sedition statute, and to gather evidence for possible prosecution under existing firearm statutes" (*ibid.*, 501).

Information gathering at the national level was focused on impeding movement activity, meanwhile at the local level intelligence gathering was done to aid with these goals, providing an ongoing threat analysis as well as feedback on the effectiveness of their tactics (Bennett 2010). Brame and Shriver (2013) also found that information sharing occurred frequently with other enforcement agencies, including local police forces. This was key in assisting each agency in their individual social control efforts. For example, the "FBI was able to occasionally warn the local police of potentially violent events, while police investigation of the Panthers contributed to the FBI's efforts to monitor and track Panther activity" (*ibid.*). Ultimately intelligence gathering and information sharing played a large role in the repression of the Black Panther Party, enabling other tactics such as direct violence or arrests.

As well as targeting the Black Panther Party, COINTELPRO also set its sights on prominent civil rights activists like Martin Luther King, Jr. Though he was already on their radar, after his "famous 'I Have a Dream' speech in Washington during 1963, the FBI began to actively pursue King's 'neutralization,' increasing their surveillance campaign against him" (Boykoff 2007, 98). Some of these tactics included wiretapping King's homes, offices, and hotel rooms. Along with this, King was subject to "Black Bag Jobs" (illegal break-ins) for the purpose of gathering information (Fleming 2007, 142).

The FBI first began its campaign against King by setting out to collect information that would paint his character in a negative light, attempting to gather information about his drinking and extramarital affairs (Boykoff 2007, 99). As King continued to gain momentum, in 1965 the FBI's objectives changed from discrediting King to gathering information that would allow them to know what civil rights events would be occurring ahead of time (*ibid.*). Those closest to King noted that this had an effect on him, and caused him to alter his actions to account for the possibility of constant surveillance (*ibid.*). Surveillance was a key component of the protest policing tactics used during this time. Direct repression, like state-sanctioned violence, and subtler forms of suppression such as surveillance were often used together to preemptively neutralize alleged threats posed by activists, and minimize the risk that they posed to the existing socio-political order. Yet, due to the constraints of the technologies used, surveillance of activists was not ubiquitous. Surveillance was limited to a specific time and place, and often directed towards a suspect known to authorities beforehand.

While it is easy to draw parallels between the intent of past and present forms of surveillance, the technology available to both police and activists during this time created a very different situation. Surveillance of activists was limited to on-the ground information gathering from informants, wiretapping, and planting surveillance technologies such as microphones or recording devices (*ibid.*). Surveillance technologies were constrained by physical place, took a great deal of effort to plant, and were applied specifically to a suspected person. While surveillance of civil rights activists meant a great deal of information was collected and shared between enforcement agencies, the physical constraints of surveillance technologies used meant it was more difficult for them to be applied ubiquitously to all movement members. Information sharing between different enforcement branches was common, but it was not instantaneous.

The technology available to activists during this time was also very different, and came with problems of its own. If civil rights activists needed to get urgent news out in the 1960s, they were largely reliant on the telephone, or coverage by traditional news media, which could be monitored or censored (Stephen 2015). As mentioned previously, wiretaps were placed on the telephone lines of prominent movement targets and their conversations were monitored. If activists wanted to place a call to one of the major national civil rights organizations to relay news, there would usually be issues if they attempted to do so by dialing a standard long-distance number (*ibid.*). This entailed speaking with a switchboard operator and asking to be put in contact with one of the national civil rights organizations. Due to the hostile political climate civil rights activists were acting within, this opened up the possibility for your call to be blocked by the operator if they did not support the civil rights movement (*ibid.*).

To combat this, organizations like the Student Nonviolent Coordinating Committee (SNCC) invested in a Wide Area Telephone Service (WATS) line that "much like an 800 line, would patch directly through to the business or organization that paid for the line" (*ibid.*). These phone calls would lead to write-ups, "which would be compiled into mimeographed WATS reports, and then mailed out to other civil rights organization leaders, the media, the Justice Department, lawyers, and other friends of the movement across the country" (*ibid.*). It took a great deal of effort to disseminate news through the technology that was accessible to activists at the time. Due to the constraints of place and time, surveillance technologies of the past were not capable of enabling ubiquitous surveillance of all movement activists. These constraints enabled pockets of resistance where activists were able to subvert and escape surveillance at times.

#BLACKLIVESMATTER AND DIGITAL MEDIA SURVEILLANCE

For present-day social movements both the availability of digital media, and the potential for surveillance have changed drastically. One major difference is the emergence of contemporary forms of protest policing that rely more heavily on surveillance than those of the past. Changes in protest policing have resulted in an increased reliance on information-based policing, which has been attributed to various factors. Scholars such as Leslie Wood (2014) argue that changes in modern protest policing have occurred in response to the neoliberal transformation of social, political and economic systems. Wood claims that "as the social safety net weakened under neoliberal restructuring, the role of police became one of 'cleaning up' the damage caused by economic transformations, and that of 'securing a strong investment climate.'"[7]

Intelligence-led policing has become common in this political climate. Intelligence-led policing can be defined as a managerial approach in which "data analysis and crime intelligence are pivotal to an objective decision-making framework that facilitates crime reduction, and prevention through strategic management" (*ibid.*, 60). Intelligence-led policing changes the job of policing "from one of reacting to crime to one that preempts it, through an emphasis on intelligence gathering and analysis, and the strategic use of resources to disrupt potential disorder" (*ibid.*, 61). New socio-political and economic circumstances, as well as changing tactics being employed by protesters have resulted in police adopting what has been called the "strategic incapacitation" approach.

Under strategic incapacitation, protest-policing tactics began to emphasize preemptively planning for and defusing potential security threats before they occur.

This method of policing employs surveillance in the form of information collected on "activists and advocacy groups between protest events," as well as real time surveillance during events (Gillham 2011, 644). Contemporary surveillance can take many forms such as monitoring of activist social media platforms and websites, or much like the past, on the ground infiltration of social movements (*ibid.*). Although it is difficult to determine where and how they are used due to secrecy surrounding these methods, big data tools also "allow police to apply computer analytics to a very large collection of digitized data, in order to identify suspicious persons and activities on a massive scale" (Joh 2016, 16). For example, Joh notes that the Chicago Police Department "already uses big data tools to identify high risk persons based on the strength of person's social networks" (17). This technique does not target pre-identified suspects, but instead seeks to determine potential suspects before a crime occurs (*ibid.*). During actual protest events, "authorities sometimes align march routes with pre-existing CCTV infrastructure, and set up CCTV cameras outside 'no-go' zones and legally sanctioned free-speech zones" (Gillham 2011, 644). Similar to the past, this information is shared widely between various organizations such as federal, state, and local agencies (*ibid.*). What is different is the ease in which digital information can be collected and shared.

As mentioned above, information collection can include data taken from existing social media platforms such as Facebook and Twitter. Social media platforms provide an easily accessible means for police to record the activities and social life of protesters. By merely being active on social media, people produce data about their social interactions, interests, and personal history (Trottier 2012). Digital media provide police with a wealth of information that requires fairly little effort to obtain. Digital media monitoring usually takes the form of officers manually using or searching social media platforms. These searches can include searches for keywords and suspects (Joh 2016, 24). In other cases, instead of relying on individual officers, "a big data approach looks through all, or nearly, all, of the available data and uses computer algorithms to identify suspicious patterns of activity or to reveal previously unknown links among criminal suspects" (*ibid.*). While digital media makes activists vulnerable to police surveillance, such media also provide them with many affordances, making them a tool that is difficult to discard. On the topic of affordances, Hutchby (2001, 448) notes that,

> [C]ertain objects, environments or artefacts have affordances which enable the particular activity while others do not. But at the same time the affordances can shape the conditions of possibility associated with an action: it may be possible to do it one way, but not another.

For activists, some of the affordances of digital media include "increased speed of communication, helping outreach efforts, enabling engaging feedback loops, and cost-effectiveness" (Obar 2014, 214).

Digital media has become an important tool for contemporary social movements like Black Lives Matter, for many of the reasons listed above. The Black Lives Matter movement describes themselves as "a chapter-based national organization working for the validity of Black life, and working to rebuild the Black liberation movement" (Black Lives Matter, 2016). While their platform is complex and diverse, they depict themselves as "a call to action and a response to the virulent anti-Black racism that permeates our society" (*ibid.*). Digital media has been an integral component of Black Lives Matter from its inception. #BlackLivesMatter, "became a hashtag in the summer of 2012, when an Oakland, California, labour organizer named Alicia Garza responded on her Facebook page to the acquittal of George Zimmerman, the man who killed Trayvon Martin" (Stephen 2015). Since that moment, it has become the key phrase under which disparate organizations and individuals fight against racial inequality and injustice (Stephen 2015).

Scholars such as Bonilla and Rosa (2015, 5) argue that the "increased use and availability of digital media provides marginalized and racialized populations with new tools for documenting incidents of state-sanctioned violence and contesting media representations of racialized bodies and marginalized communities." For Black Lives Matter activists, hashtags play a crucial role in "disseminating messages, drawing global attention to issues, and attempting to bring visibility and accountability to repressive forces" (*ibid.*, 7). In the case of Ferguson, the #Ferguson hashtag was an important tool for bringing attention to "the fatal shooting of Michael Brown, for publicizing the protests that ensued, and in bringing attention to the militarized police confrontations that followed" (Bonilla and Rosa 2015, 5). Digital media are at the center of contemporary social movements, changing how protesters mobilize, disseminate messages, and document incidents of police violence. For example, during Occupy Wall Street, Twitter was used for a number of purposes, which included facilitating direct actions, reporting from direct actions, disseminating news to the public, expressing movement opinions, engaging in online discussions, making connections with others involved in the movement, and enabling online actions (Penney and Dadas 2014, 79). Yet as mentioned prior, activist use of digital media is occurring within a protest policing context that relies heavily on surveillance. For Black Lives Matter, the threat of police surveillance is continuous. While surveillance of activists in the past was constrained by place and time, as Black Lives Matter activists use social media to organize, they are subject to a more ubiquitous form of surveillance that permeates their everyday actions.

Documents obtained by *The Intercept* through a Freedom of Information Act request confirm that surveillance of Black Lives Matter activists is occurring (Joseph 2015a). The documents verify that the "Department of Homeland Security has been monitoring the Black Lives Matter movement since anti-police protests erupted in Ferguson, Missouri" (*ibid.*). Information on Black Lives Matter activists is frequently collected through social media accounts on platforms like Twitter,

Facebook, and Vine (*ibid.*). The documents show that the department has been monitoring both protest events related to Black Lives Matter, and those that are seemingly benign or mundane (*ibid.*). On this topic, a Department of Homeland Security spokesperson stated that conducting surveillance of Black Lives Matter activists is merely providing "situational awareness and establishing a common operating picture so that federal, state, and local governments are prepared in the case of terrorism or other man-made disasters" (*ibid.*). In other words, this kind of monitoring is intended to protect the existing socio-political order from potential "threats."

Experts on this topic disagree, and claim that surveillance is a problem that goes beyond "informational awareness" for social movements (*ibid.*). Baher Azmy, a legal director at the Center for Constitutional Rights, argues that, "over time there's a serious harm to the associational rights of the protesters and it's an effective way to chill protest movements. The average person would be less likely to go to a Black Lives Matter protest if the government is monitoring them" (*ibid.*). In line with the strategic incapacitation approach, police are relying heavily on information collecting so that they can monitor for and preemptively disrupt potential "threats" in order to ensure the protection of the existing socio-political structure. Surveillance enables both preemptively policing, and serves to potentially chill dissent through the knowledge that one's actions are being monitored.

Much like in the past, digital media surveillance is used alongside on the ground surveillance of activists. Documents acquired by *The Intercept* confirm that undercover police officers frequently attended Black Lives Matter protests in New York between December 2014, and February 2015 (Joseph 2015b). The nearly 300 documents obtained illustrate that more "on-the-ground surveillance of Black Lives Matter activists is occurring than previously shown, conducted by a coalition of MTA counterterrorism agents and undercover police in conjunction with NYPD intelligence officers" (*ibid.*). The documents released include content like "live updates on protests from undercover police officers, reporting on group sizes, and the tracking of protesters' movements around the city" (*ibid.*). On the ground surveillance, combined with the ease of digital media surveillance, significantly changes the context in which activists are acting.

Digital surveillance has far fewer limitations than that of the past. This is in part "a result of the technological possibilities created by digital interactivity, but also a result of economic choices about how to support the information infrastructure upon which people are increasingly reliant" (Andrejevic 2012, 91). Andrejevic (2012) describes the contemporary moment as one of "ubiquitous surveillance." He characterizes ubiquitous surveillance as, "the prospect of a world in which it becomes increasingly difficult to escape the proliferating technologies for data collection, sorting, and storage" (*ibid.*, 92). The emergence of ubiquitous surveillance has influenced security and policing organizations in a number of ways. They have become reliant upon digital surveillance technologies, as well as data collected by the private sector for commercial purposes, finding ways to make use of existing databases for information collection (*ibid.*).

The characteristics of digital surveillance technologies also alter the ways in which surveillance can be used as a protest policing tactic. For example, digital surveillance technologies are not constrained by time or place. Unlike wiretapping a phone line or bugging a room in hopes of collecting information on a suspect known beforehand, many new technologies are not "especially applied to a suspected person or place, and are commonly applied categorically" (Marx 2007, 84). Similarly, Andrejevic (2012, 92) points out that "there is a spatial component to the notion of ubiquitous surveillance: as interactivity migrates into new spaces, the capability for monitoring arrives with it." With the capacity to easily monitor large groups of people, surveillance affects a greater number of social movement actors more ubiquitously. With surveillance now being applied to large groups of people whom fall within a certain context, the term "suspect" is extended to include those that may not currently be, but could eventually become, a "threat." This phenomenon is evident in surveillance of Black Lives Matter activists. The documents obtained by *The Intercept* on this subject indicated that surveillance was not only directed at large rallies and key movement leaders, but also included monitoring seemingly mundane events which were note even directly affiliated with the movement (Joseph 2015a). These included monitoring a Funk Parade and the Avon 39-Walk to End Breast Cancer, both of which occurred in historically black neighborhoods (*ibid.*). Applying surveillance categorically serves to preemptively criminalize large groups of people, some of which are not even affiliated with the movement.

Unlike technologies of the past, police do not have to wait for the right moment to capture useful information as data collection is often integrated into routine activities. The digitization of surveillance has enabled "active sorting, identification, prioritization and tracking of bodies, behaviors and characteristics of subject populations on a continuous, real-time basis" (Graham and Wood 2007, 218). By merely owning a smartphone and being active on digital media platforms, activists are producing data about their location, social interactions, interests, and personal history. They are increasingly vulnerable to subtle forms surveillance enacted by digital systems that track, identify, and categorize them in complex ways. As Black Lives Matter activists use digital media as an organizational tool, these technologies automatically produce data that enables activists to be monitored, tracked, and sorted. Unlike the past, police do not have to wait for Black Lives Matter activists to make a call on a wiretapped phone line to collect information that might allow them to disrupt social movement activities; instead data is automatically collected as activists Tweet, use their phones, and search the Internet.

Digital surveillance also makes information sharing between systems much easier than in the past. Digitization "facilitates interconnection within and between surveillance points and systems. To be truly effective, linkage is often required so that captured and stored data can be compared" (*ibid.*, 220). This has often meant that surveillance now "transcends institutional boundaries, and systems intended to serve one purpose often find other uses" (Haggerty and Ericson 2007, 111). This is exemplified in how police organizations have secured "routine and often informal access to a host of non-police databases, such as those from insurance companies and financial institutions" (*ibid.*). For example, information collected on Black Lives Matter activists through commercial databases may be repurposed and used for policing. Information sharing is no longer limited to different branches of enforcement agencies, but occurs across institutions with ease. This is exemplified in the documents obtained by *The Intercept* on surveillance of the Black Live's Matter movement. These documents showed the Department of Homeland Security sharing information with the FBI, NYPD's counterterrorism intelligence organization, and other state police organizations (Joseph 2015a). This kind of information sharing not only expands the reach of surveillance, but diversifies the kind of information that is collected.

INTENT AND EFFECT OF SURVEILLANCE

Surveillance of social movements not only allows law enforcement to preemptively disrupt perceived threats, but it also introduces a subtle form of social control. The knowledge that one's activities are being monitored can result in social movements gradually altering their behaviors in accordance with external pressures. Foucault's concept of biopower[8] is useful for understanding the intent and effect of surveillance of social movements. Biopolitics is the process by which biopower is exerted, and refers to the control of human bodies through state discipline. Biopolitics is not "power enacted on the individual, but acts at the level of massification instead of individualization" (Ajana 2005, 2). It aims to "identify risk groups, risk factors and risk levels, and therefore anticipate, prevent, contain and manage potential risk, all through 'actuarial analysis'" (*ibid.*, 3). Power does not come from a centralized source, and biopower becomes internalized as the human subject gradually complies with subtle regulations and expectations in all areas of life, ultimately participating in their own self-monitoring and discipline through 'technologies of the self'[9] (Foucault 1997, 246–247). The concept of biopower has been used to illustrate a shift from centralized state power, towards more dispersed and hidden forms of control embedded in our everyday lives.

Related to biopolitics is Foucault's concept of the panopticon. Foucault uses Bentham's figure of the panopticon to explain how "power does not need to be enforced but merely "internalized" through mechanisms of self-regulation" (Ajana 2005, 5). Bentham's prison panopticon was an architectural figure "based on an observing supervisor placed in a central tower who can see without being seen, producing the feeling of constantly visibility for prisoners" (Ajana 2005, 4). Some scholars have contended that Foucault's notion of the panopticon is no longer a suitable metaphor for understanding how surveillance affects individuals.[10] Meanwhile theorists like Ajana (2005) argue for its continued relevance alongside the concept of biopower. She claims that panopticism "did not produce a prison-like society, but instead self-managing individuals were formed through the process of power internalization alongside a partitioning of responsibility between state and citizens" (*ibid.*, 7). She claims it is crucial to understand the ways in which "old disciplinary mechanisms are reconfigured and refashioned within the circuits of everyday existence" (*ibid.*). Biopower is diffused through past and present technologies of the self, which reproduce panoptic power structures. Both of these theories are useful for understanding the intent and effects of surveillance of social movements. Surveillance of social movements is done to preemptively identify and prevent what is perceived as a risk. Meanwhile, the knowledge that one's activities are under surveillance can sometimes lead to gradual suppression of dissent.

As open as the Civil Rights movement was, the fact that it was so heavily monitored undoubtedly had an effect on its ability to organize. Boykoff (2007, 105) notes that the surveillance of Martin Luther King, Jr. affected morale and altered movement tactics. Despite the appearance that King was unaware of or unconcerned about FBI surveillance, King and his advisors were very much aware that it was occurring and debated whether or not to make public the FBI's operation against him (Cooper 2008). According to the people who knew him best, King operated on the assumption that his every move could be recorded and later used against him (Boykoff 2007).

Others noted that fear of surveillance on the part of those not actually monitored eventually produced a sort of self-censorship, even leading to the erosion of important social movement figures (Boykoff 2007). Civil rights activist Jack O'Dell noted that, "If Martin was speaking somewhere, I'd stay clear because I'd figure they were surveilling it" (*ibid.*, 106). He eventually resigned from the Southern Christian Leadership Conference[11] (SCLC) because of the intense surveillance he was under, and how it was influencing King (*ibid.*). Surveillance and the spreading of rumors also had a negative influence on the SCLC's ability to raise funds (*ibid.*). External forms of regulation were internalized through civil rights activists at the level of human interaction, slowly influencing their ability to organize and generate solidarity. Yet it is also important to note that despite surveillance undoubtedly having a negative effect on some movement members, and King himself, Civil Rights activists still persisted despite their fears. This indicates that although the effects of surveillance are felt, and may cause social movements to alter their actions, surveillance alone does not always completely chill dissent.

Scholars have pointed out that, "knowing that agents are gathering information on it may make the social movement less open, democratic, require that limited resources be devoted to security, and may deter participation" (*ibid.*, 106). Starr *et al.* (2008) argue that contemporary forms of surveillance affect protest movements in similar ways. In a study done based on group interviews conducted in 2006 that included 71 social justice organizations, the effects of American state surveillance on social movement activity in the post-Seattle era were examined (*ibid.*, 251). The study found that rather than "hardcore activists becoming more militant while others become more moderate, signs of pervasive pacification was the norm" (*ibid.*, 267). They also note that "surveillance has caused security culture to replace organizing culture, with devastating impacts on inclusivity, solidarity, bonds of friendship, and community, and prefigurative practice" (*ibid.*, 262).

Black Lives Matter activists have voiced similar concerns on the effects of social movement surveillance. Elsa Waithe has stated that she believes one of the intended effects of intense police surveillance of the movement is to suppress dissent while collecting information that allows police to more efficiently target organizers (Joseph 2015b). On this topic, she has stated, "when you know they're recording and watching you, that's a feeling I can't ever shake. I don't know what they are doing with all of those hours of recordings because there's nothing there. It's just being used to intimidate us" (*ibid.*). Maurice Mitchell voiced similar concerns stating, "Surveillance is a tool of fear. When the police are videotaping you at a protest or pulling you over because you're a well-known activist—all of these techniques are designed to create a chilling effect on people's organizing (Joseph 2015a). Despite this, he also notes that, "The level of surveillance, however, isn't going to stop us. After all, we organize because our lives depend on it" (*ibid.*). Surveillance aims to preemptively disrupt threats, while simultaneously chilling dissent through the knowledge that one's activities are being monitored. Yet, as Black Lives Matter activists continue to persevere despite being under surveillance, it is clear that it does not always suppress dissent.

A study done by Leistert (2012) examines how activists develop digital media tactics that attempt to resist surveillance, and how the surveillance practices of police consequentially adapt. Her study examines both statements given by activists that focus on how they protect themselves from digital surveillance, and court documents detailing German surveillance practices (*ibid.*). This study found that while activists continue to develop many tactics that allow them to resist surveillance such as code words, encryption, or using their phones very rarely, surveillance adapts to these tactics (*ibid.*). The study concluded that despite taking steps to protect the content of their communications, by merely having their phones turned on, activists were producing metadata that could be used to monitor them (*ibid.*). Yet what is important to note is that despite not being able to completely escape surveillance, activists continued to attempt to resist it. This resistance is also evident in the case of Occupy Wall Street. Despite being subject to almost every aspect of the strategic incapacitation approach, including surveillance, activists continued to resist and work to develop new ways of countering protest policing tactics (Gillham, Edwards, and Noakes 2013). This indicates that although modern surveillance is distinct from the past in its expansion, ubiquity, and ability to capture and bring together diverse data from different places in order to paint an extensive picture of those surveilled, it still provides the potential for pockets of resistance. Although the panoptic effects of surveillance may be felt and are undoubtedly detrimental to social movement organizing, much like the past contemporary activists continue to persist and subvert even more ubiquitous surveillance systems.

Haggerty and Ericson's (2007) concept of the "surveillant assemblage" helps to illustrate what is unique about contemporary surveillance. Different from systems of the past, they emphasize that the surveillant assemblage is not bound by place or time, and describe it as "operating by abstracting human bodies from their territorial setting and separating them into a series of discrete flows. These flows are then reassembled into distinct 'data doubles' which can then be scrutinized and targeted for intervention" (*ibid.*, 104). In this process, an increasingly large group of people are being subject to routine surveillance (*ibid.*). They claim that "assemblages consist of a multiplicity of heterogeneous objects, whose unity comes solely from the fact that these items function together, that they 'work' together as a functional entity" (*ibid.*, 106). This theory helps exemplify how contemporary surveillance of Black Lives Matter activists differs from that of the past.

As opposed to monitoring predetermined suspects, an increasingly large group of people who may be loosely affiliated with the movement are surveilled. The information gathered on activists is diverse, but comes together to depict a more extensive picture of those surveilled. The digital data collected on movement members is abstracted from place and time, ultimately facilitating "interconnection within and between surveillance points and systems" (Graham and Wood 2007, 220). Information is collected from the content of social media accounts, location data, on the ground surveillance, etc., but ultimately works together as a functional whole to monitor and disrupt social movement activities. In combination with other information collected from on the ground surveillance and available databases, the surveillant assemblage "provides exponential increases in the degree of surveillance capacity" (Haggerty and Ericson 2007, 107).

The surveillant assemblage also increasingly relies on machines to conduct surveillance. Haggerty and Ericson argue that while past forms of surveillance relied heavily on human observation, the surveillant assemblage leans more towards machine observation. While on-the ground surveillance still plays a role in contemporary protest policing, the use of technology to conduct surveillance has increased exponentially since the 1960s. As mentioned previously, digital media technologies provide police with a wealth of accessible information due to the fact that data collection is automated and integrated into their design.[12] Despite the ubiquity of the surveillant assemblage, some scholars also highlight the resistive possibilities of contemporary surveillance.

Vian Bakir (2015) proposes the term, "veillant panoptic assemblage," which she describes as "an arrangement of profoundly unequal watching, where citizens' watching of self and others, is through corporate channels of data flow, fed back into state surveillance of citizens" (12). This concept acknowledges the potential for resistance against modern surveillance systems. Bakir notes that "this term highlights that resistance against surveillance may be attempted through different types of veillance including sousveillance[13] counterveillance[14] and univeillance[15] practices" (18). This is helpful in conceptualizing how, despite the ubiquity of contemporary surveillance, social movements like Black Lives Matter continue to grow and resist the panoptic effects of surveillance. Though digital media enables ubiquitous surveillance and its conceivably panoptic effects, it also provides activists with the potential to resist and fight back against these systems. Ultimately, although the intent and effect of past and contemporary forms of surveillance of social movements is comparable, digital surveillance is increasingly ubiquitous. The surveillant assemblage means that larger groups of people are surveilled, through more diverse and extensive means. The surveillant assemblage brings together data from multiple systems, making it difficult, though not impossible for activists to fully escape or subvert its reach. Contemporary activists continue to persevere and resist ubiquitous surveillance.

CONCLUSION

While much of the discussion around digital media focuses on how it is different from that of the past, it is important to acknowledge the similarities to better understand the contemporary moment. Past and present surveillance of social movements is an attempt to suppress dissent, and protect the existing socio-political and economic structure from perceived "threats." Although the political context has undeniably changed since the 1960s, contemporary civil rights activists are still being monitored and policed in comparable, if not more extensive ways. Modern protest policing is subtler in its approach, in part due to the affordances that digital media gives present-day activists. A considerable deal of effort went into disseminating news using the technology available to civil rights activists of the 1960s, contemporary activists are able to do so with ease. This changed how police must conduct themselves, and digital surveillance has become an appealing way to monitor large groups of suspected persons with low visibility. What sets the current moment apart from the past is the ease and capacity of digital surveillance. While past surveillance technologies were constrained by the limits of time and place, digital surveillance enables real-time collection and storage of data across vast distances. For present-day civil rights activists, surveillance is involuntary and often integrated into routine activities such as their digital media use.

As well as enabling other protest policing tactics, surveillance itself can quietly suppress dissent through the knowledge that one's actions may be being monitored. In the cases of both the Civil Rights movement and Black Lives Matter, the effects of surveillance were felt, and some activists began to self-censor or to distance themselves from the movement. In both cases, it is also clear that while surveillance poses a threat to social movements, it does not necessarily lead to their deterioration. While research indicates that surveillance causes significant damage to the organizational culture of a social movement, there are undoubtedly many individuals who choose to carry on with their work despite the knowledge that they may be monitored. In both past and the present contexts, activists were able to create pockets of resistance within surveillance systems that allowed them to grow and thrive despite the potentially chilling effects of surveillance. The effects of digital surveillance on contemporary social movements is worth further study, as events continue to evolve and unfold.

NOTES

1. Under COINTELPRO, surveillance of activists entailed wiretapping rooms, photographic surveillance, warrantless surreptitious entries, movement infiltration, and more.
2. The escalated force approach makes use of extreme violence in an attempt to disrupt and disperse protesters. This approach uses violence indiscriminately, and even against those protesting peacefully (McPhail, Schweingruber, and McCarthy 1998).
3. These covert programs targeted "The Communist Party, the Socialist Workers Party, White Hate Groups, Black Nationalist-Hate Groups, and the New Left" (Boykoff 2007, 46).
4. Legal repression typically included, "assault, loitering and weapons charges" (Jeffries 2002, 77).
5. In late 1968, "in exchange for dropping criminal charges against him, William O'Neal agreed to infiltrate the Black Panther Party for the FBI" (Boykoff 2007, 54).
6. "The Winston-Salem branch of the Black Panthers were within the jurisdiction of the FBI's Charlotte, North Carolina field office" (Brame and Shriver 2003 2013 in bib, 506).
7. For example, a 1990 report written by the Solicitor General of Canada on this topic detailed how due to cuts in social services, there would be an increase in unemployed, unskilled people in some cities, which would result in an increase in crime and civil unrest. The report recommends combatting these issues through privatization of policing, reliance on new policing technologies, and cooperation between enforcement agencies (Wood 2014).
8. Foucault (1997, 242–243) described biopower as unconcerned with the practice of power over the individual/social body, but instead acts at the level of power over the masses.
9. Technologies of the self operate through putting in practice a kind of freedom in which "individuals are made in charge of their own behaviour, competence, improvement, security, and well-being" (Ajana 2005, 3).

10. Haggerty (2011, 26) argues that "each new 'opticon' points to a disctinction, limitation, or way in which Foucault's model does not completely fit the contemporary global, technological, or political dynamics of surveillance."
11. The Southern Christian Leadership Conference was an American Civil Rights organization in which King was the president.
12. For example, "networked devices like mobile phones and laptops facilitate the collection of detailed information about user behaviour" (Andrejevic 2012, 91).
13. Sousveillance refers to "surveillance from below." This can include protesters using digital media to record videos of police violence.
14. Counterveillance refers to measures that "block both surveillance and sousveillance" (Bakir 2015, 18). These practices can include "counterveillant technologies that detect and blind cameras or going 'off grid' and disengaging with all networked, mediated, communications" (Bakir 2015, 18).
15. Univeillance is where "surveillance is blocked out and sousveillance is enabled" (Bakir 2015, 18). This can include technologies that enable "anonymization, and end-to-end encryption" (Bakir 2015, 18).

REFERENCES

Andrejevic, Mark. 2012. "Ubiquitous Surveillance." In *Routledge Handbook of Surveillance Studies*, edited by Kristie Ball, Kevin D. Haggerty and David Lyon, 91–99. New York: Routledge.

Ajana, Btihaj. 2005. "Surveillance and Biopolitics." *Electronic Journal of Sociology* 7: 1–15.

Bakir, Vian. 2015. "Veillant Panoptic Assemblage: Mutual Watching and Resistance to Surveillance After Snowden." *Media and Communication* 3 (3): 12–25.

Kahn, Kimberly Barsamian, and Karin D. Martin. 2016. "Policing and Race: Disparate Treatment, Perceptions, and Policy Responses." *Social Issues and Policy Review* 10 (1): 82–121. doi:10.1111/sipr.12019.

Bennett, Hans. 2010. "The Black Panthers and the Assassination of Fred Hampton." *Journal of Pan African Studies* 3 (6): 215–221.

Black Lives Matter. 2016. "About the Black Lives Matter Network." *Black Lives Matter*. Accessed November 18. http://blacklivesmatter.com/about/.

Boykoff, Jules. 2007. *Beyond Bullets: The Suppression of Dissent in the United States*. Oakland, CA: AK Press.

Bonilla, Yarimar, and Jonathan Rosa. 2015. "#Ferguson: Digital Protest, Hashtag Ethnography, and the Racial Politics of Social Media in the United States." *American Ethnologist* 42 (1): 4–17. doi:10.1111/amet.12112.

Brame, Wendy and Thomas Shriver. 2013. "Surveillance and Social Control: the FBI's Handling of the Black Panther Party in North Carolina." *Crime, Law and Social Change* 59 (5): 501–516.

Cooper, Frank. 2008. "Surveillance and Identity Performance: Some Thoughts Inspired by Martin Luther King." *New York University Review of Law and Social Change* 9 (1): 517–541.

Della Porta, Donna, and Herbert Reiter. 1998. "Introduction" In *Policing Protest: The Control of Mass Demonstrations in Western Democracies*, edited by Donatella Della Porta and Herbert Reiter, 1–32. Minneapolis: University of Minnesota Press.

Della Porta, Donna, and Alice Mattoni. 2015. "Pro-Democracy and Anti-Austerity Protests." In *Social Media, Politics and the State: Protests, Revolutions, Riots, Crime and Policing in the Age of Facebook,*

Twitter and YouTube, edited by Daniel Trottier and Christian Fuchs, 39–63. New York: Routledge. http://site.ebrary.com/id/10897207.

Elmer, Greg, and Andy Opel. 2008. *Preempting Dissent: The Politics of an Inevitable Future.* Winnipeg: Arbeiter Ring Publishing.

Fleming, Daniel. 2007. "Marvin Gaye, Martin Luther King, Jr, and the FBI." *Traffic (Parkville)* (9): 135–154.

Foucault, Michel. 1975. *Discipline and Punishment.* Great Britain: Penguin Books.

———. 1997. *Society Must Be Defended: Lectures at the College De France 1975–1976.* New York: Picador.

———. 2007. "Panopticism." In *The Surveillance Studies Reader*, edited by Sean P. Hier and Josh Greenberg, 67–77. England: Open University Press.

Fuchs, Christian. 2011. "New Media, Web 2.0 and Surveillance." *Sociology Compass* 5(2): 134–147.

———. 2012. "Introduction: Internet and Surveillance" In *Internet and Surveillance: The Challenges of Web 2.0 and Social*, edited by Christian Fuchs, Kees Boersma, Anders Albrechtslund, and Marisol Sandoval, 1–3. New York: Routledge.

Gillham, F. Patrick. 2011. "Securitizing America: Policing of Protest Since the 11 September 2001 Terrorist Attacks." *Sociology Compass* 5 (7): 636–652.

Gillham, Patrick F., Bob Edwards, and John A. Noakes. 2013. "Strategic Incapacitation and the Policing of Occupy Wall Street Protests in New York City, 2011." *Policing and Society* 23 (1): 81–102. doi:10.1080/10439463.2012.727607.

Graham, Stephen and David Wood. 2007. "Digitizing Surveillance: Categorization, Space, Inequality" In *The Surveillance Studies Reader*, edited by Sean P. Hier and Josh Greenberg, 218–231. England: Open University Press.

Greenwald, Glenn. 2014. *No Place to Hide: Edward Snowden, the NSA, and the U.S. Surveillance State.* New York: Metropolitan Books.

Haggerty, Kevin, and Richard Ericson. 2007. "The Surveillant Assemblage" In *The Surveillance Studies Reader,* edited by Sean P. Hier and Josh Greenberg, 104–117. England: Open University Press.

Haggerty, Kevin. 2011. "Tear Down the Walls: On Demolishing the Panopticon" In *Theorizing Surveillance, The Panopticon and Beyond,* edited by David Lyon, 23–46. New York: Routledge.

Hier, P. Sean. 2007. "Probing the Surveillant Assemblage: On the Dialectics of Surveillance Practices as Processes of Social Control" In *Surveillance Studies Reader*, edited by Sean P. Hier and Josh Greenberg, 117–129. England: Open University Press.

Hoerl, Kristen, and Erin Ortiz. 2015. "Organizational Secrecy and the FBI's COINTELPRO-Black Nationalist Hate Groups Program, 1967–1971." *Management Communication Quarterly.* 29 (4): 590–615.

Hutchby, Ian. 2001. "Technologies, Texts and Affordances." *Sociology* 35 (2): 441–456.

Jeffries, L. Judson. 2002. "Black Radicalism and Political Repression in Baltimore: The Case of the Black Panther Party." *Ethnic and Racial Studies* 25 (1): 64–98.

Joh, Elizabeth. 2016. "The New Surveillance Discretion: Automated Suspicion, Big Data, and Policing." *Harvard Law and Policy Review* 10 (1): 15–42.

Joseph, George. 2015a. "Exclusive: Feds Regularly Monitored Black Lives Matter Since Ferguson." *The Intercept*, July 24. https://theintercept.com/2015/07/24/documents-show-department-homeland-security-monitoring-black-lives-matter-since-ferguson/.

Joseph, George. 2015b. "Undercover Police Have Regularly Spied on Black Lives Matter Activists in New York." *The Intercept,* August 18. https://theintercept.com/2015/08/18/undercover-police-spied-on-ny-black-lives-matter/.

Marx, Gary. T. 1988. *Undercover: Police Surveillance in America*. Berkeley, CA: University of California Press.
Marx, Gary T. 2007. "What's New about the 'New Surveillance'? Classifying for Change and Continuity" In *The Surveillance Studies Reader*, edited by Sean P. Hier and Josh Greenberg, 83–95. England: Open University Press.
Maguire, Mike. 2000. "Policing by Risks and Targets: Some Dimensions and Implications of Intelligence-led Crime Control." *Policing and Society* 9 (4): 315–336.
McPhail, Clark, David Schweingruber, and John McCarthy. 1998. "Policing Protest in the United States: 1960–1995" In *Policing Protest: The Control of Mass Demonstrations in Western Democracies*, edited by Donatella Della Porta and Herbert Reiter, 35–49. Minneapolis: University of Minnesota Press.
Obar, A. Jonathan. 2014. "Canadian Advocacy 2.0: An Analysis of Social Media Adoption and Perceived Affordances by Advocacy Groups Looking to Advance Activism in Canada." *Canadian Journal of Communication* 39 (2): 211–233.
O'Neill, Megan and Bethan Loftus. 2013. "Policing and the Surveillance of the Marginal: Everyday Contexts of Social Control" *Theoretical Criminology* (17) 4: 437–454.
Penney, Joel and Caroline Dadas. 2014. "(Re)Tweeting in the Service of Protest: Digital Composition and Circulation in the Occupy Wall Street Movement." *New Media & Society* 16 (1): 74–90.
Roman, Meredith. (2016). "The Black Panther Party and the Struggle for Human Rights." *Spectrum* 5 (1): 7–32.
Starr, Amory, Luis A. Fernandez, Randall Amster, Lesley J. Wood, Manuel J. Caro. 2008. "The Impacts of State Surveillance on Political Assembly and Association: A Socio-Legal Analysis." *Qualitative Sociology* 31 (3): 251–270.
Stephen, Bijan. 2015. "Social Media Helps Black Lives Matter Fight the Power." *Wired*. http://www.wired.com/2015/10/how-black-lives-matter-uses-social-media-to-fight-the-power/.
Trottier, Daniel. 2012. "Policing Social Media." *Canadian Review of Sociology* 49 (4): 411–425.
Wood, J. Leslie. 2014. *Crisis and Control: The Militarization of Protest Policing*. London: Pluto Press.

CHAPTER SIXTEEN

Ubiquitous Emotion Analytics AND How We Feel Today

SUSAN CURRIE SIVEK

Emotions are complicated. Humans feel deeply, and it can be hard to bring clarity to those depths, to communicate about feelings, or to understand others' emotional states. Indeed, this emotional confusion is one of the biggest challenges of deciphering our humanity. However, a kind of hope might be on the horizon, in the form of emotion analytics: computerized tools for recognizing and responding to emotion. Technologies containing this capability—such as market research tools using webcams, and apps for mental health—are becoming commonplace, even though they are unfamiliar to much of the public. Major technology companies are working to endow their devices and platforms with the ability to understand emotion. While humans struggle to master this skill throughout their lives, the increasingly ubiquitous nature of emotion analytics may mean that our devices will soon be better equipped to understand feelings than we are.

Though shifting this emotional facility to technology could seem potentially liberating to humans, the soon-to-be-ubiquitous use of emotion analytics carries complex implications regarding humans' experience of emotion in our society. As Dourish and Bell argue (2011, 46), ubiquitous computing is "already a sociocultural object, both in its artifacts and its practices." In other words, even before we can examine the likely consequences of emotion analytics' usage, we can look closely at what the implementation of these tools says about our interactions with technology today and our contemporary regard for emotion. Our willingness to accept the growing ubiquity of emotion analytics suggests that in today's technologically saturated society, we now trust in the superiority of technology as a tool not only for recognizing emotion, but also for managing it.

This analysis explores how emotion analytics may reflect the current status of humans' regard for emotion. Emotion need no longer be a human sense of vague, indefinable "feelings"; instead emotion is in the process of becoming a "legible," standardized commodity (Scott 1999) that can be sold, managed, and altered to suit the needs of those in power. Emotional autonomy and authority can be surrendered to those technologies in exchange for perceived self-determination. Emotion analytics promises a new orderliness to the messiness of human emotions, suggesting that our current state of emotional uncertainty is inadequate and intolerable.

ABOUT EMOTION ANALYTICS

Emotion analytics gives order to emotion by using a variety of computerized methods to gather, analyze, and respond to human users' expressions of emotion. Sensors—such as front-facing cameras and heart-rate monitors–that are embedded in users' devices and environments can collect information on facial expressions, voices, word choices, social media input, physiological status, and other details. They then send those data to powerful cloud-based analysis software that match the data to established profiles of human emotions. When emotional states are identified, the software can offer appropriate responses to suit the user's feelings at the moment, such as media content suggestions or targeted advertising.

Currently, emotion analytics tools may operate with or without the user's active involvement. Emotion analytics can be implemented in ways that are passive (from the user's standpoint), meaning that they gather information from the normal device usage and daily activities of the user. For example, smartphones collect a great deal of data that can contribute to the analysis of their users' emotions, such as app usage, touch pressure, and physical movement; sensors in retail or education environments can do the same. Alternatively, emotion analytics can actively involve the user in the generation of useful data. For example, the use of emotion analytics to examine the effectiveness of advertising is usually conducted with volunteer test subjects who agree to watch ads while their expressions of emotion are monitored. Additionally, tools are emerging that engage the user in analyzing emotion for health applications or for human resources purposes. These users are knowingly engaging in the production of emotion data.

Overall, it is possible for emotion analytics to be at work with or without the user's active involvement or conscious awareness. However, as I have addressed elsewhere (Sivek 2018), emotion data are among some of the most private kinds of information about users that might be gathered, and they should be kept private and collected only with consent. Users should be informed of and specifically consent to this potential use of their information when they use devices or software with this capability.

A number of technology companies are developing emotion analytics tools. Some companies are household names; others are small startups, often spinoffs of academic research labs like the MIT Media Lab. Each company offers its own suite of emotion-related products, focusing on their own methods of emotion recognition (e.g., facial expressions, voice analysis, sentiment analysis for text) and/or a specific application (e.g., call center customer service, advertising research, media content testing). In the two case studies that follow, I will examine how one startup and one major technology company are contributing to the ubiquity of emotion analytics tools.

Affectiva

Affectiva is a Massachusetts company founded in 2009 by Rana el Kaliouby and Rosalind Picard. Both had previously conducted research at the MIT Media Lab in affective computing, which is the branch of computer science concerned with helping computers understand and respond to human emotion. Kaliouby originally sought to develop what she called an "emotional hearing aid" for people with autism, a device that could recognize and assist in responding to interlocutors' expressions (Khatchadourian 2015). Similarly, Picard was interested in the health-related applications of affective computing.

Today, however, the company they founded looks very different. Picard apparently left the company after four years when she felt its focus shifted too much toward advertising and market research (Khatchadourian 2015). Kaliouby has emphasized Affectiva's use of Affdex, its emotion analytics suite, to refine and target advertising and media content. CBS, Unilever, and candy manufacturer Mars are among the most significant clients listed on its website. Unilever and Mars both use Affectiva software to analyze test subjects' emotions upon viewing prospective advertisements. They also use the emotion data to refine the content and place ads in the most effective media. CBS tested how its ads and primetime show content generated emotional responses among viewers. Therefore, Affectiva essentially sells a computerized interpretation of emotion, and media producers can then respond by shaping their products accordingly. These uses of emotion analytics reveal that—though consumers are largely unaware of these tools' existence—the media content and ads they view have potentially been tested and altered to effectively evoke specific emotions and generate sales.

As Khatchadourian's (2015) *New Yorker* account tells it, Affectiva's founders were driven apart by their disagreement about the best use of these tools. Emotion data could be used to improve consumers' health, though some might problematize that usage for its encouragement of detachment from users' awareness of their physical bodies. However, Affectiva currently uses these data primarily to increase its clients' profits through the refinement of the emotional states evoked by marketing and media messages.

Apple

While Affectiva is a relatively new technology startup, Apple has billions of dollars in cash to spend on promising twists in its products. Apple's range of consumer technology devices and services now includes desktop and laptop computers, the iPhone, Apple TV, the Apple Watch, iTunes, and Apple Music. According to some reports, there are over a billion Apple devices currently in use around the world (Statt 2016).

The incredible success of Apple products means that their many users are now available as sources of emotion data. The webcams built into computers, the front-facing camera on the iPhone, the heart rate and Force Touch sensors in the Apple Watch—all of these could potentially provide information about users' emotional status. Apple has patented a method of using emotion data to offer targeted content (probably ads, though this could also refer to other media content, such as music or movies). Apple's approach would use this "mood-associated characteristic data collected over a period of time to produce at least one baseline mood profile for a user," and comparisons thereunto would allow for the interpretation of the user's current emotion (Greenzeiger, Phulari, and Sanghavi 2015).

In this patent, Apple argues that other methods that rely on targeting through demographic or interest information data are incomplete, because "there are many other factors that can affect an individual's responsiveness at a particular point in time. For example, if an individual is pre-occupied or unhappy, the individual may not be as receptive to certain types of content" (*ibid.*). Apple doesn't appear concerned with shifting the user toward a less preoccupied or happier state of mind. Instead, the goal seems to be offering the right marketing message to suit that negative state.

The ease with which Apple could likely gain an emotional awareness of each of its devices' users is remarkable. Apple can intimately know the consumers who "live within the Apple ecosystem," so to speak, through their interactions—passive and active—with these devices. Sitting still could be a data point for emotion analysis; so could the impact with which a user taps on the screen of a phone (detected by Apple's Force Touch sensors). Apple's patent for emotion analysis includes a lengthy list of data points (shown in Table 16.1) that can be synthesized to understand a user's emotional status (*ibid.*).

Table 16.1. Gathering Emotion Data: User Characteristics Included in Apple Patent. Source: Quoted from Greenzeiger, Phulari, and Sanghavi 2015

Physical characteristics	Heart rate; blood pressure; adrenaline level; perspiration rate; body temperature; vocal expression, e.g. voice level, voice pattern, voice stress, etc.; movement characteristics; facial expression
Behavioral characteristics	Sequence of content consumed, e.g. sequence of applications launched, rate at which the user changed applications, etc.; social networking activities, e.g. likes and/or comments on social media; user interface (UI) actions, e. g. rate of clicking, pressure applied to a touch screen, etc.; and/or emotional response to previously served targeted content
Spatio-temporal characteristics	Location, date, day, time, and/or day part
Media consumption characteristics	Music genre, application category, ESRB and/or MPAA rating, consumption time of day, consumption location, subject matter of the content

In sum, at any given moment, a user might share through device and/or media usage at least 24 data points that Apple has identified as emotion-related. And, in addition to its own patents, Apple also recently acquired the startup Emotient (Winkler, Wakabayashi, and Dwoskin 2016), which specialized in emotion analytics by way of facial expression recognition. Therefore, it is likely that Apple will integrate Emotient's software into its own tools in the near future.

In addition to Apple products available at the time of writing, the company's new wireless earbuds, the AirPods, could (now or in the future) include some of the "psychological or biometric sensors" that the company has previously patented for use in headphones or earbuds (Prest and Hoellwarth 2014). With these developments, it seems we are moving closer to the fulfillment of what technologist Chris Messina (2016) notes about Apple: "Apple is securing its future, and to do that, it must continue to shrink the physical distance between its products and its customers' conceptions of self." The devices the company produces are becoming more attached to their users' bodies and more integrated with the data those bodies generate—including their emotional status, as inferred through emotion analytics. Emotion is no longer an unknown realm of human experience, but one that has been made accessible for business. (On a related note, German technology company Bragi is collaborating with IBM and its Watson supercomputing system to offer a similarly souped-up earbud system for businesses, promising "a powerful audio and sensory interface that fits inside the ear[,] opening up a myriad of new opportunities for transforming the workplace" [Chang 2016].)

In sum, living in the Apple ecosystem means that the company potentially gathers data on one's body and activities in all locations and at all times, thereby enabling its monitoring of and response to emotion. Apple users become not only purchasers of devices and subscribers to services, but also constant generators of emotional data. They exude a trail of emotional data points that reveal their responses to their daily lives in potentially profound, personal ways. Apple can use these data to better market their own products and others' products to their devices' users. In addition, those emotional data become themselves a product that Apple can sell to any interested party seeking to understand consumers' behavior and responses to the everyday world.

The Coming Ubiquity of Emotion Analytics

In addition to Affectiva and Apple's uses for emotion analytics, many companies are exploring the use of these tools in other domains of human life. For example, the company Cambridge Cognitive is developing apps for wearable devices that collect patients' expressions of mood and send them to their doctors or psychiatrists; the apps are intended to circumvent patients' tendency to be less than forthcoming in face-to-face conversations with caregivers (Curry 2016). Honda and SoftBank are collaborating on emotion recognition for robots and self-driving vehicle software, "to harmonize mobility with people, so that drivers can feel a kind of friendship with their vehicles" (Kageyama 2016). The startup Gyana is attempting to analyze the moods of large-scale populations, combining satellite and aerial imagery; sentiment and emotion analysis of social media data; and demographic, traffic, and weather information (Gyana 2016). Amazon's Alexa, a digital assistant for shopping, smart home devices, and media, now includes emotion-recognition capability for its voice-based interactions with users (Farrell 2016). And in education, students working on computerized lessons may soon notice their computers responding to "facial cues of boredom…in an effort to motivate or boost [the students'] confidence" (Dodd 2016). Health care, transportation, robotics, governance, shopping, and education: All are potential realms for the further implementation of emotion analytics, suggesting that these tools will soon be truly ubiquitous in technology users' lives—even though their operation may not be known or noticeable.

Making Emotion Legible

The operation of emotion analytics tools requires the creation of standardized categories for emotions. No matter which kind of data a particular algorithm uses, it ultimately must decide which specific emotion is best reflected by the user's condition at that moment. For example, the facial expression recognition tools typically are based upon a typology of "basic emotions" developed by Paul Ekman (1999). Ekman argues that across cultures, emotions consistently correlate with specific movements of the face, making it possible to "code" faces for emotion (Paul Ekman Group 2016). Ekman's work is the basis for the methods underlying Affectiva's tools; he and other scholars are cited in the company's white papers (e.g., McDuff *et al.* 2013). Similarly, companies that use voice analysis (such as Cogito) identify users' emotional states based on "dynamic variations in voices, rate of speech, whether there's good participation and flow, and signs of vocal strain" (Underwood 2014).

However, human emotion is notoriously difficult to define and measure. For example, when we are upset, it can be difficult to decide exactly what mixture of emotions we're feeling; someone who is crying could be profoundly sad, or could be feeling a mixture of sadness, anger, and shame. Yet the promise of emotion analytics is that computers can more effectively tell what emotions are being expressed at a given moment. Emotion analytics companies portray their software as better able to understand and address human emotion than humans themselves. The company nViso addresses "the perceived inability of researchers to measure and interpret emotional response. 3D Facial Imaging revolutionizes how we collect and interpret data on advertising material....No complex questions or dials are required—emotional response is measured directly" (nViso 2016).

Similarly, another company, Emotient, argued (prior to its buyout by Apple) that facial expression analysis is "a profound improvement" over humans' attempts to test advertising. Emotient argued that "direct measurement of emotional state derived from facial expressions is the only way to get to the unspoken truth of how customers really feel" (Emotient 2015). Even more dramatically, Realeyes' commercial director has stated that facial expression analysis "is richer and more pure" than data gathered through other research methods (Adgully 2014). Emotion analytics are alleged to provide true, unsullied emotional perception; human interaction simply confounds the search for understanding.

The growing ubiquity of emotion analytics in market and media research, public spaces, and personal computing suggests that we have easily accepted these assertions of computers' superiority in understanding emotion. This acceptance reveals much about how our understanding of human experience is shifting as new technologies develop. As Picard and Klein (2002, 161) note, affective computing (of which emotion analytics is a small part) raises serious questions: "[I]ssues include how humans may use (or abuse) such devices themselves; how such devices might change the nature of human-computer (and human-human) interactions; and *how humans will define themselves* in a world where such devices are regularly used" (emphasis added). Picard and Klein's final item could include the question of how humans understand their own emotions in a world where computers are thought to have a "richer" and "purer" comprehension of emotion than people do. Accepting this alleged superiority suggests a kind of surrender of emotional agency to technology. This acceptance assigns the scrutiny of emotion to tools thought to garner insight into our myriad feelings more easily and effectively.

This acceptance of technological superiority in the interpretation of emotion has consequences not only for individuals, but also for the way in which those with various forms of power may seek to control them today and in the future. The enticing promise of emotional clarity also offers what Scott (1999) calls "legibility." Scott describes how the modern governmental state imposes various means of measurement, mapping, and classification onto otherwise unruly phenomena (people, natural features, and so forth). For example, Scott examines at length the effort to make German forests "legible" at the beginning of professional forestry, around the turn of the nineteenth century. He concludes:

> The controlled environment of the redesigned, scientific forest promised many striking advantages. It could be synoptically surveyed by the chief forester; it could be more easily supervised and harvested according to centralized, long-range plans; it provided a steady, uniform commodity, thereby eliminating one major source of revenue fluctuation; and it created a legible natural terrain that facilitated manipulation and experimentation. (18)

Instead of a formless mass of muddled trees, underbrush, and animals, the forest became a clearly defined entity that could be known to humans with the help of mapping and planning technologies. Along the way, though, folk understandings of these phenomena were ignored in favor of a more "rational," consistent, revenue-protecting strategy.

Emotion analytics provide legibility to those seeking similar clarity regarding emotion. Emotion analytics' legibility would allow (to give some hypothetical examples) market researchers to assert that 76% of subjects evinced happiness upon viewing a prospective advertisement; educational software designers to provide easier questions when a student demonstrates a score of 5 out of 5 for "frustration"; and retail stores to offer promotions on wine at 5:30 p.m. when the after-work crowd reads as "stressed" to in-store sensors. Legibility removes the uncertainty of humans' assessment of other humans' emotional states, neatly removing the blurry edges of human experience as it is placed in the most fitting category.

Making emotion legible through emotion analytics also suggests that emotions—like Scott's legible forests—could be subjected to further efforts toward the commodification and management of emotion. Emotion analytics make messy human emotions into a recognizable, manageable resource. Impure, untrustworthy human observations of emotion are less easily salable than "emotion data," tidily graphed and mapped with sophisticated software, particularly in an age when "big data" promises higher profits and better lives (e.g., Buckley 2015). Those with an interest in swaying emotion in a particular direction might also be enticed by freshly legible emotions, and could seek to manage the emotions of others for their own benefit.

Emotion neatly analyzed and classified through emotion analytics constitutes a product that can be bought and sold. The data that results from the application of emotion analytics could be sold to a variety of parties, including: users themselves, seeking to improve or alter their mental states; companies that manufacture consumer software and technology, such as Apple and Google; marketers and those who sell advertising space, such as manufacturers and media companies; political and issue groups, wanting to test the impact of their candidates and messages; government entities, seeking to monitor individuals or public spaces; and employers, wanting to check employee morale and improve productivity. Each of these uses of emotion data has either been documented or tested in restricted settings at the time of writing (Thomas 2015).

This commodification of emotion effectively turns the human experience of feeling into labor. Well before emotion analytics existed, Andrejevic (2002)—and many others to follow—observed the potentially exploitative nature of gathering data on the users of technology. Those data are often gathered in the course of routine usage of the technology, with little awareness on the user's part, and may be sold to other parties for a range of purposes. Andrejevic points out that there is no compensation for what is effectively labor: the manufacture by users of economically valuable data. He argues that this lack of compensation is exploitative, even if it is secondary to the usage of technology for work or play, and even if users consent to the gathering and sale of their data in exchange for (free) access to the technology.

While the gathering and sale of personal data now feel routine to technology users—exploitative or not—there has been little public discussion of the potential addition of emotion analyses to these data. A quick review of recent news coverage demonstrates little coverage of emotion analytics as they may be implemented in consumer technology; it is difficult to know how the public would respond to the idea that their emotion data—even if only ever analyzed and sold in aggregated, anonymized forms—could be made available for purchase. Is there something fundamentally different about emotion data that should cause a negative response to this prospect? The abstracted legibility of emotion data might suggest that the phenomenon of *feeling* of those emotions does not matter; rather, those feelings present merely yet another opportunity for promoting products, and what it feels like *to feel* is beside the point. This treatment of emotion represents a cheapening of human experience, even as it makes data regarding those experiences inherently valuable.

MANAGING WITH EMOTION ANALYTICS

Even if we were to conclude that emotion data should be regarded no differently from data on one's favorite movie or preferred language, its availability for sale raises another concern: the potential for efforts toward managing the emotions of an individual or group. Scott notes that forests, made legible to the state, were "also easier to manipulate experimentally" (1999, 18). Just as the legibility provided by mapping makes a forest's acreage and features more yielding to foresters' interventions, so too might the legibility of emotion offered by emotion analytics provide a way for various groups to attempt to manage emotions.

Lest this discussion sound too much like the rant of a conspiracy theorist, it is worth noting that actual efforts have already been made to try to manipulate emotion using various technologies. One of these received extensive media attention: Facebook's ill-advised experiment with emotional contagion throughout its network, which, though legally permitted through its terms of service, raised questions about the legality of manipulating emotions among unwitting users through the items shown in their News Feeds. The experiment showed that users' emotions could be effectively altered by Facebook's strategic display of positive or negative items; however, the actual effect was quite small (Kramer, Guillory, and Hancock 2014). The fact that Facebook has a business interest in testing its capability for emotional contagion suggests that digital media platforms are already realizing the prospective value of the emotion data they gather—and of potentially altering it to suit their own (or their advertisers') needs. Research has shown that certain kinds of advertising may be more effective when presented to viewers in specific emotional states (e.g., Kemp, Bui, and Chapa 2012). Therefore, Facebook's revenues could be positively affected by offering advertisers the ability to show ads to users already demonstrating, or deliberately shifted toward, the desired emotions.

Social media sites have an interest in emotional manipulation for the purposes of advertising, but all companies have an interest in maintaining a happy workforce to ensure productivity and profit. The ability to place sensors in workplaces—and even on employees' bodies—makes ubiquitous emotion analytics potentially a powerful tool in managing a workforce. A couple of technology companies have begun developing or already offer such tools, and they market them as means of improving workplace quality and removing forms of bias from humans' evaluative processes. For example, the Hitachi Business Microscope system uses sensors in employee ID badges to track movement and to collect other data. The analytics software then looks for "distinctive patterns in physical movements that have strong correlations with a group's happiness…quantifying [the] 'happiness level'" (Hitachi 2016). This information can ostensibly help managers create better conditions for workers, though such data-gathering is potentially invasive and controlling. Another startup, Kanjoya, applies sentiment analysis to textual responses to employee surveys in order to seek the "truth" behind what employees say (Captain 2015). Finally, the company HireVue uses facial expression analysis to help managers evaluate job applicants, partly by comparing the applicants' expressions to those of successful employees at the organization (*ibid.*).

This latter example points to another issue in managing emotion using ubiquitous emotion analytics: To what degree should workers' emotions be "policed" and required to fit within a particular set of norms? Such omnipresent surveillance and analysis of emotion are problematic, particularly when tied to one's work and livelihood. Those whose emotional expressions are outside of an "acceptable" range may feel that they must learn to display the standardized, "legible" emotions of the mainstream, or risk marginalization. Illouz (2007, 66 argues that today's popular concept of "emotional intelligence" is especially reflective of "the emotional style and dispositions of the new middle classes which are located in intermediary positions, that is, which both control and are controlled, whose professions demand a careful management of the self, who are tightly dependent on collaborative work, and who must use their self in both a creative and a productive way." The emotional expressions likely to be valued and receive positive responses from employers and others in power are likely to be similar to their own emotional norms and preferences. The standardization of emotion required for emotion analytics, if implemented more widely for the purposes of emotion management and policing, could reinforce existing societal circumscription of emotional expression, confining acceptable expressions within class-constrained norms.

MECHANIZING EMOTION

This critique has suggested that the ubiquitous use of emotion analytics tools, in their varied current and potential forms, represents a contemporary effort to standardize, commodify, and constrain emotion in ways that ultimately result in a narrowed range of human emotional expression. These new tools for looking at and classifying human experience provide another example of what Meštrović (1997) calls the "mechanization" of emotion in contemporary society. Just as other human activities have been made industrial or mechanical in nature, Meštrović argues that we also now live in a "postemotional" society, in which not only ideas, but also emotions, are manipulated by those in power to serve their own needs: "emotions have been McDonaldized, petrified, routinized, and otherwise made artificial. Mechanization has extended its imperialistic realm from technology and industry to colonize the last bastion of nature: the emotions" (146). Indeed, the deployment of ubiquitous emotion analytics does indeed seem to follow this progression, suggesting a uniform experience of standard emotional classifications to be experienced and managed as needed.

Though he crafted this theoretical perspective well before the introduction of emotion analytics, Meštrović describes how "work, family, play, leisure, church: these and other social domains increasingly come to resemble the functioning of a machine based on pre-determined rules for engaging in emotional exchanges" (150). Today, ubiquitous emotion analytics means that the world might not only resemble, but could literally be guided by machines with rules regarding emotion. The end result of the mechanization of emotion, Meštrović argues, is a postemotionalist society "designed to avoid emotional disorder; to prevent loose ends in emotional exchanges; to civilize 'wild' arenas of emotional life…to order the emotions so that the social world hums as smoothly as a well-maintained machine" (150). Some of the applications of emotion analytics described here do certainly claim to eradicate areas of human doubt, inconsistency, indecision, and bias—as in the interpretation of market research test subjects' reactions, or in the assessment of job candidates. Emotion analytics allows computers to tidy the chaos caused by human emotion and to resolve the concomitant disorder in human affairs, asserting algorithmic certainty over processes currently flawed due to human involvement.

EMOTION ANALYTICS AS A TECHNOLOGY OF THE SELF

Further insight into our contemporary acceptance of emotion analytics is provided by Foucault's (1988) analysis of the history of what he calls "technologies of the self," various methods people may use to scrutinize their own "bodies and souls, thoughts, conduct, and way of being, so as to transform themselves in order to attain a certain state of happiness, purity, wisdom, perfection, or immortality" (18). Foucault traces the movement of Western culture toward a fundamental belief in the significance of "self-knowledge" and identifies different means of achieving that knowledge. The Christian understanding of the self, he says, focuses on the "deciphering of inner thoughts…there is something hidden in ourselves and…we are always in a self-illusion which hides the secret" (46). Release from this self-illusion, and an increased closeness to God, can be found only through constant examination of one's thoughts, with the aid of verbalized confessions to an authority figure (such as a monk's confession to the abbot of a monastery). In this tradition, individuals obey religious authority—renouncing their own will and autonomy—and accept guidance regarding performing penance or changing their ways (47). Significantly, though, Foucault notes that modes of verbalization of the self have been changed "from the eighteenth century to the present…by the so called human sciences in order to use them without renunciation of the self but to constitute, positively, a new self" (49). Foucault here observes that the social sciences eventually suggested ways people could reshape their own selves—autonomously and independently—without the intervention of, and obedience to, a religious authority figure.

In our contemporary society, acceptance of ubiquitous emotion analytics as a new "technology of the self" implies another intriguing cultural shift — this time, toward computers as authority figures that can capture and classify verbal and non-verbal expressions of emotion, then respond accordingly. The adoption of emotion analytics as a technology of the self augurs the dawn of that civilized, well-ordered, but emotionally sterile society that Meštrović describes. If only Foucault were here to offer his insights into this new development. I would suggest that he would critique our apparent willingness to accept the implementation of emotion analytics and to trust in the promise of greater digital insights into ourselves. During rapidly changing times, it is tempting to delegate our understanding of emotion to a new technological power, thinking that we have somehow regained technical superiority over our challenging emotions through the legibility provided by analytics. Emotion analytics suggest a new way to "constitute, positively, a new self," with external discernment of what we "really feel"; however, in lieu of an abbot serving as confessor, we have placed ubiquitous sensors and devices—and their designers—in the place of authority, and may sacrifice our emotional autonomy to satisfy their needs.

CRITIQUING THE "EMOTION LAYER" OF UBIQUITOUS COMPUTING

The company Affectiva (2016) describes the data gathered through their emotion recognition tools as an "emotion layer" that enhances "any aspect of your work…it can be used anytime, anywhere, and on any device." Indeed, the growth of emotion analytics and the likelihood of these tools' widespread implementation add a new layer to theory and research on ubiquitous computing.

As our technologies become both ever present and aware of our feelings in new ways, we must begin to consider the ramifications not only for the technicalities of their development, but also what they suggest about the larger human regard for the experience of emotion today, and how that experience may be shaped by those creating and using these new tools. As Dourish and Bell (2011, 195) write, "When we think of sensing technologies as devices that order the world, rather than devices that describe it, then alternative relationships between the social and technical are strikingly brought to light." This perspective highlights the need to examine emotion analytics as a technology that both represents our current regard for human emotion and will shape that perspective in the future.

REFERENCES

Adgully Bureau. 2014. "Ormax Media Launches Content Testing Tool—Ormax Xpressive." *Adgully*. June 25. https://www.adgully.com/ormax-media-launches-content-testing-tool-ormax-xpressive-58126.html.

Affectiva. 2016. "Solutions." http://www.affectiva.com/solutions/overview/

Andrejevic, Mark. 2002. "The Work of Being Watched: Interactive Media and the Exploitation of Self-Disclosure." *Critical Studies in Media Communication*. 19 (2): 230–248. doi: 10.1080/07393180216561.

Buckley, Jonathan. 2015. "How Is Big Data Going to Change the World?" *World Economic Forum*, December 1. https://www.weforum.org/agenda/2015/12/how-is-big-data-going-to-change-the-world/.

Captain, Sean. 2015. "How Artificial Intelligence is Finding Gender Bias at Work." *Fast Company*, October 10. https://www.fastcompany.com/3052053/elasticity/how-artificial-intelligence-is-finding-gender-bias-at-work.

Chang, Lulu. 2016. "Watson Will Soon Be in Your Ear with 'Hearables' from Bragi." *Digital Trends*, September 4. http://www.digitaltrends.com/cool-tech/ibm-watson-bragi-the-dash/.

Curry, David. 2016. "New Mental Health Technology Tells Your Doctor What You Won't." *ReadWrite*, August 23. http://readwrite.com/2016/08/23/wearable-mental-health-kit-hl4/.

Dodd, Tim. 2016. "Bored with Study? The New Wave of Edubots Will Find a Way to Spark Your Interest." *Australian Financial Review*, June 5. http://www.afr.com/ technology/apps/education/bored-with-study-the-new-wave-of-edubots-will-find-a-way-to-spark-your-interest-20160602-gpa9em.

Dourish, Paul, and Genevieve Bell. 2011. *Divining a Digital Future: Mess and Mythology in Ubiquitous Computing*. Cambridge, MA: MIT Press.

Ekman, Paul. 1999. "Basic Emotions." In *Handbook of Cognition and Emotion*, edited by Tim Dalgleish and Mick Power, 45–60. New York: Wiley.

Emotient. 2015. "Emotient AdPanel Product Brief." Accessed September 11. http://www.emotient.com.

Farrell, Nick. 2016. "Amazon's New AI Can Tell If You Are in a Bad Mood." *TechEye*, June 14. http://www.techeye.net/news/amazons-new-ai-can-tell-if-you-are-in-a-bad-mood.

Foucault, Michel. 1988. "Technologies of the Self." In *Technologies of the Self: A Seminar with Michel Foucault*, edited by Luther H. Martin, Huck Gutman, and Patrick H. Hutton, 16–49. Amherst, MA: University of Massachusetts Press.

Greenzeiger, Michael F., Ravindra Phulari, and Mehul K. Sanghavi. 2012. Inferring User Mood Based on User and Group Characteristic Data. US Patent 8,965,828, filed July 23, 2012, and issued February 24, 2015.

Gyana. 2016. "About Gyana." Accessed September 11. http://www.gyana.space/story/index.html

Hitachi. 2015. "Hitachi High-Technologies Has Developed a New Wearable Sensor." February 9. http://www.hitachi.com/New/cnews/month/2015/02/150209.html.

Illouz, Eva. 2007. *Cold Intimacies: The Making of Emotional Capitalism*. Cambridge: Polity Press.

Kageyama, Yuri. 2016. "Asimo Meets Pepper: Honda and Softbank Partnering in Robots." *U.S. News & World Report*, July 21. http://www.usnews.com/news/news-articles/2016-07-21/asimo-meets-pepper-honda-and-softbank-partnering-in-robots.

Kemp, Elyria, My Bui, and Sindy Chapa. 2012. "The Role of Advertising in Consumer Emotion Management." *International Journal of Advertising* 31 (2): 339–353. doi:10.2501/IJA-31-2-339-353.

Khatchadourian, Raffi. 2015. "We Know How You Feel." *The New Yorker*, January 19. http://www.newyorker.com/magazine/2015/01/19/know-feel.

Kramer, Adam D. I., Jamie E. Guillory, and Jeffrey T. Hancock. 2014. "Experimental Evidence of Massive-Scale Emotional Contagion Through Social Networks." *Proceedings of the National Academy of Sciences* 111 (24): 8788–90. doi:10.1073/pnas.1320040111.

McDuff, Daniel, Rana El Kaliouby, Evan Kodra, and Laurent Larguinat. 2013. "Do Emotions in Advertising Drive Sales? Use of Facial Coding to Understand the Relationship Between Emotional Responses to Ads and Sales Effectiveness" (white paper). http://www.affectiva.com/

wp-content/uploads/2014/09/Do_Emotions_in_Advertising_Drive_Sales_Use_of_Facial_Coding_to_Understand_The_Relati.pdf.
Messina, Chris. 2016. "Why Silicon Valley Is All Wrong about Apple's AirPods." *Medium*. September 14. https://medium.com/chris-messina/silicon-valley-is-all-wrong-about-the-airpods-8204ede08f0 f#.9k4wpwjc7.
Meštrović, Stjepan. 1997. *Postemotional Society*. London: Sage.
nViso. 2016. "Solutions for Creative Agencies." Accessed September 11. http://www.nviso.ch/solutions-for-creative-agencies.html.
Paul Ekman Group. 2016. "Facial Action Coding System." Accessed September 11. http://www.paulekman.com/product-category/facs/.
Picard, Rosalind, and Jonathan Klein. 2002. "Computers That Recognise and Respond to User Emotion: Theoretical and Practical Implications." *Interacting with Computers* 14 (2):141–69. doi:10.1016/S0953-5438(01)00055-8.
Prest, Christopher, and Quin C. Hoellworth. 2008. Sports Monitoring System for Headphones, Earbuds and/or Headsets. US Patent 8,655,004, filed August 21, 2008, and issued February 18, 2014.
Scott, James C. 1999. *Seeing Like a State: How Certain Schemes to Improve the Human Condition Have Failed*. New Haven, CT: Yale University Press.
Sivek, Susan C. (2018). "Media That Know How You Feel." In *Ethics for a Digital Age* (Vol. 2), edited by Bastiaan Vanacker and Don Heider. New York: Peter Lang.
Statt, Nick. 2016. "1 Billion Apple Devices are in Active Use Around the World." *The Verge*, January 26. http://www.theverge.com/2016/1/26/10835748/apple-devices-active-1-billion-iphone-ipad-ios.
Thomas, Elise. 2015. "Are You Happy Now? The Uncertain Future of Emotion Analytics." *Hopes & Fears*. Accessed September 11. http://www.hopesandfears.com/hopes/now/internet/216523-the-uncertain-future-of-emotion-analytics.
Underwood, Ryan. 2014. "How This Entrepreneur Knows When Your Customers Are Angry." *Inc.*, September. http://www.inc.com/magazine/201409/ryan-underwood/inc.500-joshua-feast-uses-real-time-measurements-to-improve-customer-service.html.
Winkler, Rolfe, Daisuke Wakabayashi, and Elizabeth Dwoskin. 2016. "Apple Buys Artificial-Intelligence Startup Emotient." *Wall Street Journal*, January 7. http://www.wsj.com/articles/apple-buys-artificial-intelligence-startup-emotient-1452188715.

Contributors

EDITORS

Michael S. Daubs is a Senior Lecturer in Media Studies at Victoria University of Wellington in New Zealand where he teaches courses on interactive media, mobile and ubiquitous media, and media and activist movements. He has published on a variety of topics including digital labour, mediatisation and social movements, and mobile apps. His recent publications include "Forgetting History: Mediated Reflections on Occupy Wall Street" (*Media and Communication 5.3*; with Jeffrey Wimmer) and "HTML5, Digital Rights Management (DRM), and the Rhetoric of Openness" (*Journal of Media Critiques 3.9*).

Vincent R. Manzerolle is an Assistant Professor in the Department of Communication, Media and Film at the University of Windsor, Ontario, Canada. His teaching and research focuses on the history, political economy, and theory of media. He has published on a range of topics including credit technologies, consumer databases, apps, wireless connectivity, mobile payment systems, and is a co-editor of *The Audience Commodity in a Digital Age* (Peter Lang, 2014).

AUTHORS

Mark Andrejevic is Professor and Department Chair of Media Studies at Pomona College. He is also a Visiting Professor at Monash University's School of Media,

Film, and Journalism. He is the author of three books and numerous articles on digital media, surveillance, and popular culture.

Kris Belden-Adams is Assistant Professor of Art at the University of Mississippi, USA. Her scholarly work on the history of art, photography and visual culture has been published by the Metropolitan Museum of Art, Photographies, Southern Studies, Afterimage: The Journal of Media Arts and Cultural Criticism, The International Journal of Technology, Knowledge and Society and Cabinet.

Susan Bryant is a Professor in the Department of Communication, Media and Film at the University of Windsor in Windsor, Ontario, Canada. Her research interests include the social relations of new media in everyday life, gender and technology, labour/gender/technology, as well as the natural environment and digital culture.

Marco Centorrino is a Researcher in Communications Sociology at the Faculty of Letters and Philosophy, Messina University, Italy. He is the co-author (with Angelo Romeo) of *Sociologia dei digital media. Concetti e percorsi di ricerca, tra rivoluzioni inavvertite e vita quotidiana* (Franco Angeli, 2012).

Edward Comor is a Professor in the Faculty of Information and Media Studies at the University of Western Ontario. Among other works, he has authored or edited five books on political economy and communications.

Julián de la Fuente is an Assistant Professor of Audiovisual Communication at Universidad Europea de Madrid and the University of Alcalá. He has worked as an independent producer and director since 2002, has several publications on film and history, and has conducted several outreach projects for film heritage.

Jacqueline H. Fewkes is an Associate Professor of Anthropology at the Harriet L. Wilkes Honors College of Florida Atlantic University. She has conducted research in many different parts of the world, including India, Indonesia, the Maldives, Saudi Arabia, and the United States. Dr. Fewkes has written a number of articles on topics as diverse as gender, visual ethnography, transnational economic histories, development, and Islam. She is the author of the book *Trade and Contemporary Society along the Silk Road: An Ethno-history of Ladakh*.

Sarah Harney is a PhD student in the School of Journalism and Communication at Carleton University in Ottawa, Ontario, Canada. Her dissertation project will examine how technological developments in neoliberal context are influencing how activists use social media as well as how protest policing is executed in Canada.

Abdul Nasir Khan is an Affiliate Research Scholar at the Harriet L. Wilkes Honors College of Florida Atlantic University. He is the author of several articles on culture, history, and media in India and has directed and produced multiple documentaries on social issues globally, including *The Culture of Here: Preserving Local History in a*

Local Museum and *Migration and Human Rights Among the Guatemalan Maya*. His forthcoming book, *Focusing on the Local, Connecting to the Global*, explores the role of local television in Kargil, India and its uses of new digital media in more detail.

Pilar Lacasa is a Full Professor of Audiovisual Communication and Researcher at the Faculty of Humanities at the University of Alcalá. She has coordinated the Culture, Technology and New Literacies Research Group since 1998. She has been a visiting at the Comparative Media Studies program (MIT), the University of Southern California, Annenberg Innovation Lab. Currently she's a visiting researcher at the Digital Ethnography Research Centre (RMIT, Melbourne). Pilar is the author of *Learning in virtual and real worlds* (Palgrave, 2013) which includes a foreword by Henry Jenkins.

Eric Lehman is a Masters student in English (Public Texts) at Trent University in Lakefield, Ontario, Canada where he is working on discourses on theft in filesharing. He is a music industry veteran having worked as a royalties and licensing coordinator for the Canadian Musical Reproduction Rights Agency (CMRRA) and in merchandising with Pindoff Record Sales.

Katiuska Manzur is a graduate student at the University of Alcalá and a visiting student at the iMinds-MICT Gaming and Immersive Media Lab at the University of Gent (Belgium). She has a Degree in International Business from Intec University of Santo Domingo, and specializes in marketing and communication. She is interested in video games, social networks, and online gaming.

Tanner Mirrlees is the director of the Communication and Digital Media Studies program at the University of Ontario Institute of Technology. He is a critical political-economist of communication and the author of *Global Entertainment Media* (Routledge, 2013) and *Hearts and Mines: The US Empire's Culture Industry* (University of British Columbia Press, 2016), co-editor of *The Television Reader* (Oxford University Press, 2012).

Ana Rita Morais is a Doctoral Candidate in the Communication and Culture Program at Ryerson University, Toronto. She has devoted much of her academic and professional career to investigating mobile media through investigations of archival material, cartography, digital culture and space/place. She has published and presented her research at several international conferences including at both MIT and Oxford.

Sebastiano Nucera is a Researcher and Assistant Professor of the Department of Cognitive Sciences, Psychology, Education and Cultural Studies at Messina University and the Managing Editor of *Reti, Saperi, Linguaggi. Italian Journal of Cognitive Sciences*. His research activity has been concerned with ecologies of clothing evolution, wearable technologies, virtual and augmented reality, and cultural influences on moral behaviour.

Maggie Reid is a PhD student in the department of Communication and Culture at Ryerson University in North York, Ontario, Canada.

Aaron Shapiro is a PhD candidate at the Annenberg School for Communication at the University of Pennsylvania. His research focuses on the cultural politics of urban data infrastructures. His article, "The Mezzanine" was published ahead of print in Space and Culture in March, 2016.

Susan Currie Sivek is an associate professor in Mass Communication Department at Linfield College in McMinnville, Oregon, USA and the magazine correspondent for PBS' *MediaShift*, where she writes about magazines' transition to the digital age.

Laura Steckman is a fellow with the University for Wisconsin-Madison, affiliated with the Center for Southeast Asian Studies. She currently works for Whitney, Bradley and Brown as the Command Social Scientist at the Marine Corps Information Operations Center (MCIOC).

Turo Uskali is the Head of Journalism, Senior Research Scholar and Adjunct Professor at the Department of Communication/University of Jyväskylä, Finland and an Associate Professor at the Department of Information Science and Media Studies, University of Bergen, Norway. His research focuses on innovations in journalism including mobile data journalism, drone journalism and smartwatches. He has authored or co-authored seven books about the evolution of journalism and the changes in media industries (in Finnish).

Index

A

advertising, 1, 33, 42–43, 51–52, 54, 60–61, 79, 85, 121, 129, 131, 133–134, 168, 184, 189, 191, 192, 194, 222, 252, 254, 259, 288–89, 293–96
affective labor, 205, 209, 210–11
Al Jazeera, 46, 49, 232
algorithms, 28, 54, 79, 82, 83, 110, 117, 241, 244, 273, 292, 298
Amazon, 252-3, 254
    Alexa, 252, 253, 292
    Echo, 252, 254
Andrejevic, Mark, 44, 52, 54, 80, 83, 132, 133, 135, 275, 276, 295
Appadurai, Arjun, 97, 223, 224, 230
Apple, 5, 6, 9, 24, 35, 47, 290–92, 293, 295
    iPhone, 35, 47, 148, 154, 157, 290
Arab Spring, 23
ARPA, *see* DARPA
ARPANET, 7–8
artificial intelligence (AI), 5, 252
audience commodity, 54, 128, 132, 133, 136
augmented reality (AR), 5, 10, 98, 99, 100, 112–13, 117, 118, 119, 120, 251, 254
aura, 163–76
automation, 84, 87, 97
    in journalism, 244

B

Babbage, Charles, 19–20
Bakhtin, Mikhail, 143–45, 148, 150, 152, 157
Barthes, Roland, 146, 154
Bateson, Gregory, 79, 254, 255
Bauman, Zygmunt, 67, 79
BBC, 241
Benjamin, Walter, 162, 163, 164, 166, 167, 169–71, 172–75, 176
Bennett, Jane, 260
bias of communication, 186, 187
big data, 28, 81, 258, 263, 273, 294
biometric technology, 6, 259, 291
biopower, 268, 277–78
Black Lives Matter, 268, 274–77, 279, 280, 281
blogging, 54, 55, 128, 240, 241
    microblogging, 148, 240
Bluetooth, 19, 21, 24, 25, 28, 29
Borges, Jorge Luis, 258, 261

Bourdieu, Pierre, 130, 146, 154
Bush, Vannevar, 6

C

calm computing, 20–21
camera drones, *see* drones
cameraphones, *see* mobile phones
Castells, Manuel, 2, 7, 9–10, 94, 119, 241
chronotope, 143–44, 145, 148, 150, 152, 157–58
citizen journalism, *see* journalism, citizen journalism
city forensics, 83–84, 87
CNN, 23, 43, 47, 51, 52, 239
cognitive surplus, 95–96, 97
commodification, 44, 127, 131, 133–38, 294–95, 297
consumerism, 230
consumption, 23, 52, 63, 100, 109, 127, 164, 174, 175, 191, 193, 225, 230, 253–54, 263, 291
convergence, 3, 52, 112, 129, 130, 220, 223, 225–26, 232
　　convergence culture, 3, 43
cookies, 33, 253
cumulativity, 94, 96–98
customization, 23, 84, 133, 252
customized society, 252
cyberspace, 63, 67, 251

D

DARPA, *see* Defense Advanced Research Projects Agency
data,
　　collection of, 6, 26, 33, 61, 251–55, 258, 259, 261, 263–64, 273, 275, 276–77, 280–81
　　data visualization, 82, 109, 111, 112–13, 115, 121, 122, 147, 264
　　See also big data

databases, 9, 81, 83, 87, 115–17, 121, 258, 276, 277, 280
deconstruction, *see* Derrida, Jacque
Defense Advanced Research Projects Agency (US), 7, 55
Department of Defense (US), 32, 41, 45
Derrida, Jacque, 171, 260–61
　　deconstruction, 260–61
desire, 175, 189, 262–64
digital,
　　digital cameras, 152, 240
　　digital humanities, 164
　　digital labor, 44, 50, 127, 129, 132, 134–135, 137, 202, 213
　　digital photography, 80, 146, 154, 164, 172, 174
digital rights management, 59–67, 70–71
double articulation, *see* surveillance
DRM, *see* digital rights management
drones, 253, 263
　　camera drones, 243, 245

E

E-mail, 7–8, 267
Elmer, Greg, 80, 134
emotion analytics, 287–99
Empire and Communication, *see* Innis, Harold
encryption, 19, 29, 33, 35, 63, 279
entrepreneurial journalism, *see* journalism, entrepreneurial journalism
everyware, 97, 109, 111, 112, 113–15, 122

F

Facebook, 34, 43, 48, 50, 52, 54, 55, 80, 133, 146, 165, 169, 174, 225, 241, 243, 244, 258, 261, 273, 274, 275, 296
　　Facebook Live 243
fake news, 244, 256, 257, 261
FBI, *see* Federal Bureau of Investigation

FCC, *see* Federal Communications Commission
Featherstone, Michael, 1–2, 3, 6, 10, 42, 53, 60, 78, 128, 226, 230
Federal Bureau of Investigation (US), 35, 267, 269–71, 277, 278
Federal Communications Commission (US), 23, 24, 28–32
Flickr, 81, 82, 87, 165, 169
Foucault, Michel, 62, 268, 277–78, 298–99
Fuchs, Christian, 44, 48, 54, 133, 135, 240

G

geolocation, 28, 79, 86
   see also Global Position System
Gitlin, Todd, 255
Global Position System, 19, 21, 24, 27–29, 79, 112, 115, 253
Google, 1, 33, 34, 43, 55, 81, 82, 117, 133, 171, 263
   Google Android, 6, 71
   Google Earth, 81
   Google Glass, 100
   Google Home, 254
   Google Maps, 81, 87, 96
   Google Play, 71
   Google Street View, 12, 81, 84, 86
   Google Translate, 117–18, 121
GPS, *see* Global Position System
Guattari, Felix, 116

H

Hardt, Michael and Negri, Antonio, 133, 205, 210
Hayles, N. Katherine, 164, 173, 174, 230
Heidegger, Martin, 62, 85, 118–20
Hesmondhalgh, David, 135, 136
HTML, *see* Hypertext Markup Language
Hypertext Markup Language, 30

I

IEEE, *see* Institute of Electrical and Electronics Engineers
immaterial labor, 127, 133, 205, 209, 213–14, 230
infography, *see* mobile infography
information
   information collection, *see* data, collection of
   information overload, 52,
   information visualization, *see* data visualization
   infovis, *see* data visualization
infrastructure, 6, 45, 67, 68, 79, 240, 273, 275
Innis, Harold, 85, 183–198
   Empire and Communication, 188
Instagram, 48, 80, 148, 149, 152–54, 169, 174
Institute of Electrical and Electronics Engineers, 24
Internet of Everything, 10, 22
Internet of Things, 21, 26, 27, 32, 251, 252, 254
IoE, *see* Internet of Everything
IoT, *see* Internet of Things
iPhone, *see* Apple, iPhone

J

Jenkins, Henry, 3, 43, 52, 94, 128, 150, 225–26, 240
   See also convergence, convergence culture
journalism
   citizen journalism, 128, 129, 239
   entrepreneurial journalism, 129–32
   public service journalism, 130

K

Kittler, Friedrich, 84
Kurzweil, Ray, 260

L

labor, *see* affective labor; digital labor; immaterial labor; unpaid labor
Lacan, Jacques, 262
Latour, Bruno, 119, 260
LifeLogger, 259
live streaming, 238, 240, 244
location-based applications, 21
Luhmann, Niklas, 79

M

Manovich, Lev, 81, 110, 111, 112, 118, 165
Marx, Karl, 134–35, 198n4, 199n11, 199n16
Mauss, Marcel, 94
McLuhan, Marshall, 93, 94, 95, 97, 109, 110, 115, 197
mechanization of knowledge, 191, 197
mediascape, 2, 219, 221, 222, 224, 228, 230, 234
memes, 169, 170–71, 174
Merleau-Ponty, Maurice, 114
metadata, 81, 82, 83, 112, 116, 122, 263, 279
micro-stories, 144, 156–57, 158
microblogging, *see* blogging, microblogging
Microsoft, 34, 100
mobile camera, *see* mobile phones, mobile camera
mobile infography, 110–120
mobile internet, 228, 241
mobile phones, 1, 4, 19, 22, 23, 28, 29, 113, 143, 150, 154, 155, 225, 240
    mobile camera, 109–111
    smartphones, 5, 9, 23, 26, 27, 43, 44, 50, 52–53, 96, 115, 116, 118, 146, 147, 163, 183, 202, 221, 241, 244, 288
    See also Apple, iPhone
monopolies of knowledge, 183, 184, 186, 188, 189, 194, 196

N

National Security Agency (US), 35, 254
neoliberalism, 14n2, 127, 130, 131, 135, 136
network centric warfare, 45
network society, 2, 9, 10
Nokia, 23, 242
NSA, *see* National Security Agency

O

Occupy Wall Street, 268, 274, 280, 243

P

P2P, *see* peer-to-peer
Panofsky, Erwin, 110
panopticon, 61–62, 134, 277–78, 280, 281
Parikka, Jussi, 60, 62, 66, 68, 69
peer-to-peer, 63, 64
Periscope, 242–43, 244
pervasive computing, 21, 78, 112, 113–15, 122
Pokémon Go!, 99, 113, 120
privacy, 20, 28, 29, 33–35, 60–61, 66–67, 71, 252, 263
propaganda, 42–43, 45, 47, 49, 52, 195
prosumer, 44, 50–54, 133, 137
public service journalism, *see* journalism, public service journalism

Q

Qualcomm, 1, 28

R

radio-frequency identification, 19, 21, 22, 24, 26–29, 86
remediation, 3
RFID, *see* radio-frequency identification

S

self-branding, 128, 132, 146
selfies, 164, 165–166, 168, 170, 171
sensorium, 115, 163, 172–74
Shirky, Clay, 95–98, 129, 131
smart homes, 253, 292
smartphone, *see* mobile phones, smartphones
smartwatch, 244
    See also wearables
Smith, Dorothy, 201–02, 203, 214
Smythe, Dallas, 51, 54, 128, 132, 133, 136
Snowden, Edward, 35
social media, 23, 28, 43, 47–49, 50, 52, 55, 79, 80, 94, 98, 121, 127, 129–30, 132–35, 137, 146, 148, 149, 152, 154, 156, 158, 164, 165, 168, 171, 173, 174, 176, 223, 227, 233, 238–41, 243, 273, 274, 280, 288, 291, 292, 296
    See also Facebook; Instagram; Twitter; Vine
social movements, 267–69, 272–81
social networks, *see* social media
Sontag, Susan, 69, 146
spectrum management, 19, 29, 30–33
spreadable media, 43, 240
surveillance, 80, 133–34, 254, 267–81
    double articulation of, 80, 84
surveillant assemblage, 280–81

T

time-shifting, 52
Trump, Donald, 254, 256–57, 261
Turkle, Sherry, 53, 202–04, 209, 210–11, 214
Twitter, 23, 48, 29, 50, 55, 133, 135, 166, 169, 241, 242, 273–74

U

UbiComp, see ubiquitous computing
ubiquitous communication, 238, 241, 243, 244
ubiquitous computing, 4–6, 20–23, 25, 29, 78–80, 84, 88, 94–95, 111, 113, 226, 244, 251–52, 287, 299
ubiquitous connectivity, 1, 10
UGC, *see* user-generated content
unpaid labor, 127, 132, 135, 203
user-generated content, 128–30, 132

V

Vine, 149, 275
virtual reality, 5, 77, 244, 251, 254, 255, 258, 259–61, 264

W

Wajcman, Judy, 203, 204, 205, 208–09
wearables, 5, 21, 244
Web 2.0, 44, 47–48, 50, 55, 240
WhatsApp, 219, 228–29, 231, 232, 234
Wi-Fi, 21, 24–5, 28, 29, 252, 25
Wikileaks, 49
Wikipedia, 96, 121, 169

X

Xerox Palo Alto, 4, 77

Y

YouTube, 44, 48, 49, 50, 51, 55, 128, 135, 156, 159, 223, 225, 228, 232, 234

Z

Žižek, Slavoj, 261, 264
Zuckerberg, Mark, 258, 261

General Editor: **Steve Jones**

Digital Formations is the best source for critical, well-written books about digital technologies and modern life. Books in the series break new ground by emphasizing multiple methodological and theoretical approaches to deeply probe the formation and reformation of lived experience as it is refracted through digital interaction. Each volume in **Digital Formations** pushes forward our understanding of the intersections, and corresponding implications, between digital technologies and everyday life. The series examines broad issues in realms such as digital culture, electronic commerce, law, politics and governance, gender, the Internet, race, art, health and medicine, and education. The series emphasizes critical studies in the context of emergent and existing digital technologies.

Other recent titles include:

Felicia Wu Song
    Virtual Communities: Bowling Alone, Online Together

Edited by Sharon Kleinman
    The Culture of Efficiency: Technology in Everyday Life

Edward Lee Lamoureux, Steven L. Baron, & Claire Stewart
    Intellectual Property Law and Interactive Media: Free for a Fee

Edited by Adrienne Russell & Nabil Echchaibi
    International Blogging: Identity, Politics and Networked Publics

Edited by Don Heider
    Living Virtually: Researching New Worlds

Edited by Judith Burnett, Peter Senker & Kathy Walker
    The Myths of Technology: Innovation and Inequality

Edited by Knut Lundby
    Digital Storytelling, Mediatized Stories: Self-representations in New Media

Theresa M. Senft
    Camgirls: Celebrity and Community in the Age of Social Networks

Edited by Chris Paterson & David Domingo
    Making Online News: The Ethnography of New Media Production

To order other books in this series please contact our Customer Service Department:

(800) 770-LANG (within the US)
(212) 647-7706 (outside the US)
(212) 647-7707 FAX

To find out more about the series or browse a full list of titles, please visit our website:
WWW.PETERLANG.COM

www.ingramcontent.com/pod-product-compliance
Ingram Content Group UK Ltd.
Pitfield, Milton Keynes, MK11 3LW, UK
UKHW021328180426
11947UKWH00017B/1501